The Acrobat

ALSO BY JOHN STEWART
AND FROM MCFARLAND

Italian Film: A Who's Who (2012)

Antarctica: An Encyclopedia, 2d ed. (2011)

Byron and the Websters: The Letters and Entangled Lives of the Poet, Sir James Webster and Lady Frances Webster (2008)

Confederate Spies at Large: The Lives of Lincoln Assassination Conspirator Tom Harbin and Charlie Russell (2007)

African States and Rulers, 3d ed. (2006)

Broadway Musicals, 1943–2004 (2006)

The British Empire: An Encyclopedia of the Crown's Holdings, 1493 through 1995 (1996)

Moons of the Solar System: An Illustrated Encyclopedia (1991)

The Acrobat

*Arthur Barnes
and the Victorian Circus*

JOHN STEWART

McFarland & Company, Inc., Publishers
Jefferson, North Carolina, and London

LIBRARY OF CONGRESS ONLINE CATALOG DATA

Stewart, John.
    The acrobat : Arthur Barnes and the Victorian circus / John Stewart.
        p.   cm.
    Includes bibliographical references and index.

    ISBN 978-0-7864-7023-5
    softcover : acid free paper ∞

2012014081

BRITISH LIBRARY CATALOGUING DATA ARE AVAILABLE

© 2012 John Stewart. All rights reserved

No part of this book may be reproduced or transmitted in any form or by any means, electronic or mechanical, including photocopying or recording, or by any information storage and retrieval system, without permission in writing from the publisher.

On the cover: acrobats from print entitled *Thirteen Men Doing Acrobatics,* Calvert Litho. Co., 1891 (Library of Congress); background images © 2012 Shutterstock

Manufactured in the United States of America

McFarland & Company, Inc., Publishers
  Box 611, Jefferson, North Carolina 28640
    www.mcfarlandpub.com

Contents

Acknowledgments   vii
Preface   1

Presenting   3
The Somersaulting Record   6
Powell's Circus   14
Hughes's Circus Royal   23
The Disappearance of Mr. Arthur Barnes   40
The Return of Mr. Arthur Barnes   51
Wallett   54
Cooke's, 1849–1850   62
Cooke's, 1851–1852   85
The Hernandez Years   116
America   142
The Hengler Years   150
Music Halls   175
Retirement   206

Bibliography   213
Index   217

This is the seventh book I've dedicated to
Gayle Winston

which tells a story

Acknowledgments

For Gayle, of course.

For my brother Dave. Dave and I started this whole project. The book's mine, of course, but without Dave, this book would not have got off the ground; in fact, we would never have known about the Acrobat in the first place.

For my parents, especially my mother in this case, the granddaughter of the subject of this book.

For my sister Mary Young; my brother-in-law Willie Young; and my nephew William Young.

For my brother Pete, as always; and Marion, and George.

For Tom Barns, my uncle.

For John Turner, a very generous friend, and a great contributor to the world of the circus. Dr. Turner wrote about Arthur Barnes quite a lot; he put the Arthur Barnes entry into the *Dictionary of National Biography*, and he threatened never to talk to me again if I didn't finish the book, and then it was all over. We all miss you, John, but the book's out, and you'll enjoy it, wherever you are.

Preface

When my brother Dave and I started this project 20 years ago, we knew virtually nothing about our mother's grandfather. We thought we knew his name, Arthur Henry Barns, but that turned out to be his son's name. The Acrobat's name was Arthur Barns—just like that. His professional name was Arthur Barnes, with an "e," but, back then, we didn't even know he had a profession, let alone a professional name. All we knew was that he used to do cartwheels, or forward rolls, on the village green—whatever village that was. He was described as an active lad. There was not the faintest mention of the circus. Our mother has a wooden mirror of his with "Madrid" carved in the back, and the date 1858. She remembered, growing up, glass bowls which had been awarded to her grandfather for his little somersaults. She even remembered black-framed photos, but they were destroyed by her stepmother.

We knew the old boy had married our great-grandmother (name possibly Catherine), and that she was the second wife, that he had married her when he was in his forties, and that the first wife was Danish, named Alexandrina (turned out to be Alexine), and that by her he had had a daughter, Nancy, who had lived into my mother's time, in Birmingham. Nancy used to make iced lemonade, my uncle told me, and she died unmarried. Someone mentioned that the Danish lady's name was Cobb. Another lead was that the old man had had another daughter, by his second wife, in other words, my grandfather's full sister—another Alexandrina. This younger Alexandrina married a Mr. Jewiss, and had a son named Harvey, a naughty boy who used to pull my Aunt Mary's hair (she deserved it). Harvey's mother died in childbirth. This name Jewiss would play hell with our research—it turned out to be Dewis.

Our uncle owned a silver snuff box which had wording on it. That was the beginning of this book, really. "Presented by W.F. Wallett, Esq., to Arthur Barnes, on the occasion of his throwing the unprecedented number of 73 somersaults. Leeds. June 28, 1849."

Dave and I were sitting outside the library, discussing the wording on the snuff box. Suddenly it hit us—"unprecedented number." "World record." Not little cartwheels. Maybe this was the circus. Maybe Wallett was a circus owner. We dashed into the reference section, went to the British circus—and found Wallet. It was an epiphany. Arthur Barnes was an acrobat, and he'd obviously been a star. We looked for him in George Speaight's book, and found him — the greatest acrobat of his day. This led us to the magazine *Bandwagon*, for which John Turner had written articles, and Mr. Barnes started to come to life, especially after we followed the references to the *Era* magazine, with the help of which we tracked Arthur Barnes' career. It remained only to research in more newspapers, as well as other repositories, to put the whole story of the Acrobat together.

Presenting

Of all the "champion" acrobats of the Victorian circus—Barnes, Connor, Dale, McFarland, Franklin, Price, North, and the rest—only one was the true "Champion Vaulter of All the World"—and that was Arthur Barnes. He was known as "The 100-Somerset Man" because he threw 100 summersets, one after the other, "in one trial" as they used to say.

A somersault, at least the way they did them in those days, involved standing on a narrow, wooden "elastic board"—as the name implies, a springboard, highly-elasticated, level (i.e., not inclined in any way)—jumping up and down a few times with both feet, to get going, and then propelling yourself vertically into the air. Just like today's trampoline, but considerably more difficult. You waited for the moment of maximum height, then rapidly raised your knees to your chin, encircled your shins with your arms, threw yourself forward (or backward if you were doing a backward somersault), completing a 360-degree turn in the air, and then straightened out before landing back on the springboard. Part of the skill of this movement included landing back in the right place to be able to take the next jump with the minimum amount of time lost. In a series, or "trial," you repeated this feat again and again, one somersault after the other, with no significant interval between efforts. In those days, this was called "still-vaulting." To perform even one such somerset was highly dangerous, and very difficult, for the untrained. For the trained acrobat to do any number of these was just a matter of stamina, maintaining some sort of equilibrium, and, of course, ignoring the always present threat of breaking your neck. In order to do several one had to be incredibly fit. To add to the legend, Arthur Barnes would do a long trial of forward somersaults and finish with a reverse somersault, or the other way around. He did both.

Arthur Barnes began as a top line pro at the age of 15, performed in front of King Pedro V of Portugal, Queen Isabella of Spain, the Emperor Napoleon III, King Oscar I of Sweden and Norway, King Frederick VIII of Denmark, the Emperor of Russia, Abraham Lincoln, hundreds of the nobility, and literally millions of paying customers all over Britain, Europe and the United States, during a 22-year career that lasted until 1866. He worked with all the greats of the day—Pablo Fanque, Wallett the Clown, William Cooke, the Henglers, Lord George Sanger, Hernandez and Stone, and especially his great friend Harry Connor. He threw an estimated 1 million somersaults in his day, retired well-off, at the age of 38, and never had anything to do with the circus again.

In truth, despite the "100-Somerset Man" tag, Arthur Barnes never did a hundred. No one ever did. Speaking for himself, Mr. Barnes admitted as much during an interview he gave in 1860, when he was in the twilight of his career. It's just that when he went to the United States for his 1856 tour, the American promoters had to dream up some catchy and exciting tag line for him, and "The 95-Somerset Man" wasn't it. The neat, hackneyed, but inaccurate, term, "100-Somerset Man" had been used in the States for years, for various artistes, so they simply reapplied it to Arthur Barnes. Notwithstanding, there was and is universal agreement that Arthur Barnes was the greatest somerset man of all time.

The origins of the circus as we know it today lie in the 1760s, when former cavalryman Philip Astley formed his establishment in London. The main thrust in those days was equestrianism, i.e., horses. In the 1770s other impresarios sprang up, on both sides of the Atlantic, adding acrobats, comedians, and other acts. The word "circus" as applied to a moving establishment of performers, as opposed to a fixed amphitheatre, would be first used in the United States, but not until about 1824; however, even after the 1820s the term "equestrian establishment" would linger for decades, especially in Great Britain. And the term "equestrian," indicating any circus performer, would similarly hang around. Astley's, at the Amphitheatre, Westminster Bridge, in London, ran an ad in the October 25, 1785, edition of the *Morning Chronicle*, in which it says: "For the first time, and never performed in England, an exercise called still vaulting, invented by young Astley [this is John Astley, Philip's son], and performed by himself, demonstrating what ought to be practiced by every horseman in order to familiarize more effectually the body to the various actions of the horse." So, that was how the term "still-vaulting" came about. Actually, back then, "still-vaulting" meant putting one's foot in the stirrup and then vaulting, but, over the years, the term took on a different meaning, and, even before Buonaparte was finally vanquished, the term had come to mean vaulting on the elastic board. Mr. Powell's touring circus was offering still-vaulting competitions before 1820, and Bill Smith, of Astley's, was still-vaulting in 1825, when he landed badly, and broke his neck.

A million light years from the glittering life of the circus lurked the dreaded inferno of the brass and iron foundry, a business which, like the mines, mercilessly used up its men in its noble drive to contribute to the magnificence of the British Empire. The Barnes family, Midlands all the way, were denizens of this underworld—casters, founders, moulders, whatever you want to call them — men trapped by their class, not always stupid men, by any means, not always men without dreams, but men confronted and preoccupied with the daily nightmare of having to make a living the hard way. And they dragged their wives along with them, reproducing as they went, always reproducing, to bring more and more misery to more and more children equally doomed to the foundry. Two brothers had arrived in Birmingham in the mid-1700s: Sam and Henry. Henry died in late 1792, quite well-off—so it didn't have to be an unprofitable world, this world of hot metal and sparks, not if you used your head. But then, not many iron casters used their heads. That's when it became deadly.

These boys, Henry and Sam, were the ones who adopted the spelling Barns in 1770. Intrinsically the names are the same — Barnes and Barns— and in those old days, long before the Acrobat's time, it didn't matter at all how you spelled a name. English was essentially a spoken language back then, and the written word was reserved for clerics and scholars— hence the expression "benefit of clergy"— and their written interpretation of a name they heard could vary widely, depending on certain factors, not the least of which was how much they'd had to drink the night before. But, truly, spelling was not a big deal back then. Barnes or Barns, it only made a difference if you were the one who'd changed it. In the 1840s, when Arthur Barnes began his circus career, he soon learned that *Barns* caused confusion on the marquee, so, keeping *Barns* for his personal life, he settled on the much more well-recognized and widely accepted *Barnes* as the spelling of his professional name.

Sam Barns begat Henry and Henry begat Henry, the Acrobat's father, in 1792. He too became a caster. In 1818 this caster married Jane Williams at Aston Juxta, Birmingham, and they moved into a house on the corner of Green Street and Birchall Street, in the immediate vicinity of the Britannia Inn, in Deritend, the old part of Aston. Henry and Jane Barns had six children. First was Tom, in 1822; then Henry, in 1824; and then the Acrobat, in April 1828. He was named for Arthur Wellesley, the Duke of Wellington, who became prime minister that year. There were a lot of Arthurs born in England that year. Tom was baptized at St. Martin's, the big Birmingham church, in 1823; Henry was baptized at home in 1825; and Arthur Barnes was not baptized at all, which is unfortunate in that we have no precise record of his birth date. We know it was April, from triangulating various bits and pieces of information; it was nine years before civil registration came into force in the United Kingdom. The next Barns child was Mary Ann, born in 1829, and baptized in 1830, at St. John's Church, Deritend. Finally, two more, Richard and Jane, born in 1833 and 1836 respectively, but, again, not baptized.

The Somersaulting Record

Jem Ryan had only one eye, but it was an eye to the main chance. He was a London lad, of Irish extraction, and his circus was one of the big touring outfits in the 1820s and would become even more famous next decade. In that generation prior to Arthur Barnes, no proprietor in the equestrian world was as big as Mr. William Batty, of Astley's, but Jem Ryan was right up there in the next echelon. In the November 22, 1831, edition of the *Belfast News-Letter*, Ryan's Circus advertised a grand trial of skill to be contested on the elastic board, when a number of somersets would be performed by Mr. Ryan, the manager, and assisted by other performers, including Bill Randall, the clown, John Bridges, the first man ever to turn a somersault on the tightrope, Tom Moseley, who will pop up occasionally in this story, and Loughran, the clown. Another ad for Ryan's, in the *Manchester Times* of March 29, 1834, tells of "Champions of agility," who included Messrs. Ryan, Bridges, Alfred Hengler (brother of the future great circus owner, Charles Hengler), Moseley, Randall, and Williams, the popular clown, who "will distinguish themselves in a surprising manner on the Elastic Board, by introducing forward and backward somersets to an amazing height and number."

The *Pittsburgh Manufacturer* of August 8, 1835, introduces one of the great somersault throwers, Levi James North, a Long Island boy, then 21, who, at the age of 12 had been apprenticed to Quick & Mead's Circus. On the morning of August 3, 1835, while performing with Brown's Mammoth Circus in Pittsburgh, the celebrated young American equestrian gave an extraordinary exhibition of his prowess in the science of gymnastics. He had bet $500 that he could throw 30 somersaults, or tourbillions, in succession, from a battute, or springboard, in the space of 30 minutes. On the first trial he accomplished 28, and on the second trial 28, falling in the 29th without receiving any injury. On the third trial he executed the extraordinary number of 32, thereby winning the wager, "being the greatest number of summersets ever done by any performer in the world," making in all 88 summersets in three successive trials, "which is unprecedented in the annals of gymnastics."

Another great still-vaulter of those days was W. B. Wilkinson, who performed with Tom Price ("the Bounding Ball") at Ryan's Circus in 1835. "Two of the first summerset throwers in the world." Mr. Wilkinson also had an original act he called the Inca of Peru, in the course of which he depicted, on a naked horse, and in splendidly appropriate costume, the peculiar maneuvers of a Peruvian warrior.

The *Brighton Patriot* of October 4 and 11, 1836, tells us, regarding Ryan's Circus, which was appearing in that town, that Tom Price, the very prince of tumblers, who was appearing during the evening as one of the clowns, was striving every night "to accomplish a task never yet, we are informed, executed by man — that is, to throw, in one attempt, thirty summersets." One night the previous week he had thrown, in the course of the evening, 65 in three attempts — namely 11, 25, and 29. Then came the morning performance of Thursday, October 6. Tom did 28, then, minutes later, with the crowd going berserk, he finally broke the 30 barrier, by doing 31 in one trial. For this wondrous feat, his fellow performers presented him with a silver snuff box, and Mr. Ryan gave him a medal and a £5 note. This British all-comers' record made big news, even in the Metropolitan newspapers. By September 1837, Tom Price was, so to speak, still still-vaulting with Ryan's, and was nightly throwing between 30 and 50 somersaults. "Gymnastic competition!," yelped the *Bristol Mercury* ad of November 1837. "Extraordinary trial of aerial flights from the board elastic by the best company of vaulters in the kingdom, including the superior exertions of the celebrated Price, the first summerset thrower in the world." A warning here: Unless the figures are attested, as, say, at the Brighton gig, they must be taken cautiously, especially in ad blurb. With this in mind, on June 4, 1838, at Astley's, in London, Tom Price threw 26, to the astonishment of the audience.

In 1838 Levi North arrived in England from the States, to perform at Astley's with Tom Price. These two great somersaultists vaulted against each other for 12 days (taking breaks, of course), and North threw 31 on June 30; 32 on July 2; and a phenomenal 44 on July 19. Price won only one of the 12 nights' competitions. In August, now with Ryan's Circus in Leeds, Mr. North did 36 somersaults, to much acclaim. The November 8, 1838, edition of Edinburgh's paper, the *Caledonian Mercury*, tells us that Price had recently done 42 at Astley's. On November 5 Tom opened with Batty's touring circus at Edinburgh, "ably assisted by Lavater Lee and the other Swiss Acrobats [Whitton, Billy Bonaker, and Morris]." That opening night Tom threw 25 and then 23 somersaults. On the following night he did 34. The *Mercury* was impressed with the easy manner with which he performed this astonishing feat and the great height he reached each time he rebounded off the elastic battute.

The November 8, 1838, edition of the *Bradford Observer* carried an ad for Ryan's Royal Circus, which tells us: "The whole company of Chinese vaulters will most particularly exert themselves in their various trials of competition, including the wonder of the world, the celebrated Mr. North, who has thrown, in rapid succession, the unprecedented number of thirty to forty summersets, making the astonishing number of seventy in two trials, alighting each time on his feet, within the compass of a pocket handkerchief." The next week, in Bradford, Mr. North did 91 in two trials, so it is said. He would have had to have done at least 46 in one of the two trials, which, if true, would have been a new world record.

Meanwhile, back in the States, the *Daily Commercial Bulletin* of St. Louis, of December 1, 1838, declared: "Wonderful vaulting. The celebrated North and the whole world beaten. We have, at the present time, in our city, a gentleman attached to the circus, who has thrown forty-six somersaults, beating North's great effort at Astley's Amphitheatre by five summersets. This great feat was performed by Mr. Richard Sands at Mackanaw, Ill., very recently. This is certainly the most wonderful vaulting on record." Dick Sands, whose early career somewhat paralleled that of Arthur Barnes, was also from Long Island. He was 24 when he broke the world record. We will hear more of Mr. Sands.

It was in the late 1830s, on both sides of the Atlantic, that the whole concept of the circus expanded, took on a new vigor, with the introduction of more novelty acts. The menageries were enlarged, and promotion became a big part of touring life, with gilded advertising wagons replete with handbills being sent out into the rural districts. Everything was enlarged and embellished. Vaulting and somersaulting became bigger than ever. Still-vaulting commanded huge attention, and would continue to do so for another 25 years or so, before it eventually died out as an act. "'Still-vaulting' is another acrobatic act that was very popular with the circus audiences some time ago, but never seen now. It consisted in throwing somersaults in rapid succession within a small space marked off on a level springboard. Arthur Barnes, an English performer, thus threw 100 consecutive somersaults" [from an article about old circuses in the October 18, 1896, edition of the South Carolina newspaper, *The State*].

The March 19, 1839, *Brighton Patriot* tells us of major new ground being broken. "Our readers doubtless remember the vaulting of Mr. Price, a member of Mr. Ryan's equestrian company. It appears, by the *Glasgow Herald*, that he has excelled himself in throwing summersets, for on one occasion he threw fifty summersets in succession, a feat unequalled in the annals of gymnastics. He is, says the paper, to be presented with a gold medal by Mr. Batty (with whose troop he is now performing)." Hard on the heels of this, the *Derby Mercury* of April 3, 1839, tells us that "at Ryan's Circus in Birmingham one night last week [it was actually March 21] a person named North threw the extraordinary number of fifty summersets [it was actually 55, and he received a medal for it], which elicited strong approbation and has caused much interest."

Freeman's Journal and Daily Advertiser (of Dublin) tells us, in their June 25, 1839, edition, "Mr. Price ... will throw twenty-one somersaults, without the aid of a springboard, never attempted by any other performer." In July 1839, in London, Mr. North did 55 again [on the board, of course], and got a silver snuff box. The *Cork Advertiser* (August 1839) tells us that Mr. Price, the celebrated acrobat of Mr. Batty's company, won a wager of £20 that month, by executing 56 somersaults at one trial in a morning practice, that being the greatest number ever accomplished.

In 1839 Henry Barns and his family moved to London, together with a hinge maker named Spencer Smith and his wife Charlotte. The future Acrobat was then 11 years old. The house they all moved to was a squalid Finsbury tenement in the ward of St. Barnabas (named for the local church), in St. Luke's parish. Masons Place, a mean, narrow alleyway that God forgot, ran between York Road and Goswell Road, behind Charles Street. No. 25 was a two-story brick terraced house with the iron foundry right across the way. Spencer Smith and his wife lived on one floor, and the Barnses on another. The old man, and his two eldest sons, Tom and Henry, went straight to work in the foundry, up early in the morning, never seeing the sun, slaving inch by inch toward a certain death, only to stagger back across the alley at night at the end of yet another day in the iron pit. There must be something better than this, and there was, but not for them.

The June 6, 1841, census at 25 Masons Place lists Henry Barnes, 45, moulder; Jane, 45; Thomas, 18; Henry, 15; Arthur, 13; Mary, 11; Richard, 8; and Jane, 4. At No. 7 lived Sarah Freeth, a schoolteacher, with her 15-year-old daughter, Jane, then working as a button tie binder. Jane would later marry the Acrobat's brother, Henry.

The *Liverpool Mercury* of November 1, 1839, says: "Mr. Batty has, in his company at Sheffield, a person named North, who, it is said, can throw fifty-five summersets with ease." The *Bristol Mercury* of December 14, 1839, talking of Ryan's Circus there, tells us that he [this North person] has thrown the "almost incredible number of fifty-five summersets." But that was all old news now, and by 1840 Mr. North was back in the States.

Lavater Lee, born Steven Lavater Lee in 1817, some say in Valparaiso, was one of the great vaulters. The *Bristol Mercury* of October 10, 1840, tells us (in an ad) that on October 12 "the great summerset thrower who has, in two successive trials, thrown the astonishing number of sixty summersets" made his bow with Ryan's, in Bristol. That opening night he was the Air Diver of Venice. His partner those days was Billy Bonaker, the clown [they had been two of the four Swiss Acrobats with Mr. Batty's circus a couple of years before, when Lee was the Bounding Salamander and Billy was the Monkey Man]. In 1841 Mr. Lee was back with Batty's, in Dublin, and, later that year, with Batty in London, playing with Master Polaski (more of whom later), and Mr. Nunn, the Patagonian Samson. In 1842, Lee was with Batty's again in Dublin, performing with Jem Newsome and Paul Masotta. Mr. Lee and the clown, Felix Carlo, were the Bounding Athletae. In addition, the Four Persian Acrobats went through "the entire of their gymnastic exercises." *Freeman's Journal* ran an ad on May 30, 1842, in which was claimed: "Lavater Lee will appear in his most prominent feats of still-vaulting, throwing frequently seventy-five somersets." He may have done, but not in one trial. Mr. Lee came to grief in Barnstaple, later in 1842, while playing with Cooke's Circus. His horse slipped, and he was thrown into the woodwork. His life was despaired of, but he pulled through, and by 1843 was part of Henry Cornwall's circus, with, among other performers, John Samwell.

Three of the great vaulters of the early 1840s were Americans—Mr. North, of course, Tom McFarland of Virginia (already, in 1839, being touted as the best), and William Owen Dale, of Cincinnati, who had begun vaulting in 1836. The *New York Herald* of December 4, 1840, reported, "There was a most animated display of gymnastics at the Amphitheatre last evening, in the arena contests. McFarland, the champion vaulter, threw 51 successive somersets, the greatest number ever thrown in this country." Indeed, he was being billed as the 50-somerset man.

The *New York Herald* of December 10, 1840, trumpeted, "The Champion Beaten." It goes on to tell us that there had been a great sensation in the Bowery the last day or two, in reference to the rival vaulters in the opposition shows. Bets amounting to several thousand dollars had been made upon the greatest number of somersets to be thrown by the champion, McFarland, of Down East, and young Dale, of Philadelphia, the former being attached to the Amphitheatre, and the latter to Welch's Company, performing at the Bowery Theatre. Each night the vaulting at both houses was watched as narrowly and with as much excitement as the progress of a pair of Arabians on a race course. On Tuesday evening, the following dialog took place at "the Branch": "Well, Tom, I've won that hat of you tonight. Mac threw his fifty easily, and had a fine beat of the board for half a dozen more, if he had been of a mind." "What if he did?" was the reply, "Dale threw more somersets over to Hamblin's than there were people in the house." The paper then says, "Of course, the champion is floored." People actually spoke like that in those days.

The Boston *Daily Atlas* of December 20, 1841, reported that McFarland, the great vaulter, had a benefit that evening at the Tremont Circus, and would throw 50 somersets, on a wager of 100 dollars. The *New York Herald*, of January 25, 1843, referred to "McFarland, the greatest vaulter in the known world," when he appeared with Welch's Park Circus in New York.

In 1842, Levi North returned to England and the following year, with

Tom Price, put together Price & North's Circus. At the end of the summer season, they disbanded, and North went home, to join Rockwell & Stone's Circus. He would be back in England on occasion, over the years.

In 1843 W. O. Dale and Tom McFarland came over to England. The highlight of this act was when the two vaulted against each other. These two boys were constantly swapping the record, and, by now, had both gone over 60 at a swing. McFarland was already being billed as the "60 Somerset Man"; by 1845 he was being billed as the 80-Somerset Man, which is plainly ridiculous blurb.

It was around 1843 that Arthur Barns made his move out of the grisly Finsbury tenement. Astley's New Royal Amphitheatre of Arts opened on Westminster Bridge Road, London, that year, and would be the home for Batty's Circus until 1853. Arthur Barns went to it one evening, and was mesmerized. The circus revealed another world, a world of excitement and glitter, something as far removed from the drab life of Masons Place as the human mind could imagine. It showed him that there was another kind of life out there, that he wasn't necessarily doomed to the foundry. What caught his imagination more than anything else at Astley's was the vaulting: acrobats springing into the air, turning head over heels, and landing back on their feet. In competition with one another, and to the ever increasing roar of the crowd, they would carry on somersaulting until one of them dropped. The survivor would then keep going, in an attempt to break the world record of the day. Sometimes he'd do it, sometimes he'd run out of steam before he got there, but the audience went wild every time.

Inspired after Astley's, Arthur Barns went home and immediately started to vault. This could be his one-way ticket out of the slum. Finally he mastered one somersault, then two, then three, on and on until he was able to do 20 at one throw. There's a quote from Peter Paterson's book *Glimpses of Real Life; Theatrical and Bohemian* (Nimmo, Edinburgh, 1864), chapter "Circus People on the Stroll" and sub-chapter "What Acrobats Can Do" (a piece that appeared in the *Glasgow Herald* of May 3, 1864, as well as in the *Preston Guardian* of May 7) which refers to this period. Arthur Barnes virtually speaks to us in this article. Paterson says,

> I can remember how great a man he was thought who could turn off the springboard ten consecutive somersaults; but now there is an acrobat (I have seen him do it in Sanger's Circus) who can turn seventy without once pausing to look over his shoulder. Surely that is thoroughly sensational! To throw a somersault on horseback, aided, as the performer is, by the velocity of the horse, is comparatively easy; but to turn heads over heels seventy or eighty times from a common spring-board, and in about as many seconds, is a feat that must have taken a long time to achieve. I once asked Mr. Barnes as to this, and he told me that for a

long time he could only do from twenty to thirty, but that, by constant practice and hard work, he eventually one day contrived to make out the fifty, and he does not despair of some day accomplishing the hundred!

Another insight into the Acrobat comes from William C. Honeyman's book *Strathspey Players, Past and Present* (1922, Larg & Sons). "Once, when I was a boy, I asked Arthur Barnes, the champion vaulter of the world, who could turn eighty somersaults in succession, if he could do all the other feats of the circus riders. 'Oh, yes,' he answered, 'but it is better to do one feat better than everyone else in the world, and get highly paid for it, than to do what thousands can do.'"

While the rest of Arthur Barnes' family, without exception, eked out the rest of their lives in the grim twilight of the East End, he was the only one to make it out into the big bright world. He apprenticed as a circus acrobat, and it wasn't long before he entered the ranks of the contenders.

The October 14, 1843, issue of the *York Herald* tells us that Tom Price, "the English Champion Vaulter," had done 60 somersaults, but this may be an exaggeration, as it was in an ad. The same paper, of precisely a week later, ran an ad for Price & North's British and American Circus, in which it proclaims that Bill Dale, the Champion American Vaulter [who was visiting the UK at that time], "has likewise performed a similar number of summersets, being the only man in England capable of competing with the British champion." By the 1840s the big vaulters were regularly doing over 50 somersaults at one throw, and the world record was an obsession, not only with the vaulters themselves, but with the circus-going public. Vaulting was where the excitement was, the big time, the fame, and the money.

The *New York Herald* of December 15, 1843, described those who would appear soon with the Broadway Circus at Niblo's Gardens, including "that man of 100 somersets, McFarland." However, by 1845 he was being billed as the 80-Somerset Man again. The same paper of March 8, 1844, referring to the upcoming Chatham Circus, which was going to perform that night, says, "McFarland turns his 50 somersets, and one more, with perfect ease." The *Herald* of a week before had said, "McFarland, the champion vaulter of the world, the man who makes nothing of turning 70 summersets, is engaged." The same paper of September 6, 1844, says, "McFarland throws 50 somersets at a spell" [at the Bowery Amphitheatre]. On the night of January 11, 1845, McFarland threw the unprecedented number of 66 somersets, and received a gold watch for this world record. All of which goes to show that McFarland's 80-Somerset Man and 100-Somerset Man tags had been blurb, pure and simple. Not an ounce of truth to it. But, Mac's 66 was genuine, all right, a new world record.

Meanwhile, Moses Lipman, the great American vaulter, did 50 somersaults in one trial, on January 3, 1844, while with Van Amburgh's circus in London. Lipman, it is said, was born in London in 1811, so he was 17 years older than Arthur Barnes. By 1842 he was reputed to have done 71 somersaults, but this is blurb, as was his "72-somerset man" moniker. Isaac A. Van Amburgh, born on March 11, 1801 (or was it May 26, 1808?), in Fishkill, New York, started as a lion tamer and by the age of 23 was a circus owner. In 1838, he took his show to England, survived a tiger attack at Astley's, and performed in front of Queen Victoria, who was a circus fan all her life. The *Liverpool Mercury* of March 8, 1844, tells us that Lipman threw the unprecedented number of 41 somersaults while performing in that city with Sands' and Van Amburgh's joint circus; and his 48 somersaults at Banbury on June 4, 1844, would still get rave notices.

About this time, Jem Ryan, the circus owner, bit off more than he could chew in a speculative amphitheatre in Birmingham, and went bust. He never recovered, going from a few more feeble attempts as proprietor to a long career as supporting player, to poverty, to squalor, to the courtroom.

Powell's Circus

William Powell was an equestrian. Born in 1815, in Edinburgh, he had been with Batty's Circus as a teenager, and in 1837, while performing with Jem Ryan's Circus in Birmingham, he married Elizabeth Anne Hengler, of Hengler's circus family. From 1841 to 1843 he was co-owner of Price & Powell's Royal Circus, then, when the partnership was dissolved on April 18, 1843, sole owner. The new Powell's Royal Circus played in Hammersmith and Stepney; in August and September they were in Dover; and in October in Canterbury. John Henderson and Alfred Hengler were with them then. By December 1843 they were at London Street, Greenwich.

While Powell's had been touring Kent, one of Mr. Batty's several touring companies was playing in Jersey. On August 18, 1843, while attempting a double somersault there, John Aymar, the great American vaulter, landed on his neck and was killed. This was not the first time this had happened to a vaulter. It was a dangerous game. Also at this period, Ducrow's was on tour, featuring Messrs. Kemp, Smith, Taylor, and Holyoake, the Antipodean Professors, going through their wonderful gymnastic feats. The term Antipodean was quite a common one in the 1840s circus, used by a welter of different performers. A man called the Antipodean Vaulter appeared at the New Marylebone Theatre, Lisson Grove, on January 8, 10 and 13, 1844. Among his fellow acts was Charles Dillon, with whom Arthur Barnes would appear five years later. Another was Tom Lee, the Irish comedian. Unfortunately, however, we don't know the identity of this particular Antipodean Vaulter. It may have been Arthur Barnes, but, more probably, the young Mr. Barnes was with Powell's at this time.

In January 1844 Van Amburgh and Dick Sands were drawing good crowds in Manchester with their joint circus. Price & North's British and American Circus played Newcastle on January 19, 1844. In February, Jimmy Carter, the American lion king, encouraged by the successful issue of his lions, tigers, and leopards, ventured to try his hand on a wife; Van Amburgh was his groomsman. In public, the two lion kings were fierce rivals, but, of course, in private life, they were best of friends.

Lloyd's London Weekly Newspaper [printed on a Sunday; known henceforth as *Lloyd's*], to whom we are indebted for the notices on Powell's at this period, tells us that at Greenwich, in the week February 5 to February 10,

1844, Powell's show commenced with the spectacle of *Mazeppa*, which was followed by Master Polaski as the Little Grenadier on a swift courser; Mr. Dewhurst's celebrated feats, including those on the Magic Ladder; John Samwell as Napoleon, and as Nimrod, the Fox Hunter; Charles Adams, the clown, as Jim Crow and his Granny; John Milton Hengler in his flights of fancy; and, of course, Mr. Powell, the equestrian.

The King of the Clowns, William F. Wallett, opened with Powell's at Greenwich on Monday, February 12, 1844. Also featured were Mr. Powell, as Don Juan the Libertine, and "Vaulting, led by Mr. [John] Henderson, the Spirit of the Air." This was a company of vaulters, a common thing in the circus in those days. During the run at Greenwich, there was "some most surprising summerset throwing by Messrs. Connor and others." The Connor is Harry Connor. The "others" might include Arthur Barnes, but we don't know for sure. However, usually, where there was Connor there was Barnes, and vice versa, even in those early days.

Harry Connor, born in Dublin in 1821, burst on the scene in 1843, a year before Arthur Barnes did. The *Era* of April 30, 1843, says: "Astley's Royal Amphitheatre. Mr. Batty begs to inform his patrons, and the public generally, that he will produce the greatest wonder of the present day, Mr. O'Conner [sic], the double summerset thrower, who will positively throw two summersets in the air from one beat, a feat never performed by any other artist." In 1844, in Manchester, Harry married Hannahbella Williamson, daughter of a publican in Salford.

The time came in every circus's long run at a town when benefit nights followed each other rapidly. This usually signified that the end of the visit was drawing near. There were two types of benefit. One was for a local charity, which was calculated to gain the sympathy of the local bigwigs, which it always did, of course. The other type of benefit was a tried and tested custom whereby the night's receipts, or part of them, would go to an individual, either a performer or the proprietor, or perhaps some other person connected with the circus. By the middle of February, Powell's was making grand preparations for a removal to Woolwich. The architect Frederick James was progressing rapidly at Woolwich with the new arena. The manager, Mr. Powell, had done well at Greenwich, and finally closed the doors on Monday, February 19, 1844, taking his leave, respected by the inhabitants. The affability and gentlemanly bearing of the whole company had won for them the most earnest wishes for their future success. However, Mr. Powell had been experiencing financial troubles even before Greenwich, and it wouldn't be long before his days as a circus proprietor were over.

On February 24, 1844, T. P. Cooke's Circus opened in Glasgow, for a three-week run there. One of the acts was Harry Walker, the "beautiful Acrobatic Vaulter," on the Flying Cord. Mr. Walker would often perform with Arthur Barnes over the years. Tom Lee, the daring and graceful somersault horse rider from Astley's, was another performer at Cooke's that opening night in Glasgow, as was Lavater Lee, the great somersault thrower, not to mention James Carter, the Lion King. Thomas Potter Cooke, one of the great circus proprietors, was born in 1786, and died in London in 1864.

On February 28, 1844, Powell's duly opened at Beresford Street, Woolwich, for a run that would last a couple of months. Another paper published every Sunday was the *Era*, both that paper and *Lloyd's* carrying news of circuses. As silent as the *Era* is on Powell's at this point of time, *Lloyd's* is voluble, if not always illuminating on all points of interest, notably that of Arthur Barnes. It is at Woolwich that we first definitely pick up Mr. Barnes as a professional performer. He was 15.

On Monday, March 11, 1844, and for the rest of the week, the performances commenced with John Henderson, as the Air Diver of Venice. In the course of the evening the following classic acts were introduced: Master Polaski, the Infant Prodigy, as the Little Jockey (this is Jean Polaski, otherwise known as Young Polaski, brother of equestrian Antoine Polaski); Mademoiselle Carolina as the Sylph of the Circle (this was her opening night); vaulting by the whole company, led by Mr. Henderson, the Spirit of the Air, and Harry Connor, the renowned double-summerset thrower; Master W. Samwell as Chifney, the Racing Jockey (Bill Samwell, born in 1827 in Mildenhall, Suffolk, was son of the Samwell's Circus Company people, and brother of John Samwell; he was playing the real-life jockey, Sam Chifney); Mons. Hengler, who introduced the beautiful cream-colored steed Prince George, and put him through his incredible performance; Mr. Paddington upon the slack rope, as the Flying Gymnasiast; Mr. J. Samwell, the much admired equestrian, appearing as Masaniello, upon a blood steed (John was born in King's Lynn, Norfolk, in 1820); the magnificent entree of *Sir Roger de Coverley*, introducing the whole stud of richly mounted steeds; Mr. J. Samwell and Mademoiselle Carolina appeared in a celebrated act called *The Swiss Milk Maid and Her Lover*; Mr. Powell, the Prince of English Riders, appeared in his favorite act, *The Tar of All Weathers*; the whole concluded with *The Chinese Law*. Doors opened at 6:30, performances to commence at 7:00. Front boxes: 2/6; side boxes: 1/6; pit 1/-; gallery 6d. Half-price, to the boxes, at 9:00—front boxes: 1/6; side boxes: 1/-. No half-price to the pit or gallery. Children under 10 years of age, to the front box: 1/6; side box: 1/-. Architect to the establishment, Frederick James. Acting manager, Mr. Stanley.

Pablo Paddington deserves a little more inspection, especially under his trousers. Back in the 1820s, he and John Clifford, both "colored men," were touring with Cooke's circus. In fact, Clifford had been 15 years with Cooke's, from the time he was five. Pablo had a long affair with Miss King, an affair that became somewhat scandalous. In the meantime, Mr. Clifford became pregnant, and had a child in the workhouse on January 2, 1827. Several newspapers, including the *Leicester Chronicle*, picked up the story "Two Female Impostors [sic]." In 1838 Pablo was with the Samwells, and in 1840 with Jem Ryan, billed as "the extraordinary slack rope vaulter, Mr. Paddington, the man of colour," displaying his surprising evolutions on the corde volante, and concluding his feats by riding on his head upon a quart pot with the horse at full speed. Ryan's big equestrian romantic spectacle was *Raymond and Agnes; or the Bleeding Nun of Lindenberg*. What a title! Another of the acts with Ryan's then was Mr. Price, the first summerset thrower in the world. William Powell was also a member of the troupe, as was Mons. Hengler on the tightrope. Pablo Paddington would continue to perform all over the country for some years.

The first mention of Arthur Barnes, by actual name, is in *Lloyd's* of March 17, 1844, which describes Powell's at Woolwich as a "brilliant concentration of novelty and attraction." The ad announces the reengagement of Miss C. O'Donnell, the celebrated equestrian; the first appearance of Mr. James Furr, the celebrated clown; the first appearance of the renowned Herr Hengler, the Operatic Tight-Rope Dancer, whose performances have created an astounding sensation in every town and city upon the Continent. This is Edward Henry Hengler, more of whom soon. It also tells us that tomorrow (Monday) the performances will commence with the appearance of Master J. Hengler (this is John Michael Hengler, younger brother of Charles Hengler; his relationship with Arthur Barnes would continue over the decades), as The Little Horticulturist, and that Mr. Samwell and his brother will appear as The Olympian Riders upon two blood steeds. Mr. Powell, in his classic masterpiece of equestrianism, appeared as Falstaff, Shylock, and Richard III, and "Messrs. Conner [sic], Elliott, H. Elliott, and Barnes, as The Acrobats of Albion." Also billed were the laughable scene of Cupid in a soot-bag; Mr. Samwell and Miss O'Donnell appeared as Jockey and Jenny upon two Arabian steeds, and the Grand Cavalcade of the Mamaluke [sic] Chief, introduced the whole stud of horses. Mr. Henderson appeared in his pantomime scene as *The Merry Corporal*, and Miss O'Donnell was the Circassian Flower Girl. The show concluded with *Sir Gilpin Cabbage*. The Brothers Elliott, who will figure so strongly in this story, were Timothy and Henry, both born in Islington, sons of a furrier, Tim in 1824, and Harry in 1826. Miss O'Donnell had begun her circus career as an infant prodigy in the 1830s, working with, among others, the polander Edwin Hughes, in Batty's Circus.

At the time Powell's was playing Woolwich, the old champion pugilist Tom Cribb was living there, retired, of course, and flat broke. On that very evening, Monday, March 18, 1844, the fancy gave him a benefit at the National Baths, on Westminster Road, in London. Unfortunately, Tom couldn't attend, being indisposed, and it is equally likely that he was too unfit to attend the circus in Woolwich, even if he could have afforded the price of admission. Poor old Tom, he only had four years to live on this Earth, but, as a consolation, his name would rightly live on forever in all the boxing halls of fame.

In those days, there were no performances on a Sunday, but every other evening of the week Powell's continued to play at Woolwich. On Monday, April 1, 1844, and for the rest of that week, the circus commenced with "the appearance of Messrs. Conner [sic], Elliot, H. Elliott, and Barnes, as the Jingling Jumpers." This term "Jingling Jumpers" was not new; Jingling refers to Peking. There was animated architecture by the whole company; Mr. Samwell and Miss O'Donnell as the Greek Warrior and the Circassian Maid, upon two blood steeds; Mr. Furr, the modern Samson, performed his giant-like feats of strength, and introduced his wonderful trained dog Blutherrups; Mr. Powell appeared in his *Olio, or Masquerade*, in full gallop, introducing six different characters; Master Polaski appeared upon a swift courser, as the Little Grenadier. Mr. Samwell introduced his much admired act, descriptive of the life and exploits of Napoleon Buonaparte. The new grand spectacle, introducing the whole stud of horses, was entitled *Europe, Asia, Africa and America*. Mr. Paddington executed her wonderful acts of dancing upon the slack rope. Also on the bill was the laughable extravaganza of *Old Giles's Wedding Day*. The whole concluded with the laughable scene, entitled *Lubin and Annette*, in which Mrs. Powell appeared upon the tightrope. Doors opened at 7:00, performances to commence at 7:30.

On Thursday, April 4, 1844, under the kind and distinguished patronage of Colonel Sir George Hoste, KCB, and the officers of the Royal Engineers, a brilliant evening amusement took place by desire at Powell's, with the brass band of the regiment attending at intervals during the program, playing some beautiful overtures, national airs, etc. On Good Friday, there were no performances, and the night of Monday, April 22, was a benefit for Mrs. Powell. The performances commenced with the appearance of Mr. Henderson, in his equestrian act, *The Corporal of the 41st, or Tom Late for Drill*. Mons. Hengler introduced the diminutive pony, Jim Crow, and put this astonishing animal through a variety of feats. Miss O'Donnell appeared in an elegant equestrian scene, entitled *An Act of Fancy*, and concluded with the scarf dance upon horseback. Mrs. Powell, by particular desire, appeared on the tightrope, and, with Miss O'Donnell, danced a pleasing pas de deux. Master John Hengler threw backward and forward summersets upon the tightrope. Master Polaski appeared on two rapid coursers as The Old English Gentleman and took several surprising leaps. Mr. Samwell was The Italian Bandit. Mr. Powell, as *The*

Sprite of the Morning Star, introduced his talented infant family. *Sir Roger de Coverley, or The Flitch of Bacon* was performed, and the whole concluded with the laughable extravaganza of *Sir Gilpin Cabbage*.

Dick Sands broke away from Van Amburgh, and the two circuses each began an 1844 summer tour. On April 29 and 30, 1844, Van Amburgh's Roman Amphitheatre played at Macclesfield, and on May 2 and 3 at Shelton. On May 3 and 4, 1844, Richard Sands' American Circus opened at Worcester, with Mr. Lipman vaulting. Later in May, Van Amburgh's were in Stourport, then Droitwich, and finally Gloucester, taking in £140 a day at the latter place. From May 22 to the 25th, they played Cheltenham, and Sands played Watlington on May 22.

According to *Lloyd's* of May 12, 1844, "Powell's has left Woolwich, and on Monday [i.e., May 13] opens a splendid pavilion for equestrian performances at Chatham." *Lloyd's* of May 19, 1844, tells us that they were at Globe Lane, Chatham, open every evening. Triumphant success of the present season. Second week of the appearance of the great French rider, Paul Masotta, from Astley's. A complete change in the performances given every two evenings. Ladies and gentlemen taught the polite art of riding by Mr. Hengler, riding master, of whom cards of terms may be had, or at the box-office of the circus. Acting manager, Mr. Walker.

At that time, May 1844, Pablo Fanque's was playing at Chadwick's Orchard, Preston, in Lancashire (*Preston Guardian*, May 18, 1844; Preston was always an important venue for circuses, and, unless otherwise stated, our guide over the years for events in this town is the faithful *Guardian*). Some of Pablo's acts were the Flying Man, the Antipodean Brothers, Athletic Tour de Force, Sauteurs, and Gymnastic Interludes. Tom Swann (a Birmingham boy) and John Griffiths (a Shrewsbury boy) were the clowns. Pablo Fanque, who would become an important employer of Arthur Barnes, was really William Darby, a mulatto born in Norwich on February 28, 1796, and he had started his own circus in 1841, based out of Lancashire. There is a playbill for February 14, 1843, for Pablo Fanque's Circus Royal at Town Meadows, Rochdale, the evening being for the benefit of Mr. Kite (that is, William Kite, late of Wells's Circus) and Mr. John Henderson, the celebrated acrobat, who threw 21 somersets on the solid ground. On Monday, June 3, 1844, Pablo took his own benefit, but, perhaps more important, it was the first night there of the Virginian Brothers, "from Mr. Batty's Olympic Circus in London, who have been acknowledged by all who have seen them to be the first-rate somerset throwers and acrobats in England." Who the Virginian Brothers were we don't know, probably just a nonce name, like the Olympic Circus, which was really Astley's Amphitheatre, in London, where Mr. Batty was the manager. However, the Virginians may have been the trio later called the American

Brothers. Pablo's last performance in Preston was on Thursday, June 6, and he left town next day.

Mr. Cornwall's circus was playing Falmouth at that time, followed by Launceston, where Mr. Cornwall found himself in financial difficulties, and borrowed £60, which he couldn't pay back. On June 28, 1844, while the company was playing Truro, the bailiffs came in and seized the circus, selling it piecemeal by auction the following Saturday. A lot of innocent players were left stranded. Mr. Cornwall retired to his home in Jersey, eventually becoming the landlord of the Seaton House, and, in his spare time, opening the Theatre Royal there, which never really worked. Henry Cornwall had had an interesting start in life. Born in 1810, he was a foundling in Redruth, Cornwall, and his adopting mother, Nanny, named him after the county. He trained as a musician, and worked as such with Wombwell's Menagerie before starting his own circus. In 1838, in Preston, he married Mary Ann Samwell, sister of John and Bill of equestrian fame.

Van Amburgh's were in Wootton-under-Edge on June 1, 1844, and on Monday, June 3, they opened in Bristol, with Tom Moseley, Harry Walker, and Nunn the strongman as attractions. Wallett was with them then, as was a giraffe. On June 20, one of the monkeys escaped, and, boys being boys, they stoned the critter to death. Welcome to Bristol. On June 25, 1844, Van Amburgh's opened in Salisbury, and on the 26th in Warminster. Meanwhile, Dick Sands played Market Harborough on June 8, 1844; one of the equestrians threw 37 back somersets in quick succession, and Mr. Sands himself threw 21. They were in Pontefract on June 19, Selby on June 20, Wetherby on June 21) and Boroughbridge on June 22. On June 24, 25, and 26 they played in a field at the Lord Mayor's Walk, in York, and this gig was followed by Knaresborough (June 27), Harrogate (June 28), and Ripon (June 29).

On July 8, Van Amburgh's began a stint at Windsor, and on July 11, by royal command, they performed in front of the Queen at the castle. It was a big moment for Wallett the clown, as, in the absence of Van Amburgh, he was chosen to present a pair of new lion cubs in the Queen's drawing room to not only Her Majesty, but also Prince Albert, the Duchess of Kent, the Countess Wratislaw, and a pride of other dignitaries.

In the meantime, Dick Sands played Driffield, but we don't have the exact date. Another circus to visit Driffield was Ginnett's, on July 19, 1844. For Sands it was on to Stockton-on-Tees (July 16) and Hartlepool (July 17). On July 29, 1844, Van Amburgh's entered Southampton. Then it was on to Portsmouth, and along the south coast to Brighton by mid-August, following the lousy weather. In August 1844, Powell's Circus was in Maidstone, and doing very well attendance-wise, presumably still with Arthur Barnes. We next pick up Price & North's in Chelmsford, on August 19, 20, and 21. On

August 18, 1844, a Sunday, as they were on their way into Chelmsford, the wagons passed through the sleepy little parish of Margaret Roothing, just as the Rev. William Shepherd was conducting morning service. The noise was absolutely deafening, and God could not hear his flock. This so upset the priest that he brought suit against Price & North. Mr. Price appeared in court at Dunmow Petty Sessions on August 26, Mr. North being absent, and was fined a pound for conveying goods by wagon on a Sunday.

On August 22, 1844, Sands was in Bangor, and on August 28, Van Amburgh's played Sevenoaks, and the following day, Tunbridge Wells. An elephant has big testicles, which comes as no surprise to anyone, except perhaps the horn player with Van Amburgh's during that summer tour. He would amuse himself by firing little balls at the objects of his fascination, a dangerous business, as many of the other lads warned him. While the troupe was in Canterbury, in September, Bolivar got hold of the musician with his trunk, trumpet and music book and all, and, lifting him up as high as he could, slammed him to the ground. The trumpeter was lucky on this occasion.

Sands was in Hereford on September 23, 1844, and we next pick up Van Amburgh's in Colchester (October 2 and 3, 1844), Manningtree (October 4), Harwich (October 5), Ipswich (October 7 and 8), and Stowmarket (October 9). On October 25, while Van Amburgh's were in Norwich, Bolivar opened the door of his elephant house and went for a quiet evening stroll down a country road. Scared the hell out of everyone, but they got him back without any trouble.

Lloyd's of November 10, 1844, says: "Hastings. Mr. Powell has seceded from the business of the circus; Mr. Robinson, the well known horse dealer having, on Saturday last [Nov. 2] sold by public auction the whole of his stud and properties which, with a few exceptions were bought by Herr Hengler, the celebrated rope-dancer [i.e., Edward Henry Hengler], who commenced his management on Monday night [i.e., Nov. 4], having put forth a bill which drew a crowded and fashionable house [i.e., in Hastings]." The purchasers were actually Edward Hengler and his brother Charles, and this marked the beginning of the career of the Henglers as proprietors. On Monday, December 2, 1844, Hengler's closed at Hastings, that night being under the patronage of Lady Montgomery and Sir Charles Lamb. The circus "is about to commence at Greenwich" [*Lloyd's*, December 8, 1844].

Hengler's was one of the great circus dynasties. It all started with Michael Hengler, a German artillery officer who came to London, becoming a pyrotechnist at Astley's Circus. He died in 1802, but his widow carried on Hengler's Fireworks, dying in a spectacular fire at her factory in 1845. Henry Michael Hengler, their son, was a rope dancer, apprenticed at an early age to Jean Richer, the French harlequin, acrobat, and rope dancer. In 1789 he appeared before Louis XVI and Marie Antoinette, and, after much success in Paris, returned to London at the time of his father's death, and appeared in major English circuses. His children included Georgianna, who married James Henry Frowde and was mother of Jem Frowde, later circus owner and employer of Arthur Barnes; Eliza, who married William Powell, the future circus owner and employer of Arthur Barnes; Henrietta, who married Richard Beacham, the equestrian; Edward Henry Hengler; Charles Hengler (real name Frederick Charles Hengler, born August 12, 1821, Cambridge), future circus owner and employer of Arthur Barnes; Alfred Hugh Hengler; Agnes, who married Lambeth boy John Henderson, future employer of Arthur Barnes; and John Michael Hengler (1831–1919), also known as John Milton Hengler, the famous tight-rope artiste, and colleague and traveling companion of Arthur Barnes. Incidentally, Charles Hengler married Mary Ann Frances Sprake, daughter of circus bandmaster Jacob Sprake and his wife Susannah Cooke, the sister of William Cooke, the famous circus owner and future employer of Arthur Barnes. Also, incidentally, Charles and Mary Ann's eldest daughter, Susanna Jane Hengler married William Powell's son William Henry Powell. So, it was a tight knit shop.

On October 29 and 30, 1844, Dick Sands was in Exeter, and on November 5 and 6, Van Amburgh's were in Bury St. Edmunds. In late November 1844, they were playing at Midsummer Common, in Cambridge. Sands opened in Bath on November 25, 1844, for a twelve-night run.

Hughes's Circus Royal

Edwin Hughes, one of the great circus proprietors of those days, was born in Birmingham in 1813, the son of a steel toy manufacturer. As a younger man, Master Hughes had sold lucifer matches on the street. Mr. Batty, the circus manager, hired him in a pub, and Hughes became one of the great polanders. In 1831 he was with Jem Ryan's circus, standing on his head, on a pole 14 feet high, without the aid of his hands, surrounded by a brilliant display of fireworks. Hughes was proprietor of a company at Donnybrook Fair, in Dublin, for two years, 1842–44, and then at Cheltenham started his Mammoth Circus. Hughes's Circus Royal had been playing at the back of North Street, in Bristol since November 25, 1844, when, on December 4, 1844, the great somersault thrower Levi North opened with them for a brief time. And Jem Ryan was appearing for a while on the tightrope. Then, on Monday, January 6, 1845, Arthur Barnes, still only 16, opened with them.

The question is: Where was Arthur Barnes over the Christmas and New Year period of 1844–45, before he joined Hughes in Bristol on January 6? It seems unlikely that he would be at leisure over the period of the Christmas entertainments, but if he was performing, we can't find him. We know he wasn't yet with Hughes. William Cooke's Circus Royal was performing in Poplar, and several performers are mentioned by name, but not our man. Same with Astley's, in London, where Tom Barry was clowning. At the City of London National Theatre, two clowns were appearing in the pantomime *The Fairy Gnomes of the Golden Caves*— Signors Barnesconi and Carterini (or Casterini, or Carlorini, depending on which paper you read), leaving "the audience in a continued roar of laughter." Despite being clowns, it is tempting to think this Barnesconi might be our man, but these two clowns were still appearing there on January 6, 1845, the day Arthur Barnes opened with Hughes in Bristol.

The *Bristol Mercury* of January 4, 1845, has this to say (and, for this period of time, we rely heavily upon that illustrious newspaper, as well as, to some extent, on the *Era*):

> Hughes's Circus-Royal. Monday, Jan. 6, 1845. Decidedly the greatest combination of talent ever produced in this city will be brought forward on the above night, introducing for the first time the great French riders, Monsieur and Madame Dumos, whose astonishing performance, having created so great a sensation on

the Continent, induced His Majesty, the King of the French, to give his royal command that they should appear before him at Franconi's Cirque Olympique, Paris, in order that His Majesty might have an opportunity of witnessing their miraculous prowess. In addition to the above artistes, Messrs. Barnes, Elliott, Conner [sic] and S. Elliott, will make their first appearance. They have been engaged, at an enormous expense, for a limited period, and will display their feats of La Tranca Hispaniola, Gymnasia, etc. The whole strength of the company will be brought into requisition.

It goes on to say:

> Notice: Mr. Hughes respectfully begs to acquaint the nobility, gentry, and public in general, that, in compliance with numerous requests from families residing in the country, who are prevented from attending the evening entertainments, he has arranged that two day-performances shall take place next week on the following days: Thursday and Saturday, January 9 and 11, commencing at 2 o'clock. The polite art of riding taught. Doors open at half past six o'clock, performance to commence at half past seven precisely.

As for the equestrians Mons. and Madame Dumos, when it says "introducing for the first time," what it means is in Bristol. In 1843 they had toured Britain with Francois Tourniaire's Royal Olympic Arena of Arts, going over to Cooke's Circus in early 1844. In April 1846, they would be at Astley's, in London, along with star Austrian equestrienne Pauline Hinne, who was Madame Dumos' sister. Mons. Dumos, who looked somewhat like Napoleon, had two performing children — Caroline and Master Dumos. In 1846, in Lambeth, Pauline Hinne married another of the Batty performers, Jem Newsome, a Newcastle lad. The Newsomes would shortly depart for Le Continong, and, aside from the occasional visit, would not return until 1852.

On January 7, 1845, there was a grand fashionable fete in Bristol for Hughes's Circus, being under the distinguished patronage of Philip William Skinner Miles, Esq., M.P. The *Mercury* of January 11, 1845, says (of the upcoming week): "Last week but one of Hughes's Circus Royal." This night, Monday the 13th, and for four successive evenings, the troupe performed the grand romantic melodrama *Timour the Tartar*, in which male and female elephants appeared in harness. Also on the bill was Harry Connor, "the only double somerset thrower in the world, will positively throw two somersets at one bound!" Harry was, perhaps, the only double somerset thrower in Britain, but not in the world; Bill Stout had performed the act at the Bowery Theatre the year before, and it is said that Tomkinson the vaulter (not the clown) had done the first ever double off a springboard, as early as 1835. The paper says "the performances will be varied by the introduction of the Antipodean Professors, Messrs. Barnes, Elliott, Conner [sic], and S. Elliott." Signor Paul

Masotta, the Italian equestrian professor from the Cirque Olympique, in Paris, made his debut with Hughes that night, "one of the most intrepid and daring riders we ever saw," said the *Mercury* of January 18, 1845.

In addition to these amusements, Wombwell's Grand National Menagerie had just arrived in Bristol, at the Grove, with 14 wagons of animals and birds, and were exhibiting their portable zoo to the masses. Old Mr. Wombwell was still alive then.

In January 1845, at the Royal Amphitheatre in Liverpool, Mr. Batty's troupe, including Jem Newsome and Madame Isabelle, had been pulling them in since late the previous year. They would play there until Easter, people flocking in to see Lavater Lee a-leaping, Mr. Charlton a-clowning, Alfred Cooke equestrianing, Herr Maus (Friedrich Adolf Maus) strongmanning, Mons. Plege tightroping, Professor Dewhurst and his infant sons gymnasticizing, and General Tom Thumb being — well — small.

On January 6, 1845, Dick Sands' American Equestrian Company opened at the Theatre Royal, in the same town (i.e., Liverpool), going head to head with Batty. Aside from the gymnastic feats of Mr. Sands and his little brother, Maurice, star attractions included Messrs. Joe Pentland and Rockwell, the Yankee clowns. Mr. Caulfield, the transatlantic Hercules, joined Sands on January 13 and left on February 7. At that time the circus was also featuring Madame Fraustinia on the tightrope and the two vaulters Levi North and Moses Lipman. In February 1845, Dick Sands went over to the Queen's Theatre, Manchester, where he and Maurice came in for raves.

On Thursday, January 16, 1845, Mr. Hughes drove through the city of Bristol, 20 horses in pairs in hand, and then they performed the morning show (morning shows were almost always at 2 o'clock in the afternoon, and were also called day performances). The *Mercury* of January 11, 1845, warned its readers that Friday night, the 17th, would be the last performance of *Timour the Tartar*, but the warning was groundless (in fact, an old circus trick — need one say more?). The show was decidedly successful, and nightly drew crowded houses. That Saturday, January 18, 1845, they presented their last morning performance, and that evening, by particular desire, was a grand fashionable dress-box night, under the distinguished patronage of Mr. Miles, M.P.; J. Harding, Esq., high-sheriff; H. Bush, Esq.; Peter Maze, Esq.; John Kerle Haberfield, Esq.; and G. Goldney, Esq. *Timour the Tartar* commenced the performance. The *Bristol Mercury* of January 18, 1845, mentions (of the upcoming week, beginning Monday, January 20) that "the four amphigymnasiarchs [i.e., Barnes, Connor, Elliott and Elliott] will exhibit a curious combination of muscular power." The same ad tells of displays of agility by revolving antiscii. The show concluded with the *Battle of Waterloo* (a spectacle, by J. H. Amherst, first produced at Astley's, on Easter Monday, 1824). Nightly crowded houses, the paper says. "The four Acrobats perform many wonderful acts, and one of them (Mr. Connor) takes some extraordinary leaps, and throws two, and even three, somersaults at a single bound." The paper calls Madame Dumos an elegant rider, and tells us that Mr. Davis, in a little piece called *The Cockney Sportsman*, "exhibits considerable comic powers."

At Hughes's Circus, the receipts of Friday (January 24, 1845) evening's performance, amounting to £14, went to the Bristol Infirmary and General Hospital. The following day Hughes presented a grand fashionable night, for the benefit of Master Ryan, on which occasion Ryan made his first appearance on horseback. *The Battle of Waterloo* got very good reviews in the *Mercury* of January 25.

The ad in the *Mercury* of January 25, 1845, says, of Monday, January 27, "Positively the last week of Hughes' Circus Royal" in Bristol. "Grand fashionable night on Monday, January 27, for the benefit of Mrs. Hughes, and during the week, when the entertainments will commence with the celebrated national sport of the Terreo, or Spanish Bullfight, in all the splendour which crowned its long and brilliant career at Astley's Royal Amphitheatre, London, for one hundred successive nights." It featured Leon Davis, the "the champion matador." The bull was actually played by a horse dressed up as el toro. Also on the bill were the juvenile equestrienne Miss Brown, and the Protean Artistes. Elliott did the Tranca Hispaniola, and although Arthur Barnes is not mentioned, one assumes that because Elliot and the Tranca are mentioned, Barnes, Connor, and the other Elliott were there too. The ad also says "Signor Massotta will execute his peculiar and daring exercises."

It seems Hughes's last night at Bristol was February 1, 1845, but, being the last night, Hughes did not see fit to advertise in the local paper. Hughes left Bristol on Sunday, February 2, 1845, and one has to assume that because Arthur Barnes was with Hughes at the beginning of 1845, and also at the end (which he was), then he was with him throughout the entire year. This would make sense, given his youth and need for steady employment. With this in mind, all we can do is piece Hughes's itinerary together, from existing press reports. As the winter season ended in late March as a rule, it is possible that after Bristol they didn't gig again until April, when we begin to pick them up on their summer tour, a grind of the country towns, one village after another. Curiously, they just missed performing in the same city as General Tom Thumb, who arrived on the 6th, for a three-day gig at the Assembly Rooms, Prince's Street, Bristol.

On February 8, 1845, Mr. Lewis, performing as Harlequin in the pantomime *Johnny Gilpin*, at Astley's, in London, made his usual jump through a window on stage, but, tonight, there was no one to catch him. It shook him up a bit. Only four days later, at the same theater, a lad named Edward Woods, aged 12, a general gopher around the stage, had his leg broken when a trap door fell on it. They rushed him to the Westminster Hospital, where the surgeon, Mr. Beaumont, fixed him up.

About that time, Van Amburgh was at the Theatre Royal, Nottingham. This from the *Era* of March 9, 1845: "Although the attractions at Van Amburgh's are great, the business has been but indifferent. Mr. O'Dale and Mr. Lipman, the former the greatest summerset thrower extant, and the latter one of great pretensions, gave unequivocal satisfaction. The public, however, seem to prefer stage spectacles, combined with horsemanship, in preference to the latter only." This was an acute observation, and circus proprietors took notice. On March 24, W. F. Wallett, the clown, who had recently been with Van Amburgh's, in Manchester, opened a circus at Ashton under Lyne (it didn't last long). On Whitmonday, 1845, Jem Ryan and Edward Hicken, in partnership, opened at the Amphitheatre, Birmingham, with a talented company.

As for Arthur Barnes's family back in the East End, his parents carried on at 25 Masons Place, with the children getting older all the time, as sometimes happened in the slums of London. Henry, Richard, Mary Ann, and Jane were all still living at home. Henry was at work at the foundry, of course, and the girls were doing millinery work. The Acrobat's eldest brother, Tom, was living with a young shoebinder, Mary Ann Walker, at nearby George Street, and on March 17, 1845, at the district parish church of St. Paul's, Islington, they were married.

On March 24, 1845, William Cooke's Amphitheatre opened in Manchester, with Mons. Leonard and Bill O'Dale, both poached from Van Amburgh. On April 14, 1845, the circus opened at Stockport, during an enormous storm, but would return to Manchester at Whitsuntide. Wallett was with them then, as were Messrs. Dale, Rochez, Hume, and Jackson. Wallett left for the United States on April 27, 1845.

In April 1845, while performing in *The Fox Hunt* at the Royal Amphitheatre in Liverpool, Mr. Somerville had a nasty accident. While in the act of drawing a loaded pistol from his belt, the trigger, which was on full cock, caught in a button, and one of the balls was discharged into, well, you know.

We next pick up Hughes in the Cotswolds, even though Barnes is not mentioned in the article in the April 26 edition of *Jackson's Oxford Journal* (henceforth known as *Jackson's*), which tells us that Mr. Hughes, the equestrian, visited the pretty little Oxfordshire town of Chipping Norton (the word "chipping" meaning "market") on Thursday (i.e., April 24, 1845). The long train of carriages and horsemen, with several ladies on horseback, moved in grand procession through the town soon after 11 o'clock — the lead was taken by Mr. Hughes driving 14 pied horses in hand, with a splendid carriage containing his band of musicians, and the rear was brought up by the Burmese Imperial State carriage and throne, drawn by two elephants, the whole forming a spectacle exceedingly grand and imposing. A pavilion was erected in a close belonging to the White Hart Inn, where the parties performed in the afternoon and evening, many hundreds of persons attending to witness it. Five days after the circus had left Chipping Norton, that town would celebrate its annual Fair Day. The circus, of course, used the road; Chipping Norton's town council, like those of so many local towns, was pushing hard for a railway connection.

In 1883 Richard Hemming, by then a retired circus proprietor, was in the United States, reminiscing in "The Sawdust Circle," an article picked up by the *St. Louis-Globe Democrat*. Hemming, a Birmingham lad, six years younger than Arthur Barnes, had often performed with the world's greatest vaulter back in England in the old days. "Very few of the present generation have any idea of the complete change which circuses have undergone within the past twenty years. The mode of travel, the tent, the ring, the performance, the salaries paid, the method of training riders, are all very different. All circuses twenty years ago traveled in wagons drawn by horses; now all but the smallest and most insignificant travel by rail." He then explains that the size of the modern circus would render road transportation impossible. "The labor, anxiety, and possible loss with even the small-sized wagon shows of the past were terrible. In bad weather, on muddy roads, horses would become exhausted and have to be left to die; wagons would be broken to pieces, and the show would often fail, day after day, to reach in time the towns where it was advertised to perform." He continues,

> Still, traveling with a wagon show had its pleasures for the performers. Those of them who received large salaries had their own conveyances, and could choose their own time for making their journeys, provided they arrived at their destination in time to perform, and in pleasant weather it was by no means disagreeable to drive a fine team over good roads, through a beautiful country, in the cool of a summer morning, from twelve to thirty miles, which was about the range of the distances. But in very hot weather the drives were made at night to spare the horses, and thus the people often lost a great deal of rest. The way through the country was found by two men who, in a buggy, preceded the show and, aided by a synopsis of the route furnished them by the advance agent, inquired the way and marked doubtful parts of the road with rails taken from the neighboring fences.

At Yarmouth, at 6:15 in the evening of Friday, May 2, 1845, Nelson the clown, a performer at Cooke's Circus in that town, undertook to swim in a tub drawn by four geese from the drawbridge on the quay to the suspension bridge across the North River, the bridge having been erected in 1829 on the site of an ancient ferry, near the Bure. This tub and geese idea was not new by any means, it having been introduced on the Thames in 1809 by the late Liverpool circus clown Dickie Usher. And, to boot, in 1843, Mr. Nelson had performed a similar stunt of naval quackery in Guernsey, with twelve ducks. And Astley's clown Tom Barry had done it with geese on the Thames in 1844. Thousands of people flocked both banks of the river to witness Nelson's exploit. The clown commenced his feat with the floodtide at the drawbridge, and had entered the North River. There were many persons on the bridge, and that number grew as Nelson approached. They all wanted to see him as he passed beneath them, and, hundreds of them shifted suddenly to the south side of the bridge as Nelson got to Bessey's Wharf. With the sudden shift, the chain holding up this side of the bridge collapsed, and the assemblage plunged into the water, over a hundred dying. It was the greatest tragedy to hit Yarmouth since the plague of 1759. Although the papers lashed out at Nelson's stupidity in performing such a stunt, it wasn't his fault at all. He was just a clown doing a stunt that had already been performed by himself and others to the delight of all. It was the bridge that was woefully inadequate, and the police should never have allowed such a number of persons on it at any one time. However, the following morning, at a first court hearing, Mr. William Cooke told them he had decided to leave town. The court thought that was a jolly good idea.

Nothing on Hughes until Saturday, May 24, 1845, when we are told by the *Leicester Chronicle* that Hughes's Great Mammoth Establishment entered Market Harborough that day, a few minutes before 11 o'clock, and was admitted by all who witnessed the procession to be one of the grandest sights ever seen in that town. Although the rain had been falling in torrents nearly all the morning and the previous night, there were several thousand spectators present on the occasion. The procession was headed by the original "Prince of Whips" Hughes, driving 14 beautiful horses, two abreast, attached to a splendid carriage, in which was seated the band; after this followed several other horses and carriages in succession, consisting of about 40 horses. These were followed by the Rath, or Burmese Imperial state carriage and throne, drawn by the royal male and female elephants, on which was seated a native of the Birman empire, dressed in his full native costume. The Rath on which he was seated was richly and deeply carved, and much admired for its exquisite workmanship. The male elephant, which was the smaller, took the lead; he stood about seven feet high, was eight years of age and weighed about two tons twelve hundredweight. The female elephant, which was twenty years old, stood about nine feet six high and weighed more than five tons. Both were very handsomely equipped in harness, and when going along the streets, seemed very quiet and manageable. In consequence of the rain falling very heavily there was a very small attendance at the afternoon's performance, which took place under a canopy in the Cherry Tree Yard, but that in the evening was rather better attended, though the circus was not half full. Jem Guest, the clown, sustained the character of Mr. Merryman, and he certainly was in one of his merry moods on the occasion. The company was kept in continual roars of laughter at his wit and comicalities. The elephants took part in the performances. At the close, one of them was ordered to lie down, and the youths present invited to get on his back; on his rising, three youths fell therefrom, and one of them, named Pollard, had the misfortune to be at the bottom, and got his shoulder dislocated.

The same paper tells us that the company left at an early hour on Monday, May 26, 1845, for Northampton. That same day, Mr. Batty opened at Chippenham, featuring the great lion tamer Mr. White. For Hughes's June 2 gig in Oxford, we are indebted to *Jackson's* of May 31 and June 7, and also to the London *Standard* of June 3, 1845. Hughes's Circus came into the great university town at about 11 o'clock on June 2, from the town of Thame, with their troupe of horses and elegant car, drawn by elephants. They entered the town over Magdalen Bridge, passed through High Street, Corn Market Street, Beaumont Street, and returned down St. Giles', Broad Street, Hollywell Street, to the Star Hotel, causing the shops to be closed in consequence of the thousands of persons who were congregated to witness this singular procession, every window and available point being occupied. That afternoon the performances of Mr. Hughes and his company took place in a large arena erected in Walton Close and were attended by an immense number of persons. Everything passed off very satisfactorily till about the middle of the performances, when a thunderstorm came on, and the rain poured down in such torrents that the canvas covering of the amphitheatre would not repel it, and those who were enjoying the dignity of the boxes were thankful to avail themselves of the humbler but drier accommodations of the pit. In the evening there was a second performance, which was even more numerously attended than the first, and there could have been not much less than a thousand persons present; the amusements were varied, and consisted of bold and elegant riding, extraordinary feats of tumbling, and surpassing acts of docility, on the part of ponies, horses, and elephants.

We next pick up Hughes's Great Mammoth Equestrian Establishment in Hampshire in late June, and for the information about their appearances in that county we rely on the *Hampshire Advertiser and Salisbury Guardian*, the *Hampshire Telegraph and Sussex Chronicle*, and the *Portsmouth Herald*. The circus left Fareham on the 26th, arriving in Portsmouth — it was their first time there — at 11 o'clock, making a grand procession through Landport, Queen Street, Common Hard, Portsea, through the Quay Gate, down Lombard Street, up St. Thomas Street, down High Street, Broad Street, and then returning to the Globe Inn, Oyster Street, Portsmouth, when the nobility, gentry, and public in general had the opportunity of witnessing one of the most costly and magnificent cavalcades ever exhibited in Europe. Their Royal Arena had been erected in St. George's Square, Portsea, and doors opened at half past one in the afternoon and half past six in the evening. Performances began at 2 o'clock and 7 o'clock. Mr. Sheffield was the advance agent. They played there Thursday, Friday, and Saturday, June 26, 27, and 28. Positively for three nights only! The first night brought out upwards of a thousand spectators. "It is worthy of a visit." The elephants bathing upon Southsea Beach attracted some thousands daily.

James Cooke, William Cooke's brother, after a long stay in Newcastle, left that town on June 27, 1845, and on the 29th opened in Stockton-on-Tees, with a splendid stud and numerous troop of equestrians. It was a good night. The rival clowns, Seal and Tomkinson, kept the audience "all alive" as usual (*York Herald*, July 5, 1845). Billy Seal, born in Durham in 1808, would later work with Arthur Barnes.

Hughes's Equestrian Establishment left Portsmouth on Sunday, June 29, 1845, bound for Southampton, and on Monday opened there, in the Fair Field, for two days. In July, according to John Turner's book *Victorian Arena*, Hughes was in Hastings, and on August 12, the circus seems to have been in Chatham. Several papers ran an article reporting that a musician with the establishment, named John Verry, dropped dead of a heart attack on the pavement of High Street, while walking through that town.

In July, 1845, Pablo Fanque opened a large circus in Leeds. On September 9, 1845, William Cooke's Royal Circus was performing in Manchester when, at about nine o'clock, during the intermission, the floor fell through, about thirty men, women, and children plunged, and one man was severely injured, one of the violinists, Edward Sudlow, aged 59. He died on September 16.

On September 18, 1845, Hughes's Oriental Equestrian Company entered Ely with their usual procession. The performances were well attended, and richly deserved the plaudits bestowed upon them (*Era*, September 21, 1845). The troupe was expected to play Cambridge in October, but the mayor arbitrarily refused to allow them in, on the grounds that the people of his fair town had no money to spare for sight-seeing (*Newcastle Courant*, October 10, 1845).

On October 16, William Cooke's Circus entered Burnley, in order to perform there in a marquee erected on the cricket ground. The following day, Pablo Fanque entered the town from Todmorden, with a much bigger circus. This was merely a case of one-upmanship on Fanque's part, and he returned to Todmorden the same day.

For Hughes's Gainsborough gig, we depend on the *York Herald* of October 25 and the *Hull Packet* of October 31, 1845. Wednesday, October 22, 1845, Fair Day, the day Hughes's Equestrian Establishment entered the town amid a vast concourse of juveniles, was the main day of the famous October Mart. The performances took place in the Mart Yard in the afternoon and evening. The October Mart itself would continue until the 28th.

Then it was on to Worksop (October 25, 1845), Mansfield (October 27, 1845), Chesterfield (October 28, 1845), and Alfreton (October 29, 1845). Then into Derby on Thursday the 30th. We are indebted to the *Derby Mercury* of October 29 and November 5, 1845, for all this information on Hughes's Grand Oriental Equestrian Establishment, and that which follows concerning Derby itself. This really fine establishment of equestrians entered Derby on Thursday morning in grand procession, to the manifest delight of the inhabitants, who were quite on the qui vive for some time before the cavalcade, with its costly trappings, made its appearance.

The first object of attraction was a large carriage, containing a band of musicians, drawn by 14 horses, and driven in excellent style by Mr. Hughes. This carriage (upon which are some beautifully painted equestrian devices) was followed by three other vehicles, all well finished, the horses being gaily caparisoned. These were followed by the ponies, and the male and female artistes, mounted on various-coloured horses. The procession was wound up by the Rath, or Burmese Imperial state carriage and throne, drawn by two fine elephants in rich trappings. It attracted very great attention, and the ornamental portions were much admired. On that Thursday and Friday, the 30th and 31st of October 1845, they played in a large circus erected on the Swan Inn Bowling Green, St. Peter's Street, by permission of Right Worshipful the Mayor of Derby. "From what we have heard of the extraordinary talents of the principal performers, we have no doubt that the inhabitants of Derby have had a rich treat." As an instance of Mr. Hughes's liberality, he sent free tickets of admission to the circus to the governor of the Union Poor House, for the use of the children.

Then it was on to Wirksworth, for their presentation of November 1, 1845. The following day, Sunday, Hughes's Great Mammoth Equestrian Establishment, still with Arthur Barnes as part of the company, traveled to the village of Ashbourne, where they played on Monday, November 3, 1845. Shrewsbury was next, and they opened there at New Market Hall, on Howard Street, on November 10, 1845. We know this from a poster of that date printed by Hughes. Adolphe Maus (later a circus owner), Massotta, Wallett, Messrs. M. Conner and T. Barnes (sic), were still with the troupe. The *Era* of November 23, 1845, reports that the circus was open and that it continued to be liberally supported. "Its artists are of first-rate celebrity." From the *Hampshire*

Advertiser of November 29, 1845, we learn that Hughes was still in Shrewsbury on that very date.

In November 1845, at William Cooke's Circus, at the Amphitheatre on North Street in Bristol, the four amphi-gymnasiarchs, also advertised as the rival Gymnical Nonsuchs, were exhibiting "their school of exercises" (*Bristol Mercury*, November 22, 1845). These lads were, in reality, Alfred Palmer (the equestrian), Nelson Lee (the clown), Jem Buckley (the Wild Indian), and Bill Barlow. Others on Cooke's bill were Tom Swann (the grotesque), and Mr. Adrian and Harry Brown (clowns). Henry Brown, the clown, was born December 17, 1814, in Droxford, Hants, and Henry Adrian in Islington, in 1825. Adrian was traveling with his wife, Eliza, who was now quite pregnant. As for Nelson Richard Lee, he was born on January 8, 1806, at Kew. After a career as an actor and conjurer, he became the most famous of all the pantomime writers, with, to his credit, no fewer than 209 produced pantos. Cooke's performed St. *George and the Dragon*, and Bill Dale (the "Champion Vaulter of America") was with the company. They would be here until December 27, 1845. "Mr. W.O. Dale will throw a summerset over a broad canvass, alighting on the back of a horse going at full speed." Incidentally, St. *George and the Dragon* had first been produced by Andrew Ducrow on December 26, 1833, for the Christmas entertainments at Drury Lane, with the producer as St. George. Incidentally, on December 5, 1845, Bill Randall, the clown, died broke, in Birmingham, aged 42.

On December 15, 1845, Professor Hemming and his two sons opened at Gloucester for six nights before heading back to London. Who this Professor Hemming was remains a mystery. He was appearing in London theaters in 1844, with a son, Master Hemming, and in 1845 was touring the country, now with two sons. This surely cannot be the James John Hemming, a Birmingham tailor, who married Liverpool girl Sarah Wilson in 1830, in Edgbaston, and who had several children, all born in Birmingham, most of whom would become circus folk — Harry Wilson Hemming (born June 21, 1831), Richard Hemming (born January 4, 1834; named after his grandfather), James John Hemming (born February 21, 1836), Susan (born May 4, 1838), Hannah (born 1840), Jane (born 1844; she became a dancer), and finally William Edward Hemming (born September 17, 1849). In 1850 the James John Hemming family moved to Lambeth, in London.

Then, for Hughes's Great Mammoth Equestrian Establishment, it was back to Derby on December 26, 1845, where they opened that night at Babington Lane, by kind permission of the Right Worshipful William Eaton (Call Me "Eaton") Mousley, Mayor of Derby. They would be there for a month, and, again, we rely on the *Derby Mercury*, who reviewed the circus on the last day of the year: "We have visited this place of fashionable resortment, and more than realized our expectations; but space will not allow us going into more than a limited detail." That limited detail included the following: "On Monday was presented to a most numerous audience the magnificent historical spectacle of Queen Elizabeth's visit to Kenilworth Castle, with all the gorgeous splendor of bygone days." The procession of Queen Elizabeth on her road to the Castle was beautifully portrayed, and the various costumes and dresses of the cavaliers and dames were very costly and of very superior make, as were the trappings of the horses. In the piece was introduced the ancient dance of the men of Coventry, pastoral ballet of the season, introducing four infant actors as Spring, Summer, Autumn, and Winter; the whole concluding with a grand combat between Sir Walter Raleigh (Mr. Wallett) and Master Richard Varney (Mr. Bateson: John Bateson on the slack rope; his wife, the former Selina Wild from Oldham, whom he married in Leeds in 1845, was the younger sister of Edwin Hughes's wife, Sarah Ann). "The above splendid piece will be performed for the last time this (Wednesday) evening, in order to make room for further novelties." Herr Maus, "undoubtedly the strongest man in the world," appeared and performed some extraordinary feats of horsemanship, which met with considerable applause.

> We have no hesitation in saying it is the best company of equestrians that has ever visited Derby. As to the structure of the building, we, without hesitation, confess it is one of the largest, most complete, and undoubtedly the most expensive ever erected in this town; the interior being fitted up with an evident degree of taste; the boxes are well cushioned and lined; and the whole of the place is well warmed. The proprietor, it appears, has left nothing undone that would ensure comfort to his patrons who, we trust, will duly appreciate his enterprising exertions. If crowded houses honored by some of the most influential families in this locality is a criterion as to ultimate success, we should say Mr. Hughes has a sufficient guarantee that such will be the case. It will be seen by the advertisement in another column, that Mr. W. O. Dale, the great American rider and vaulter, will appear tomorrow evening. On Tuesday evening next the performance will be under the patronage of His Worship the Mayor of Derby.

The "advertisement" referred to, adds that Dale executed the miraculous feat of throwing a summersault from feet to feet whilst his horse was going at full speed. It also informs us that the first grand mid-day performance took place at two o'clock on Friday, January 2, 1846.

George Speaight, in his *History of the Circus*, tells us, "By 1846 Hughes's Mammoth Equestrian Establishment was mounting a particularly impressive parade with fifty horses, of which 32 were driven in hand, the sacred Egyptian Dragon Chariot pulled by four camels, and the Burmese Imperial Carriage and Throne pulled by two elephants. These had been designed by Wallett."

As an example of some of Arthur Barnes's fellow acts with Hughes at

Babington Lane, Derby, on Tues., January 6, 1846: Mr. and Mrs. and Master Hughes; Messrs. Wilde (Jim and Sam Wild, equestrian clowns; brothers; Jim was born in 1810, in Nottingham, and Sam was born in Huddersfield, in 1814; oddly, they were not related to the Wild Sisters, who married Messrs. Hughes and Bateson, respectively); William F. Wallett (clown); Mr. Bateson; Bill & John Samwell (equestrians); Jem Guest, the clown (a Birmingham lad, actually from Yardley, 13 years older than Arthur Barnes; he had married Elizabeth Richardson, an equestrian from Sunderland, on Christmas Day, 1838, and they were touring with their growing family, which would finally settle in Birmingham); Tim Elliott (balancer and foot juggler); Bill Dale and Harry Connor (vaulters); Morton, the Flying Horseman; and Herr Maus. So here, for the first of many times, we find Arthur Barnes in company with Dale, Wallett, and Connor, and Tim Elliott. "The vaulting of Messrs. W. O'Dale [sic], Conner, and Barnes, was first rate, but it was very perceptible that Mr. O'Dale was by far the best performer" (*Derby Mercury*, January 7, 1846). The mayor of Derby attended the performance that night.

On Monday, January 5, 1846, *Timour the Tartar* was performed for the first time in Derby. The following evening was the first fashionable night under the immediate patronage of the mayor, while the performance of January 7 was under the patronage of the Right Hon. Lord Scarsdale. The ad in the *Derby Mercury* of that date says,

> The grand Oriental magnificent [equestrian] spectacle of *Timour the Tartar* is received with the most unequalled marks of approbation from the largest and most respectable audiences that ever graced an arena; consequently will be repeated this evening, in which four gigantic Egyptian camels !!! will appear, and two of them in harness, being the first ever seen in Europe, drawing Timour [Mr. Wild] and the Princess Zorilda [Mrs. Hughes], in his triumphal state carriage to the tournament, with all the Eastern pomp and circumstance of the time!!

Mr. Guest played Oglou. After the show, Mr. and Mrs. Hughes appeared in a pantomimic equestrian act, as the Swiss milk maid and Tyrolean shepherd. Mr. Hughes also personated several well-known characters on horseback. "The rest of the performers acquitted themselves very satisfactorily. A superior band is stationed in the orchestra."

On Friday, January 9, 1846, a mid-day performance began at two o'clock, under the patronage of Sir Henry S. Wilmot, Bart., on which occasion the children belonging to the various charity schools of the town were admitted free. The evening's performance was by command of the officers of the Derby and Chaddesden Troop of the Yeomanry Cavalry. On January 12, Hughes presented *The Battle of Waterloo*, with Mr. Guest playing Wellington and Wallett playing Napoleon. The performance of January 13 was under the patronage of E. S. Chandos-Pole, Esq., of Radbourn Hall, while that of January 14 was under the patronage of Edward Strutt, M.P., and the day performance (2 o'clock) of Friday, January 16, 1846, was under the patronage of Sir John Harpur Crewe, Bart.

The *Derby Mercury* says, in an ad: "Positively the last night but three, of this pre-eminent company performing in this town, this present (Wednesday) January 21st. The proprietor feels a degree of pleasure in announcing that the proceeds of this evening will be applied to the Derby Race Fund, and the Mechanics' Institution." On the following day, Thursday, January 22, 1846, the proprietor, Mr. Hughes, took his benefit under the distinguished patronage of the Worshipful Master and members of the Tyrian Lodge of Freemasons, who had signified their intention of honouring Mr. H. with their presence, he being a member of that Loyal Body. On Friday, January 23, was a grand mid-day performance, under distinguished patronage. It commenced at two o'clock.

Saturday, January 24, 1846, was Hughes's last night in Derby, and then it was on to Leicester, where we pick up the *Leicester Chronicle*. "The Amphitheatre will be opened for a fortnight on Monday next, by Mr. Hughes, with his Great Mammoth Equestrian Company." Mr. Briggs had already applied to the bench (at Leicester) for a license enabling Mr. Hughes to perform equestrian spectacles on the stage of the Amphitheatre for one month. The application was granted. The paper, reviewing the week's performance, said, "This place of amusement, during the last week, has been well attended. The performances are first-rate, and have been received with well-merited applause. The feats of Herr Maus are truly astonishing."

On January 31, 1846, Saturday, for the last time in Leicester, was presented *Queen Elizabeth's Visit to Kenilworth Castle*, and on Monday, February 2, *Timour the Tartar* was shown for the first time there. The evening performance of Tuesday, February 3, which included *Timour the Tartar*, was by desire, and under the patronage of the mayor, and members of the St. John's Masonic Lodge, who honored Brother Hughes with their presence on the occasion. Also in Leicester, that evening, at New Hall on Wellington Street, Mr. Wilson was giving one of his celebrated entertainments on the songs of Scotland. Mr. Land accompanied him on piano. Front seats were 2 shillings, and back seats were a shilling. Not to be minimized, this Wilson, the Prince of Scottish Song, who was on a monstrously successful tour. Royalty loved him, especially the Queen.

On the Wednesday, February 4, 1846, which once again showed *Timour the Tartar*, the performance, under the patronage of Mr. Edward Weston, the mayor, was the first fashionable box night and was well attended, while the next night, February 5, the circus played to a "delighted and crowded house."

The feats of the French (i.e., German) Hercules were wonderful. On Saturday, February 7, 1846, a mid-day performance took place at 2 o'clock.

Hughes was still in Leicester on Thursday, February 19, 1846 (he would leave two days later), with Wallett taking his benefit that evening and assuring the crowd that he would be running for the Leicester Town Council. That day, Mr. Hughes gave a donation to the dispensary, with the regret that the sum would have been bigger if it hadn't been for the fact that several performers were not there any longer, owing to previous engagements elsewhere. Arthur Barnes was one of them. He was now with William Cooke's Circus.

According to the CFA (Circus Friends Association) Archives, Scrapbook 609, page 47, Barnes was with Cooke's in Bath on Monday, Tuesday, and Wednesday, the 16th, 17th and 18th of February 1846. Mr. Cooke played the character of St. George. Bill Barlow, who had been a performer since 1838, was the lion-horseman; Clarissa Cooke (niece of William Cooke) was an equestrian pas chinois; Henry Russilli, ball on horseback; John William Cooke (son of William Cooke) as Young Meltonian; Barnes, Connor, Russilli and Hemming as Elastique Sauteurs; Albert and Henry Cooke; Chatteris Jackson (musical and talking clown; he would die in Dublin in 1859); Kestler and Green; and Adams. So, here we find Harry Connor again, and Jackson the clown, and Hemming. This is either Richard Hemming or his older brother Harry. Harry was 15 at this stage, so it's probably he. Charles Adams was the equestrian clown, born in 1828, the "Grimaldi of the Arena." He married Mary Cooke, Mr. Cooke's niece. Unfortunately, for any confirmation of this Bath gig, *Lloyd's*, the *Era*, and the *Bristol Mercury* are totally useless.

Henry Russilli was born Henry Russell, of course, on January 15, 1823, in Shrewsbury, son of James Russell and Elizabeth Weston. In 1845, in Ipswich, he married Susanna Page, but they had no children. He would remain in the business for years, a good friend of Arthur Barnes. Jack Russilli seems to have been his brother.

Just as it is desirable to have at least an elementary grasp of the Hengler family and its genealogical tentacles within the world of the British circus, so it is with Cooke's, the other great dynasty, and one, indeed, intertwined with the Henglers. Thomas Cooke, Scottish circus owner, begat Thomas Taplin Cooke, equestrian, rope walker, strongman, and circus proprietor. T. T. begat 19 children, took a show to Lisbon in 1816, and 20 years later established a great circus in New York. He died in 1866. Those 19 Cooke children included Thomas Edwin Cooke (born 1800), equestrian; William Henry Cooke (born 1808), who would become the great circus proprietor and employer of Arthur Barnes; James Thorpe Cooke (born 1810), circus owner; Henry Cooke (1814–1901), the tightrope walker and later animal trainer; Rebecca Cooke (born 1816), the equestrian, who married (first) George Woolford on September 15,

1835, in Glasgow, and had Mdlle. Rebecca, and (second), James Clements Boswell (born January 4, 1826, Halifax, one of the all-time great clowns; and Alfred Cooke (born 1821, one of the great equestrians). There was also Mary Ann, who married W. H. Cole and became the mother of W. W. Cole, the famous American circus proprietor. William Henry Cooke, for so long Arthur Barnes's boss, married Mary Ann Spicer and had Kate Cooke, the famous equestrian with her father's circus, and John William Cooke, also an equestrian. Henry Cooke (William's brother) was the father of equestrians Harry Welby Cooke and John Henry Cooke. Harry Welby married Ellen Hughes, daughter of circus proprietor Edwin Hughes (Arthur Barnes's boss in 1845), while John Henry (billed as master John Cooke when he was a child), became a circus owner and died in 1917.

Sometime in 1846 Barnes and Connor left Cooke's and went over to Pablo Fanque's Circus, but we don't know when that was exactly. William Cooke's Circus Royal opened at Queen Street, Exeter, on March 23, 1846, soon after which Le Petit Adrian's daughter was born. They closed in Exeter on Friday, May 8, going on from there to Tiverton on May 9, Wellington on May 11, and Taunton on May 12 and 13, 1846. We don't know if Barnes and Connor were still with them at that stage, but it's not a good bet. Many of the performers are listed in various press reports, during their stay in Devon, but not Barnes and Connor. In March Pablo was at Bolton, doing roaring business in their magnificent circus in the market place. Madame Camille Leroux, the celebrated equestrian, joined them late that month. On Saturday, May 30, 1846, Pablo's Circus opened at Chadwick's Orchard, Preston, for 12 nights only. Unequalled equilibrists were advertised in the local paper, as were the Antipodean Brothers (which may mean Barnes and Connor, but it's unlikely). On June 14 (Sunday) they were traveling from Preston to Bradford, for the fair. On June 13, 1846, Cooke's opened at Salisbury, for what that's worth. However, as with Cooke's, it's doubtful if Arthur Barnes and Harry Connor were with either company until July. In Preston, for example, every night seemed to be a benefit night, and the lucky lads were all mentioned. Not Barnes and Connor, however.

Pablo began advertising in the *Leeds Mercury* on July 11, 1846. On July 27, 30 and 31, 1846, Connor and Barnes were definitely both with Pablo Fanque's Circus Royal at King Charles Croft in that town. Connor was billed as "air diving"; Messrs. Williams and Charles Adams equestrianism; Mr. Elliott; Mr. Sylvester (equestrian); Mr. Butler; clowns John Griffiths and Mr. Bowman; Ringmaster Joseph Daly. Mdlle. Laurena was making her Leeds debut fresh from Franconi's, in Paris. The *Era* of August 2, 1846, informs us of a monumental moment in the history of still-vaulting: "Leeds. Circus Royal. Mr. Barnes, of this theatre, on Monday last [i.e., July 27], performed the difficult operation of throwing sixty-six somersaults at one trial," thus equaling James McFarland's record.

Fanque's Circus Royal (and Arthur Barnes) was still in Leeds on August 7, 1846 (or at least part of the company was; the other part was in Dewsbury), when the repeal of the Corn Laws was celebrated with a show by Pablo Fanque's Circus on Woodhouse Moor, at the end of which there was a huge display of fireworks.

> The chief feature of the entertainments on the moor was the equestrian performance of the company of Mr. Pablo Fanque. The arrangements had been under the superintendence of Mr. Silvester, and had been suitably and judiciously carried out for the intended purpose. When the spectators were gathered on the moor, it presented the most animated, joyous, and spirit-stirring scene that has ever been witnessed at that theatre of so many great demonstrations, in former times of public rejoicing and political excitement. The intended entertainments not only appeared to have been attractive to the Leeds public, but drew large numbers from distant places [*Leeds Mercury*, Aug. 8, 1846].

The paper goes on to say, "The performance of Mr. Fanque's company occupied from six to nine o'clock. Too high a compliment could scarcely be paid to their endeavours in every branch." It wraps up by saying that "not one of the least memorable tasks was accomplished by Mr. Barnes, who at one trial turned 60 somersets in a most clever style."

The *Mercury* of August 15, 1846, when referring to Pablo's Circus, used the word "was" instead of "is," which must mean they had gone by then. However, "A peep at the circus": On August 18, Pablo appeared in court in Leeds, to prefer a complaint against two boys, Charles Wood and John Peacock, who had been found on top of the circus, cutting a hole in the canvas so they could see the show. The damage came to five pounds. Mr. Fanque was lenient, demanding only a flogging, which, with the parents' consent, the lads duly and humbly received.

The Disappearance of Mr. Arthur Barnes

That date of August 7, 1846 is the last date we have for Arthur Barnes performing in the circus, any circus, for over two years. In fact, the distinct lack of mention of the name Arthur Barnes, at a time when he was an up-and-coming star, is absolutely glaring. There can be no question that he and Harry Connor split up, went their separate ways, over this period of time, or, at least, part of it, for we find several mentions of Mr. Connor from late 1847 on, but no Arthur Barnes. Given the major event that would happen in his personal life in July 1848, it is almost certain that he was performing in Copenhagen. Undisturbed by Mr. Barnes's invisibility, or at least, as undisturbed as we can be, we can at least weave a tapestry representing the British circus, with a strong emphasis on Mr. Fanque, over that two-year period, so that when Mr. Barnes does come back onto the scene, we have not missed anything of import while he was away. However, during these two years there are certain references—oblique and fraught with numerous possible interpretations—which may indicate an Arthur Barnes presence in England, and these will be mentioned, although not altogether hopefully. The first is Dundee, August 10, 1846, when Hughes's Mammoth Equestrian Establishment entered the town by the Perth Road, performing there that night for one day only. Mentioned in the *Dundee Courier* of the following day is "Master Elliott," only about six or seven years old, and Herr Maus, the French Hercules. The paper also mentions the "beautiful evolutions and figures of the Protean Artistes." This expression "Protean Artistes" is of interest merely because Arthur Barnes was mentioned as being on the same bill as Elliott and the Protean Artistes back in Bristol in January 1845. Hughes performed in Edinburgh on September 1 and 2, 1846.

On August 31, 1846, Alfred Cooke's Equestrian Establishment opened in Dublin. On September 11, Pablo Fanque's Pre-eminent Equestrian and Gymnastic Establishment commenced its run at the new Circus Royal, Dock Green, Wellington Street, in Hull. They would be there for almost two months, and we rely on the *Hull Packet* for this period. The bill, as advertised, included Master O'Donnell (as the Hunting Boy of Bohemia, on his spotted charger); Pablo Fanque, introducing his celebrated trained monkey jockey and his pet steed; Mr. Charles Adams (the dauntless equestrian, as "the Red Man of the

Far West"); Grayham Smith singing "Lucy Neal" and accompanying himself on banjo; then the grand vaulting act (unlikely, but this may be Arthur Barnes and Harry Connor); and Richard Hemming on the tightrope.

On September 14, 1846, Mr. Newsome, the premier horseman of Astley's, made his first appearance in Hull, with Pablo's Circus; on Monday, September 21, Pablo made a grand procession through the streets of that town, and a grand day performance was given at 2 o'clock, while the evening of September 25 was the first of two benefit nights for Mr. Williams, the Centaur Horseman. Another grand day performance was given on Tuesday, the 29th. It had been scheduled for Monday, the 28th, but public demand forced the change. Monday, October 5, was for the benefit of Mr. Pablo Fanque. This was "positively the last night" of Fanque's circus at Hull, predicted the paper of October 2, but they were wrong, of course. The night of October 9, 1846, was under the patronage of the Hull District of the Independent Order of Odd Fellows, Manchester Unity, and the cirque finally wrapped up at Hull the following night. There is more on Fanque's engagement at Hull in Samuel Wild's book, *The Original, Complete and Only Authentic Story of Old Wild's*, published by Vickers, London, in 1888, in which Arthur Barnes is not mentioned. In the meantime, while Pablo was playing Hull, Hughes's Circus opened in Preston on October 3, 1846.

Meanwhile, back in the States, the October 5, 1846, edition of the *Cleveland Herald* carried an ad for Rockwell & Stone's Mammoth Circus. It says, "McFarland, the King of Vaulters. The only one ever known to achieve 67 successive somersets. His competition with his only rival, Hiram Franklin, is a sublime sight." This is all blurb, of course.

On Saturday, October 3, and Monday, October 5, 1846, Thomas Cooke's Circus played in Beverley, then moved on to Grimsby, and then Hull, where they opened on Monday, October 12, 1846, at the new amphitheater, on Paragon Street. Thomas Cooke was William Cooke's brother. Harry Walker, the "Vaultigeur Phenomenon," was with them.

There is reason to believe that Pablo's company was in Preston in late October 1846. The *Preston Guardian* of October 31, 1846, mentions a donation by Mr. Fanque of five pounds to the Preston Dispensary (thanks for this donation were expressed during the dispensary's meeting of October 26).

The *York Herald* of October 31, 1846, says this:

> On Tuesday last [i.e., Oct. 27], at the Guildhall, John Brown was charged with having assaulted Pablo Fanques [sic], the proprietor of the circus in St. George's Field, in this city [i.e., York], on the previous night. The complainant stated that on Monday night [i.e., the 26th], about half past eight o'clock, a number of boys were on the roof of his circus, when he went to the outside, and succeeded in capturing one of them. The defendant immediately seized him by the collar,

struck him over the shoulder, and knocked him down. The complainant, however, said that he did not wish the bench to be severe with defendant, as he had merely brought him before them, in order to learn him and others that such an assault and outrageous proceeding were not to be committed with impunity. The defendant was discharged after having apologized for his conduct, and paid the costs.

The ad for Pablo Fanque's Circus Royal in the *York Herald* of October 31, 1846, tells us that the following Monday (i.e., November 2) would be the first night of the Grand Greek Entree, and also the first night of Mrs. Pablo Fanque. The *Leeds Mercury* of November 21, 1846, tells us that Pablo's Circus was about to visit Wakefield, to play on vacant ground in Wood Street, near the courthouse. The company seems to have opened there on November 23. For sure, Pablo's Circus Royal was in Wakefield on December 29, 1846 (*Bradford Observer*, January 7, 1847). Meanwhile, James Cooke's Circus opened in Edinburgh on November 9, 1846, and then it was on to Aberdeen. On November 25, 1846, Ginnett's circus played Chesterfield on a most miserable, drizzly day. John Ginnett, a Frenchman, had been taken prisoner during the Napoleonic Wars, and had settled in England. He became Andrew Ducrow's master of horses, and married an Essex girl named Ann Partridge. His children included Madame Macarte, and Gentleman George Ginnett. On December 11, 1846, Hughes's Circus entered Worcester.

On February 15, 1847, Cooke's Circus began its last week at King Charles's Croft, in Leeds. As for Mr. Fanque, his circus was running at Wigan. We know this from the *Liverpool Mercury* of March 19, 1847, which tells us that on the morrow (i.e., Saturday, March 20) Barry the clown would close a 12-day engagement at the "circus of Mr. Pablo Fanque" (in Wigan). We also know it from an article in the *Manchester Times* of May 14, 1847, which relates a criminal incident which took place in Wigan, when the defendant claimed to have been at Pablo's Circus that night. Meanwhile, Mr. Fanque himself made his London debut on March 8, 1847, at Astley's, for a 12-day stint as a solo act. March 20, 1847, was Fanque's last night at Astley's, then he had to head back to Wigan to fulfill his provincial engagements, beginning in Stockport. Incidentally, on March 3, 1847, at St. Martin's, Birmingham, Edwin Hughes's daughter, Cattie, was baptized.

Later in March 1847 Pablo Fanque was heading Darby's Royal Tenting Company, this time back at Wigan. Wigan was followed by Huddersfield in the same month. In March, Edwin Hughes was playing Birmingham, with Wallett and Professor Jameson. "The somerset-throwing was also good" (*Era*, March 7, 1847). On March 1, 1847, in Birmingham, Herr Maus, the strongman, married Joanna Louisa Noack, and, later that month, Pablo and his company were taking Wigan by storm, while on March 15, Mons. Tourniaire replaced

The Disappearance of Mr. Arthur Barnes 43

Thomas Cooke at the Amphitheatre, in Hull. Appearing with Tourniaire was an act called The American Brothers. In late May, Mr. Wallett, the clown, was with Tourniaire's for a few nights, enough nights to collect a benefit. By late June, Mr. Fanque was appearing with Tourniaire's, and the troupe left Hull after their last performance of July 7, 1847, the three American Brothers still with them. It is tempting to think that these brothers might have included Arthur Barnes, but this cannot be. A year earlier, while they were performing in London in January 1846, Barnes had been with Edwin Hughes in Derby.

On March 9, 1847, Bill Dale opened in Boston with Sands, Lent & Co.'s American Circus Company. His fellow acts included Hernandez, Tom Moseley (in his Pickwickian scenes), Dick Sands, of course, and the famous British pugilists Deaf Burke and Tom Spring. Curiously, the British pantaloon and pantomimist, W. A. Barnes, was appearing in Boston, Massachusetts, at the same time, at the National. This Barnes was the second pantaloon named Barnes, the first, Jim Barnes, known as Old Barnes, having died at his lodgings in Pentonville, on September 28, 1838, aged 49.

On April 12, 1847, Pablo's Circus opened at the City Royal Amphitheatre, Knott Mill, Manchester, in competition with Cooke's Circus, which was playing the same town. We rely now on the *Era* and the *Manchester Times*, for coverage of this period. "Splendid and unrivalled entertainments for Monday, April 12th, and during the week. The wondrous mare Beda." The ad goes on to mention George and Madame Ryland, the jugglers and horseback riders from Astley's Amphitheatre (George F. Ryland was born in 1826, in New York. He would later be a circus owner in Arizona.) "Great vaulting, tight and slack rope performances, by the most eminent professors." This Monday, at 12, Mr. Fanque drove 14 horses in hand through the principal streets of Manchester, returning to the circus at one, when the doors were thrown open for the grand day performance at two. Boxes, 1s; pit, 6d; gallery, 3d.

What seems odd is that the same paper of the same date (i.e., April 9) gave a review of this circus that had not yet opened. "Knott Mill Fair. Mr. Pablo Fanque. Though no great sight-seeing folks, we were not a little delighted on witnessing one day this week the performance at Mr. Pablo Fanque's Circus. This spirited gentleman, who has selected a first-rate band of artistes unequalled in their several departments, has lately attracted considerable attention in the metropolis and elsewhere." It goes on. What is clear is that the reviewer saw the circus somewhere else, probably in Wigan.

Incidentally, on April 12, 1847, White's Equestrian Company, from Astley's, in London, opened at Blackburn, for one day only. They had played Chorley on the 9th. They boasted "the most talented corps of vaulters in the world," as well as "acrobatic and gymnastic artistes." This seems to have been a very short-lived company.

The *Manchester Times* of April 16, 1847, says: "Mr. Pablo Fanque's Circus. This place of amusement, as will be seen by advertisement, will continue open for a short time to the inhabitants of the town and district, at very reasonable charges of admission." That evening, i.e., Friday, April 16, was patronized by the officers of the garrison stationed here, while the evening of the 21st was patronized by "our benevolent townsman, Daniel Grant, Esq.," and that of the 23rd by Elkanah Armitage, Esq., mayor of Manchester, and R. P. Livingston, mayor of Salford. Cooke's closed in Manchester on April 24, with Wallett, who had taken his benefit the night before. On April 29, Pablo's closed.

The morning performance of April 29, 1847, put on by Hughes's Circus, which had been playing at the Theatre Royal, Drury Lane, London, since April 1, was by command of the Queen. Prince Albert came too, as did the Prince of Wales, the Princess Royal, and Princess Alice, as well as the Duke and Duchess of Bedford, the Duke and Duchess of Montrose, the Marchioness of Douro, Lord and Lady Howe, Lord James Stuart, the Baron de Rothschild, and a whole set of notables. It was a big day for Hughes. On May 1, Hughes left London, for a tour.

On May 11, 1847, Carter, the lion king, died. He was 34. On Sunday, May 16, 1847, Pablo's arrived in Preston, opening there the following day. The May 15 edition of the *Preston Guardian* mentions "two of the first vaulters in England, Messrs. Ryland and Walker [this is Harry Walker]." It also mentions Madame Ryland (the intrepid and graceful female artiste) and Master Burnham (the great equestrian tightrope dancer), as well as Mr. C. Adams (the rider of merit) and Mr. Williams (the great Centaur horseman). This opening night, May 17, was to a crowded house. Thursday (May 20) there was a change in the performances, commencing with a piece entitled *The Demon Rider*, in which the celebrated mare Beda took part.

As for Edwin Hughes's tour, we don't actually pick them up until Warminster, on May 20, 1847. Then it was Frome (May 21, 1847), Shepton Mallet (May 22, 1847), Wells (May 24, 1847), Glastonbury (May 25, 1847), Bridgwater (May 26, 1847), Taunton (May 27, 1847), Wellington (May 28, 1847), Cullompton (May 29, 1847), Exeter (May 31 and June 1, 1847), Teignmouth (June 2, 1847), Newton Bushel (June 3, 1847), Torquay (June 4, 1847), and Brixham (June 5, 1847).

On Thursday, June 3, 1847, Pablo Fanque's Leviathan Equestrian Company entered the village of Leyland at half past 11 o'clock, driving 14 horses in hand, accompanied by his brass band, and afterwards performed at two o'clock under his Royal Leviathan Marquee, erected in the Cabin Croft. The company returned to Preston in time for the evening performance. The Leyland gig was performed to an overflowing house, and "to the apparent satisfaction of the inhabitants of that village." That day, in Preston, while the troupe was in Leyland, James McCarter stole a cloth coat, a waistcoat, two pistols, and a box of caps from Job Taylor, a tailor with Pablo Fanque's circus. Two days later, McCarter was charged, the items having been found in his lodgings, and he was committed for trial.

Mr. Fanque devoted the proceeds of June 3rd's Preston evening performance to the benefit of the widows and orphans fund of the Ancient Order of Foresters, and on Saturday, June 5, 1847, Fanque's circus entered the village of Bamber Bridge, as they had done at Leyland on the 3rd, for a morning performance only, at two o'clock. That evening they were back doing a night performance at Preston. The *Preston Guardian* of that day ran an ad: "Pablo Fanque's Leviathan Equestrian Company, New Circus, Orchard, Preston. Notice! Only a few more performances remain to be given at this fashionable resort of the pleasure-seeking inhabitants of Preston."

The evening performance of June 7, 1847, was for the benefit of Bowman the clown. There was no night performance on the 9th, 10th and 11th, because on Wednesday, June 9, they were playing Kirkham, on the next day in Poulton, and on the Friday in Garstang. On each occasion in these three towns, Mr. Pablo Fanque announced his arrival by driving 14 horses in hand through the principal streets, accompanied by his brass band.

On June 19, Saturday, the company entered Burnley, with Pablo driving 14 in hand. He proceeded through the town, and on the Todmorden Road, to his splendid marquee, which had been erected on the cricket ground near Turf Moor. Two performances were given during the day, which were very numerously attended. Then, on the Sunday they were off to Bradford, where we pick up the *Bradford Observer* as our guide through this part of Yorkshire. Fanque's Leviathan Equestrian Company roared into town at 11:30 that day, making a grand procession through the main streets. Doors opened at one in the afternoon, and again at seven in the evening. Although Barnes is not mentioned by name on the bill, he might be one of the elastique sauteurs advertised, but it is highly doubtful. Those named on the bill were Madame Ryland, the first female equestrian in England; Master Burnham, the extraordinary tightrope dancer; Mr. Williams, the intrepid equestrian, the justly famed Centaur horseman; Miss Brown, the elegant little female equestrian; the equestrian Master O'Donnell, the "Prince of the Antipodes"; and Messrs. Bowman and Lomas, the clowns. Everyone else was named, but no Arthur Barnes. Just for the record, Pablo Fanque was at Idle on the 22nd, at Brighouse on the 23rd, and at Halifax on the 24th. In late June, Pablo (by himself) was in Hull, doing a solo act for circus proprietor Francois Tourniaire. On July 10, 1847, his troupe entered Otley in the same manner they entered every other town — in grand style. Their evening's performance there was attended by a vast number of spectators who witnessed their exploits with wonder and astonishment.

Meanwhile, Hughes was still touring in the West Country: Totnes (June 7, 1847), Tavistock (June 11, 1847), Callington (June 12, 1847), Liskeard (June 14, 1847), Lostwithiel (June 15, 1847), St. Austell (June 16, 1847; his stables caught fire here), Redruth (June 17, 1847), Hayle (June 18, 1847), Penzance (June 19, 1847), Helston (June 21, 1847), Falmouth (June 22, 1847), Truro (June 23, 1847), St. Columb (June 24, 1847), Wadebridge (June 25, 1847), Bodmin (June 26, 1847), Camelford (June 28, 1847), Launceston (June 29, 1847), Hatherleigh (July 1, 1847), and Axminster (July 10, 1847).

On July 10, 1847, Batty's Circus arrived in Portsmouth from Southampton, opening two days later. By August, Wallett was with them. On July 27, 1847, William Cooke's circus, then on a tour of the south of England, entered Ramsgate. This was followed by Margate on July 31, and then, in early August on to Canterbury and Faversham.

Meanwhile, back in the States, in August 1847, Howes' Circus was appearing. Bill Dale and Tom McFarland were vaulting against each other. The blurb claimed that Dale held the world record of 87, and that McFarland had done 79. From this blurb (example: the *Cleveland Herald*, of July 30, 1847), we learn that Dale had performed with Batty's Circus in England, and that no British performer had ever done even 50 somersaults, which, of course, we know to be false, as Arthur Barnes had done 66. When Mr. Dale is meant to have done his 87 is not known, likewise McFarland with his 79. However, the *Dover Gazette and Strafford Advertiser* (New Hampshire) of September 16, 1848, makes this even more confusing, when they ran an ad for Howes's Circus, due to open on September 22: "Mr. Thomas McFarland, the champion vaulter of both hemispheres, and the hero of 87 successive somersetts, will eclipse all previous efforts."

The book *Here We Are Again: Recollections of an Old Circus Clown*, by Robert Edmund Sherwood, published in 1926, claims that the author saw Dale do 89 (he claimed he actually counted them), and that Tom McFarland had done 78. The story of 89 somersets by Bill Dale is repeated in the September 1848 ads in the United States drawn up by Rockwell's Circus, with which Dale was appearing. "Mr. Dale has thrown the astonishing number of 89 consecutive somersaults."

Hughes was still on tour, in Essex and East Anglia: Hertford (August 3, 1847), Bishop's Stortford (August 4, 1847), Dunmow (August 5, 1847), Chelmsford (August 6, 1847), Braintree (August 7, 1847), Coggeshall (August 9, 1847), Colchester (August 10, 1847), Hadleigh (August 11, 1847), Ipswich (August 12, 1847), Woodbridge (August 13, 1847), Aldeburgh (August 14, 1847), and Saxmundham (August 16, 1847).

On September 6, 1847, Pablo's company left Garstang for Poulton-le-Fylde and pitched their marquee in a field belonging to Mr. Robert Taylor, of the Golden Ball Inn, performing in a very satisfactory manner before a respectable audience in the evening. Pablo was not there, despite being billed (*Lancaster Gazette*, September 11, 1847). No mention of Arthur Barnes.

The week beginning October 11, 1847, Edwin Hughes played Barking, then traveled via West Ham to Stratford, Essex. Then the circus wrapped up. Starting November 1, 1847, Hughes sold off his circus at Vauxhall Gardens, and retired, well-off.

Then, for Pablo's, it was on to Manchester, where the *Era* and *Manchester Times* pick up the story. The company opened on October 25 at the Royal City Amphitheatre (late Cooke's Amphitheatre), which establishment Mr. Egerton, from the Queen's Theatre, Hull, had taken over, and obtained a license for, for twelve months. The Manchester paper of October 23, 1847, says: "Pablo Fanque. It will be seen, by advertisement, that this spirited equestrian is about to pay us another visit, having engaged the Amphitheatre in Mount Street for a limited period. In addition to his unrivalled band of artistes, that 'king of clowns,' Mr. W.F. Wallett, is announced as having been engaged for six nights, and will doubtless keep the visitors 'in a roar,' with those mirth-exciting jests and smart repartees for which he is so eminently celebrated." Business boomed, and Saturdays were packed. In fact, Saturday, October 30, was the night of the incident of the pig. They were going to run a pig in the ring, and the first six blindfolded persons in the ring stood a chance of securing the porker for supper. However, there was a crush, and an alarm that the gallery was giving way. It didn't, but it was enough for Wallett to stop the performance. By the middle of November, the Bedouin Arabs were the main attraction.

This was the second group of Bedouin Arabs to play Britain. The first group had come over from Paris in 1836, opening at the Colosseum in London on May 5 of that year, and playing various other theaters in the metropolis until 1838, when they did a tour of the United States. That first troupe included Abdullah, the leader, a notorious ladies' man, who left them before they went to the States. The others were Hussein, Hassan ben Abdallah, Ahmad, and Sidi Ali. Their interpreter was Mons. Salame, and their manager was a Jew named Moses Davousie. On February 4, 1838, the youngest of them, aged 16, died as the result of an accidental gunshot wound. In 1839, they returned to England, fulfilled some more engagements, and then went back to wherever they had originally come from, which may or may not have been an Arab country. One of the American papers described them as looking more Malay or Chinese than Arab. In July 1839, when they were about to return to their native homeland, one of them, Ben Mohamed, refused to go. His two wives back home offered nothing compared to the delights of London. In 1847, the new Bedouin Arabs appeared. A third group with the name created a sensation in Paris before making their triumphant British debut at the Royal Lyceum Theatre, in London on November 27, 1856. There were 10 of these lads (14 if you include the priest, the interpreter, and a couple of children), reputedly imported from Morocco by Van Hare, the showman. Unlike ordinary vaulters, who used a springboard, these Bedouin Arabs would throw somersaults over 20 men, making their bound from a solid stone. There is much more on these lads as we go through this book. Yet another group would be playing in England in the 1890s, and well into the 20th century.

On Monday night, November 15, 1847, at Manchester, Pablo Fanque took his benefit. It was a bumper night. Wallett and the Bedouin Arabs were still on the bill. Meanwhile, William Cooke's British Royal Circus opened at Bristol on November 15, 1847, and Batty's Equestrian Company, as well as Franconi's, were performing in Liverpool. Pablo closed in Liverpool on November 20, 1847, and the following day they were traveling to Hull. Near Sheffield, that afternoon, there was an accident on the Glossop Road, near the Fulwood tollbar, in which one of Pablo's wagons hit a carriage with three men in it, one of whom was much injured (*Sheffield and Rotherham Independent*, November 27, 1847). Meanwhile, on November 22, 1847, Harry Connor opened with Batty's troupe at the Adelphi (the old Olympic Circus), on Christian Street, in Liverpool. They finished their run there on December 17. Still no mention of Arthur Barnes. Pablo opened at the Queen's Theatre (late Royal Amphitheatre), Paragon Street, Hull, on November 22, 1847, and the *Hull Packet* is our guide through that town.

That paper, of November 19, 1847, says:

> The manager has great pleasure in informing the public that he has formed an engagement, for eight nights only (the last of the season), with Mr. Pablo Fanque, and his celebrated mare Beda. In conjunction with Mr. W.F. Wallett, the celebrated comedian and clown, from Astley's Royal Amphitheatre, London, who will make their first appearance on Monday, November 22nd, in a splendid drama in three acts, called *The Arab and His Steed, or the Pearl of the Euphrates*, from the pen of the late L. Rede, Esq. It will be produced with all the original music by John Cooke, Esq., as performed at Astley's Amphitheatre 108 nights to crowded and brilliant audiences.

The whole was arranged and produced under the superintendence of Mr. W. F. Wallett and Mr. Pablo Fanque. Also presented was the new drama, from Cruickshank's Illustrations, entitled *The Bottle*. The show was concluded with a melodramatic romance called *The Brigand Chief*, with Mr. Emery in the title role. Doors opened at half past six o'clock; performances began at seven precisely. Children in arms were not admitted. Meanwhile, Harry Connor was still with Batty's, at Liverpool, with Mr. Bridges and Mr. Powell. Still no mention of Arthur Barnes.

Monday, November 29, 1847, at Hull, was a benefit for Mr. Wallett, and the following night (the 30th) for Mr. Egerton, the lessee and manager of the theater, by desire and under the patronage of Joseph Jones, Esq., and the tradesmen of Hull. The new drama, *The Pride of Birth*, had its debut here that night, and that was followed by the farce *The King's Gardener, or Nipped in the Bud*.

They extended their run in Hull. In early December, the following personnel are mentioned by name: Miss Brown, the graceful little equestrian; Mr. Pablo Fanque, Jun., the extraordinary tightrope dancer; Mr. Richards, the modern Samson; the celebrated Olympic youths, Herr Ludovic and Mr. O'Donnell, Ludovic being the modern Agonistes and Olympic Ball Tosser; the Amphi Arabs, whose extraordinary feats have filled every spectator with wonder, at their unsurpassed excellence, appeared in their routine of performance, which neither pen nor language could adequately describe; the Antipodean Wonders; Harry Walker, the Aerial phenomenon, slack rope tourbillionist, and astonishing leaper; and Mr. Palmer, the Star Rider of the world. "Mr. Pablo will introduce his matchless mare Beda, whose wonderful performance at Astley's Royal Amphitheatre, London, secured for Mr. Pablo the distinguished honour of appearing by special command before Her Majesty, Prince Albert, and the Royal Family. In estimation of her [i.e., Beda's] extraordinary merits, Mr. Pablo has been presented by W. Batty, Esq., with a massive gold cup, value 100 guineas." The clowns mentioned were Messrs. Wallett, Bowman, and Adams. No Arthur Barnes.

On December 15, 1847, while Rockwell & Stone's Mammoth Circus was in St. Louis, Harrington, one of the acts, shot Hiram Franklin, wounding him slightly. Harrington then shot himself twice in the head, which did more than wound him a little (the *Emancipator*, New York, December 29, 1847). A note on Hiram W. Franklin, the "American Apollo." He had begun as a clown in the circus in 1835, when Arthur Barnes was a lad. By 1841 he was clowning with Joe Pentland at the Bowery, in New York. He was also doing the slack rope and light riding. Tom McFarland was doing the vaulting. Franklin is said to have thrown 76 somersaults at one trial.

Pablo Fanque's Royal Circus was at Hull on Friday evening, January 7, 1848. Mr. George Cooke, the daring equestrian, appeared, as did Messrs. Bowman and Adams, the clowns. No smoking allowed. The last grand day performance there was January 8, under the patronage of Sir Clifford and Lady Constable. Pablo took his benefit there on January 10. They closed in Hull on January 15, 1848, moving over to Sheffield, where they opened at the Adelphi on January 17 (*Sheffield and Rotherham Independent*, January 15, 1848), closing there on Saturday, February 12 (*Era*, February 13, 1848), and heading to Wakefield. On January 24, 1848, Harry Connor opened at the Amphitheatre, Liverpool, with the Elliott Brothers and Mr. Wells, as part of Mons. Dejean's Circus, in an act called The English Wrestlers. Mr. Newsome was also with Dejean at this time, as was Auriol. No Arthur Barnes.

In March Pablo's opened at Leeds, at the arena that had been built for Hengler's Circus in November 1847. For information about the Wakefield and Leeds gigs, see Thomas Frost's book *Circus Life and Circus Celebrities* (London: Tinsley Brothers, 1875).

On March 13, 1848, from Leeds, Pablo announced in the paper that one of his apprentices, answering to the names of Pablo Fanque, Jr., or Master Burkham [sic], had absconded, and that anyone hiring him would be subject to the penalty of the law (*Leeds Mercury*, March 18, 1848). One doesn't quite know how to interpret this. Fanque had a son named Pablo, who was about 12 at this time. Anyway, he was evidently soon back with the company. This advertising in the papers about a runaway apprentice happened with a frequency that suggests that, in some cases, it may have been a publicity stunt.

On Saturday night, March 18, 1848, the pit collapsed at King Charles Croft, during Wallett's benefit, and right in the middle of a performance by Pablo Fanque, Jr. on the tight rope. The pit had been built in a sloping position on a framework of wood, and without warning, just caved in. Mrs. Fanque and Mrs. Wallett were in the lobby underneath the pit as it crashed on them. Mrs. Susannah Darby (i.e., Pablo's wife) was killed outright. The jury returned a verdict of accidental death. On Wednesday afternoon, March 22, 1848, they held the funeral at Woodhouse Lane Cemetery. This from the *Leeds Intelligencer* of March 25, 1848, and from all the other papers that picked up the story, and also, of course, from Wallett's autobiography, published by Bemrose & Sons, in London, in 1870.

The show must go on. On Monday, March 27, Fanque's Circus was in Rotherham (*Leeds Intelligencer*, March 25, 1848; *Era*, April 16, 1848), and they were still there in April, whence they left for a gig at Sheffield for 12 nights. During the summer the troupe visited the fairs of Lancashire, Cheshire and adjoining counties (*Era*, May 14, 1848).

On May 12, 1848, Arthur Barnes and McFarland lost their joint world record to Harry Connor, who threw 68. For this, he was awarded a huge gold medal by circus owner William Batty. On May 2, 3, and 4, 1848, William Cooke's Circus was playing Ipswich.

The Return
of Mr. Arthur Barnes

Finally, in June 1848, we track down Arthur Barnes by name. It has been since August 1846 that we have had a definite bead on him, and that is an extremely uncomfortable situation in a supposed biography. In June 1848 he was in Copenhagen again, staying at Narbrø with Pettoletti's Circus. Pettoletti was the famous Danish equestrian family. Philip Pettoletti had originally come to Copenhagen with the Casorti Troup, a Waldensian pantomimist outfit, in May 1800. By 1827 he'd set up for himself and was licensed to perform acts in the Pantomimist Hippodrome in Copenhagen. This theater burned down, but within a month the Pettolettis had rebuilt and were performing again. Philip married Johanne Laurenze Kobke on February 6, 1827, at Frederiksberg, and their eldest child, Alexiné Wilhelmine, was born in June 1829 and baptized on July 3, 1829, at Vor Frue Kirke (Church of Our Lady) in Copenhagen.

Arthur Barns married Alexiné in Der Danske Volkekirke in Frederiksberg on July 4, 1848. He'd put the banns out on June 17. Just prior to the marriage, the minister had asked to see Arthur's baptism certificate, just for the record, but as the Acrobat had never been baptized in a church, and therefore had no proof of his existence (he had been born nine years before the advent of birth certificates), he was forced to go to the Anglican Church in Copenhagen, on June 27, and be dunked by the British chaplain, Rev. B. J. Ellis, M.A. The Danske Volkekirke required proof of baptism, not of age, so the Acrobat indulged in a little prevarication. Well, he was in his 21st year, after all, so one could argue that he told the truth when he said he was 21. If he said he was under 21, he would have required his parents' permission to marry, which would have been not only horribly inconvenient, but also somewhat humiliating, as he had been a star in an adult world for half a decade. The witnesses for the marriage (both supplied by Miss Pettoletti), were her relatives, H. J. Westermann and T. B. Ebbesen.

On July 10, 1848, Tom, the Acrobat's recently widowed elder brother, tied the knot with the widow Porter at the parish church of St. Mary's, in Haggerstown, in the parish of Shoreditch. In the United States, the *Natchez (Mississippi) Semi Weekly Courier* carried an ad for Rockwell's Circus, in which it talks about Hiram W. Franklin having thrown the unprecedented number of 76 somersets, "a number never equaled by any performer in the world." Talking of the U.S., Lavater Lee had arrived there on September 29, 1848.

On October 2, 1848, William Cooke's Circus was at Hadleigh; on the 3rd they were in Sudbury; on the 4th in Halstead; in Braintree on the 5th; at Thaxted on the 6th; and at Haverhill on the 7th. The *Era* of November 5, 1848, tells us that James Cooke's Circus was playing in Dundee, with Madame Macarte, Mr. Ryland, Tom Lee, and Mr. Seal, the clown, among others. Franconi's was playing Liverpool. William Cooke's circus opened in Bristol on Monday, November 20, 1848. James Cooke was still in Dundee, and Franconi's in Liverpool. From November 13, for the week, Van Amburgh's was appearing at the Theatre Royal in Edinburgh.

After getting married, Barnes returned to Pablo Fanque's outfit. This is the first performing mention we have of Arthur Barnes by name in over two years. On December 23, 1848, Fanque's Company, including Arthur Barnes, and the clowns Harry Brown, Charles Stonette, and John Griffiths, opened at the Royal Amphitheatre, the building Pablo had had specially constructed in Victoria Gardens, in Norwich. The *Era* will illuminate this long gig for us. On December 26, Mr. Connor threw 67 somersaults, Barnes threw 51, and Bill Fenner (born 1827, Ireland, son of the equestrian Theophilus Fenner and his wife Mary) threw 49. Herr Hengler (Edward Hengler, brother of Charles), the great rope dancer, appeared, from Batty's Circus.

The *Era* of January 7, 1849, says: "Pablo Fanque's Circus Royal continues to attract crowds of visitors every evening, the doors being closed before the performances commence, to keep the crowd out. It is the best equestrian company that has visited Norwich since the late Mr. Ducrow was in the city [Andrew Ducrow; 1793–1842; circus performer, and manager of Astley's from 1824 until his death in Lambeth]." The circus was honoured with the presence of the mayor, Samuel Bignold, Esq., and family, the officers of the 16th Lancers (quartered in the city), and the principal nobility and gentry of the city and county.

The *Era* of January 21, 1849, says:

> Pablo Fanque's Circus Royal. A variety of new performances have been produced to the staple productions of this establishment, the most successful are the three American Brothers, rival Risley's, also Messrs. Conner [sic], Barnes, and Fenner. The latter gentleman's feats of strength are almost beyond credibility. The summerset throwing has been good; the average throws were from fifty to sixty-six. Next week Mr. Pablo will introduce stage pieces, having already engaged a dramatic company. A new piece will be brought out, called the *Arab and his Steed*, with new scenery and costumes.

The *Era* of January 28, 1849, says: "Pablo's Circus. Crowded houses are witnessing the performances of Mr. Pablo's black mare Beda in the new spectacle called the *Arab and his Steed*. The piece is excellently got up, and the principal characters are well played by Mr. and Mrs. Lomas, Messrs. Stephens, Stonette, and Brown. The Mayor, S. Bignold, gives a bespeak on Tuesday next [i.e., January 30, 1849], when an overflowing house is anticipated."

The *Era* of February 18, 1849, says:

> Pablo Fanque's Circus Royal. The equestrian troupe here have brought out another equestrian spectacle, entitled *Mazeppa, or the Wild Horse*, with new scenery by Kemp, artist to the establishment. Principal characters by Messrs. J. Stephens, Brown, and Lomas; Mrs. Stephens, Mrs. Lomas, and Mrs. Hulse. Herr Hengler (from Batty's), the great rope dancer, has been starring here for a week. The benefits are on this week, and have been well supported up to the present time. On Friday next [i.e., Feb. 23, 1848], H. Chamberlin, Esq., Sheriff of the city, will patronize the Circus.

This was, in reality, Robert Chamberlin.

Wallett

On March 1, 1849, Arthur Barnes left Norwich and Pablo Fanque, after a successful winter season. On March 2, 1849, Pablo was at Wisbech. Later that month Arthur Barnes was with Wallett's Royal Circus in the north of England. We don't know exactly when he joined Wallett, but he was certainly with him by April 7, in Nottingham, as we shall see. William Frederick Wallett, "The Talking Clown," was a vile, humorous and successful individual whose autobiography, *The Public Life of W.F. Wallett; the Queen's Jester*, is full of self-importance and pomposities. He was born in 1813 in Hull, and, after taking the lion cubs to show to the young Queen Victoria (as we have related), henceforth called himself the "Queen's Jester." He didn't like the term clown (as applied to himself), so he called himself "The Shaksperian Jester" (in those days, the standard spelling for *Shakespeare* was *Shakspere*). In 1848 he was a clown at Astley's Amphitheatre in London, and the following year saw him take the plunge and become a circus manager.

So, in 1849 (says Wallett), "I commenced my managerial career at Yarmouth, where I erected a very fine amphitheatre. The support I received was very meagre, for the entertainment was too good for the taste and capacity of the people." They then went to Colchester, where, Wallett tells us, he "was well received and properly appreciated." However, during the second night's performance (i.e., on January 10, 1849), a storm blew up and the roof fell on the audience. There were no deaths, but the several injuries caused an appropriate number of lawsuits that bedeviled Wallett for a couple of years. The performance of January 17, 1849, was a benefit for the Essex and Colchester Hospital (*Essex Standard*, January 19, 1849). With business dead in Colchester, he moved on, with the intention of taking a spot in Ipswich. However, a friend of his was playing that town, and didn't want the competition, so he provided Wallett, free of charge, another space, the Theatre Royal, but in Bury St. Edmunds. This last gig was undertaken while Wallett was waiting for a space at his desired venue—Leicester.

On February 14, 1849, the large circus opened at Leicester. "A New Circus. Mr. Wallett will open a new circus, in Market Street, on Wednesday next, when he will bring before the public his equestrian and other performances. Mr. Wallett is well remembered by our townsmen as a clever and amusing clown in the circus, who has often drawn down the applause and laughter of crowded houses" (*Leicester Chronicle*, February 10, 1849). They were in Leicester for a couple of weeks. The *Leicester Chronicle* of March 10, 1849, has this gem: "Public House open too late. S. Elson, of the Dog and Gun, was charged with having his house open for the sale of liquors after midnight on Saturday [i.e., March 3, 1849]. He admitted that the house was open, but pleaded that it was for the accommodation of Mr. Wallett, who was paying his men. Sergt. Tarratt stated that several persons were in the house, and that drinking and smoking were going on when he went there. Fined 10s." Wallett's left there on or after March 14, 1849. However, Wallett himself admits that Leicester was a mistake. After the dismal showing he vowed he would never go back.

"My next visit was to dear old Nottingham, where I was most kindly received. I did a great business here." The *Nottinghamshire Guardian* of March 29, 1849, says:

> Wallett's Royal Temple of Equestrianism. An advertisement in our paper will show that Mr. Wallett, the very popular clown, our old friend Rex jocundi, who well deserves so distinguished a title for the truly original style of the witticisms he so glibly pours from his ever-ready and eloquent tongue, will pay us a visit at Easter for a short season, with "the best company in the world." A huge place is substantially erecting on the vacant ground in Thurland Street, and will be fitted up replete, as the auctioners [sic] say, with every comfort, for an immense auditory. Of the opinion formed of his establishment in other towns, we give, with great pleasure, the following complimentary letter, which has been handed to us, addressed to our very worthy chief magistrate: "Leicester. March 14, 1849. Thomas Carver, Esq. Dear Sir, I have pleasure in introducing and recommending to your patronage, the bearer, Mr. Wallett, who has been performing in Leicester for the last few weeks, during which time his performances have been no less distinguished by their talent and ingenuity than by the decorum and respectability of the whole establishment. I remain, dear Sir, yours truly, W. Briggs, Mayor." This real tribute of respect to Mr. Wallett is a proof of his deserts. His stud, we understand, is well selected, of great beauty, and in admirable training. His artistes of metropolitan and provincial fame, and his whole establishment superior to any thing we have latterly seen in Nottingham. As a townsman, and a man of genuine talent, he has our best wishes for a prosperous season.

It was Saturday, April 7, when they finally opened in Nottingham, in an arena the exact same size as Astley's—120 feet long by 54 feet wide, one of the largest and best booths ever built in Nottingham (*Nottinghamshire Guardian*, April 5, 1849).

The same paper of Thursday, April 12, 1849, gave Wallett's Royal Circus a nice write-up: "This place of amusement, which bids fair to be the most popular establishment of the kind ever opened in Nottingham, commenced a short season on Saturday last. The whole arrangements are on a scale of magnitude and excellence to which we have hitherto been strangers in our town." The building, erected by the very clever architect, Mr. Frederick James, was described as ample, elegant, substantial, and secure; while the whole arrangements for the comfort of the audience "are as perfect as in a well arranged theatre." The report continued:

> The performances have been chastely elegant, and we affirm the different artistes are perhaps the very best, in their respective performances, we ever saw together in or out of the metropolis; this is great praise, but it is well earned and really deserved. Mr. Wallett in his appointments cannot be excelled; his management is admirable — the whole establishment most gentlemanly — the dresses rich and elegant enough for a drawing-room performance, and down to the subordinates appropriate and uniform. Of Mr. Wallett himself we have no need to speak; his long well-earned reputation here as the first man of his class is proverbial, and his public cognomen of "Rex jocundorum" speaks for the opinions formed of his peculiar talents elsewhere. Russelli is a good second to him as a witty clown, while in other respects he exceeds him. To hear Russelli's variation on the air "The flaxen-headed Cow Boy" on the flute is a performance worth an express visit to the circus alone to hear.

The paper informs us that Mr. Ducrow, Mr. Moseley, Miss Wells, young Polaski, and Mr. Wells are splendid riders in their various styles, and that Moseley is equal to any equestrian that has "preceded him in our locality." Harry Walker excelled on the slack rope and as a vaulter; while the brothers Russelli, in their performances with two globes, astonished the audience by the cleverness and the exquisite perfection with which they went through their pleasing display.

> The ladies of the establishment have not yet graced the arena, but we have no doubt they excel on an equality with those who have appeared before us. The infant troupe are a fascinating little group, and their scenes most pleasing and effective. Of the vaulters, who truly are the best in the world, we cannot speak in terms too highly of their skill and prowess. Hemming, Walker, Connor, and Barnes, more especially who severally threw, the nights we were present, the astounding number of 35, 45, 51, and 61 somersaults clearly and perfectly, as if winding themselves round an ariel [sic] machine. The whole establishment is worthy the most extensive and best patronage our county and town friends can give. On Tuesday last we were glad to find that a distinguished audience honored Mr. Wallett by their presence at his day performance; among the party were Sir Juckes Granville Juckes Clifton, Lady Clifton, Sir Hervey Bruce, Lady Bruce, and other fashionables. We understand Mr. Wallett has also been honoured by several bespeaks from the most influential in our neighbourhood, and we trust his season will produce to him what he so truly deserves for his spirit and liberality — a bountiful harvest.

The same paper of April 19, 1849, said:

Royal Temple of Equestrianism. This popular place of entertainment is crowded every night with delighted audiences, and the performances, of which we have spoken so highly, continue to give the greatest satisfaction. On Monday, Tuesday, and Wednesday nights [i.e., April 16, 17, and 18] was produced the spectacle of St. *George and the Dragon*. That the make up of the monster was admirable was evident from the terror he was gazed at by the children and women in the lower seats of the pit and gallery. The combat was exceedingly well sustained, exciting an intense interest in the minds of the spectators for the safety of the champion. During the fight, the effect was considerably increased by frequent flashes of lurid flames being sent into the arena. Mrs. Wallett made a graceful fairy, and Mr. Wallett, as the Knight's attendant, was exceedingly ludicrous. Tuesday night was under the patronage of Sir Juckes Clifton, Bart., and Sir Hervey Bruce, Bart., and to-morrow (Friday) night, the performances are under the patronage of the Mayor of Nottingham (T. Carver, Esq.), when the splendid Oriental spectacle of *Timour the Tartar* will be produced.

The same paper, of April 26, 1849, had this item:

Wallett's Vauxhall Company. The whole performances throughout the week, at this splendid and extensive establishment, have been of first rate excellence. Mr. Wallett, on his benefit night last Monday [April 23, 1849], though labouring under severe illness, excelled even himself. His Mesmeric Lecture was grotesque and admirable, and the illusion of obtaining a stranger to operate upon was capitally carried out by Russelli. It was a splendid burlesque upon so incomprehensible a science, and a fine hit at a well known lecturer. All the other performances were so excellent that we shall not individualise. To-night and following evenings the bill of fare is a most attractive one, the great focus resting on Mademoiselle Rosina, whose graceful flights and classical feats have gained her a name among the first of female equestrians. The company is the very best we have ever had in Nottingham, and the arena the largest and most comfortable. Of the management, we emphatically state that it is beyond all praise, and highly deserves the patronage of the wealthy and respectable, the general performances being classically chaste and elegant [chastity was quite clearly a big deal in Nottingham]. To-morrow evening, as will be seen by advertisement, Colonel Arthur and the officers of the 3rd Dragoons give their valuable patronage, when the splendid band of the regiment will be present. On Saturday [i.e., April 28, 1849] there will be a grand day performance, at two o'clock, under distinguished patronage, when the inmates and children of the union will be admitted, through the kindness of the spirited manager. Monday next is set apart for the benefit of Mrs. Wallett, our amiable young townswoman, when we trust the compliment of a crowded house will show the estimation in which the conduction of the establishment is held.

It sounds as if Wallett himself wrote these articles, but, regardless of that, it was in Nottingham that Wallett was presented with a silver snuffbox. On

May 1, 1849, the Nottingham Board of Guardians met, and, very impressed with Wallett's generosity to the workhouse kids, voted to give him a benefit.

By May 10, 1849, prices had been reduced to attract the last stragglers from the country. The day before, May 9, as the result of a wager with two of the officers of the 3rd Dragoons, Wallett had driven eight cab horses in pair that had never been coupled together before through the narrow, awkward, hill and dale streets of Nottingham. That evening, Wallett took his benefit from a grateful town. On Monday, May 14, 1849, *Turpin's Great Ride* was the special feature, with the newly engaged James Harwood and his wonderful thoroughbred black mare Bonny Black Bess, from Astley's, in London. On the 19th, at 2 o'clock, there was a select day performance. Then, after a party on May 22, it was off to Bradford.

"Wallett's Royal Circus. A large, temporary, but at the same time firm and substantial, structure, is now in course of erection, on the fair ground in this town [i.e., Bradford], by Messrs. Demaine and Johnson, carpenters, for the reception of Mr. Wallett's renowned Company of Equestrians. During the next week, the holiday folk will not only have an opportunity of witnessing extraordinary feats of horsemanship, but of enjoying the drolleries of the prince of clowns—Wallett" (*Bradford Observer*, May 24, 1849). Frederick James was again architect.

Wallett's Royal Circus (or Wallett's Royal Vauxhall Company) opened on the fairground at Darley Street, Bradford, that night, Whitmonday, May 28, 1849, and the house was crowded to the ceiling each evening. The *Observer* of May 24, 1849, tells us that roof of the circus was perfectly impervious to the wet, the place was aired, and good fires kept. The crowd was astonished by the performances of the equestrians and acrobats. "Vaulting wonders" were mentioned. During the short run the troupe performed St. *George and the Dragon*. Those mentioned were: Clown, Mr. W. F. Wallett; Merry Musical Momus, Mr. John Russilli; Jester, Mr. Swann; Leader of the Orchestra and Composer, Mr. Clements; Stud Groom, Mr. Bannister; Property Maker, etc., Mr. Parish.

On May 29, May 30, and June 7, 1849, the day performance began at 2 o'clock. Doors opened at one. And a performance in the evening, at 7:30. Doors opened at 7:00. On Monday, June 11, 1849, still at Bradford, Mr. James Harwood, and his celebrated mare Black Bess, both from Astley's, made their debut with Wallett's, in the drama *Dick Turpin's Ride, or The Death of Black Bess*, for six nights only. He played this show for three consecutive nights, and then the next three he appeared in *Mazeppa*. The *Bradford Observer* of June 14, 1849, has this: "Wallett's Circus Royal has had overcrowded houses during the present week, and promises to be a source of general attraction during the fair. The fund of amusement provided—wonderful feats of horsemanship and of vaulting, in vast and strange variety, blended everlastingly with wit and drollery of the richest kind — render this exhibition superior to any predecessor in this town. More novelties are in store for next week."

June 27, 1849, was a performance for the Oddfellows' Literary Institution, and June 29 was a benefit for the poor folk in the workhouse. By that June, Arthur Barnes had regained his title of champion vaulter of the world, when, at Bradford, he stunned the circus world by throwing the first ever 70. He reached 73 to be precise, a new world record. No one had ever been over 70 before, not officially anyway.

On Monday, July 2, 1849, there was a fashionable juvenile performance in the afternoon, under the patronage of the mayor and magistrates of the borough of Bradford. The audience included many of the elite of the town. The performance passed off greatly to the satisfaction of all parties, if we except a trifling mishap which occurred to Miss Wells, while performing some of her equestrian feats. In the evening, when Mrs. Wallett took her benefit, the circus was well filled. On Tuesday evening the performances were patronized by Col. Tempest, D.L., and the West Riding magistrates of the district, and there was again a crowded house. The *Observer* of July 5, 1849, reminded its readers that Mr. Wallett's stay in Bradford would terminate with the present week. Interestingly, since Wallett's opened, many of the beer houses in Bradford were deserted, a phenomenon that would afflict other pubs in other towns over the years, which would sometimes lead committees of publicans to object officially to the appearance of a circus in town.

July 7, 1849, was their last night at Bradford, and the next day, Sunday, was spent traveling to Leeds, where they opened on the 9th. It was during this gig that Wallett presented Barnes with a silver snuffbox for his amazing stunt in Bradford. The wording on this box, which still exists, says "Presented by W.F. Wallett, Esq., to Arthur Barnes, on the occasion of his throwing the unprecedented number of 73 somersaults. Leeds. June 28, 1849." This wording is wrong. It should have said Bradford, not Leeds, or the date should say July not June. One or the other.

The *Leeds Intelligencer* of July 7, 1849, has this to say: "Mr. Wallett who, with his highly accomplished corps, has been winning 'golden opinions' in Bradford, will open a spacious arena near the Infantry Barracks in Woodhouse Lane on Monday [July 9], and will remain in Leeds for some weeks." This new arena in Woodhouse Lane could hold 3,000 people, according to Wallett.

For most of July, 1849, Wallett's Circus Royal was in Leeds. It was the depression and the cholera epidemic that forced the circus to move on, this time to the Riding School in Huddersfield. Just to make things worse, a seating disaster forced him to leave Huddersfield, for Burnley. When Wallett got to

Burnley he found no roof on the arena. He had to wait two and a half weeks, during which time he went to Manchester, and contracted with Franconi's to do a week from August 27 to September 1. Franconi's Circus had been playing at the Free-Trade Hall since July 26, to first-class business. The attractions were Steve Ethair and children, Steve, Charles, and Rose; clowns Tomkinson, Wallett, and Courteau; the equestrians Dick Bell and his wife Madame Isabelle Bell; Mademoiselle Amelie and John Bridges; and, of course, Messrs. Bastien and Henri Franconi themselves. On the 27th of August, while Wallett was making his bow with Franconi's, his own circus finally opened at Burnley. The next night, Tuesday, at Burnley, the evening performance was under the patronage of Capt. Vigro and his fellow officers who were stationed there. On the night of Friday, the 31st, Wallett took a benefit at Franconi's. However, business was disastrous in Burnley, so, on September 2, Wallett moved them to Wigan, renting a building in the Ship Yard which Pablo Fanque had erected.

At the Royal Gardens at Vauxhall, in London, on August 27, 1849, and the following four days, one could, for the price of a shilling, see "the celebrated Arab Mohammed Ben al-Hagghe, the most extraordinary vaulter in the world, who will go through his astonishing feats of Gymnastics, in which he will leap as a tiger, lion, etc., and throw the most wonderful somersaults ever witnessed." Also engaged there, over the same period, was Master Hernandez, the greatest wonder in the world. The *Morning Post* of August 27, 1849, in the ad, tells us that Hernandez will be leaving the country at the end of the engagement (i.e., the last day of the engagement was August 31). At the same time, in Cremorne, London, Tim and Harry Elliott were doing globe dancing in an outfit that included equestrians Francois Tourniaire and George Cooke.

That Sunday, September 2, 1849, Wallett returned to Manchester, and made an arrangement for his circus to join Franconi's, as a double troupe. However, this would not become effective until the 10th, so, in the meantime, they played Wigan. But here, too, business was ruined by the epidemic. Wallett says, "We were greatly assisted by Mr. James Hernandez, the great American rider, who here made his debut before an English audience, and achieved a success unparalleled in the history of equestrianism." In the meantime, Wallett's crew had been pressing him for money, some more than others, Arthur Barnes the most vociferously, and Jack Russilli not far behind Barnes. Wallett was disgusted with them for this, which is why Arthur Barnes is painstakingly omitted from Wallett's book. Arthur Barnes jumped ship and went over to Franconi's, and Harry Connor joined him there. The two famous vaulters made their bow at Franconi's on September 3, 1849 (*Manchester Times*, September 1, 1849). "On Monday, an engagement commences with Messrs. Connor and Barnes, whose summersaults are amongst the most wonderful agile feats of the day." On September 7, "the two incomparable artists" Connor and Barnes had their benefit night. That night they leaped over nine horses. Their last night there was Saturday, September 8, and they did a grand day performance that day as well. So, when Wallett's opened with Franconi's, at the Free-Trade Hall, on the 10th, Barnes was no longer with them. Saturday, September 15, 1849, was the last day for Wallett at Franconi's, but he reengaged for another week (*Era*, October 14, 1849). On September 17, 1849, Young Hernandez made his debut at Franconi's, and on September 22, Franconi's wrapped up in Manchester.

The *Era* of October 7, 1849, says of the Queen's Theatre, Manchester: "A domestic drama, entitled *The Blighted Troth*, has been produced this week, in which Mr. and Mrs. Dillon [i.e., Charles Dillon and his wife, Clara Conquest] have sustained the principal characters with great effect. The entertainments have been varied by the performance of the Brothers Hutchinson and Mr. G. Thompson. An attractive bill is issued for their benefit on Friday [Oct. 12, 1849] when Mr. E. Hemming and his pupil, and the celebrated vaulters Messrs. Connor and Barnes will appear." At that time Wallett was playing in Sheffield, with Franconi's. On the 15th Mr. and Mrs. Charles Dillon opened at Ashton, and on October 29 at Sheffield, and then from there the rest of the tour. We don't know if Barnes and Connor were still with them, but it's highly unlikely. The Dillons were well-advertised wherever they went, and the supporting players were liberally (but not exhaustively) mentioned. Not a squeak from the Barnes-Connor corner, which means they probably only played that one night in Manchester with the Dillons. The Brothers Hutchinson were, like Arthur Barnes, Birmingham lads, Thomas Proctor Hutchinson (born October 23, 1820), and his brother Edward, born in 1821. In 1856, Edward would have a son in Birmingham, named Arthur.

Wallett's first stint as an owner had caused him more headaches than he could handle, and he gave it up at the end of the summer season, going to the United States on what is now known as Wallett's first American tour. But, he would be back.

Cooke's, 1849–1850

The huge and new William Cooke's Equestrian Circus entered Manchester in procession from the Ashton Road on Saturday, November 10, 1849, Mr. Cooke driving 16 horses in hand. They set up at Museum Street, where they opened the following Monday (i.e., November 12, 1849), to provide "Rational Amusements for the People." We now have as our guide not only the *Era*, but also the *Manchester Times*. Those with the show included Le Petit Adrian, the clown; Jack Russilli, who had joined Cooke's immediately after the last Wallett gig, in November 1849; Mr. Cooke's brother, Alfred Cooke; Mr. Cooke's sister, Mrs. Woolford, and her daughter, Mdlle. Rebecca; Mr. Cooke's daughter, Miss Kate Cooke; Mr. Cooke's nephew, Master John Henry Cooke; Mr. Cooke's niece Miss Emily Cooke; and Mr. Cooke's brother-in-law, Boswell the clown.

On November 17, 1849, a gas-illuminated grand day performance was given, with the *Steeple Chase* being enacted. There would be a day performance every Saturday. The night of Monday, November 19, was when the Champion Vaulters, Arthur Barnes, Harry Connor, and Harry Walker, made their debut with Cooke's. The *Steeple Chase* was meant to be performed for the last three nights on the 19th, 20th, and 21st, but public demand put back that schedule to the 22nd, 23rd, and 24th. On Saturday, the 24th, charity schools were admitted gratis to the two o'clock day performance, and the night of November 26, 1849, was a fashionable box night, under the distinguished patronage and presence of Lt. Col. Hodge and officers of the 4th Dragoon Guards. The evening performance of December 1 was under the patronage of R. Norreys, Esq., and several families of distinction, that being the night William Cooke played George in St. *George and the Dragon*. The week beginning Monday, December 3, 1849, they presented *The Chinese War Junk, and Feast of Lanterns*. For every night beginning Monday, December 10, 1849, they put on *Lady Godiva and Peeping Tom of Coventry*, while Monday, December 17, 1849, saw the first of six nights' worth of *Robin Hood and Little John*, complete with a real stag hunt, featuring the only performing deer in the world. On the 22nd, they had to contend with the awesome drawing power of Mr. J. C. Byrne at the Athenaeum, who was recruiting immigrants for Natal, as men similar to Mr. Byrne were all over Britain. December 26, 1849, Boxing Day, started with a bang when Mr. Cooke drove 20 horses in hand around the town, getting back to the circus by 1:30 to open the doors for the day performance. That evening was produced Nelson Lee's new pantomime, *Yankee Doodle on His Little Pony.*

Arthur Barnes, Harry Connor, Harry Walker, and Jack Russilli were still with Cooke's in Manchester in January 1850, the holiday folks at Manchester, having, at this circus, had amusement to their heart's content. On Wednesday, January 9, 1850, and Saturday, January 12, Grand Juvenile fetes took place, commencing at two o'clock each day, the vaulting of Messrs. Barnes and Connor adding not a little to the feast of entertainment. Meanwhile, at the Athenaeum, Mr. Gallagher, the ventriloquist, enjoyed his last night in Manchester. Monday, the 14th, Cooke's began *Cinderella* and *Turpin's Ride to York*. At that time, great preparations were making to produce on Monday, the 21st, the grand spectacle, St. *George and the Dragon*. Monday, January 28, 1850, was benefit night for Mr. Cooke, and also the opening night of *The Rigs of Mr. Briggs. Little Red Riding Hood* was performed at the day performance on February 2, while the night performance of Tuesday, January 5, 1850, was under the distinguished patronage of The Worshipful the Mayor, John Potter, Esq., and the Corporation, being for the joint benefit of the Night Asylum (Juvenile Refuge and School of Industry) and the Ragged School. Mr. Cooke donated £10 to the Asylum. February 11 was Alfred Cooke's benefit night. However, that night, an indeterminate number of potential patrons were lured away by Rymer Jones giving a lecture on "A Wander Through the Ocean" at the Mechanics' Institution. If it wasn't Rymer, it was Mr. Royal playing the flute at the Free-Trade Hall, accompanied by Mr. D. W. Banks banging away on his old organ, and Mrs. Winterbottom belting out "The Meeting of the Waters." The *Era* of February 17, 1850, reported from Manchester that "This fine equestrian circus has closed for the season." In fact, that was a rather typical case of bad predictive reporting. Mr. William Cooke's Circus was due to close on Saturday, January 16, but, in consequence of some arrangements not being completed as early as anticipated, this equestrian establishment remained open another week, until Saturday, February 23rd, their last night. The *Manchester Times* of February 20 says: "William Cooke's Royal Circus. Positively the last four nights." The last Wednesday, Friday, and Saturday, they presented *The Battle of Waterloo.*

They left Manchester by special train, arriving at the Wellington Street Station in Leeds at 11 o'clock on Monday, February 25, 1850. About noon they made their public entree into the town, passing through the principal streets in procession, with Mr. William Cooke driving 16 horses in hand. For this Leeds gig we rely basically on the *Leeds Mercury* and the *Era*. They opened, by permission of the Worshipful the Mayor, in a large and substantial circus built by Mr. Cooke on the north side of Boar Lane. Doors opened at half past six, and the show began at 7:15. The show concluded with the *Steeple Chase!, or England's Harvest Home!*, produced under the direction of Mr. Alfred Cooke. The ballet department was under the direction of Signor Zamezou (Tom Jameson; born London, 1820; the name *Zamezou* is also seen as *Zamesou* and *Zameso*). Business was only moderate that first week. In the afternoon of March 5, 1850, the circus gave free performances for two Leeds charity schools. Business picked up, and on March 8, the performance was under the patronage of the Earl of Harewood, when St. *George and the Dragon* was presented. Business really started to improve, and on the evening of March 22, 1850, the performance was under the patronage of Captains Grant and Wardlow and officers of the Artillery and the Dragoons, and the band of the Royal Artillery played some of the most popular music of the day. The week beginning Monday, March 25, they performed *Mazeppa, or the Wild Horse of Tartary*, every night except the Friday. On Easter Monday (April 1, 1850), William Cooke drove 20 horses in hand through the principal streets of Leeds, starting from the circus at 11 o'clock, and that day (and the following day) there was a grand day performance, with doors opening at half past one, with the show commencing at two. At these day performances, the juvenile branches of the troupe performed the grand fairy spectacle *Cinderella, or The Little Glass Slipper*. At night, the main troupe was now performing *The Rigs of Mr. Briggs* (taken from *Punch*), and a little later they presented *Lady Godiva and Peeping Tom of Coventry*. On the evening of April 11, 1850, under the patronage of the mayor, they did a benefit for the Leeds Strangers' Friend Society. On April 21, 1850, William Cooke took his benefit, and leaped over 14 horses, presumably out of sheer gratitude. Mr. Adrian, the clown, injured his hand when a pistol burst, presumably out of sheer carelessness.

The London *Standard* of April 27, 1850, tells of an extraordinary wager of £10 made in Leeds on April 24, when Mr. Baker, the attitudinarian at Cooke's, bet that he could compress himself into a basket 2 feet 7 inches long, one foot seven inches wide and the same deep, and to be conveyed thus on a car to the railway station, to be mailed to Bradford at half past two at luggage price, and to return to Leeds before half past six. Mr. Baker, who was 5 foot 10, was a touring performer known as The Red Man, and, like a later performer named Houdini, was able to dislocate himself at will. He placed his great coat at the bottom of the basket, and, wearing a crimson suit, got in with a bottle of brandy and a few oranges. In this manner, he was duly posted to the Bermondsey Hotel, in Bradford. He made it back to Leeds in time to win the wager. This great story was carried in several papers.

Wednesday, May 1, 1850, was Cooke's last performance in Leeds, and then it was on to Bradford, where they opened on May 2, playing to full houses (*Era*, May 5, 1850). For some reason, no ad appeared in the *Bradford Observer*, either on April 25 or May 2. Anyway, then the tenting season began, the tent capable of holding 2,000 persons. The *Era* tells us where they were, at any given time, through regularly placed ads and reports. We also pick the troupe up through ads, notices, or articles in local papers, as we do for James Cooke's Circus, which began, at the same time, a tour of Scotland and the north of England, and whose itinerary appears at the end of the year. The ad William Cooke's circus used (in the *Era*, anyway) was a basic template consisting of "William Cooke's Royal Colossal Equestrian Establishment of fifty horses and ponies, reindeer, &c, will make their grand entree into" and then the name of the town and the date. Below that was a list of the towns and dates for the next five days. This was followed by "Two representations will be given each day by the first ladies and gentlemen of equestrian art; the first, at two P.M., including the brilliant entre of the Dames of the Chase; the second, at seven P.M., terminating with the military spectacle of The *Battle of Waterloo*. Programme in circulars." This ad remained constant throughout the tour. We will give the approximate distances between towns, so the reader can get an idea of the sheer grind of the travel. But we will do this only for this year.

On May 13, 1850, they were in Skipton, where the performances were under the patronage of Sir Charles Robert Tempest, Bart. Meanwhile, that evening, the Henglers opened in Newcastle, with, among others, Mons. Polaski, the equestrian. They were there for some time, but didn't do a summer tour, as such. There used to be a Roman road running the five miles between Skipton and Addingham, the latter a beautiful, but rapidly declining mill village on the Wharfe, where William Cooke's Circus played their next gig, on May 14, 1850. Then they moved on to the old market town of Otley (May 15, 1850), eight miles away. Otley is about seven miles from Leeds, and eight from Bradford. Only two nights before the circus opened here, the inhabitants of Otley had sustained another thrill, the last of three lectures delivered in the courthouse by Mr. Somerville of London on the most popular of Shakspere's dramas. Then it was Wetherby (May 16, 1850), 12 miles away, after which they traveled the 12 miles to Tadcaster, for the May 17 performances. Tadcaster is about six miles from Harrogate, and the little town was still reeling from the coffee bean that had only very recently killed the child of Mr. Utley, the mason. After Tadcaster, it was on to Aberford (May 18, 1850), about five miles away, on the Great North Road, exactly halfway between London and Edinburgh. Then came Sunday; they had just over 11 miles to journey to get from Aberford to their next gig at Wakefield (May 20, Whitmonday). The *Bradford Observer* of May 23, 1850, tells us about that day in Wakefield: "On this day nearly all the shops were closed, and the town assumed quite a holiday appearance; a few, however, were, we regret to say, opened. The town was enlivened by the visit of Mr. Cooke's equestrian establishment. The splendid stud of animals was greatly admired, and the performances during the day were well attended."

After Wakefield, it was on to Barnsley (May 21, 1850), about 10 miles away. The *Sheffield and Rotherham Independent* of May 25, 1850, tells us that at noon, many persons assembled to witness the entrance of Mr. Cooke's equestrian establishment into Barnsley, at which they were highly gratified. This was Whit Tuesday, the main holy day of Whitsuntide. After Barnsley, it was on to Rotherham (May 22, 1850), almost 10 miles away, and then on to Sheffield, another four miles. The Sheffield paper of May 25, 1850, reported that on Thursday and Friday Mr. Cooke paid a visit to that town, with his splendid stud of horses, mounting to upwards of 50. On Thursday, the whole company entered in full procession, which had a very imposing appearance. The performances each day were of a very superior character. The Royal Stag Hunt, by the ladies of the establishment, on their cream-coloured coursers, concluding with the *Battle of Waterloo*, were striking spectacles. They observed that young Mr. John Cooke "promised to be a very superior equestrian, and the laughter-waking Shaksperean clown Jackson is deserving of the highest praise for his originality."

Just over a week before Cooke's played Sheffield, a local lad, Charlie Peace had just had his 18th birthday. With his father once having been a very talented lion tamer with Wombwell's Menagerie, one would think young Charlie was destined for bigger things than rolling steel. He thought so, especially after a piece of steel had crippled him for life at the tender age of 14. By the time the circus arrived, Charlie had already begun to steal into houses at night and rob his fellow Sheffieldians. Within a few years, when he wasn't doing porridge, Charlie was burglarizing and killing, rapidly becoming a legend. They got him in the end, and hung him. But he almost certainly saw Arthur Barnes somersaulting.

After the two days in Sheffield, it was on to Chesterfield (Saturday, May 25, 1850), 10 miles away. Then the Sabbath again, during which they traveled the 15 miles from Chesterfield to Belper for their May 27 gig. Then to Derby, about six miles away, while Henglers were still playing Newcastle. The *Derby Mercury* of May 22, 1850, advised its readers that under the immediate patronage of His Worship the Mayor, James Haywood, Esq., for one day only!, Wm. Cooke's Royal Circus and Colossal Equestrian Establishment would appear on Tuesday, May 28, 1850, at the Swan Inn Bowling Green, St. Peter's Street, Derby, in a spacious royal tent, on an improved construction, illuminated with portable Gas. The company "will arrive in this town, precisely at twelve o'clock, forming a grand equestrian procession, with new carriages led by the proprietor in his char-a-banc." The announcement that Mr. W. C. would make a public entree gave an impetus to the town and country, and at the appointed time, the streets and windows were lined with the fashion and beauty of Derby, in expectancy for their arrival; and truly the procession had a very imposing appearance, doing just credit to the spirit and taste of the proprietor. More precisely, the procession consisted of the Dragon Carriage; a cavalcade of spotted, white and golden dun steeds and ponies; the elegant miniature curricle, drawn by two dwarf ponies, expressly made for and driven by the talented child, Miss Kate Cooke; the ladies of the stag Hunting Chase!! mounted on their cream-coloured Arabian coursers, in scarlet costume; handsome sledge, drawn by trained Russian deer; state chariot, drawn by four Lilliputian ponies; Miss Kate Cooke's celebrated menage pony, Black Diamond; unique pagoda car, conveying Queen Mab's Fairy Chariot, drawn by the smallest horses in the world, only 24 inches high, a complete model curiosity; the superb war carriage. The horses were among the finest ever seen in Derby; everything was carried out with elegance, and wore the appearance of reality divested of all gaudy gingerbread show. Nor were the performances of this talented company and numerous stud of superb horses of a less distinguished character. "To use an everyday phrase, they were first-rate. Mr. Alfred Cooke was himself a host, being one of the most daring and masterly riders of the present age." Master John Cooke was a promising youth, treading close on the heels of Hernandez. Pretty Miss Kate Cooke and Miss Woolford won great favours with their graceful and talented performances, while Jackson — the inimitable Jackson — brought down roars of laughter and applause. The Champion Vaulters were perfect wonders. The result of such sterling talent was two overwhelming houses. The *Royal Stag Hunt*, by the ladies on their cream-coloured Arabian coursers, and the *Battle of Waterloo* (most effectively got up) were the great cards; won golden opinions; "and will doubtless win for Mr. W. Cooke a golden harvest wherever he pitches his Royal Tent."

It had to have been after Derby that William Cooke split his troupe into two, one to head southwest and the other to head south. Arthur Barnes stayed with the main branch, the one heading south. Using the *Derby Mercury* of May 22, 1850, and various editions of the *Era*, we are able to plot their course for the next few weeks (the other, southwestern branch) we will pick up occasionally along the way. First, it was from Derby to Nottingham, about 12 miles away, where we also pick up the *Nottinghamshire Guardian* of May 30, 1850. There were upwards of 50 beautiful horses and wonderfully small ponies, with truly splendid carriages, the whole forming a procession worth the trouble of the thousands who hastened out to gaze upon it. The troupe played Nottingham on May 29 and 30, 1850, and from there it was on to Southwell (May 31, 1850), 11 miles away. From Southwell, on to Newark (June 1), another six miles on. Then it was Sunday again, during which they shifted to Lincoln for the June 3 gig. They also played there the following day. From Lincoln, it was on to Gainsborough (June 5, 1850), about 15 miles away. Here, Arthur Barnes shattered his world record by doing a phenomenal 87 back somersaults, during an exciting evening patronized by Sir Charles Anderson, Sir Thomas Beckett, and a full house. Harry Connor did 75, and one forward. "The Champion Vaulters are perfect wonders." The boxes had to be enlarged.

From Gainsborough, it was on to East Retford (June 6, 1850), about nine miles away. As they arrived there, they, along with everyone else, heard the shocking news that John Simpson, formerly John Bridgeman, brother of Orlando Bridgeman, Earl of Bradford, had, just that night, died at Babworth Hall, on the outskirts of Retford. That put a damper on the circus, at least for the afternoon performance. The evening one, however, was a "bumper," and gave great satisfaction. After Retford, it was seven miles on to Worksop (June 7, 1850), which, lying on the northern edge of Sherwood Forest, on the River Ryton, has perhaps the ugliest name of any town in England. From there, it was on to Mansfield (June 8, 1850), 12 miles away, then came Sunday again, when they were traveling the 11 miles to their next gig, Ripley (June 10, 1850), the day the southwestern branch opened at North Street, Bristol, for a few nights, with a troupe of equestrian performers and a small, but well-trained, stud of horses. Hernandez, who, until April 24 was at Astleys, and then, perhaps, in Paris, had joined them as the main attraction.

For Arthur Barnes and the southern branch of Cooke's traveling cirque, from Ripley, it was nine miles on to Matlock, the county town of Derbyshire, where they played the June 11 gig. Incidentally, that evening, Astley's in London was patronized by the Nepalese princes, and, to mark the occasion with appropriateness, Mr. Batty presented a piece called *The Afghanistan War*. For William Cooke's it was on to Bakewell (June 12, 1850), about seven miles from Matlock. There were tarts in Bakewell, the town was well known for it, but Arthur Barnes was too health-conscious for all that. Wirksworth was next, about 10 miles away, a Derbyshire market town; they played there on June 13, then on to Ashbourne (June 14, 1850), about eight miles away. They had to cover 15 miles to get to their next performance, at Burton-on-Trent (June 15, 1850). Then it was Sunday. Cooke's traveled the eight miles to Ashby de la Zouch, and played there on the 17th. Then on to Nuneaton (June 18, 1850), about 16 miles away. From Nuneaton, it was eight miles to Coventry (June 19, 1850), then on to Warwick (June 20, 1850), another nine miles. From Warwick, it was on to Royal Leamington Spa (June 21, 1850), only three miles away, where they performed under the patronage of Lord Somerville, and a numerous and fashionable company, who left delighted. From Leamington it was over to Stratford-upon-Avon (June 22, 1850), a distance of 11 miles.

Seven miles from Stratford is the village of Bidford-on-Avon, one of the nearby villages from which the populus flocked into Stratford for market days, baptisms, weddings, funerals, and circuses. A boatman living in Bidford, one William Edgington, had a substantial family, including an eight-year-old daughter named Catherine (born in Bidford on May 16, 1841, and baptized in Stratford on February 26, 1846). The Edgingtons, like everyone else in Bidford, would have gone to see Arthur Barnes vaulting. Twenty-four years later, Catherine Edgington would become the second Mrs. Barnes.

Then came Sunday, which they spent traveling to Kington, 11 miles away. They played Kington on June 24, 1850, and then it was off to Banbury, about 30 miles farther on. *Jackson's* of June 29, 1850, tells us, about the Banbury gig of June 25: "Mr. Cooke's body of equestrians performed twice here on Tuesday last, in a pavilion erected in the cricket field on the Oxford Road, which was crowded each time. The company arrived in Banbury at 12 o'clock, and formed a procession round the town." From Banbury, it was on to Chipping Norton (June 26, 1850), 13 miles away, then to Woodstock (June 27, 1850), a 10-mile trip. From Woodstock, it was on to Oxford (June 28, 1850), eight miles away, and then on to Abingdon (June 29, 1850), another six miles. On Sunday they stayed in Abingdon, and the following day, July 1, traveled to their next gig, Reading, 20 miles away. *Jackson's* of July 6, 1850, says, "Reading. Mr. Cooke's Circus. Mr. Cooke's splendid equestrian troop made a grand entree into the town on Tuesday last, and created quite a sensation; Mr. Cooke drove in with sixteen horses in hand, drawing a carriage, in which was seated a very fine brass band. He gave a morning performance at two [of course, in the afternoon], which was well attended; and in the evening at 7; the immense marquee was crowded."

July 3, 1850, was taken up with traveling the long distance by train to Southampton for a July 4 gig. The *Era* of July 7, 1850, tells us: "Southampton. Wm. Cooke's Circus. This first-rate equestrian troupe, after making a great hit at Oxford, have visited this town, performing under the patronage of the mayor. A morning exhibition took place last Thursday [i.e., July 4], the proceeds of which Mr. Wm. Cooke has added to the subscription now being raised for the Exhibition of 1851. The *Battle of Waterloo* is still represented, and has lost none of its interest and attraction."

July 5 and 6, 1850, do not seem to be covered by the press. Cooke's Circus may have played Andover and/or Salisbury, but more than likely they were taking a break before their next exertion at Winchester on the 9th. The *Era* of July 14, 1850, tells us:

> Winchester. Mr. Cooke's triumphant entry into this place (for really the procession resembled more what one reads of an ancient ovation than what may be looked for at the opening of a traveling exhibition) was witnessed and admired by many thousands on Tuesday last [i.e., July 9]. The tent was numerously and

fashionably attended at the day exhibition, under the distinguished patronage of the Right Worshipful the Mayor. In the evening it was crowded to suffocation, under the honorable patronage of Colonel Ferguson and Major Raines. The procession and equestrian performances are certainly the finest which were ever exhibited in the provinces.

They may have done a second night in Winchester, on the 10th, but certainly, on the 11th, they were back in Southampton, where they also played on the 12th. From Southampton, it was on to Fareham (July 13, 1850), about eight miles away. Then came Sunday, which they used to move the circus to Portsmouth. The *Hampshire Telegraph* of July 13, 1850, says:

> William Cooke's Royal Circus. Collossal [sic] Equestrian Establishment of foreign and British artists, and a stud of 50 highly trained horses and ponies. Positively for two days only. Landport [i.e., in Portsmouth], July 15th and 16th, 1850. Mr. W. Cooke respectfully announces this Leviathan Entertainment of Equestrian Sports, Revels, Tournays, Chases, Gymnastic Festivities, Europe's choicest male and female artistes of the Hippodrome, Champion Vaulters, the greatest clowns of the day, the smallest ponies in the world, trained Russian rein-deer etc, combining the most extensive concentration of talent ever produced in this country in our day's amusement. This gorgeous fete will be the ne plus ultra of horsemanship. The first performance to commence at two o'clock precisely. Entire change, commencing at seven in the evening, the second entertainment. To conclude with the grand military piece, replete with historical events, and appropriate dresses, flags, uniforms, bivouacs, etc, entitled the *Glorious Battle of Waterloo*. Terrific combat between Shaw the Lifeguardsman and his opponents, Shaw's horse shot from under him (this is considered the most difficult act of horse training) — death of Shaw — the battle raging in the distance — Napoleon's last hope completely routed — his flight — Wellington's splendid victory — Grand Finale. Shaw the Lifeguardsman ... Mr. W. Cooke. Prices of admission: first class seats, 2s; second class, 1s; arena, 6d; children under 10 years of age and schools at half-price to the seats only.

Then the paper lists upcoming gigs for the troupe, which match exactly those given in the *Era* of July 7 and 14.

From Portsmouth, it was on to Havant (July 17, 1850), about five miles away, and from there another nine miles to Chichester, for the July 18 gig. Then six miles on to Bognor Regis (July 19), and from there to Arundel (July 20), seven miles away. Then came Sunday, and it was on from Arundel to Worthing, nine miles away. They played Worthing on July 22, 1850. It was a pity that one of Worthing's leading citizens, Dr Fred Dixon, the surgeon and famous paleontologist and dinosaur hunter, was not there to see the circus. He had died the previous October. His great-great-grandnephew would, in 1948, marry Arthur Barnes's granddaughter.

From Worthing, it was on to Brighton, 10 miles away. They did two nights at Brighton, July 23 and 24, 1850, then it was off the seven miles to Lewes, for the July 25 performance. From Lewes, it was on to Eastbourne (Friday, July 26), 13 miles away, the same day Cooke's southwestern branch opened at Plymouth. The *Era* of August 4 says that Cooke's Circus has been drawing overflowing houses ever since Friday last, when it first located here (i.e., Plymouth). "The principal object of attention is the young Hernandez, whose brilliant performances on horseback we never before saw equalled. On Friday we saw him throw a double summersault while the old horse that he rides — a well proved favorite of course — was in full swing round the ring."

For Cooke's southern branch, it was on from Eastbourne to Battle (July 27), 14 miles away. On the Sunday they traveled the next six miles, to Hastings, for their July 29 gig, and from there on to Rye (July 20), nine miles away. From Rye, it was on to Tenterden (July 28), eight miles away, and then on to Ashford, another 10 miles. They played Ashford on August 1, 1850, and then it was a further 11 miles to Hythe (August 2). From Hythe, it was on to Folkestone (August 3), only four miles away, and then, on the Sunday, it was a six-mile trip to Dover.

Dover they played for two nights, August 6 and 7, 1850, then it was up the road to Deal, eight miles away, for the night of August 8. From Deal, they continued the five miles over to Sandwich (August 9), and then the 11 miles up to the famous seaside resort of Ramsgate, for their August 10 gig. August 11 was a Sunday, on which they were at liberty in Ramsgate before doing their second night there on Monday, August 13, 1850. Then four miles across the so-called Isle of Thanet, to Margate. They did two nights at this fashionable seaside town, August 14 and 15, before moving off along the north coast of Kent, to Herne Bay (August 16, 1850), 11 miles away. Then a straight seven-mile shot into Canterbury (August 17), the home (so to speak) of the Anglican church. The *Era* of August 18, 1850, tells us that "William Cooke's Equestrian Troupe has visited Ramsgate and Canterbury with immense success, a morning performance at the latter town being patronised by Col. Ricketts and officers of the Royal Scotch Greys."

Sunday was spent traveling to their next engagement, Faversham (August 19, 1850), eight miles away, and from there it was another seven miles on to Sittingbourne, for the August 20 gig. They were now heading inexorably toward the Metropolis. From Sittingbourne, it was on to Maidstone (August 21), the county town of Kent, 10 miles away, and from Maidstone to Sevenoaks (August 22), another 15 miles. Then on to Croydon (August 23), 14 miles away, and then another six miles to Bromley (in Kent), for their August 24 gig. On Sunday, they shifted the nine miles to Stratford, Essex, where they played on the 26th, and then five miles to Woodford (August 27, 1850). From there it was on to Romford (August 28, 1850), another eight miles farther on. From Romford they went to Billericay, 11 miles away, for the gig of the 29th, and from there eight miles to Chelmsford. The *Essex Standard* of September 6, 1850, says: "On Friday last [i.e., Aug. 30] Mr. Cooke and his equestrian company made their entry into the town of Chelmsford; and the easy manner in which Mr. C. drove sixteen horses in hand through the crowded streets was the theme of admiration among the immense crowd of spectators who turned out to witness the spectacle. The performances morning and evening were numerously attended."

From Chelmsford, it was on to Maldon, Essex (August 31, 1850), nine miles away, then on the Sunday they traveled the five miles to Witham, on the River Brain. This gig was actually in Witham, as reported in the *Essex Standard* of September 6, 1850, and not in Braintree (as reported in the *Era* of September 1, 1850): "Witham. Circus. On Monday [i.e., Sept. 2] Mr. Cooke's Grand Equestrian Stud entered the town, and gave afternoon and evening entertainments. In the evening it was estimated there were not fewer than 2000 persons present, the surrounding villages for some miles having contributed largely to the number."

From Witham, it was on to Great Coggeshall, Essex, seven miles away, on the old Roman road of Stane Street, for the evening of September 3, 1850. Despite the fact that today the town of Coggeshall is the town of Coggeshall, in those days there were Great Coggeshall and Little Coggeshall. There were 13 drinking establishments in the Coggeshalls at that time, which seems somewhat excessive until one remembers it was England, and perhaps because of this, the town was still reeling from the effronteries of the recently captured Coggeshall Gang. To add insult to injury, only the day before the circus arrived, the Coggeshall cricket team had lost to Bocking yet again, in an away match, by seven wickets. Cooke's was here to cheer them up. From there the nine miles to Colchester. The *Essex Standard* of August 30, 1850, advertised: "William Cooke's Royal Circus," positively for two days only at Castle Bailey, Colchester, Weds. and Thurs., September 4 and 5, 1850. Two performances each day, at 2 and 7 o'clock. The *Era* of September 1, 1850, wondered bleakly about Cooke's future in the town of Colchester: "Mr. W. Cooke's Equestrian Establishment will make their entrance into Colchester on Wednesday [i.e., Sept. 4], and we trust Mr. Cooke will receive, at any rate, a *little* [in italics] patronage from the inhabitants of this usually dull and almost lifeless town." The *Era* needed have no fear. The *Essex Standard* of September 6, 1850, reported: "The Circus. Colchester proved no exception to the stir and bustle which Mr. Cooke's circus has been causing in our Essex towns. His entree on Wednesday [i.e., Sept. 4], sixteen in hand, was witnessed by some hundreds of spectators, and on both evenings of his stay the immense pavilion in which the equestrian dexterity of his troop is displayed was crowded to the fullest extent, beside large musters of juveniles at the day performances. Mr. Cooke will next pay a visit to Harwich."

It was actually Manningtree (September 6, 1850) next, nine miles from Colchester. They hadn't had so much fun in Manningtree since Charles Sinclair, the ventriloquist, presented his act two weeks earlier, in the Lecture Hall. Incidentally, that Friday, the 6th, Young Hengler was in Hull, playing Hamlet at Mr. Rignold's Queen's Theatre. After the performance, he threw a double somersault on the tightrope. For Cooke's, from Manningtree it was on to Harwich (September 7, 1850), another nine miles traveling. On Sunday they left Harwich on the nine-mile trip to Ipswich, where we pick up our new guide, the *Ipswich Journal*.

On Monday, September 9, 1850, William Cooke's Royal Circus, the colossal and dashing equestrian establishment of foreign and British artists, and a stud of 50 highly trained horses and ponies, paraded the streets of Ipswich. It consisted of several beautifully painted caravans, and miniature phaetons and coaches, with male and female equestrians, Mr. Cooke, the proprietor, driving 16 horses in hand, with the ease, apparently, of a most accomplished whip. Then on to the gigantic marquee, in a meadow abutting upon the Woodbridge Road, for positively one day only! But two performances. The first took place in the afternoon, beginning at 2 o'clock precisely, when the whole of the charity children of the town, amounting to several hundreds, were admitted gratuitously—an act of liberality which appeared to be well appreciated. The second entertainment, entire change, commencing at seven in the evening, was patronised by the Mayor, T. B. Ross, Esq., and Capt. Douglas and officers of the 11th Hussars. That evening show, the marquee was crowded almost to suffocation. There could not have been fewer than 2,000 people present. The performances in the ring progressed, under the circumstances, as steadily as could have been expected; but upon two occasions, owing to the pressure, and to the space allotted to the horses being invaded by great numbers, the performances were brought to a standstill. Indeed the pleasure which the box audience might have derived from the equestrian exhibitions was very much marred by the cries of distress which proceeded from the dense crowd pent up in the standing-places around the ring. Many times apprehensions were entertained of some most painful accident to this portion of the audience, who literally rolled to and fro like a field of corn when agitated by the wind. Fortunately, the mayor was present, and the gentleman, fully alive to the fact that his interposition was needed, very properly made a peremptory order that no horse should be allowed to gallop until the ring was effectually cleared of people. The duty of restoring order was entrusted, under the mayor's supervision, to the police, by whom it was efficiently performed with great good temper, though it evidently proved most laborious. Under such circumstances there was little of a very striking character in the performances. However, Mrs. Cooke put one of the horses forming the beautiful stud through some most graceful evolutions; and in the gymnastic exercises, one of the performers made *sixty-one summersets!*—a feat before unparalleled at any former exhibition of the kind in Ipswich (this was, of course, Arthur Barnes). As for the representation of the concluding Grand Military Piece, replete with historical events, and appropriate Dresses, Flags, Uniforms, Combats, Bivouacs, etc., entitled the *Battle of Waterloo*, and embodying the grand stud of horses, Double Company, and numerous auxiliaries engaged, which the pressure of the crowd caused to be shorn of many of its adjuncts, it turned out literally an affair of "fire and smoke," alternating with Stentorian voices, and the explosion of firearms and rockets, leaving the audience at the close bewildered and half suffocated in a dense body of smoke.

From Ipswich, it was on to Woodbridge, Suffolk (September 10, 1850), eight miles away, and from there another nine miles to Orford (September 11, 1850). From Orford it was six miles to Aldeburgh (September 12, 1850), and then on to Saxmundham (September 13, 1850), six miles away. Southwold (September 14, 1850) followed, 11 miles away, then it was Sunday again, during which they traveled the eight miles to Halesworth, Suffolk, for the September 16 gig. That day, Monday, September 16, 1850, Tom Matthews, the celebrated pantomimist, opened, as manager, a new establishment in Gravesend. It was also the 80th night that Astley's, in London, had presented *Mazeppa*. At the Tivoli, in Margate, that night, Mdlle. Ricardo made her first terrific ascent up the tightrope. Then, for Cooke's, it was eight miles further to Bungay, Suffolk.

Using the *Era* and the *Ipswich Journal*, we learn that the entree of Cooke's equestrian establishment into Bungay, on the 17th of September, 1850, caused the streets to be crowded with spectators, among whom were most of the town's leading families, the juveniles having found accommodation at the King's Head Inn and other houses in the market place. The whole thing caused quite an excitement in this usually quiet town. The condition of the horses, the elegance of the carriages, and the general appointments of the procession were admirable. The procession was headed by the band chariot drawn by 16 beautiful fancy horses, which were driven in fine style by Mr. Cooke, the proprietor. This was followed by several unique and elegant vehicles, among which a Lilliputian chariot drawn by a very "Tom Thumb" of a pony, and a Russian sledge, drawn by a reindeer, excited universal admiration. With great liberality, the children of the National and British Schools, numbering about 200, were admitted gratis to the day exhibition, which was most genteelly and well attended. The various feats of strength and agility of the performers and the high training and docility of the horses, excited the warmest applause. In the evening the circus was filled to an overflow, no fewer than 1,700 or 1,800 persons being present. The performances in the ring were more than usually good. "On leaving Bungay, we are informed," says the *Era*, "Mr. Cooke intends to make the tour of Norfolk, and visit all the leading towns."

From Bungay, it was the six miles on to Beccles, Suffolk, for the gig of September 18, 1850, and from there to Lowestoft (September 19), eight miles away. From Lowestoft, it was on to Great Yarmouth (September 20, 1850) another eight miles on, and from there the 18 miles to Norwich, where they played on September 21, 1850. From Norwich it was 12 miles to Aylsham, and that Sunday they made the trip there, playing on September 23. From there on to Cromer (September 24, 1850), where they made their equestrian procession through the town at 12 o'clock on Tuesday noon, to the great delight of many hundreds who had thronged every avenue, and filled the church square, for the purpose of witnessing the motley cavalcade. Steeds of various sizes and colors; carriages of all dimensions and forms; ladies in their scarlet hunting dresses; gentlemen in troubadour and chivalric costume; these, headed by a band of wind instruments, discoursing good and exhilarating music, driven in a gigantic char-a-banc (16 horses in hand) by the spirited proprietor himself — the centre of the column of march exhibiting miniature curricles and miniature quadripeds [sic], of the equine species, daintily harnessed to them — besides the unique feature of a reindeer also acting as a beast of draft — while the rear was brought up by vehicles fanciful in shape and showy in decoration — these were the chief components of a midday pageant. On that date, September 24, 1850, Hernandez arrived back in London after a successful tour with Cooke's southwestern branch, thus implying that the southwestern branch tour itself was over, and that they had rejoined the main branch of Cooke's Circus.

From Cromer, it was eight miles on to Holt, Norfolk, for the performance of September 25, 1850. Then the 11 miles to Wells-next-the-Sea, for the September 26 gig. It would be another six years before a railway station opened in Wells, so it was by road the five miles from Wells to Burnham Market (also known as Burnham Westgate), still in Norfolk, where they performed on September 27, 1850. Then on to Fakenham, nine miles away, on the River Wensum, for the September 28 show. Local iron and scrap founder John Garrood must have got away from his home in the Pound Houses, to see the circus. If his son John had been born — and he wouldn't be for another two years yet — he would have gone along too. The son would later become an engineer, and make improvements to the penny farthing bicycle. On the Sunday, the 20 miles to King's Lynn for the performance of September 30, 1850.

October 1, 1850, saw them playing Downham Market, Norfolk, just over 10 miles from King's Lynn, on the edge of the Fens. It was here that Charles I had hidden after the battle of Naseby. From Downham it was on to Swaffham, Norfolk (October 2, 1850), just over 12 miles away, and the town most identified with pugilist Jem Mace. After Swaffham, it was on to East Dereham, Norfolk (October 3), 10 miles away, and then the eight miles to Watton, still in Norfolk, where they played October 4, 1850. From Watton it was 11 miles to Thetford (October 5), and then it was Sunday again. They traveled from Thetford to Bury St. Edmunds (October 7, 1850), 11 miles away, the same day Hengler's Circus was opening up north, in Sunderland. Also that evening, in London, Mr. Batty was presenting *Mazeppa* for the 99th time at Astley's, and Herr Maus was performing with Franconi's, up in Dundee. From Bury St. Edmunds, it was on to Lavenham, Suffolk (October 8, 1850), which was another 10 miles, and then, on October 9, 1850, they played Sudbury, just on the Suffolk border, six miles from Lavenham and eight miles from their next destination, Halstead (October 10). Then another five miles to Braintree for the performance of October 11, and from there to Thaxted, 11 miles away, for the gig of October 12. On the Sunday, they traveled the six miles from Thaxted to Great Dunmow, Essex (October 14), and from there it was on to Bishop's Stortford (October 15), eight miles away; Saffron Walden (October 16), another 11 miles; Linton, in Cambridgeshire (October 17, 1850), another six miles; and then, on Friday the 18th, a further nine miles into Cambridge itself.

There was a bit of fuss at Cambridge, according to the *Bury and Norwich Post* of October 23, 1850. Mr. Cooke applied to the mayor for permission to bring his circus to town, which was readily granted. Cooke then asked the vice-chancellor for his sanction, and was refused. Cooke then went back to the mayor, who said come anyway, he would take responsibility. The circus duly came to town, and the vice-chancellor, very upset, had printed an inordinate number of copies of a spiteful leaflet warning students that if they attended the circus they would be expelled, or worse. Notwithstanding, Cooke's did roaring business on their two days there, October 18 and 19, 1850.

On October 20, 1850, Sunday, William Cooke's Royal Circus, with Arthur Barnes, traveled the 12 miles from Cambridge to Newmarket, still in Cambridgeshire, where the *Era* of October 27, 1850, tells us that a vast number of persons assembled on the Monday, October 21, to witness the entree of this extensive establishment. The cavalcade extended nearly the whole length of High Street, and the manner in which Mr. C. managed his team of 16 highbred horses and turned them twice in that narrow thoroughfare excited the wonder and admiration of the beholders. The interesting child, Miss Kate Cooke, in her miniature curricle drawn by two dwarf ponies, appeared an object of great attraction, and the whole procession afforded a great treat to those assembled. The day performance was well and fashionably attended. In the evening the immense circus was filled to overflowing, and the performances gave unbounded satisfaction. From here Mr. C. proceeded to Ely, 12 miles away, where he performed next day, the 22nd; at Chatteris, another 12 miles, on Wednesday, October 23, 1850; at Ramsey, another seven miles (which put them in Huntingdonshire) on Thursday, October 24; at Whittlesey, Cambridgeshire on Friday, the 25th; and on Saturday the 26th of October, 1850, at Peterborough, five miles away. Peterborough has formed the fulcrum of several counties over the years, depending on administrative gerrymandering, but, being a cathedral town, it has always managed to retain its identity as the soke of Peterborough.

On the Sunday, it was on to Market Deeping, eight miles away, for the performance on Monday, October 28, 1850. They were now in Lincolnshire, but more specifically in the area of the country that revolves around the Peterborough-Stamford nexus, where Lincs, Rutland, Leicestershire, Northants, Hunts, Cambridgeshire, and the northwestern part of Norfolk all come together, in a manner of speaking.

Then, from Market Deeping, it was on to Stamford, six miles away. The *Era* of November 3, 1850, has this to say: "Stamford. William Cooke's Circus. The name of Cooke, as caterer for the public of equestrian amusements has been well known and respected by the inhabitants of Stamford for a period of thirty years, and on each visit he has received a welcome." The reception Mr. William Cooke met with in the above town, on Tuesday, October 29, 1850, was gratifying in the extreme, and on no previous occasion did the inhabitants assemble in such large numbers to give their countenance to an equestrian performance, upwards of 2,000 persons having visited the circus in the evening. Both the day and evening representations gave the highest satisfaction, and the manner in which Mr. Cooke acknowledged the liberal patronage awarded to him by the Stamfordians showed that he fully appreciated the support tendered. Next day, October 30, 1850, the colossal troupe visited Uppingham (some sources mistakenly say this gig was in Oakham), and thence proceeded the 14 miles to Melton Mowbray, Leicestershire; this gig took place on October 31, 1850. Then it was on to the town of Leicester itself, 14 miles away.

They played Leicester on November 1 and 2, 1850, and then November 3 was a Sunday, during which they traveled to Hinckley, 12 miles away, for their gig of Monday, November 4, 1850. Only 15 years before, the first hansom cab had been built at Hinckley. From there it was seven miles down the road to Atherstone, in Warwickshire. Then on to Tamworth, Staffs (November 6), seven miles away, and another eight miles into Lichfield, for the November

7 gig. That night, in Lichfield, a young solicitor's clerk named Arthur Barnes would have gone to see his namesake performing. Actually, the clerk was four years older than the Acrobat, but the curious thing is that, although not related, both were born in Birmingham. And, to make it odder, the clerk was not the only Arthur Barnes living in Lichfield. There was a baby of that name, son of carpenter Tom Barnes, living on St. John Street. The clerk Arthur Barnes would soon become one of the leading legal lights in Lichfield. Then, for Cooke's, it was on to Walsall, another nine miles away. They played Walsall on November 8 and 9, and then on the Sunday they traveled the seven miles to Dudley, Staffs, for their November 11 gig. Then it was on to Bilston, still in Staffs, only four miles from Dudley. They played Bilston on November 11 and 12, then it was the 10 miles into Arthur Barnes's hometown of Birmingham.

The *Era* of November 17, 1850, says:

> Amusements in Birmingham. William Cooke's Equestrian Visit. Mr. William Cooke entered Birmingham for a visit of two days, on Thursday last [i.e., Nov. 14], heading his extensive stud by driving sixteen in hand. He took up his quarters at the New Exhibition Hall, Broad Street (Bingley House), and on that day and Friday, presented an equestrian fete of such talented attractions that is rarely witnessed in the provinces. That gorgeous military piece, the *Battle of Waterloo*, concluded each performance, and the troupe were highly successful in rendering a novel description of that great historical event. The stud, constantly in requisition, both for extent, beauty, and sagacity, is unrivalled by any similar exhibition in this part of the country.

So, after playing the two days at Birmingham, November 14 and 15, their 1850 summer tour came to an end. They left Birmingham on the Saturday, bound for Bristol, where we pick up the good old reliable *Bristol Mercury* again.

That Saturday, November 16, 1850, Mr. W. Cooke's talented and really colossal equestrian company arrived in Bristol by special train, at one o'clock, making a public entry into the city and proceeding in a grand equestrian procession from the terminus to the Royal Circus, North Street, attracting large crowds in the streets through which they were expected to pass. The cavalcade, with various new carriages, and accompanied by Mr. Cooke's brass band, was a very imposing one, comprising the principal members of the equestrian corps on horseback, the splendid and elaborately carved dragon carriage, drawn by 16 richly caparisoned horses all driven in hand by the proprietor in his music char-a-banc, a sledge drawn by a reindeer, and numerous petite pony and other carriages. One of the crowd standing opposite the terminus, waiting for Cooke's train, was Mary Ann Gibbs. She felt someone touch her pocket, and in turning around, saw Sarah Smith withdrawing her hand. Mary Ann searched her pocket immediately, and found missing a silk handkerchief and the sum of 11 shillings and sevenpence. She handed Sarah over to Police Sergeant Yates, who found the money in the prisoner's hand. The handkerchief was found at her feet. It was a fair cop.

The Circus Royal had undergone extensive alterations under the superintendence of S.B. Gabriel, Esq., architect, and had been thoroughly redecorated and embellished. Monday, November 18, 1850, the very fully attended opening night for the new building, was also opening night in Bristol for Cooke's, the first day of their wintering-season. The equestrian cavalcade called *The Roman Warriors* was presented (as it would be also for the next two nights). Mr. Hemming appeared in his juggling acts. Henry Cooke presented the comedy *The Clown and His Granny of Eighty on Horseback*. Mons. Ethair and his family appeared in their drawing-room entertainment. Master John Cooke in his act of riding backward, and Mademoiselle Rebecca on her steed of beauty. Mr. Alfred Cooke, the premier horseman of the day, appeared as "The Andalusian, or Cheval Conqueror." "The Champion Vaulters Messrs. Barnes, Connor, and Hemmings [sic]" performed. William Cooke introduced his Hanoverian mare, and the entertainment concluded with *The Rigs of Mr. Briggs, or The Pleasures of Housekeeping and Horsekeeping*, with Alfred Cooke as Mr. Briggs and Mrs. W. Cooke as Mrs. Briggs. "Our old favorite Jackson is here as a clown," said the paper.

On one of the days this week Barnes threw 87 somersaults at one trial, and Connor threw 75. The first day exhibition took place at two o'clock on Saturday, November 23, 1850, and two days later began another week with Mr. Barnes and Mr. Connor. The new cavalcade *The Swiss Entree* was presented (as it would be also for the next two nights). Mr. Cooke instructed his spotted barb, Prince. Master John Cooke appeared as "Monopologue on Horseback." Masters Stephen and William Ethair, surnamed "The Elfin Sprites," sustained themselves on a rapid revolving globe. "This act will introduce the most daring vaulters, Messrs. Barnes and Conner [sic]." Mrs. G. Woolford appeared in the "Act of the Menage." Mr. Boswell performed an Antipodean maneuver on the Magic Ladder. Mr. W. Barlow in a comic scene entitled *A Night with Punch*. Mr. Henry Cooke on the tightrope, and Mdlle. Rebecca as the Leaper of Streamers. The entertainment concluded with *The Rigs of Mr. Briggs*.

The next day performance was on Saturday, November 30, again at two o'clock. "Messrs. Barnes and Connor defy competition as the champion vaulters," cried the *Mercury* of that day, not necessarily referring to that day's performance specifically, but rather to the two acrobats in general. The *Era* of December 1, 1850, has this to say:

Bristol. William Cooke's Circus. Mr. William Cooke's leviathan and talented equestrian troupe are carrying all before them at the North Street circus. Mr. Briggs, *Punch*'s equestrian and sporting hero, has been brought out in excellent style, Mr. Alfred Cooke eliciting shouts of laughter and applause by his clever embodiment of the humours, eccentricities and mishaps of the ill-fated Mr. Briggs, in which Mrs. Cooke shares as his cara sposa. The champion vaulters, Barnes and Connor, excite wonderment and delight, whilst the riding of Mrs. G. Woolford, W. Barlow, Mdlle. Rebecca, and Master John Cooke is truly graceful; added to which we have the tight rope performances of Mr. H. Cooke, and feats of agility and strength by Masters Ethair, Mr. Boswell, etc. Crowded audiences reward the efforts of the proprietor to cater for the public amusement.

On December 2, 1850, Mr. Barlow appeared as the Alpine Springer, Mr. Russilli as the bottle equilibrist, and La Petite Emily Cooke as the Parisian Masquerader on horseback. "Messrs. Barnes, Connor, and Hemmings [sic], will throw an immense number of summersaults," predicts the *Mercury* of November 30 safely. Mr. A. Cooke, assisted by his daughter, appeared in a spectacle entitled *A Midsummer Night's Dream*. On December 5, *Mazeppa* was presented. About this time, in Bristol, Boswell the clown married the widowed Rebecca Woolford, thus becoming, by a stroke of the pen, both the stepfather of Mdlle. Rebecca and the brother-in-law of the great William Cooke.

The *Era* of December 15, 1850, tells us: "Bristol. Mr. W. Cooke's Circus. On Thursday last [i.e., Dec. 12], the clever and liberal proprietor gave the proceeds as a benefit to the Exhibition of 1851," the show being under the distinguished patronage of the Right Worshipful the Mayor, John Kerle Haberfield, Esq., and the Corporation of Bristol. The usual varied entertainment, including *Turpin's Ride to York*, was well patronized and deservedly applauded by a delighted audience. "Miss Clarissa Cooke, Mdlle. Rebecca, Messrs. Hemming, H. Cooke, Boswell, and W. Cooke, are all painstaking and extraordinary artists." The fund came to £50.

Saturday, December 14, 1850, also offered a day performance at two o'clock. On Monday, the 16th, the evening's entertainment began with *The Village Lovers, or The Old Ones Outwitted*, and concluded with *Turpin's Ride to York*, as it did also on Tuesday and Wednesday, Wednesday being the last night for *Turpin's Ride to York*. Nelson Lee, the greatest and most prolific of all the panto writers, was busy preparing the great Christmas Pantomime. On December 23, 1850, *Lady Godiva & Peeping Tom of Coventry* was presented, the following night (Christmas Eve) being the last production of that piece. On December 24, 1850, at Toxteth Park, Liverpool, at the church of St. Clement's, Edwin Hughes's son Fred was baptized.

They never performed on Christmas Day, of course, but Boxing Day was always a big event. A holiday fete took place at two o'clock, and that evening was reviewed in the *Mercury* of the 28th.

> Mr. Nelson Lee's new pantomime, *Punch and Judy*, was produced at this establishment as a treat to the holiday folks, and, combined with a very attractive series of equestrian and other amusements, it drew together one of the most crowded houses that has been known in the history of the establishment in this city. Hundreds—perhaps thousands—were obliged to be turned away from the doors, and so crowded was the building that some portion of the ring was taken possession of by a number of the densely-packed audience, an occurrence which in some measure interfered with the effective representation of a portion of the performances. The pantomime is arranged to combine, according to the programme of its author, "wit, mirth, frolic, fun, harmony, melody, eloquence, grace, talent, flexibility, neatness, precision, fraud, deceits, dupes, victims, laughter, joy, gladness, and applause," and it may readily be believed that out of such elements a clever playwright and wit like Mr. Lee has succeeded in producing an entertainment replete with varied and changing incident, and calculated to draw largely on the risible faculties of those who witness it. Mr. Jackson made a capital representation of Punch in the opening, nor was he less happy, after the transformation, in portraying the whimsicalities and humor of "Mister Merryman," who cracked his witticisms and played his pranks with a degree of good humor which made all his "jokes go free." Mr. Lehman made a clever Judy, and Pantaloon Mr. Boswell a most amusing and mirth-provoking sprite; Mr. Barlow an effective Punch, Jun. and Harlequin, and Mdlle. Rebecca a light and airy personation of Columbine. The other characters, and particularly the Fairy Queen of Mrs. Cooke, were well sustained, and the pantomime, which passed off with éclat, was got up in a manner reflecting the highest credit on the management.

The paper failed to mention the idle weeds, the sprites—Chickweed, Groundsil, Soursorrel, and Nightshade, in the midst of whom revels the Fairy Snowdrop. Barnes and Connor played two of the sprites.

For the record: James Cooke's Circus left Edinburgh, and their 1850 summer tour looks like this: Portobello (May 6, 1850), Dalkeith (May 7, 1850), Musselburgh (May 8, 1850), Haddington (May 9, 1850), Linton (May 10, 1850), Dunbar (May 11, 1850), Ayton (May 13, 1850), Berwick-upon-Tweed (May 14, 1850; the Brothers Elliott opened with them here), Belford (May 15, 1850), Alnwick (May 16, 1850), Felton (May 17, 1850), Morpeth (May 18, 1850), Newcastle (May 20 and 21, 1850), North Shields (May 22, 1850), Sunderland (May 23 and 24, 1850), Houghton-le-Spring (May 25, 1850), Bishop Auckland (May 29, 1850), Darlington (May 30, 1850), Stockton-on-Tees (May 31 and June 1, 1850), Guisborough (June 3, 1850), Whitby (June 4 and 5, 1850), Scarborough (June 6 and 7, 1850), and Filey, June 8, 1850.

The next week is incomplete, but they had to have headed south, to

Bridlington, then over to Driffield, and on to Fridaythorpe, perhaps playing one or two small towns along the way, before going up to Malton for the June 15 gig. Playing with them at this time were Joe Gee, Billy Seal, Jim Barlow, and the Brothers Elliott. After Malton, it was on to Pickering (June 17, 1850), Kirkbymoorside (June 18, 1850), Helmsley (June 19, 1850), Thirsk (June 20, 1850), Easingwold (June 21, 1850), York (June 22 and 24, 1850), Selby (June 25, 1850), Howden (June 26, 1850), Goole (June 27, 1850), Snaith (June 28, 1850), Thorne (June 29, 1850), Doncaster (July 1 and 2, 1850), Pontefract (July 3, 1850), Sherburn (July 4, 1850), Thorner (July 5, 1850), Harrogate (July 6 and 8, 1850), Knaresborough (July 9, 1850), Boroughbridge (July 10, 1850), Ripon (July 11, 1850), Masham (July 12, 1850), Bedale (July 13, 1850), Richmond (July 15, 1850), Barnard Castle (July 16, 1850), Middleton-in-Teesdale (July 17, 1850), Kirkby Stephen (July 18, 1850), Appleby (July 19, 1850), Penrith (July 20, 1850), Keswick (July 22, 1850), Cockermouth (July 23, 1850), Whitehaven (July 24, 1850), Workington (July 25, 1850), Maryport (July 26, 1850), Allonby (July 27, 1850), Wighton (July 29, 1850), Carlisle (July 30 and 31, 1850), Annan (August 1, 1850), Dumfries (August 2 and 3, 1850), Thornhill (August 5, 1850), Old Cumnock (August 7, 1850), Ayr (August 8 and 9, 1850), Kilmarnock (August 10, 1850), Irvine (August 12, 1850), Stewarton (August 13, 1850), Paisley (August 14 and 15, 1850), and Greenock (August 16 and 17, 1850).

Then a gap before we pick them up again: Stirling (August 26, 1850), Alloa (August 27, 1850), Dunfermline (August 28 and 29, 1850), Kirkcaldy (August 30, 1850), Leven (August 31, 1850), Anstruther (September 2, 1850), St. Andrews (September 3, 1850), Cupar (September 4, 1850), Auchtermuchty (September 5, 1850), Newburgh (September 6, 1850), Perth (September 7, 1850), Errol (September 9, 1850), Dundee (September 10, 1850), Arbroath (September 11, 1850), Montrose (September 12, 1850), Brechin (September 13, 1850), Forfar (September 14, 1850), Kirriemuir (September 16, 1850), Alyth (September 17, 1850), Blairgowrie (September 18, 1850), Coupar Angus (September 19, 1850), Stanley (September 20, 1850), Methven (September 21, 1850), Auchterarder (September 23, 1850), Dunning (September 24, 1850), Kinross (September 25, 1850), Tillicoultry (September 26, 1850), Bridge of Allan (September 27, 1850), Falkirk (September 28, 1850), Linlithgow (September 30, 1850), Bathgate (October 1, 1850), Airdrie (October 2, 1850), Hamilton (October 3, 1850), Strathaven (October 4, 1850), Lanark (October 5, 1850), Biggar (October 7, 1850), Peebles (October 8, 1850), Galashiels (October 9, 1850), Melrose (October 10, 1850), Selkirk (October 11, 1850), Hawick (October 12, 1850), Jedburgh (October 14, 1850), Kelso (October 15, 1850), Lawder (October 16, 1850), and then into Edinburgh on the 20th. They opened there the following day, Monday, their punishing tour at an end.

For the record: Ginnett's Circus, on their first Welsh tour, on this occasion through the shires of Angelsey, Carnarvon, and Denbigh, entered Wales from Wrexham, and passed through Llangollen on June 29, 1850 (without, however, playing there), on their way to Anglesey, to begin the tour at Llanerchymedd on July 6, 1850. Then it was on to Amlwch (July 8, 1850), Holyhead (July 9, 1850), Bryngwran (July 10, 1850), Llangefni (July 11, 1850), Menai Bridge (July 12, 1850), Bangor (July 13, 1850), Bethesda (July 15, 1850), Llanrwst (July 16, 1850), Conway (July 17, 1850), Abergele (July 18, 1850), Rhyl (July 19, 1850), St. Asaph (July 20, 1850), Denbigh (July 22, 1850), Ruthin (July 23, 1850), Mold (July 24, 1850), Holywell (July 25, 1850), Flint (July 26, 1850), Hawarden (July 27, 1850), and finally into Chester. On September 5, 1850, Ginnett's arrived in Leicester, but weren't allowed to erect their building. We pick them up again in Melton Mowbray (September 7, 1850), Stamford (September 11, 1850), Lincoln (September 16, 1850), and Aylesbury (September 19, 1850).

For the record: Another circus that had toured in 1850 was Macarte and Bell's Grand American Circus, not a big one, but a good one. Madame Marie Macarte (wife of Michael McCarthy, known as John, who with his brother Dan McCarthy, and also with Dick Bell, owned the circus) was performing as an equestrian with Pablo Fanque's at the beginning of the year, in Liverpool. Born Mary Elizabeth Ginnett in 1827, in Leigh-on-Sea, Essex (her mother's hometown), the daughter of John Ginnett, later proprietor of Ginnett's Circus, she was a pupil of the late Andrew Ducrow, and had appeared for years on both sides of the Atlantic, with and without her husband (whom she had married in Birmingham in 1841). From January 28 to February 2, 1850, she was with Franconi's, in Birmingham, which is where Messrs. Macarte teamed up with Bell. On March 23, they left Birmingham for Wolverhampton, Dudley, West Bromwich, etc., and by May 11 were in Burton-on-Trent, featuring such acts as Mr. Bell and his wife Madame Isabelle; Madame Macarte; the Zamezou family; equestrians Herr Smidt and his wife Rose; and Harry Crouesté and Jim Doughty, the clowns. Their gimmick however was that they were "the only real troupe of lady equestrians." All societies need a sexual outlet for the male of the species, otherwise the obvious will happen. This is even more true in a repressive environment, such as the Victorian Era, where such outlets abounded in spades, one of which was the circus. "In olden days a glimpse of stocking," etc. After Burton-on-Trent, Macarte & Bell's were in Derby (May 13 and 14, 1850), and Uttoxeter (May 15). On July 1, 1850, they entered Bristol, but the unexpected paucity of female performers disappointed the gentlemen in the audience. The week beginning Monday, July 8, they played Honiton, Taunton, Weston-super-Mare, and Bridgwater. From July 15 through the 20th they were in Exeter, then, from July 22 to August 4, in

Plymouth. Then Callington (August 6, 1850), Liskeard (August 7, 1850), Bodmin (August 8, 1850), St. Austell (August 9, 1850), Truro (August 10, 1850), Falmouth (August 12, 1850), Helston (August 13, 1850), Penzance (August 14 and 15, 1850), Camborne (August 16, 1850; here the seating collapsed; a human agency caused the disaster; he had been hiding under the seats; Mrs. Vivian of Baripper broke her leg in the fall), Redruth (August 17, 1850), Truro again (August 19, 1850), St. Columb (August 20, 1850), Wadebridge (August 21, 1850), Camelford (August 22, 1850), Launceston (August 23, 1850), Okehampton (August 24, 1850), Crediton (September 4, 1850), Exeter again (September 5, 6, and 7, 1850), Exmouth (September 9, 1850), and Sidmouth (September 10, 1850). From October 28 to December 16, 1850, they were in Southampton. J. W. Doughty (this is Jim Doughty, born in Bristol in 1819) would get a job at the Standard Theatre, in Shoreditch, with another great clown, Mr. Buck, for the Christmas festivities of 1850. At the same time, M. Silvani would be a sprite there. From Southampton, Macarte & Bell went to Winchester, where they played the week before going to take up winter quarters in the building erected especially for them in Portsmouth.

Cooke's, 1851–1852

The New Year came and went in Bristol, as they usually do. On January 4, 1851, Saturday, there was a morning performance by William Cooke's Circus, at which the pantomime was repeated by desire. The evening's performance of Monday, January 6, began with Mr. Barlow as the Springer of Rialto. Then there was Mr. Henry Cooke as a drunken soldier on horseback, followed by Mdlle. Rebecca as the Sylphide. The male artistes in a scene entitled *The Pyramidical Devices*. Mr. Alfred Cooke in five characters—Old Weller, the Prince of Whips; the Fat Boy; bustling Mr. Pickwick; Mr. Sam Weller; and the Aerial Puck. Miss Kate Cooke, in the "Act of the Menage." Master John Cooke as the Last of the Mohicans. Mons. Ethair's performance with the Magic Barrel. Miss Emily Cooke as Esmeralda. The entertainment concluded with *Punch and Judy*. This bill was repeated on the following two nights. Friday offered both a day and evening performance, both being patronized by Bristol's chief magistrate. The evening show of January 13 began with *The Dames of Athens*. Miss Clarissa Cooke as Diana, goddess of the chase. Others billed included the Young Godolphin (i.e., Alfred Eugene Godolphin Cooke, son of Alfred Cooke) as the Venetian Clown. Mr. Jackson dancing in the character of the Hippopotamus. The shows of January 14 and 15, 1851, began with *The Dames of Athens*. The evening of January 20 kicked off *Cinderella*. Then there was Mr. Russilli in his act with the dancing globe, Mr. Barlow as the Racing Jockey, La Petite Emily Cooke in her exercise La Cracovienne, Mr. H. Cooke and son as the Roman and his pupil, Mr. Ethair and sons in their classical entertainment, Mr. A. Cooke as the Masquerader on Horseback, Mr. W. Cooke on his Hanoverian jet-black steed, Master John Cooke in trick act riding. *Cinderella* was presented again on January 21 and 22, and, on the 23rd, the night St. *George and the Dragon* was presented, William Cooke took his benefit. On the 27th, the night Alfred Cooke took his benefit, *The Rigs of Mr. Briggs* was presented for the last time. On January 29, someone took a benefit. We don't know who it was, but £5 of the receipts went to the Bristol Royal Infirmary. Cooke's were in Bristol until Saturday, February 8, 1851, when they packed up, ready to go to Birmingham. In the meantime, in January 1851, The Brothers Francisco (who will reappear in our story) were playing at Astley's, in London, and Hengler's was in Sunderland.

Meanwhile, Ginnett's Circus played Reading between January 13 and

January 18, then opened in Windsor on January 20, 1851, with Knight the clown being featured. In late January 1851, they opened at Derby Road, Nottingham, with Harry Walker and John and Bill Samwell as stars. In January 1851, Henri and Bastien Franconi's Circus was still playing at the Amphitheatre in Liverpool, with various attractions, including Herr Maus and his two infant sons.

In January 1851, Pablo Fanque's was in Ireland. In Maynooth, a strolling beggar sold his 14-year-old son to Pablo Fanque's circus, for 2 shillings, for equestrian purposes. The man only took the money in order to assuage the "wound caused to his paternal feelings." On January 27, 1851, Pablo opened at the Music Hall, Lower Abbey Street, in Dublin. Featured were Mr. John B. Bridges, the English Hernandez, from Astley's Royal Amphitheatre, in London; Mdlle. Amelie, niece of the late Andrew Ducrow, and late of Franconi's Cirque Olympique, in Paris; Mons. Klare, on the globe roulant; the equestrians Miss Brown and Miss Cotterell; Tamborino Voy, the Ebony Wonder; Prof. Milner and his acrobatic pupils; Mr. William Banham on the tightrope; Mr. Stevens, the barrel equilibrist, and Mrs. Stevens, both from the Theatre Royal, Manchester; Tom Moseley as Mr. Pickwick; Harry Brown, the clown; Bill Fenner, the vaulter; and the equestrian Mr. Williams.

For William Cooke's Circus, Sunday, February 9, 1851, was occupied making the long trip, by train, north out of Bristol, and the following day they opened at Bingley Hall, Broad Street, Birmingham. We rely on the *Era* of February 9, 1851, for a cast list. It was still Messrs. Barnes and Connor, together. Madame Barnes is noted as part of the company, as are Mesdames Russilli (with her husband, Harry Russilli), Jackson (with her husband, the Shaksperian clown), Russell (with her husband, Bill Russell, the agent for the circus), Lehman (with her husband, Mr. Lehman, the strongman), and Beattie (with her husband, Mons. Beattie). Richard Hemming was along too. Madame Clementi was there, as was Bill Barlow, the lion horseman. Also featured were Masters Stephen and William Ethair and Mdlle. Rose Ethair, with young Steve playing a gorilla. Their parents were part of the company too. The father, Steve Etheridge, had worked as a groom in London for years before venturing into the circus business, taking his children with him and changing the name to Ethair. And then there were the Cookes themselves, of course — Mr. and Mrs. Cooke, Henry, Emily, Alice, Rosina, Kate, Alfred, Master A. E. Cooke, Master John Cooke, Mdlle. Rebecca, Miss Clarissa Cooke, and Boswell the clown and his wife, Mrs. Boswell. The interior of the theatre had been fitted out like an ancient Roman amphitheatre and could seat 3,000.

On March 1, 1851, Franconi's Cirque wrapped up in Liverpool and headed for Huddersfield, where they embarked on a six-week gig beginning on March 4, Shrove Tuesday, at the Riding School on Ramsden Street. The clowns

Tomkinson and Stonette were with them then. On March 25, 1851, Pablo Fanque's Circus wrapped up in Dublin and moved on to Belfast, where they opened on March 27.

On March 31, 1851 (Monday), William Cooke's commenced yet another week attracting full audiences and also introduced *The Chinese Junk, or the Maid of Pekin*. On April 21 was produced *Punch and Judy*. April 24 was William Cooke's benefit night, and on Monday, May 3, 1851, they closed at Birmingham, after a successful season.

On March 21, 1851, back in London, the Acrobat's brother, Tom, died, spent, thus, failing, by nine days, to make the 1851 census. Mr. William Cooke's youngest brother, Tertius John, was a Birmingham coal dealer and tobacconist, and it was in his house that Arthur Barnes and his wife Alexiné were lodged while the Acrobat was performing. They did make the census.

On April 9, 1851, Ginnett's played Newark, and on April 14, Mansfield, with Jem Guest as the clown. Virtually no one came to the day performances, but, in both towns, the evening was packed. On April 21, 1851, they were in Retford. In Huddersfield, Franconi's gig had extended until April 17, and, on the morning of the 18th, they shifted, by special train, to Manchester, where they opened at the Free Trade Hall on Saturday, April 19, 1851. On May 1, 1851, Mr. Batty opened his enormous Grand National Hippodrome in Kensington, the same day that great American vaulter Hiram Franklin made his European debut at Vauxhall Gardens in London, in company with Hernandez.

The *Era* of May 4, 1851, which tells us that William Cooke's Colossal Equestrian Establishment of 60 horses and ponies was to launch their summer tour the following day, ran a front page ad: "Mr. W. Cooke respectfully announces that this highly talented company will exhibit ... their Olympic wonders in a spacious royal tent, on an improved construction, illuminated with gas." The same publication of May 11, 1851, ran this ad: "All the world is not in London. William Cooke's Grand National Equestrian Exhibition and Pageant of sixty horses and ponies—elegant carriages—sixteen horses in hand—Russian sledge drawn by reindeer—First ladies and gentlemen of Equestrian Art, etc, etc.." Then it goes on to list the venues for the upcoming week, and mentions that the troupe will enter in grand procession at 12 o'clock. Performances at 2:00 and 7:00 each day. Concluding with the spectacle of the *Battle of Waterloo*. The price of admission for first class was 2/-; second class 1/-; promenade 6d. Children under 10 and schools at half price to seats only. The agent in advance of the establishment was Mr. William Russell.

Their 1851 summer tour, like all summer tours, was exhausting and demanding. We rely mostly on the *Era* for details, not only of William Cooke's tour, but also those of the other circuses touring Britain that year. On Sunday,

May 4, 1851, William Cooke's were on their way to Stourbridge for the May 5 gig, then to Kidderminster (May 6, 1851), 17 miles southwest of Birmingham and 15 miles north of Worcester. Then it was into Bewdley for the May 7 performance, and Bromyard (May 8, 1851), Hereford (May 9, 1851), and Welshay (May 10, 1851). On Sunday, May 11, they made their way to Kington. The *Era* of May 11, 1851, has this to say:

> William Cooke's colossal equestrian exhibition creates so great a furore [sic] that it may justly be termed the National Exhibition of equestrian art; all that can be produced in the noble art of horsemanship is exemplified. The superior training of the steeds, the graceful and daring feats of the artists, among which stand most prominent the ladies of the chase, whose matchless cream steeds, proud of their lovely burdens, fly over the barrier gates like aerial visions to the view. Europe's premier horseman, Mr. Alfred Cooke; the British Hernandez, Master John Cooke; the unequalled juvenile equestrian abilities of Miss Kate Cooke; the Tom Thumb horseman Godolphin; the equestrienne Miss Woolford; the champion vaulters of the world, Messrs. Barnes and Conner [sic]; the renowned clowns, Jackson and Boswell; the beauteous steed Raven, are in themselves a host daily, drawing thousands of admirers at the various towns Mr. Cooke is now visiting.

They played Kington on May 12, 1851, the same night Young Hengler played Hamlet and took his benefit at Blackburn. For William Cooke's it was on to Leominster (May 13, 1851), Ludlow (May 14, 1851), Church Stretton (May 15, 1851), and then into Shrewsbury, where they played the 16th and 17th of May 1851. Then it was Sunday again, and they traveled to Wellington, in Shropshire, for the evening of Monday, the 19th. Then it was on to Broseley Way (May 20, 1851), Shifnal (May 21, 1851), Albrighton (May 22, 1851), Brewood (May 23, 1851), and Great Bridge (May 24, 1851). This past week, down in Kent, there was some prodigious gymnastic entertainment on offer at the Royal Terrace Gardens, at Gravesend, with Harry Walker, and John and Bill Samwell, as well as the clown, Mr. Twist. On the Sunday, William Cooke's traveled to Dudley, for the gig of the 26th, and from there it was on to Bromsgrove (May 27, 1851), and then into Worcester for the gig of May 28, 1851.

The *Era* of June 1, 1851, tells us that William Cooke's Colossal Equestrian Establishment visited Worcester on Wednesday last, attracting by their grand entree many thousands of spectators, who afterwards flocked to the entertainments until hundreds were unable to gain admission. The whole of the performances were of a very superior character; "but the great climax of this talented establishment was the wonderful achievement of ninety-one somersaults, thrown by the champion vaulter, Mr. Barnes, which unprecedented feat completely electrified the audience; and had not the attraction of the admired ladies of the chase made their timely appearance, we doubt whether the performance could have been resumed for the deafening plaudits and cheers which assailed Mr. Barnes's unrivalled feat."

From Worcester it was on to Tewkesbury (May 29, 1851), and on May 30 they pulled into Cheltenham to play that night and also May 31. June 1, 1851, was a Sunday, and they left Cheltenham, bound for Gloucester, where they played the evenings of June 2 and 3, 1851. On June 4, 1851, they played Coleford, and then it was on to Lydney (June 5, 1851), over the Severn into Wales, where they played Chepstow on June 6, 1851, and Newport on the 7th. On the Sunday they traveled to Pontypool for the gig of the 9th, and then it was on to Tredegar (June 10, 1851), and two nights in Merthyr Tydfil (June 11 and 12, 1851). On June 13, 1851, they were in Newbridge, and on June 14, 1851, in Cardiff. That day, June 14, Franconi's left Manchester, and on June 16 opened at the Cremorne Gardens, in London. Tim Elliott was with them by then, and the other Brothers Elliott soon would be.

On Sunday, June 15, 1851, William Cooke's circus traveled to Cowbridge for the June 16 gig, eight days before Cowbridge Fair, and then it was on to Bridgend (June 17, 1851; 11 days after Bridgend had held their fair), Aberavon (June 18, 1851; where David Evans was just taking over as the new vicar), Neath (June 19, 1851; on the very day of Neath Fair), and on into Swansea for a two-night gig, June 20 and 21, 1851, 10 days after Swansea Fair. They left Swansea on Sunday, June 22, bound for their Monday gig at Llanelli, then it was on to Carmarthen (June 24, 1851), Narberth (June 25, 1851), Haverfordwest (June 26, 1851), Pembroke (June 27, 1851), and Tenby (June 28, 1851). They left Tenby on the Sunday, heading for Llandeilo and the June 30 gig, then it was on to Llandovery (July 1, 1851), Brecon (July 2, 1851), Crickhowell (July 3, 1851), Abergavenny (July 4, 1851), and Monmouth (July 5, 1851). The Sunday took them to Ross for the gig of July 7, 1851, and then it was on to Ledbury (July 8, 1851) and Newent (July 9, 1851).

Pablo Fanque's Circus wrapped up in Belfast on July 1, 1851. From there it was on to Glasgow. Around this time, Tom Swann, the clown, was building a circus on Edward Street, Brighton, to be open in August in time for the races.

William Cooke's establishment closed on the 10th, 11th and 12th of July 1851, Mr. Cooke giving his players a free trip to the Great Exhibition at the Crystal Palace in London. Their admission to the exhibition was on the half crown day. We also learn that they enjoyed a breakfast at Soyer's Symposium, and visited many of the principal sights in town. We learn, from the *Bristol Mercury* of July 19, 1851, that wives went too. All expenses came out of Mr. Cooke's pocket. Mr. Cooke's people later presented him with a massive silver tankard, out of gratitude. On the tankard were the words, "Presented to Wm.

Cooke, Esq., by the equestrian members of this establishment as a small return to express their gratitude for his kindness and generosity for treating the ladies and gentlemen of his company to the World's Fair, July 10, 1851, liberality unprecedented in the profession."

On Monday, July 14, 1851, William Cooke's opened at Cirencester, and on the 15th at Wootton-under-Edge. On the 16th they were in Minchinhampton, and on the 17th at Malmesbury. On July 18, 1851, they were in Chippenham, and on July 19, 1851, they pulled into Bath, where they played that night. On Sunday they were at liberty in Bath, and played there again the following day, Monday the 21st. The *Bristol Mercury* of July 19, 1851, advises its readers that the Grand National Colossal Exhibition of William Cooke's Equestrian establishment will play at the Circus, Bristol, for two days only, Tuesday and Wednesday, July 22 and 23, 1851, by the kind permission of His Worship the Mayor. The Tuesday evening performance was under the patronage of Sir John Kerle Haberfield and his lady.

On July 24, 1851, William Cooke's circus played Clevedon, then it was down to Weston-super-Mare (July 25, 1851), down to Burnham-on-Sea for July 26, and, on the Sunday they moved to Bridgwater for the gig of Monday, July 28, 1851. On July 29, 1851, they played Langport, on July 30, Yeovil, and on July 31, Beaminster. August 1, 1851, brought them to Dorchester. One mile northeast of Dorchester, on the road to Puddletown, is the village of Higher Brockhampton, at that time the home of a twelve-year-old Thomas Hardy, who must have seen Arthur Barnes somersaulting that night. Then it was on to Weymouth (August 2, 1851). On Sunday, Cooke's traveled to Bridport for the gig of August 4, 1851, and from there to Lyme Regis (August 5, 1851). On August 6, 1851, they played Colyton, and, on the 7th, Honiton. Sidmouth was Cooke's next stop, for the gig of August 8, and on August 9, 1851, they were in Exmouth. On Sunday it was on to Exeter. *Trewman's Exeter Flying Post* (henceforth known as the *Flying Post*) of August 7, 1851, advises us that William Cooke's Colossal Equestrian Establishment would play on Queen Street, Exeter for two days only, Monday and Tuesday, August 11 and 12, 1851.

While all this was going on in England, Hiram Franklin was in Paris. There is an astonishing (and, seemingly accurate) report from the Paris correspondent of the Boston *Daily Atlas*, dated July 16, 1851, which appeared in the August 14 edition of that Beantown paper, "An American has the honors of aristocratic Paris at the moment." The reporter reminds us of the great vogue of the cirque at the Champs Elysees that summer, and tells us that "of all the personnel of the Cirque, Hiram Franklin is the favorite. On a springboard of extreme elasticity, which he calls Bataude, he executes leaps and somersets which surprise even the Arabs of the Circus. I saw him the other evening jump up about 25 feet, and turn somersets at that height, 46 times successively."

For Cooke's, after Exeter it was over to Dawlish (August 13, 1851), Teignmouth (pronounced Tinmuth) for the August 14 gig, and then into Torquay. The *Flying Post* of August 21, 1851, reported that Cooke's equestrian troupe made their grand entree into Torquay on Friday (i.e., August 15), and by the two days' performances (i.e., they played Torquay on the 15th and 16th) realized £150.

On Sunday it was off to Newton Bushel, nine miles away on the River Lemon, for the August 18 Monday gig. With Newton Abbot on the other side of the river, these twin towns were finally joined in 1901, as Newton Abbot. But, in Arthur Barnes's time, Newton Bushel was still a valid venue. From Newton, they went to Ashburton, the old tin town on the Yeo, for the performance of August 19, 1851. From Ashburton it was on to Totnes (August 20, 1851), the famous market town on the Dart, and then in to Dartmouth (August 21, 1851), followed by Kingsbridge for the gig of August 22, 1851. In those days Kingsbridge was just one long street descending to the water of the Salcombe estuary. Having a very pleasant climate, it is said that white ale was first brewed here, in the part of the town called Dodridge. From Kingsbridge, Cooke's wagon train took the Modbury road northwest out of town, wending their way up the big hill leading to Churchstow, with its conspicuous tower, on through the village of Aveton Gifford (pronounced, of course, Awton Jifford), near the Avon, and then up hill and down dale to the old world little town of Modbury, where they played on August 23, 1851, the same day Ginnett's Circus was playing Burnley, up in Lancashire. On Sunday, the 24th, they climbed out of Modbury, heading west toward Plymouth. After two miles they crossed the Erme, and three miles later passed through the village of Yealmpton (pronounced, of course, Yamton). From the road, as they looked left, they could clearly see the beautiful sylvan dingle which carried the Yealm to its estuary. From Yealmpton, still heading west, they had to exercise great caution with the wagons as they descended the alarmingly steep Kitley Hill into Brixton, and from there the rather dull route five miles straight into the southeast part of Plymouth, which they reached later that day.

The *Era* of August 31, 1851, tells us that Mr. W. Cooke, with his talented company of equestrians, visited Plymouth for two days, Monday and Tuesday, the 25th and 26th of August, when the circus was filled to overflowing mornings and evenings. The entertainments were select, and met with the warmest approval from all parts of the house. The morning's performance was honored with the presence of the Countess of Morley, attended by the rank and fashion of Plymouth. The extraordinary performance of Mr. Cooke's black mare, Raven, was astonishing. Mr. Alfred Cooke, the premier horseman to this establishment, carried the audience with him in his surprising act of managing four horses. Miss Emily Cooke was warmly received, and rode with great taste. Miss Kate Cooke, the sylph of the circle, was as enchanting as ever. "Mr. W.C. has taken a piece of ground in Union Street, Plymouth, for his winter quarters, and intends erecting an elegant and spacious Amphitheatre, for the performance of his Colossal Equestrian establishment."

The *Flying Post* of August 21, 1851, gives us an insight into permissions and licenses to perform in a town. Mr. Elliott, belonging to Cooke's Equestrian Troupe, asked for permission for the proprietor of that establishment to be allowed to perform in Plymouth during the winter, and if he might obtain the permission of the Bench and the site of ground in Queen Street, a building would be erected for the purpose. The Bench asked how long it would be required for. Mr. Elliott said about two months. The troupe would be here in November, and probably remain until February. The Mayor said the Bench would grant permission for two months. If Mr. Cooke wished to remain longer he must renew the application; leaving it to them to extend the time or not. Mr. Elliott casually mentioned that he understood another company was coming here, and was about to ask that that company be not allowed to compete against Mr. Cooke, when he was stopped short by one of the Bench. Mr. Woolmer asked if it were the Hippodrome that was coming here. Mr. Elliott said he understood a company was coming here out of their direct road to oppose Mr. Cooke. The mayor remarked that competition was recognized in these days, to which Mr. Osborne added it was free-trade times. Mr. Elliott was about to say that he was the first who had applied, and hoped permission would not be granted to a second, when he was curtly told he had had his answer and could retire.

For William Cooke's circus, from Plymouth, it was over to Tavistock (August 27, 1851), then to Callington (August 28, 1851), Liskeard (August 29, 1851), Lostwithiel (August 30, 1851), and then it was Sunday again, which they spent traveling to their Monday gig at St. Austell (September 1, 1851). From there it was on to Truro. The *Royal Cornwall Gazette* of August 29, 1851, has this to say: "Equestrian performances. It appears that on Tuesday next [i.e., September 2] the public of Truro and its neighbourhood will have the opportunity offered them of witnessing the excellent equestrian performances of Mr. William Cooke's Company; who will enter the town in grand procession, at noon, at the eastern entrance. The varied performances of the company can hardly fail to attract crowded assemblages of spectators." They did, indeed, arrive in the town precisely at noon, formed a grand equestrian procession, and held two performances in Mr. Reid's field, top of Lemon Street, one at 2:00 and the other at 7:00.

Jim Fitzsimmons was an Irish police constable living in Truro with his wife and rather large and ever growing family. They, like everyone else in Truro, must have gone along to see Arthur Barnes doing his somersaults. Jim Junior was 12, but already apprenticed to a bootmaker. The younger kids, John, Mary, Jane, Billy, and the baby Arthur, all went along. The policeman and his wife would later move to Helston and continue to produce children until 1863, when their last son was born. Soon after that they emigrated to New Zealand, where the youngest son, Bob, went into the prize ring, and ultimately became heavyweight champion of the world.

After Truro, William Cooke's Circus moved on to the famous harbor town of Falmouth, at the mouth of the River Fal, where they played two nights (September 3 and 4, 1851), and then on to Helston (September 5, 1851), the same day Ginnett's Circus was playing Farnsfield, in Nottinghamshire. On September 6 and 8 Cooke's played the fine town of Penzance, being at liberty there on the Sunday that fell between their two dates. The *Royal Cornwall Gazette* of September 12, 1851, tells us that Cooke's Equestrian Circus paid St. Just a visit on Tuesday, September 9, 1851, and performed to immense assemblages, giving general satisfaction.

From St. Just, William Cooke's moved over to St. Ives (September 10, 1851), Hayle (September 11, 1851), and then on to the tin-mining town of Camborne for September 12, and Redruth on September 13, 1851. Redruth is not, of course, pronounced as if the name implied a communist girl. However, the name does mean "red ford," but the word *red* comes not from the original *rhyd* (which means "ford"), but from the old Cornish *ruth*, which means "red." One hopes this is as clear to the reader as it is to the writer.

From Redruth, William Cooke, on the Sunday, made his way back to Truro. The *Royal Cornwall Gazette* of September 12, 1851, says:

> All the world is not in London. Re-appearance of William Cooke's Colossal Stud & Co. W. Cooke most respectfully announces to his kind patrons that in compliance with numerous applications, and hundreds being unable to gain admission for the 2nd inst., he will have the honour of again visiting Truro for one day more, on Monday, September 15th, by the kind permission of the Worshipful the Mayor, N.F. Bassett, in entering the town from the top of Lemon Street, a full procession, at 12 o'clock precisely, Mr. W. Cooke driving sixteen horses in hand, followed by the splendid cortege, and talented company, with the dames of Stag Hunting Chase, mounted on beautiful palfreys, etc., etc., etc.

The same paper of September 19, tells us that Mr. William Cooke's company of equestrian and other performers, on Monday last, September 15, made another processional entry into Truro and gave two performances, several portions of which were clever and interesting and afforded amusement to large assemblages of spectators. It was about this time that the conception of the Acrobat's first child, Alexine Caroline, would take place, so it certainly looks as if the Danish Alexine was traveling constantly with her husband.

Meanwhile, Franconi's finished at Cremorne on September 13, 1851, and, two days later, began a guest stint for a while with Mr. Batty at his Kensington Hippodrome. Portions of Franconi's troupe would perform in various towns over the next month or so, including Nottingham, where their huge circus was slowly being built.

From Truro, William Cooke's Circus traveled on to St. Columb (September 16, 1851), where a four-year-old lad named Dickie Bullock lived at the shop his father ran. Dickie later went to the States, to Deadwood, actually, where he became known as Deadwood Dick. One likes to think he would have been inspired by an early visit in life to Cooke's Circus. After St. Columb, Cookes then went to Wadebridge (September 17, 1851), and then into Bodmin for the performance of September 18, 1851. On September 19, they played Camelford, which some deluded persons think is King Arthur's Camelot. Then it was on to Launceston (September 20, 1851), pronounced, of course, "Lanson," unlike its Tasmanian counterpart, which is pronounced correctly. The Sunday they traveled to Stratton for the gig on Monday, September 22, and, on September 23, now in Devon, they performed at Holsworthy, on the River Deer. On September 24, 1851, they were in Bideford.

That day, September 24, 1851, in the little village of West Woodlands, three miles out of Frome, Somerset, a fifteen-year-old girl, Sarah Watts, was brutalized in the most scandalous fashion in the dairy barn of her parents' farm. Will Maggs, Bill Sparrow, and Bob Hurd (a prizefighter known as Frome Bob) then killed her, which, given the circumstances, was a fortunate thing. The girl's father and mother found her on their return from Frome Market. There was blood everywhere.

Franconi's opened at Brighton on September 29. On October 9, 1851, Young Hernandez commenced a short stay with them there, to compete with the ostriches of that troupe. The *Era* of October 5, 1851, tells us that Mr. W. Cooke and his Leviathan Equestrian Establishment visited Barnstaple on Thursday and Friday, the 25th and 26th of September. The circus was well attended, and the entertainment received the approval of delighted audiences. Mrs. Cooke, the manageress, kindly presented Miss Emily Cooke, the talented juvenile equestrian, with a massive gold bracelet, enamelled, as a reward for her spirited and graceful riding. Such generous acts were frequently shown by Mrs. Cooke, gratifying the receiver, and giving a stimulus to the different members of the profession, thereby endearing the hearts of all to the donor. After Barnstaple it was on to Ilfracombe for the gig of September 27, 1851. On the Sunday they traveled to South Molton.

That Sunday, September 28, 1851, Smith of the Yard (so to speak) came down from London to investigate the Frome murder. His inquiries led him to suspect Messrs. Maggs, Sparrow, and Hurd. On Monday, September 29, 1851, William Cooke's circus was playing South Molton, on the 30th they were in Bampton, and on October 1, 1851, it was Wiveliscombe. On October 1, Sgt. Smith took his first statement from Frome Bob. On October 2, 1851, William Cooke's were in Minehead, and, on October 3, 1851, at Williton. That day, October 3, Sgt. Smith took a statement from Will Maggs in Frome. Cooke's then shifted over to Taunton, for the gig of Saturday, October 4, 1851. They rested in Taunton on Sunday, and played there again on Monday the 6th. That day, the 6th, Sgt. Smith swooped down on his three suspects — taking Maggs in Frome, Sparrow in Feltham, and Frome Bob in Westbury. For Cooke's, it was on to Somerton (October 7), Wincanton (October 8), then north up the road through Bruton and Evercreech to Shepton Mallet.

The *Bristol Mercury* of October 18, 1851, tells us that Mr. Cooke's equestrian company visited Shepton Mallet on Thursday, October 9, 1851. Although the rain descended in torrents during the day, a number of people came from the surrounding villages. From the appearance of many of the countrymen, who were armed with large sticks, it was evident a row of some sort was premeditated. About 12 o'clock a party numbering nearly 20 assembled in the marketplace and commenced knocking the shutters and making all kinds of hideous noises. The constables were soon on the alert and succeeded in capturing four of the party, who were taken before the magistrates on the following day and fined £2 each or two months' imprisonment, and to "find bail to keep the peace for three months." It was Shepton Mallet jail otherwise, and that well-known establishment was bulging, with 155 male prisoners and nine females.

A 16-year-old orphaned Jewish draper's apprentice named John Lewis would have certainly gone to see the circus that night in Shepton Mallet. Young Lewis would eventually go to London, where in 1864 he opened his own company, which would become the famous John Lewis department store.

Out of Shepton Mallet, Cooke's took the road east, through Doulting and Cranmore, over to Frome (pronounced Frume), at the eastern end of the Mendips. Here they played the evening of October 10, 1851. In the audience at Frome that night had to have been a boy named Benjamin Baker, aged 11, with his sister Fanny and their widowed mother Sarah. Young Baker would become an engineer, designer of the Forth Bridge, and the man who designed the cylinder which carried Cleopatra's Needle from Alexandria to London in 1877–78, that bizarre voyage much bedeviled by the "Flaming Vulture," the vengeful spirit of the Pharaohs. Frome was, of course, reeling from what the papers called "the horrible Frome murder" (as opposed to, say, the delightful Frome murder).

For William Cooke's, from Frome, it was on, via a series of complicated byways, to Bradford-on-Avon, near Bath, but in Wiltshire. They played here on October 11, 1851. The 12th was a Sunday, and they traveled the couple of miles to the striking little town of Trowbridge, on the River Biss, where they played on the 13th, the same day the murderers were brought up before the bench in Frome.

After Trowbridge, Cooke's cut across to Devizes (October 14, 1851). Then it was back west to Melksham (October 15, 1851). Then a nine-mile cut across country to Calne, in the River Marden (October 16, 1851), up to Wootton Bassett (October 17, 1851), and then the couple of miles into Swindon (October 18, 1851), the great railway town. On the Sunday they traveled a straight shot south to the historic town of Marlborough, with its recently opened school. Here they played their gig of the 20th, and then it was on to Hungerford, on the River Dun, in the Kennet Valley, where they played on October 21, 1851. From Hungerford, the most westerly town in Berkshire, they moved on to Newbury for October 22, 1851. "Lord" George Sanger, the great circus owner, and future employer of Arthur Barnes, had been born and raised in Newbury. From there, they pressed on to Whitchurch, Hants, for the gig of October 23, 1851, then covered the seven miles to Andover (October 24, 1851). On the 25th they pulled into the famous cathedral town of Salisbury, playing the evening there. The following day, Sunday, they were at liberty in Salisbury, and, on Monday, October 27, 1851, again played that city. Then it was off to Fordingbridge, on the edge of the New Forest (October 28, 1851), and then into Southampton. The *Era* of November 2, 1851, says: "Mr. W. Cooke, with his gigantic stud of sixty ponies and horses, visited Southampton on Wednesday last, October 29th." The entertainments were under the patronage of the Right Worshipful the Mayor. The house was filled to excess. The respected equestrian ladies of this establishment presented the liberal manageress with a massive gold bracelet, enamelled and inlaid with rubies. The inscription engraved thereon was as follows, "Presented to Mrs. Wm Cooke as a token of esteem, by the Ladies of the Chase of 1851."

From Southampton it was on to the historic market town of Ringwood (October 30, 1851), and Christchurch (October 31, 1851). On November 1, 1851, William Cooke's circus opened at Poole, and, while they were playing there, Franconi's Cirque closed in Brighton, and headed for Nottingham. Their huge circus building, on the Derby Road, had been a long time in the building, what with bad weather, accidents, shoddy construction work, and other delays, but they finally opened there on November 10, 1851. Sunday, November 2, 1851 saw Cooke's traveling to Wimborne, where they played on Monday, November 3. From Wimborne, Cooke's moved on to Blandford Forum (November 4, 1851), Shaftesbury (November 5, 1851), Sherborne

(November 6, 1851), Crewkerne (November 7, 1851), and Chard (November 8, 1851). On Sunday they shifted to Wellington, and while they were on the road, Franconi's Cirque was about to open in Nottingham. In November, Pablo Fanque's Circus left Glasgow, and opened in Edinburgh, where they closed the year.

Cooke's played Wellington on November 10, 1851. The *Flying Post* tells us that Cooke's equestrian troupe arrived in Tiverton on Tuesday, October 11, and that the performances were well attended. On the 12th they played Cullompton, Devon; on the 13th Crediton; on the 14th Okehampton, at the northern edge of Dartmoor; and then, on the 15th of November, arrived in Plymouth, their tour at an end, to take up residence at their new winter quarters on Union Road, in the huge amphitheatre recently erected for the purpose. That was a Saturday, but they didn't perform that night, or the next day, of course, being a Sunday. On Monday, November 17, 1851, the Grand New Circus Royal opened, and, from this time on, covering their stint at Plymouth, we rely principally on the *Era*.

The programme was extensive, the clowns happy, the riding first-rate, and the whole performances, which were good, commenced each evening at seven. Mr. Cooke had, in addition to a numerous stud of up to 70 horses and ponies, three ostriches and a zebra, purchased from the celebrated collection of the late Earl of Derby. Other animals included monkeys, elephants, and, of course, the reindeer. They put on Roman Games, and even had a live stag brought in for the stag hunt — all on the stage. Cooke's was justly called "colossal." The building in which the troupe performed was itself very remarkable "and deserves a particular notice, as being unlike any structure before erected in Plymouth." Its dimensions were very large, the total length being 132 feet, and the width 88 feet — affording accommodation for upward of 3,000 persons. The arena had a diameter of 42 feet (equal in size to Astley's), which gave ample scope for the evolutions of the most high-mettled coursers. There was, besides, within the building, excellent stabling provided for the entire stand of horses and ponies, with compartments for the zebras and ostriches, and convenient lodgment for the carriages of the establishment.

Mr. William Cooke's Leviathan Equestrian Establishment was nightly crowded to the ceiling. The company, comprising the most talented of the day, was well selected. Mr. Wm. Cooke, with his highly trained mare, Black Raven, astonished the audience nightly, and elicited the approval of all parts of the house. "Mr. Alfred Cooke, as premier horseman, is one of the most daring riders we have ever witnessed." Miss Emily Cooke and Master A. Cooke were very clever, while the clowns were also very grotesque, and rich with original witticisms.

For the first six days in December 1851, Cooke's were doing *St. George and the Dragon*, under the able superintendence of Mr. Alfred Cooke. William Cooke played St. George. Edmund Jackson played Tom of Coventry. On December 3, there was a grand morning performance, under the patronage of Commodore Superintendent M. Seymour, of Her Majesty's Dockyard, Devonport, on which occasion the dress circle was filled to overflowing. The band of this establishment presented their manager, Mr. William Cooke, with a handsome riding whip, mounted with a beautiful representation of St. George and the Dragon, richly embossed in silver, as a token of respect. On the night of December 18, 1851, the performances were under the patronage of Col. Egerton and the officers of the 77th Regt., on which occasion, by the kindness of their colonel, their band was present. The house was filled to excess, hundreds not gaining admittance. Mr. Cooke presented the sum of 20 pounds to the South Devon and East Cornwall Hospital, to be devoted for charitable purposes. From December 22 to December 27 they were presenting *Mazeppa*, which was deservedly well received. Hundreds of people were unable to get in to see the performances for Boxing Night, there being simply not enough seats.

Meanwhile, on the night of December 8, 1851, Young Hernandez joined Franconi's at Nottingham, and on December 23 had a serious accident. He was so excited by the presence and applause of the Earl of Cardigan and the officers of the 11th Hussars that he exerted himself with such reckless energy that he received a fall on the edge of the ring. He sprang back into the circle and groaned most piteously. Several medical gentlemen present rushed into the circle, and he was borne into the dressing room. Everyone wanted him to desist, but Hernandez, ever the trouper, got back on his horse, and was thrown again, with his head and sides against the boards. He tried it again, with the same result. It was not his night. He was then taken away. Franconi's were going to winter-over at Nottingham, but they closed there on December 23, on December 26, 1851, their Cirque National de France opening at Leeds. It was a blow to the economy of old Nottingham.

For the record: James Cooke's Circus finished a stint in Dundee, then a long one in Aberdeen (where Mr. Cooke personated George, in St. *George and the Dragon*), and then embarked on their 1851 summer tour, beginning in the north of Scotland: Ellon (May 19, 1851), Peterhead (May 20 and 21, 1851), Fraserburgh (May 22, 1851), Strichen (May 23, 1851), Banff (May 24, 26, and 27, 1851), Portsoy (May 28, 1851), Cullen (May 29, 1851), Buckie (May 30, 1851), Fochabers (May 31, 1851), Elgin (June 2 and 3, 1851), Forres (June 4, 1851), Nairn (June 5, 1851), Inverness (June 6, 7, 9, and 10, 1851), Dingwall (June 11, 1851), Tain (June 12, 1851), Invergordon (June 13, 1851), and Beauly (June 14, 1851).

Then a gap in our knowledge. However, we can reasonably put forward a good proposal for the towns he visited during the missing week before he was back in Aberdeenshire on the 23rd. From Beauly, he had to retrace his steps to the town of Inverness, but, from there, instead of traveling back along the coast via Nairn, the way he had come, he would surely have taken the southerly roads of Nairnshire and Morayshire, thus taking him through such obvious venues as (in order), Aviemore, Grantown, Bridge of Avon, perhaps Aberlour and Craigellachie, Dufftown, and then from there into Huntly, which is where we pick them up again, on June 23 and 24, 1851.

Then it was on to Old Meldrum (June 25, 1851), Inveraray (June 26 and 27, 1851), Upper Banchory (June 28, 1851), Stonehaven (June 30, 1851), Laurencekirk (July 1, 1851), Montrose (July 2, 1851), Brechin (July 3, 1851), Arbroath (July 4, 1851), Forfar (July 5, 1851), Kirriemuir (July 7, 1851), Alyth (July 8, 1851), Blairgowrie (July 9, 1851), Coupar Angus (July 10, 1851), Broughty Ferry (July 11, 1851), Dundee (July 12, 1851), Errol (July 14, 1851), Perth (July 15 and 16, 1851), Auchtermuchty (July 17, 1851), Cupar (July 18, 1851), and St. Andrews (July 19, 1851).

There is then a gap for a week, before Alloa (July 28, 1851), Stirling (July 29, 1851), Falkirk (July 30, 1851), Linlithgow (July 31, 1851), Bathgate (August 1, 1851), Currie (August 2, 1851), Portobello (August 4, 1851), Dalkeith (August 5, 1851), Musselburgh (August 6, 1851), Haddington (August 7, 1851), Linton (August 8, 1851), Dunbar (August 9, 1851), Ayton (August 11, 1851), Duns (August 12, 1851), Coldstream (August 13, 1851), Berwick (August 14, 1851), Wooler (August 15, 1851), Alnwick (August 16, 1851), Warkworth (August 18, 1851), Morpeth (August 19, 1851), Blyth (August 20, 1851), North Shields (August 21, 1851), Newcastle (August 22, 1851), South Shields (August 23, 1851), Sunderland (August 25 and 26, 1851), Durham (August 27, 1851), Castle Eden (August 28, 1851), Hartlepool (August 29, 1851), Stockton-on-Tees (August 30, 1851), Middlesbrough (September 1, 1851), Stokesley (September 2, 1851), Yarm (September 3, 1851), Darlington (September 4, 1851), Richmond (September 5, 1851), Barnard Castle (September 6, 1851), Middleton (September 8, 1851), Alston (September 9, 1851), Penrith (September 10, 1851), Keswick (September 11, 1851), Cockermouth (September 12, 1851), Whitehaven (September 13, 1851), Workington (September 15, 1851), Maryport (September 16, 1851), Aspatria (September 17, 1851), Wighton (September 18, 1851), Carlisle (September 19 and 20, 1851), Annan (September 22, 1851), Dumfries (September 23 and 24, 1851), Dalbeattie (September 25, 1851), Castle Douglas (September 26, 1851), Kirkcudbright (September 27, 1851), Gatehouse (September 29, 1851), Newton Stewart (September 30, 1851), Wigton (October 1, 1851), Whithorn (October 2, 1851), Port William (October 3, 1851), Stranraer (October 4, 1851), Girvan (October 6, 1851), Maybole (October 7, 1851), Ayr (October 8 and 9, 1851), Kilmarnock (October 10, 1851), and Mauchline

(October 11, 1851). Then there is a gap, followed by Brampton (October 20, 1851), Haltwhistle (October 21, 1851), Haydon Bridge (October 22, 1851), Hexham (October 23, 1851), and Sunderland (October 27, 1851).

For the record: Hengler's had begun a tour in the north of England, playing Thirsk (June 2, 1851), Northallerton (June 3, 1851), Richmond (June 4, 1851), Darlington (June 5, 1851), Bishop Auckland (June 6, 1851), Durham (June 7, 1851), Newcastle (June 9 and 10, 1851; Whitmonday & Tuesday), Hexham (June 11, 1851), Haydon Bridge (June 12, 1851), Haltwhistle (June 13, 1851), and Brampton (June 14, 1851). Then there is a gap before we pick them up again: Kendal (June 23, 1851), Burton (June 24, 1851), Kirkby Lonsdale (June 25, 1851), Settle (June 26, 1851), Skipton (June 27, 1851), and Keighley (June 28, 1851). Then another gap before Bingley (July 7, 1851), Shipley (July 8, 1851), Pudsey (July 9, 1851), Horsforth (July 10, 1851), Hunslet (July 11, 1851), Birstal (July 12, 1851), Holmfirth (July 14, 1851), Barnsley (July 15, 1851), Wath (July 16, 1851), Rotherham (July 17, 1851), Tickhill (July 18, 1851), and Bawtry (July 19, 1851).

Then a gap before we pick them up again in Northwich (July 28, 1851), Middlewich (July 29, 1851), Over (July 30, 1851), Tarporley (July 31, 1851), Chester (August 1 and 2, 1851), Flint (August 4, 1851), Holywell (August 5, 1851), St. Asaph (August 6, 1851), Rhyl (August 7, 1851), Abergele (August 8, 1851), Conway (August 9, 1851), Bangor (August 11, 1851), Beaumaris (August 12, 1851), Llanerchymedd (August 13, 1851), Amlwch (August 14, 1851), Llangefni (August 15, 1851), Holyhead (August 16, 1851), Bangor again (August 18 and 19, 1851), Carnarvon (August 20 and 21, 1851), Pwllheli (August 22, 1851), and Tremadoc (August 23, 1851).

Then there is a gap of two weeks, followed by Shrewsbury (September 8 and 9, 1851), Wellington (September 10, 1851), Newport (September 11, 1851), Stafford (September 12, 1851), Rugeley (September 13, 1851), Lichfield (September 15, 1851), Tamworth (September 16, 1851), Sutton Coldfield (September 17, 1851), Walsall (September 18, 1851), Wednesbury (September 19, 1851), West Bromwich (September 20, 1851), Dudley (September 22, 1851), Wolverhampton (September 23, 1851), Stourbridge (September 24, 1851), Kidderminster (September 25, 1851), Bromsgrove (September 26, 1851), Henley-in-Arden (September 27, 1851), Leamington (September 29, 1851), Rugby (September 30, 1851), Market Harborough, October 1, 1851), Uppingham (October 2, 1851), Stamford (October 3, 1851), Peterborough (October 4, 1851), Market Deeping (October 6, 1851), Oundle (October 7, 1851), Thrapston (October 8, 1851), Kettering (October 9, 1851), Northampton (October 10, 1851), Towcester (October 11 and 13, 1851), Brackley (October 14, 1851), Bicester (October 15, 1851), Woodstock (October 16, 1851), Abingdon (October 17, 1851), Wallingford (October 18, 1851), Reading (October 20, 1851), Ilsley

(October 21, 1851), Wantage (October 22, 1851), Farringdon (October 23, 1851), Bampton (October 24, 1851), Burford (October 25, 1851), Stow (October 27, 1851), Moreton (October 28, 1851), Campden (October 29, 1851), Evesham (October 30, 1851), Tewkesbury (October 31, 1851). On Monday, November 3, 1851, they opened at their newly constructed circus at Cheltenham, thus bringing the summer tour to an end.

For the record: At the beginning of 1851, Macarte and Bell's Grand American Circus was playing at Landport, Portsmouth. Adrian the Clown was one of their performers. In late February, early March 1851, they left Portsmouth. By late March they were in Bath; on July 7 and 8 they were in Leicester; and on July 10 and 11, they were in Nottingham.

On Sunday, July 20, 1851, they passed through the village of Howden, en route to Hull, where they would be playing the next day. At a pub in Howden, a likely lad sold a dog to one of the troupe's musicians, Dick Holt, for three bob, except it wasn't his to sell. The usual story, except that Dick was quite a celebrated musician, leader of the brass band, and ex-trumpet player with Jullien's famous orchestra. He was also 6 foot 3. Bill Harrison, whose animal it was, tracked the pooch down to another pub in Hull, and, a constable in tow, upbraided Mr. Holt, for whom corroborative evidence saved bacon. Bill Harrison got his dog back, and Dick Holt lost three shillings. That was one day in court. The next day, Aaron Nutt Brown, another Macarte employee, appeared in the same court for savaging a man about the legs in a pub at Mytonbridge. He was fined five shillings and costs.

On July 25 and 26 the troupe was in Scarborough. On August 7 and 8, they were in Newcastle. On September 9, they were in Burnley, and the following day in Accrington. On September 25, they entered Retford, and by the end of the day wished they hadn't. For a start, some rather aggressive artists had painted on several vacant walls of the town monumentally obscene representations of men, women, and horses, evidently in a spasm of free advertising for the arriving cirque. When the reality did not match the promotion, there was distinct disappointment felt by not a small number of the inhabitants. To make it worse, just after their grand entree into Retford, it started to rain cats and dogs, and only about 25 people showed up for the afternoon performance. It couldn't be any worse for the evening show, but it was. The hordes who turned out for the event braved the increasing rain and, by now, gale force winds, and not long into the show, the center pole broke and the whole enormous tent collapsed, on top of everyone. The panic was a thing to behold, screams and moans, blood and mud everywhere, while one man was almost killed. The circus crept out of town in the wee hours of the following morning, with a take of only about £25.

In October they visited an inordinate number of towns in Lincolnshire, billing themselves as Macarte's Star Riders of the World, but too much work and no play makes Macarte's a dull cirque by any other name. The week beginning November 24, 1851, Macarte's American Circus was playing in Yarmouth. Aside from Mr. J. Macarte and Madame Macarte, the bill included the clowns Adrian and Lenton. Macarte's would go on to Norwich, where they would do the Christmas entertainments, and stay for 14 weeks.

On January 1, 1852, New Year's Day, at William Cooke's Circus in Plymouth, an ostrich race took place. The evening show of January 7 was patronized by Colonel Commander Coryton and the officers of the Plymouth division of the Royal Marines. The house was filled in all parts, and the entertainments throughout were greeted with the warmest approbation. The evening performance of January 9 was under the patronage of C. Trelawny, Esq., and the gentlemen of the Hunt. The day performance of January 14, 1852, was under the patronage of Admiral Sir John Acworth Ommanney, the recently appointed commander-in-chief at Plymouth, while William Cooke took his benefit on the night of January 19, under high patronage (i.e., the Royal Western Yacht Club). The house was crowded in every part. On February 2, 1852, Henry Cooke took his benefit, and the house was again filled to excess. The following evening, William Barlow, the Lion Horseman, had his benefit, and on the 4th there was a grand day performance under the patronage of Charles Calmady, Esq., and Mrs. Calmady, of Langdon Hall. That night, Mr. E. Jackson, the Shaksperian clown, took his benefit. This was the last performance of the season, although the troupe stayed in Plymouth, without performing, until February 7, 1852. Of interest is that Harry Connor had a daughter, Hannahbella, born about this time, in Plymouth.

On January 12, 1852, Hengler's came down from their winter quarters at Cheltenham, and opened in Exeter. Those in the cast included Miss Woolford, Jem Ryan and his daughter Susan, Mr. Barlow, Mr. Morton, Mons. Le Tort, the surprising gymnastique, and Mons. Corelli and his infant sons. Messrs. Boswell, Lewis, and Frowde were the clowns. Young Hengler (John Michael Hengler) would appear occasionally on the tightrope, when he wasn't gigging elsewhere. In January 1852, Franconi's were in Leeds. Equestrian Tom M'Collum (born 1827, Philadelphia), who for a very brief while had had his own cirque in Birmingham, featuring Hernandez, would join Franconi's on February 16, replacing Hernandez himself as the star attraction. Franconi's last night in Leeds was February 28, 1852, and they left the next morning for Hull, where they opened at the Queen's Theatre, on March 1, 1852. James Cooke's Circus had been playing in Sunderland since 1851. On January 19, 1852, they opened in North Shields.

On Sunday, February 8, 1852, William Cooke's Circus traveled from Plymouth to Bath, opening there on Monday, February 9, 1852. The circus was now being billed as Mr. William Cooke's Colossal Equestrian Establishment. By this stage of his career, aged 22, Arthur Barnes had for some time been billed as "The Greatest Vaulter in the World," or "The Champion Vaulter of All the World," and so on. Cooke's would be at Bath for over a month, and Alexine was getting more and more pregnant by the day, so to speak. They set up in one of the dwelling units that comprised 10 Kingsmead Terrace, one of the many lodging houses on that street, in Lansdown, Bath. This building was used to performers. Only the year before, the actresses Rosina Proctor and Susan Montague had occupied two units here.

On Tuesday, February 17, 1852, the Earl and Countess of Mount Edgcumbe patronized the morning show as the circus performed St. *George and the Dragon*. On Tuesday morning, March 2, the Duke of Beaufort patronized the evening's performance. On March 6, Capt. and Mrs. Farrer gave their bespeak, and March 8 was Alfred Cooke's benefit. Sir James Rivers, Bart., patronized the Thursday evening show of March 11, Jackson the clown's benefit night. At this time the daring backwards rider La Petite Emilie (who would later marry John Henry Cooke) was the main star.

According to the *Flying Post* of March 18, 1852, on Monday, March 1, M. Le Tort, of Hengler's, who was really a Scotsman with a handlebar and imperial named Bill Fitzmartin, a well-known trainer of infants for the circus, killed his own child while putting him through his paces. A verdict of manslaughter was brought in. Le Tort's wife asked the authorities if he was being accused of the killing of another child, three years before, or if this recent one was the sum total of all the charges. The Scotsman had also, not too long before, so maltreated a child that it was taken from him (in 1852 that child would be traveling with Macarte & Bell). Macarte's left Norwich on March 20, 1852, after a long stint there, and on the 22nd opened at Ipswich, with John Samwell as a main attraction.

While William Cooke's Circus Royal continued on at Bath, William Cooke's Colossal Equestrian Establishment, including Arthur Barnes, opened at the Circus Royal, North Street, Bristol, on March 15, 1852. We now have not only the *Era* to rely on, but also the *Bristol Mercury*. By now, Cooke's circus had over 100 artistes (a word that in Britain at the time was pronounced "artists").

On opening night in Bristol, to an overflowing house, the entertainment commenced with Henry Cooke, in a new act of horsemanship; Mr. J. W. Cooke on four steeds, as Le Hungarien; Messrs. Barnes and Connor, the champion vaulters; Miss Kate Cooke, in the Act of the Menage; Mr. Adams, as the Wild Indian of the Prairie; Mdlle. Zamezou, in her daring leaps over streamers, etc.; a chase of the ostriches by mounted Arabs; William Cooke introduced the beautiful, docile ponies, Blue Bell and Vesta, as well as his trained steed, Raven; Master John Cooke, in his grand act of equitation; Sig. Zamezou, in a dashing barrier act; and the entertainments concluded with the legendary representation of *St. George and the Dragon*. Clowns: Messrs. Doughty and Adams. Doors opened at 7:00, performances commenced at precisely 7:30. A grand day performance every Saturday, doors open at 1:30, show began at 2:00. No performance on Saturday evenings.

On March 18, 1852, in Bath, Jackson the Clown took a benefit. The following week, the Bristol contingent, now in their second week in that town, were doing *The Rigs of Mr. Briggs*, a popular show of the time. Doughty and Jackson were the clowns at this stage. On Thursday, the 25th, Mr. Cooke took his benefit, on a night patronized by Major Simpson and the Amateurs of Bath. The performances terminated with a grand Eastern spectacle, in which the training and docility of Mr. William Cooke's elephants were most surprising, and failed not to receive the warmest applause from an astonished and very crowded audience. On Friday, March 26, Cooke's closed in Bath, and joined the Bristol members for the grand opening there of the joint circuses. From now on, for a while, Cooke's would be described as a "double company."

James Cooke's Circus opened in Newcastle on March 29, 1852, and on April 12, 1852, Franconi's opened in Glasgow. For William Cooke's, in Bristol, the performance that night, April 12, started with the Roman Warriors, and was followed by Jack Russilli, with the globe on horseback; Mr. Adams, the "Grimaldi of the Arena," as Punch's festivities; Mdlle. Josephine in a scene d'equitation; Sig. Zamezou, in a dashing barrier act; Master John Cooke, in an act of equestrianism; Mr. Jackson, in his bloomer dance; Alfred Cooke appeared in an equestrian act entitled *Don Juan, the Libertine on Horseback*; Master Zamezou, on two ponies, as *Whenca, or Hard Heart*. The whole concluded with the spectacle called *The Kaffir War*, in which two real elephants were introduced. Mr. Jackson, Shaksperian clown; Mr. Doughty, modern jester.

April 19, 1852, was Mr. Henry Cooke's benefit night, and the evening performance of the 20th was under the distinguished patronage of Sir John Kerle Haberfield and Lady Haberfield. April 24 was the last grand day performance. On the evening of April 26, the benefit for Mr. Alfred Cooke, Young Godolphin appeared as the Prince of Wales. It was also the first night of the great performing dog, Regent, and the first night in Bristol of the gorgeous spectacle of the grand entree of *Alexander the Great into the City of Babylon*. The evening show of April 29 was patronized by W. H. Gore Langton, Esq., mayor, and Mrs. Langton, for the benefit of Mr. William Cooke. On May 1, 1852, the circus left their North Street premises, and set up in Stock's Croft. There were no performances the next day, of course, as it was Sunday, but

Monday, May 3, 1852, was the first of two nights in the Full Moon Field, Stock's Croft, Bristol, advertised as the first provincial tour. One performance on each of the two days, to commence at four o'clock. Ostriches of the desert, ridden by Arab boys; two Hindoo performing elephants; a splendid stag hunt, followed by ladies; the Sheik Riders, a comic and laughable scene; Mr. W. Cooke, with his mare Raven; "Mr. Barnes as Les Actions des Voltigeur [sic]"; Sig. Zamezou and his pupils appeared in a series of classical poses and tableaux; Mr. Barlow as a Trojan youth, driving and managing 15 furious steeds; Mdlle. Zamezou, on a single horse, in an act of equestrianism; Clowns: Jackson, Doughty, and Adams. The show concluded with *The Rigs of Mr. Briggs.*

The circus remained in Bristol until sometime in early May, 1852, probably May 8. If it was May 8, then the next day, Sunday, May 9, they would have used to travel down to their next gig, in Cirencester, which would officially kick off Cooke's Colossal Hippodrome's summer tour for the year, on Monday, May 10, with Arthur Barnes as one of the main attractions, as always. On May 11 they were in Faringdon, and then it was on to Witney (May 12, 1852), and then into Oxford.

Meanwhile, Hengler's closed in Exeter on April 8, 1852, moving on to Plymouth for Easter Monday, April 12, 1852. On May 14 they were in Paignton, then we pick them up sporadically in Torquay, on May 15, and Exeter, on May 25, 1852. Macarte's left Ipswich on April 29, 1852, after a great stay. In addition to all this, one of the great clowns decided to have a shot at being a proprietor. It didn't last long, but, in March and April 1852, George Knight's Circus was playing in Gloucester. From there, on April 24, he made his entry into Hanley, and on June 7, 1852, Signor Hendric, the equestrian vaulter from Astley's, would make his bow there with Knight's.

Jackson's of May 8, 1852, says,

> By permission of the Reverend the Vice-Chancellor and the Worshipful the Mayor, positively for one day only in Oxford, the excitement of the Great Exhibition of 1851, revived by William Cooke's Colossal Hippodrome. Unequalled for talent and magnitude in this or any other country in the world, embodying 100 horses and ponies, 30 carriages and cars, performing elephants, racing ostriches, reindeer, and monkeys, etc, etc. This Grand Equestrian Exhibition Fete will be displayed in a Colossal Hippodrome Marquee in the form of an ancient Roman amphitheatre, containing 40,000 feet of canvass, and capable of holding 11,000 persons, to be erected in a close near Worcester College, on Thursday next, May 13.

The same paper, of May 15, 1852, tells us that, on Thursday, May 13, Cooke's equestrian company made a triumphal entry into this city from Witney, at 11 o'clock. The procession came up Queen Street, passing down the

High Street, Long Wall, Holywell Street, Broad Street, Magdalen Street, to the Star Hotel, where it halted. In addition to the ordinary features of an equestrian procession, there were two elephants, an ostrich, a reindeer, and some Roman chariots, forming altogether an imposing spectacle. For the afternoon show, which began at two o'clock, between 2,000 and 3,000 persons were present, and the performances, which were clever, amusing, and varied, appeared to give satisfaction to the audience. In the evening, the performances were repeated to a still larger audience.

From Oxford it was on to Abingdon (May 14, 1852), Wallingford (May 15, 1852), and then, on the Sunday, they traveled to Reading, where they played on the 17th. It was Newbury on the 18th, Andover on the 19th (the same day Macarte's were in Chelsmford), Basingstoke on the 20th, Farnham on the 21st, and then into Alton. The *Hampshire Advertiser* of May 29, 1852, says: "Alton. May 29. Cooke's Hippodrome. On Saturday last [i.e., May 22] our town was paraded by the equestrian company of Mr. Cooke. Two entertainments were given, one in the afternoon, and the other in the evening, which were very numerously and respectably attended."

On the Sunday they shifted to Petersfield for the May 24 gig, then on to Winchester. The *Hampshire Advertiser* of May 29, 1852, tells us: "Cooke's Hippodrome. This huge equestrian establishment performed in this city [i.e., Winchester] on Tuesday and Wednesday [i.e., May 25 and 26], but the weather was unfavourable."

The *Hampshire Advertiser* of May 22, 1852, said:

Southampton. Mr. W. Cooke's Circus. This stupendous hippodrome will be erected in the Houndwell (the Fair Field not being large enough) on Thursday next [i.e., May 27] and the following day, on which day the extraordinary entertainment provided by Mr. Cooke will be given [this is slightly misleading; they played both days, as we shall see]. There are a hundred horses, two elephants, ostriches, and other performers besides the numerous actors and actresses. We recognise in the list of the company some of the most distinguished names in the equestrian ranks, besides performers of all the varied feats in gymnastics and amusement which the modern circus presents. The entertainment is equal to all that Batty or Frescati [they presumably mean Franconi] can accomplish, and is brought into towns, instead of the public being compelled to travel eighty miles to witness it.

The *Era* of May 30, 1852, reported:

Southampton. Cooke's Colossal Hippodrome. This gigantic equestrian establishment visited Southampton for a couple of days on Thursday and Friday, two performances taking place on each day in the colossal marquee erected in the Houndwell. As might naturally be expected, the performances in the arena attracted together great numbers of people, and on Thursday evening especially, when we looked in upon the scene, there were upwards of 5000 persons present. The marquee in which the performances take place forms a perfect novelty of itself. It is of gigantic proportions, being about 160 feet in length, and 102 feet in breadth, and contains 40,000 feet of canvas. Mr. Cooke seems to have gathered round him a company of ladies and gentlemen of first rank in their profession, and the scenes in the circle were of a more refined and superior order to those usually witnessed at places of this kind. The accomplished equestrianism of Mr. Cooke and his family are too well known to require further notice. The gymnastic performances were excellent, especially those of Mr. Barnes, who threw sixty-five somersaults without resting, on Thursday afternoon, and sixty-one in the evening; the graceful ease with which he accomplished these surprising feats astonished and delighted everybody, as testified by the enthusiastic plaudits of the auditory, and fairly entitle him to rank as the champion of vaulters. Nor must we omit to mention the fun and witticisms of Messrs. Doughty and Jackson, the rival clowns, who drew largely on the risible faculties of the audience. Mr. Cooke has concentrated a large amount of talent, as well as immense numerical strength, in this establishment, and we heartily wish him the same amount of success throughout his summer tour that he received in Southampton [this originally from the *Hampshire Independent*].

On the Thursday, May 27, 1852, while Arthur Barnes was doing 65 in the afternoon and 61 in the evening, his first child was born at 10 Kingsmead Terrace, Lansdown, Bath. This was Alexine Caroline, her birth being registered in Bath Registry Office on June 28, 1852, by Frederick Hanham, registrar. The father is Arthur Barns, equestrian, and the mother is A. W. Barns, formerly Pettoletti, her address being the same as the birthplace of the child.

On Saturday, May 29, 1852, William Cooke's Circus played Fareham, and the following day made their way to Portsmouth, where they performed on May 31 and June 1. It is rare that one encounters a bad review of the circus. However, the *Hampshire Telegraph* (published in Portsmouth) of June 5, 1852, when going over some of the events of the Whitsun holidays, says, "A considerable number of [persons] visited Cooke's Hippodrome, which excited, we hear very different feelings, the chief attraction being, it appears, confined to the street procession, which is made at its entrance into different towns, not unlike the shows at Bartholomew Fair, whose only feature of interest was the outside performance."

They were in Chichester on June 2, 1852, in Petworth on June 3, in Godalming on June 4, in Guildford on June 5, and then came Sunday, during which they were on the road to Dorking, where they played on June 7, 1852. A ten-year-old boy living on High Street, Dorking, was Henry Attlee. He would have seen Arthur Barnes somersaulting. Just over 30 years later, Henry Attlee would become the father of a future British prime minister.

On the 8th it was Reigate, on the 9th East Grinstead, on the 10th Horsham, on the 11th Steyning, and on June 12, 1852, Worthing. On the Sunday they moved along to Brighton, where they played two nights, June 14 and 15, 1852, the weather being very unfavorable. However, the streets were crowded with thousands of spectators as Cooke's made their entry into the town on the Monday. The rain continuing throughout the morning, the performances in the Hippodrome were unavoidably postponed. In the evening, the entertainment took place in the Royal Pavilion Circus, and was attended by numerous families of distinction, the boxes producing a dazzling display of rank and beauty. On Tuesday morning, the weather was more favorable, and by half past two p.m., the attendance at the Hippodrome was immense, the performance throughout receiving the most enthusiastic applause. In the evening, the Royal Pavilion Circus was again crowded, many hundreds not gaining admission. St. *George and the Dragon* concluded the amusements, the part of St. George being ably sustained by the spirited manager.

They were in Lewes on the 16th, in Battle on the 17th, and in Hastings for two days, the 18th and 19th of June, 1852. Then it was Sunday, and off to Rye, where they played on June 21, 1852. Tenterden was next (June 22, 1852), then Ashford (June 23, 1852), where Mr. Cooke was honored with a full and fashionable attendance, both morning and evening. Then it was on to Hythe (June 24, 1852), Sandgate (June 25, 1852), and Folkestone (June 26, 1852). On the 27th, a Sunday, they traveled to Dover, playing there two nights, the 28th and 29th. Then on to Deal, for June 30, 1852, and then into Ramsgate. The *Era* of July 4, 1852, says: "Ramsgate. William Cooke's Colossal Hippodrome. Mr. Cooke, with his extensive stud of horses, ponies, elephants, ostriches, etc., entered the town on Thursday last [i.e., July 1] for two days, and attracted thousands of the sight seeing folks together. The mid-day and evening entertainments were well attended, especially the boxes, comprising most of the aristocracy and fashion of Ramsgate and the neighbourhood."

In the general world of the circus, as opposed to say, the specific of William Cooke's outfit, on May 18, 1852, John Clarke & Palmer's Equestrian Circus, a compact company, opened in Southampton. Old John Clarke was in his mid-50s then. In early June, for Whitsun, they were in Newport, Isle of Wight. James Cooke's Circus closed in Newcastle on May 22, 1852, to commence their tenting season of that summer. Ginnett's Circus was also touring that year. Hengler's tour took in, among other places, St. Austell (June 3, 1852), Truro (June 4, 1852), Penzance (June 10, 1852), Camborne (June 14, 1852), Redruth (June 15, 1852), St. Davy (June 16, 1852), Truro (June 17, 1852), St. Columb (June 18, 1852), Padstow (June 19, 1852), and Bideford (June 30, 1852). On July 1, 1852, Franconi's opened in Sunderland. Harry Brown, the clown, was with them at that time. On June 28, 1852, George

Knight's Circus began a week-long gig in Wolverhampton, but only with tolerable success. That sounds ominous, and it was. That, and other factors, spelled finis to George's career as a proprietor, and by October he was touring the country as a jester with Welch, Hernandez & Co., later acting in a similar capacity with Hernandez & Stone.

For William Cooke's, after two nights in Ramsgate, it was Margate on July 3, 1852, and then, on July 4, a Sunday, they traveled to Canterbury, where they played the next night (July 5, 1852). Then on to Faversham (July 6, 1852), Sittingbourne (July 7, 1852), Maidstone (July 8, 1852), Tunbridge Wells (July 9, 1852), and Sevenoaks (July 10, 1852). Then, on Sunday they were off to Town Malling for the July 12 gig, where the show was patronized by the Earl Of Abergavenny and his family, as well as a host of the aristocracy. Then it was on to Rochester (July 13, 1852).

Just a couple of miles from Rochester was the village of Old Brompton, where lived a joiner named Bill Greenstreet and his wife, Eliza. The baby of the family was John J., three years old. Like everyone else in Old Brompton, the Greenstreets would have gone to see Arthur Barnes vaulting. The baby of the family grew up to become a tanner in Sandwich, married, and had a son named Sydney Hughes Greenstreet.

Then it was on to Gravesend (July 14, 1852), where Cooke's gave two performances, of course, to an immense assemblage. Then Dartford (July 15, 1852), Woolwich (July 16, 1852), and Greenwich (July 17, 1852). On Sunday it was off to Croydon, where they played on July 19, 1852. Then on to Kingston (July 20, 1852), Richmond (July 21, 1852), Wandsworth (July 22, 1852), Dulwich (July 23, 1852), and Clapham (July 24, 1852). On Sunday they traveled to Woodford, Essex, for their Monday night gig of July 26, 1852, then on to Romford (July 27, 1852), Brentwood (July 28, 1852), Chelmsford (July 29, 1852), Maldon (July 30, 1852), and Witham (July 31, 1852). On August 1, 1852, Sunday, they moved to Coggeshall for the August 2 gig, then on to Braintree (August 3, 1852), Halstead (August 4, 1852), Sudbury (August 5, 1852). For this period, we are relying not only on the *Era*, but also the *Essex Standard*.

After Sudbury it was Colchester. The *Essex Standard* of July 30, 1852, advertised:

> Positively for two days only!!! Friday and Saturday, Aug. 6 and 7. In a meadow, near the Castle, Colchester. The great sensation of the exhibition revived in William Cooke's Colossal Hippodrome, the only one traveling in England [the only "colossal hippodrome" perhaps; certainly not the only circus]. Embodying 100 horses and ponies, 30 carriages and cars, 100 male and female artistes, performing elephants, racing ostriches, trained horses, ponies, reindeers, and monkeys; Roman games taken from history; the first introduction in the provinces of

Roman car racing, Ladies' chariot racing, riding 15 horses, etc. The real stag introduced in the Royal Hunt every day.

Performances were at two and seven o'clock each day.

Throughout July 1852, Hengler's were still touring, appearing in such towns as Taunton (July 12, 1852), Langport (July 13, 1852), Bridgwater (July 14, 1852), Burnham (July 15, 1852), Weston-super-Mare (July 16, 1852), and Clevedon (July 17, 1852).

William Cooke's Circus left Colchester on the Sunday following their stint there, and traveled to Hadleigh (August 9, 1852), Ipswich (August 10, 1852), Stowmarket (August 11, 1852), and then into Bury St. Edmunds. The *Era* of August 15, 1852, says: "Bury St. Edmund's. Wm Cooke's Colossal Hippodrome. This extensive and talented company entered Bury St. Edmund's on Thursday last [i.e., Aug. 12]. The attendance at the morning and evening performances was immense, many of the first families of the neighbourhood being present. Amongst the novelties introduced is the superior training of the Burmese elephants, whose docility, combined with the difficult positions they go through with perfect ease at the simple word of command, proclaims them most clever zoological wonders."

On August 13, 1852, Cooke's Grand Hippodrome was at the great horseracing center of Newmarket, in Suffolk, and then it was into Cambridge for the first of two nights of actual performance in that town. The *Cambridge Chronicle* of August 21, 1852, reporting on the performance on Midsummer Common in that town, tells us that a pupil of Signor Zamezou threaded after the manner of a snake through the spokes of a ladder, whilst balanced on the Signor's chin. The paper then informs us that "one of the vaulters, Mr. Barnes we believe" threw 68 somersets in rapid succession, and then threw one backward. Another highlight was "Mr. W. Cooke on Raven. On Sunday, they rested in Cambridge, and did their second night there on Monday, the 16th. On August 17, 1852, they were in the cathedral city of Ely, and, from there, the plan was to head east into East Anglia. Brandon, in Suffolk, was their next stop, but, unfortunately, as there was no direct west-east road running through the Breckland, they had to detour down to Newmarket, then up to Brandon, where they performed on the 18th. Then it was only eight miles or so down the road to Tom Paine's old Norfolk hometown of Thetford, their next gig, on August 19, 1852. It was about 17 miles from there due east on the busy Lowestoft Road, until they got to their next gig, on August 20, in the old Norfolk market town of Diss, home of the old Poet Laureate, John Skelton. They then left the main road, south for just a few miles to Eye, in Suffolk, where they played on August 21. On the 22nd, a Sunday, they set out on the back road to Halesworth, going through the picturesque northern Suffolk villages of Stradbroke, Laxfield, Heveningham, and Walpole, before they reached their destination, Halesworth, where they played that Monday night, August 23, 1852. From Halesworth, they cut up due north to Bungay, back on the main Lowestoft Road, where they performed on August 24. From there it was a straight shot east into the famous Suffolk town of Beccles (August 25, 1852), 16 miles southeast of Norwich, and from Beccles to the seaside town of Lowestoft (August 26, 1852), the most easterly town in the United Kingdom. From Lowestoft it was a seaside run up the road back into Norfolk, to the famous fishing town of Great Yarmouth for two nights, August 27 and 28, 1852.

There was a train, although the circus didn't take it, that ran from Leicester to Peterborough, then through Ely, Brandon, Thetford, Wymondham, and into Norwich. From there, there were two choices, a line to Lowestoft, or one to Yarmouth. By 1852 the rail network across Britain was extensive. It was also expensive, too expensive for a large troupe traveling relatively short distances on a junket.

On August 23, 1852, Mr. Emidy's Circus Royal opened at the Donnybrook Fair, in Dublin, minus three apprentices who had fled the day before from Emidy's house at Balls Bridge—Joe Jee, his sister Janie, and Charles Bradbury. Mr. Emidy was pretty upset. Joe Jee had been born on October 15, 1838, in Clerkenwell, son of a turner. Jane was still only 11, and Charlie was only 10. The three apprentices had been taken on by Mr. and Mrs. Emidy in February 1849. Master Bradbury, to name but one, had suffered through an inordinate number of physical misfortunes during his short term as a circus apprentice with Mr. Emidy, to wit, his ribs were hurt when the box office collapsed during a mad rush into the theater one day. On another occasion, due purely to his own carelessness in the ring, he lacerated his knee and sustained a dreadful black eye while falling from his horses. Dear old Mrs. Emidy narrowly escaped injury during the box office crush incident, but no one ever accused Mr. Emidy of abusing her, not like they did with the three apprentices. Poor Mr. Emidy, to have to suffer the calumny of wicked gossips.

Meanwhile, in the States, an ad for Rufus Welch's National Circus, in the *Scioto Daily Gazette* (Ohio) of August 26, 1852, claimed that McFarland, the "greatest tumbler in the world," who was appearing, had thrown "the unprecedented number of 78 somersets in rapid succession."

On Sunday, August 29, 1852, William Cooke's left Yarmouth, bound due west for the great city of Norwich, 20 miles away, where they played two nights, August 30 and 31. Jem Mace was a young Norfolk violinist, living in Norwich at this time. He would have gone to see the circus. Jem would decide on a new career, the prize ring, and go on to be one of the great pugilists of the 19th century.

On August 30, 1852, while William Cooke's was in Norwich, Clarke &

Palmer's opened in Weymouth for the week. On Monday, September 6, 1852, they opened at the Oxford Fair. With Tom Thumb as the star, they stayed on in Oxford for the week, and then it was on to Abingdon for the week beginning September 13, 1852. This circus only operated in 1852, never again. From Norwich, William Cooke's Circus took one of the many roads leading north out of the city that would eventually take the traveler to Cromer, this one to North Walsham, the home of the famous Paston's Grammar School, where Nelson was educated prior to joining the Navy. The circus played North Walsham on September 1, 1852, and then cut across to Cromer, on the north coast of Norfolk, where they played on September 2, 1852 (the day Franconi's opened in Newcastle). They then took the busy old highway leading southwest out of Cromer toward King's Lynn, but went only as far as Holt, which they played on September 3, 1852. From there they cut south across country, down the road to East Dereham, performing there on September 4, 1852. East Dereham was a famous market town in its own right, being the place where the poet Cowper died, and the great novelist and linguist George Borrow was born. Then it was Sunday again, September 5, 1852. The next few days are a blank, as far as the circus's traveling schedule goes. They were to play Peterborough on the 8th, but Peterborough was a considerable distance from East Dereham. Probably no time for performances, which is why we can't find any gigs in this brief period. Their route would have taken them west to Swaffham. From Swaffham there was a rough road, more of a track through the woods, to Stradsett, and then a better road on to Downham Market, but, although it was August and the weather was good, it is more likely they took the safer, more traveled highway up to King's Lynn, and then cut down to Wisbech, and from there over to Peterborough. This was not an easy trip for a traveling company of this size.

The *Era* of September 12, 1852, tells us that this extensive and highly popular establishment entered Peterborough on Thursday, September 8, 1852, in grand procession. After parading the principal streets, an afternoon's performance was given in a very capacious amphitheater, erected in the Fair Meadow, which was well attended. In the evening, another entertainment took place, when the whole of the building was crowded to inconvenience. The Scenes in the Circle, the docile training of the quadrupeds, and the general efficiency of the company, called forth loud applause and enthusiastic admiration, so frequently testified by the assembly. "We have no hesitation in saying that Mr. W. Cooke's Hippodrome greatly exceeds any travelling horsemanship hitherto brought to public notice. For grandeur, extent, and extraordinary daring, the company surpass all."

Again, the next three or four days are vague, at best. Did the troupe stay in Peterborough that week, or did they move on? It seems highly unlikely that they would have missed good old Stamford while they were here, so the best bet is that they did play Stamford on at least one of these nights, and perhaps Grantham, or another largish town on another night or nights. We emerge from the dark on September 13, 1852, when they played Melton Mowbray, in Leicestershire. On the 14th they entered Leicester. "Positively for two days only, Tuesday and Wednesday, September 14th and 15th, The Cricket Ground, Leicester." Now, for the next week or so, we have not only the *Era* to rely on, but also the *Leicester Chronicle*, and, to some extent, the *Derby Mercury*.

The *Era* of September 19, 1852 tells us that Mr. William Cooke, with his colossal establishment, visited Leicester on Tuesday and Wednesday last, the 14th and 15th inst., and set the whole town a holiday making. At 10 o'clock the procession through the streets formed the most gorgeous spectacle ever seen here. The performances both days were numerously attended, the boxes in particular being crowded to overflowing by the aristocracy of town and neighbourhood. The different classical acts produced in the circle received the approval of the thousands congregated, and met with well-deserved applause.

On September 16, 1852, they played Loughborough. The *Nottinghamshire Guardian* of September 23, 1852, gave the show a lousy review:

> Cooke's Colossal Hippodrome. This large establishment visited this town last Thursday [i.e., Sept. 16]. At one o'clock a procession was formed at the Ball's Head Hotel, and proceeded through the town to the field in which the Hippodrome was erected. In the procession, the most gorgeous one ever witnessed at Loughborough, were two elephants, a reindeer, an ostrich, ladies driving Roman cars, two bands of music, and other members of the company on horseback. The performances, both of which were well attended, were of a novel but not very interesting character, and gave anything but satisfaction. Early the next morning, the company left for Burton-on-Trent.

The *Nottinghamshire Guardian* and the *Leicester Chronicle* both give Burton-on-Trent for the 17th, yet the *Era* has that date as the first of a two-day stint at Derby. In order to settle this dispute, one would think that the *Derby Mercury* of September 15, 1852, would come to our rescue: "Positively for two days only, Friday and Saturday, September 17th and 18th, 1852, on the Holmes (adjoining the Cricket Ground), Derby." However, the *Nottinghamshire Guardian* of September 23 (i.e., the lousy review above), which is actually a post facto review of the Loughborough gig, and therefore more telling, says that the troupe went on to Burton-on-Trent that next morning [i.e., September 17]. So, we really have to favor Burton-on-Trent for the 17th. Burton and Derby are neighboring towns. Definitely, the show was in Derby for the 18th, and then they were traveling north to Ripley on the Sunday. They played there on September 20, 1852, then it was up the road at the edge of the Derwent to Wirksworth (September 21, 1852), and then straight up to Chesterfield (September 22, 1852), down to Mansfield (September 23, 1852), up to Worksop (September 24, 1852), and then over to Rotherham on Saturday, September 25, 1852. The following day, Sunday, they shifted to Sheffield.

The *Sheffield and Rotherham Independent* of September 25, 1852, says: "Positively for two days only, Monday and Tuesday, September 27th and 28th, in Sampson's Cricket Ground, Headford Street, Broomhall Street, Sheffield." The *Era* of September 26, 1852, says: "Mr. William Cooke's Hippodrome. This immense and magnificent concern is announced to be in Sheffield on Monday next [i.e., Sept. 27], and there is little doubt that the popularity of the establishment will secure a large attendance."

On September 29, 1852, it was back in the beautiful town of Bakewell for Arthur Barnes; on the 30th, it was Buxton, and, continuing due west, on October 1, 1852, they were in Macclesfield. Then it was down to Leek, for the gig of October 2, 1852. This was 11 days before Leek held their Fair Day. On Sunday they went to Hanley for their October 4 performance, and then pushed on into Stoke (October 5, 1852). From there it was down to Stafford, for the gig of October 6, 1852, the same day Edwin Hughes's son William was baptized in Liverpool. From Stafford it was over to Rugeley (October 7, 1852), Brewood (October 8, 1852), and Walsall (October 9, 1852). On Sunday, the 10th, they traveled on down into Birmingham, where they opened the next day, Monday, October 11, 1852, for a two-night gig.

On October 13, 1852, they were over in Coventry, on the 14th in Rugby, on the 15th down to Daventry, and on the 16th in Northampton. On the Sunday they moved over to Bedford, opening there on Monday, October 18, 1852. On the 19th they were in Biggleswade, and then down to Hitchin (October 20, 1852), Luton (October 21, 1852), Hatfield (October 22, 1852), and Chipping Barnet (October 23, 1852). On the Sunday it was off to Watford for their October 25 gig, and then on to Harrow (October 26, 1852), Southall (October 27, 1852), Brentford (October 28, 1852), and Lewisham (October 29, 1852). Their next show was not until November 1, 1852, at the Royal Pavilion, Brighton. It was a long way to go, and they allowed themselves two days. Although he is not mentioned by name, we have to assume Arthur Barnes was still with Cooke's at this stage, for we don't pick him up anywhere else at this point of time. Brighton would be the home for Cooke's until the end of the year. It may have been the lack of press that irked Mr. Barnes. After all, he was a star by this time, and he wasn't getting the attention in the ads that he deserved.

As for Hengler's, they played Hereford (September 6, 1852), Ledbury (September 7, 1852), Malvern (September 8, 1852), Worcester (September 9 and 10, 1852), Chipping Norton (September 16, 1852), Abingdon (September 20, 1852), Henley-on-Thames (September 24, 1852), Chertsey (September 27, 1852), Chichester (October 2, 1852), and Arundel (October 5, 1852), and their winter season began in Dover on October 25, 1852. By then, they had hired the Ethair family. And, as for Macarte's, in October they were playing Reading, and by early November, they were rehearsing in Bristol, where they opened at North Street on the 15th. They would remain here through the end of the year.

The Hernandez Years

At the same time Cooke's had been touring England in 1852, another circus owner was doing the same thing, the legendary (even then) American equestrian James Hernandez. Hernandez (right name Tom Skelley), had made his first English appearance at Astley's Royal Amphitheatre, in London, on March 5, 1849, when he was 20. He met Arthur Barnes at Wigan in late 1849, while the vaulter was still with Wallett. In 1852, he teamed with Rufus Welch to form Welch, Hernandez & Co., a full-fledged circus, touring Britain. Their stars, throughout the year (most of them were with the company for the duration) included: Hernandez, of course; Hiram W. Franklin, one of the all-time great vaulters; Eaton Stone; the Brothers Elliott; Arthur Nelson, the clown; Mdlle. Fanny, the Parisian danseuse;, Burnell Runnells, the great American double-horse rider;, the Zamezou family; George Ryland; George Knight, who joined them after his own circus collapsed; Louis Courteau, the French grotesque; and, toward the end, Henri Franconi and wife.

Welch and Hernandez played Edinburgh from April 5 to April 21, 1852. On May 10, 1852, we pick them up in Alcester, which is when they began calling themselves Welch, Hernandez & Co. Until then, the company had had no real name. Then it was on to Evesham (May 11, 1852), Pershore (May 12, 1852), Worcester (May 13 and 14, 1852), Malvern (May 15, 1852), Tewkesbury (May 17, 1852), Cheltenham (May 18 and 19, 1852), Gloucester (May 20, 1852), Stroud (May 21, 1852), Wootton-under-Edge (May 22, 1852), Bristol (May 24, 1852), Clevedon (May 25, 1852), Weston-super-Mare (May 26, 1852), Bridgwater (May 27, 1852), Taunton (May 28, 1852), Wellington (May 29, 1852), Exeter (May 31 and June 1, 1852), Sidmouth (June 2, 1852), Lyme Regis (June 3, 1852), Bridport (June 4, 1852), Weymouth (June 5, 1852). Then there is a gap before South Molton (June 14, 1852), Barnstaple (June 15, 1852), Torrington (June 18, 1852), Launceston (June 21, 1852), Tavistock (June 22, 1852), Plymouth (June 23, 24, 25, and 26, 1852), Dartmouth (June 28, 1852), Totnes (June 29, 1852), Torquay (June 30, 1852), Newton Bushel (July 1, 1852), Teignmouth (July 2, 1852), Dawlish (July 3, 1852). Then there is a gap before Wells (July 12, 1852), Frome (July 13, 1852), Bath (July 14 and 15, 1852), Trowbridge (July 16, 1852), and Devizes (July 17, 1852).

The week beginning Monday, July 19, 1852, Hiram Franklin was booked at Vauxhall Gardens, in London, and for Welch, Hernandez & Co., it was on to Southampton, July 22, 23, and 24, 1852. Then another gap until Henley-on-Thames (September 8, 1852), then Aylesbury on September 10, 1852. We are blank for October, then Nottingham, November 1–20, 1852, and Leicester (November 22–27, 1852); then Derby (November 29 through December 4), and Huddersfield (December 20 through December 24).

The mutation of Welch, Hernandez & Co. into Hernandez & Stone had been some time in the planning, so, it was no great surprise when, immediately after the Huddersfield gig ended on Christmas Eve, the new proprietor team took their troupe down to Leeds over the holidays. It was a circus made up of all the best available talent in England at the time, regardless of nationality. Eaton Stone was, like Young Hernandez, young. He was also American, and was already something of a legendary "Indian" bareback rider. This was the couple's first big break. Hernandez & Stone had long ago decided that they wanted the greatest vaulter of all time—Arthur Barnes, so had made him an offer he couldn't refuse. However, life being uncertain at the best of times, especially in the circus world, Arthur Barnes found work with Madame Isabelle's Equestrian Company, at the Royal Amphitheatre, in Liverpool, beginning on December 24, 1852. We know all this from the *Liverpool Mercury* of December 17, 1852, and from the *Liverpool Albion* of December 27.

The *Liverpool Mercury* of December 17, 1852, tells us: "On Friday evening next [Dec. 24, 1852], the Amphitheatre will be reopened with a talented equestrian company under the management of Madame Isabelle." The artistes engaged were Richard Bell, Mr. Morton, Jem Newsome and his wife Pauline, the equestrians; Mr. Young, the equestrian; "Mr. Barnes, the vaulter," Mr. Mackintosh; Mr. L. Courteau, the clown; and "a French lady whose name we have not yet learnt, but whose great talent has rendered her as distinguished a favorite in Paris as the celebrated Caroline, which visited us during M. Dejean's management." Also aboard was the clown Adrian, and, of course, Mme. Isabelle herself, who was very pregnant with her second child.

Here we must introduce Dick Bell and his wife Madame Isabelle. Equestrian Richard Bell was a Birmingham lad, son of an equestrian of the same name, and four years older than Arthur Barnes. Madame Isabelle was an equestrian, real name Isabella Oliver, born in Cheltenham, Glos, in 1829, daughter of a stationer in Lambeth. She had come up through Astley's and Franconi's circuses in the 1840s, and while at Franconi's, met and married Dick Bell on September 12, 1847, at St. Mary Magdalene, Woolwich. By Dick she would have four children, one of whom, Emma, would marry into the Pinder circus family. The Bells (and the Pinders) will become a major part of our story.

We now follow the *Liverpool Mercury* and the *Liverpool Albion* as our guide for Madame Isabelle's stay at the Royal Amphitheatre in Liverpool. The

Mercury of December 28, 1852, tells us that the interior of the theater had been hung with white and gold drapery and the stage fitted for the orchestra and stalls. Those mentioned were Signor Parelli, the "Automaton Polander." His feats of agility and strength, while "suspended from a horizontal pole by his hands, are almost beyond belief." "Mr. Arthur Barnes, who has thrown as many as 91 somersaults in one trial, and who has received a gold medal, a diamond pin, and a silver snuff box for his extraordinary success in this peculiar department, is one of the company, and rightly displays his wonderful powers." Sig. Shillerett's dog, Wallace, and the horse, Prince Albert, also come in for raves. Mr. Newsome, as the shipwrecked mariner, gives great satisfaction.

For the American company, we follow the *Era* for their stay in Leeds, where Messrs. Welch, Hernandez and Company's Portable Equestrian Circus was announced to open in Basinghall-Street on Monday, December 27, with a great number of talented artists, and a numerous stud of horses. However, the tremendous gale of wind in the morning unfortunately blew down the tent and precluded the opening as intended. But all was made good on Tuesday (December 28, 1852), and a crowded audience assembled to witness the various feats of activity and ménage. Thus, in the last part of the year (1852) Hernandez and Stone's American Circus opened at Leeds. However, Arthur Barnes remained with Madame Isabelle at the Royal Amphitheatre, in Liverpool, for a while, anyway. The day after Hernandez and Stone opened in Leeds, they gave a day performance; they would give another one on New Year's Day 1853.

Meanwhile, back in Liverpool, the equestrian company at the Royal Amphitheatre was doing a good business, and, said the *Mercury*, "will, no doubt, irrespective of the many attractions in the town, continue to do so whilst they offer varied and excellent programmes. The morning performances on Wednesday and Saturday are also well attended." Those other attractions included Mons. Jullien's concerts, Wombwell's Menagerie, the Egyptian Museum on Colquitt Street, and mesmerism and clairvoyance at the Concert Hall on Lord Nelson Street. In Leeds, the American Circus (Messrs. Hernandez and Stone, Managers) were winning "golden opinions of the manufacturers of broad cloth and, no doubt, have rich reason to be pleased with their reception at Leeds. The company are not numerous, but contain some of the cleverest artists we ever saw" (*Era*, January 9, 1853). On Monday, January 10, 1853, Young Hernandez appeared at Bradford, with Franconi's. This was a morning show, crammed in en route to Halifax, presumably for a bit of quick cash flow. The American was back in Halifax that evening, because that night Hernandez and Stone's American Circus opened there. For several nights it was crowded with the elite and fashion of this populous and wealthy manufacturing town, the riding of Young Hernandez creating quite a furor, and the astonishing feats of Hiram Franklin, the great somersault thrower and slack-rope artist, hailed with enthusiasm. Mr. Eaton Stone, in his unique and original act, also received well-deserved approbation. A fire destroyed their marquee, and the circus opened in the Riding School on Tuesday, January 18, 1853, on which occasion the entertainment was under the patronage of Lt. Col. Pollard, of the 2nd West York Yeomanry Cavalry. The splendid band of the regiment (led by Mr. Sutcliffe) attended. The place was crowded in every part. On Thursday, January 25, the Shaksperian jester, George Knight, took his benefit, which attracted a full house.

In Liverpool, the grand morning performance at the Royal Amphitheatre took place on Friday, January 14, 1853, instead of Saturday the 15th, because they didn't want to clash with the grand day performance (at two o'clock) tomorrow of the new pantomime at the Theatre Royal. The evening performance of January 21 was under the distinguished patronage of the lord lieutenant of the county, the Earl of Sefton. The *Mercury* of January 25, 1853, tells us, enigmatically, that an "equestrian of great fame has this week been added to the troupe at the Royal Amphitheatre." Who could this be? On January 26 there was a day performance, beginning at two o'clock.

The mystery of the famous equestrian was solved in the *Mercury* of January 28, 1853. "Madame Isabelle has the honour of announcing to the inhabitants of Liverpool that she has succeeded in forming the engagement, for two nights only, with the most brilliant and wonderful artiste which the world has ever seen in this or any preceding age, Mr. Hiram Franklin." The same edition of the same paper says,

> During the week, Mr. Hiram Franklin's feats on the slack rope have been the principal object of admiration. His evolutions as "The Flying Man" are astonishingly pleasing, alike from their variety and the grace with which he goes through some of the most difficult positions. The extent and speed of many of his flights is terrific. On several occasions he has been called into the ring to receive the reiterated applause of the audience. Mr. Barnes' feat of rapidly making 61 revolutions of his body is more like the motion of a wheel propelled by steam than the turnings of a human frame.

Then came the famous competition between Arthur Barnes and Hiram Franklin, a contest the victor of which would emerge as the greatest somersault thrower in the world, the "champion vaulter." This duel was covered certainly by the *Liverpool Mercury*, but was picked up by every other regional paper in the country. "Rivalry of English and American Athletae. Mr. Arthur Barnes and Mr. Hiram Franklin, the great English and American somersault throwers, have entered into a grand trial of skill for 100 guineas a side."

The contest commenced on the night of January 31, 1853, at the Royal

Amphitheatre, and would be continued each evening throughout that week. The gentleman who threw the greatest number of somersaults in the six nights would be entitled to the 200 guineas. The attendance to witness the contest was rather large, and considerable curiosity was excited. Shortly after nine o'clock the two champions appeared in the circle, and Mr. Hiram Franklin, the American, was the first into the task. He commenced rapidly, and finished apparently much fatigued, after having thrown 62 somersaults. Mr. Arthur Barnes, the Englishman, then followed, and his somersaults, though not performed so rapidly as those of his competitor, were higher and more steady. He exceeded Franklin by two throws, having numbered 64 somersaults. Both men were warmly applauded by the audience. At this early stage, Barnes was now two ahead in the overall contest. That very day, Monday, January 31, 1853, Hernandez and Stone opened at Rochdale, in their new marquee, kindly furnished by Mr. Bell, of the Liverpool Amphitheatre.

At Madame Isabelle's, the next night, Tuesday, the famous contest went into its second night. Both lads threw 62 somersaults. Wednesday, February 2, 1853, was the third night. Barnes threw 62 and Franklin only threw 22, because he was ill. But, those are the breaks, and Barnes was now 42 ahead in the overall contest. On the fourth night, the Thursday, Barnes threw 55, and Franklin threw 56. Barnes was now 41 ahead in the overall contest.

A *Liverpool Mercury* ad for Friday, February 4, 1853, headed

> Madame Isabelle's Great Equestrian Company, Royal Amphitheatre. Open every evening. This evening, Friday (the 4th instant), and during the week, a magnificent change in the whole of the Entertainments. The wonders of Ancient Rome eclipsed. Rivalship of the English and American athlete. Challenge for 200 guineas. Mr. Arthur Barnes and Mr. Hiram Franklin, the greatest somersault throwers of the age, will contend in a grand trial of vaulting skill for superiority of the two nations, England and America. These matchless modern Artistes have betted one hundred guineas a side for the Championship of Somersault Throwing. This novel match commenced on Monday, and will be continued during the week, taking place every evening at nine o'clock. Competent judges are appointed to count and register the number of somersaults thrown by each party, and he who has thrown the greatest number at the conclusion of the week will receive the prize of 200 guineas. The above brilliant task will eclipse all similar feats in the known world, putting Ancient Rome, Indians, and Chinese performers in the shade. It is not possible to conceive the effect produced by this unique and extraordinary exhibition. Nothing but actually beholding this miraculous and Herculean performance will convey any idea of its marvelous reality. No further opportunity of witnessing such a display can possibly be afforded to Liverpool after tomorrow (Saturday) the 5th instant. Of itself, it is calculated to produce a triumphant and unrivalled spectacle. Mr. Franklin will also appear and represent, in a most finished style, a rapid display of equitation.

On this fifth night of the contest, Barnes threw 74 somersaults, and Franklin threw 53. Barnes was now 62 ahead in the overall contest, an insurmountable lead.

Saturday was the last night. Barnes threw 76, and Franklin threw 58. They both appeared to be very much exhausted. The *Liverpool Mercury* of February 8, 1853, gives us the overall result of the contest: "American and English Athletes. The summersault match for 200 guineas which has been contended by Mr. Arthur Barnes, an English, and Mr. Hiram Franklin, an American athlete, at the Liverpool Amphitheatre, during last week, concluded on Saturday evening in favour of the Englishman, the aggregate number of summersaults thrown being by Barnes, 393; Franklin, 313."

The *Era* of February 6, 1853, tells us that the attendance for the past week had not been as good as the performances merited. The *Liverpool Mercury* of February 8 informs us that this is the last week but one of the equestrian season. Messrs. Barnes, Shillerette, Courteau, and Parelli as the Syrian Acrobatiques. Mr. Mackintosh as the Leaper of the Rialto. Mr. Morton's celebrated trick act on a first courser. Sig. Shillerette as the Bottle Imp Pedestrian. M. Courteau, the wondrous Aeronautic Hero. Mr. Young, the famous double-horse manager, as Apollo on the Steeds of the Muses. Those were some of the acts advertised on that day at the Royal Amphitheatre, Liverpool. February 11 was the last day performance of the season, at two o'clock, and February 16 was Pauline Newsome's benefit. On February 18, 1853, Mr. Bell took his benefit, assisted by Young Hernandez. It was Hernandez's only appearance with this circus in Liverpool. Barnes played with Madame Isabelle at the Amphi until the end of the run there, on Saturday, February 19, 1853, when he went over to Hernandez and Stone.

On February 20, 1853, Arthur Barnes was making his way from Liverpool to Manchester, where we, as readers, not only continue using the *Era*, but also pick up the *Manchester Times* as our conductor through that magnificent town and its outlying villages. The American Circus, under the management of Hernandez and Stone, with a talented and powerful American troupe, and a numerous stud of beautiful horses (which created such a great sensation at the Theatre Royal, Drury Lane, London, and Bingley Hall, Birmingham) opened in Mount Street, Peter Street, Manchester, on Monday, February 21st, 1853, for 12 days only. The managers begged to call particular attention to the construction of the portable Equestrian Palace, which was on a new and novel plan, capable of accommodating three thousand persons, and which, for comfort and elegance, was not to be excelled by any amphitheater in the kingdom, being well warmed, cushioned, and carpeted, and so constructed as to seat all classes distinct who may honour the Palace with their presence. The splendid practical illustrations of the art of horsemanship introduced the following celebrated performers: the incomparable horseman and American star rider Hernandez; Jem Newsome and his wife, Madame Pauline Newsome; Mademoiselle Josephine Zamezou; Mr. Eaton Stone; Mr. Arthur Barnes; Signor Zamezou and his two talented sons (Jim and Fred); George Ryland; the Brothers Hutchinson; Mr. George Knight, the Shaksperian jester; and Mr. Russell, the modern Grimaldi — a combination of talent not to be surpassed in the world. Special notice. A grand midday performance took place on Tuesday, February 22nd, at two o'clock, by gas light. Places for the boxes could be taken at the Box Office, which was open from 11 to three o'clock daily. Doors opened at a quarter to seven o'clock, and the performance commenced at half past seven. Boxes 2s; Pit 1s; Gallery 6d. Children under 10 years of age half price to boxes and pit.

The *Era* of February 27, 1853, has this to say:

> We were perfectly astounded at the accommodation afforded in the interior of this portable equestrian palace on our visit on Tuesday evening [i.e., Feb. 22], which is sufficiently capacious to hold three thousand persons seated, divided into boxes, pit, and gallery. This unique tent is erected on a plot of ground situate in Mount Street, in the immediate proximity of the Theatre Royal, on the same site where Cooke's and other moveable establishments have made their fixture. The proprietors, we understand, are Messrs. Hernandez and Stone, who purpose remaining here for twelve nights, commencing on Monday, the 21st instant. The performances, upon the whole, are of a very superior description, Hernandez being the ne plus ultra of equestrians. His co-proprietor introduces some extraordinary feats in the Eastern fashion; and Mr. J. Newsome portrays in rapid succession the Shaksperian characters of Falstaff, Shylock, and Richard the Third. Madame Pauline Newsome displays great daring with two horses in a brilliant act of menage; and Mdlle. Josephine Zamezou is very pleasing in her equestrian performances. We must not omit Mr. George Ryland, whose dexterous manipulation with balls in all sizes in equestrian exercises must be seen to be appreciated. Brothers Hutchinson introduce many novel feats. Zameso and Russell are very clever in the pole feats, a la Risley Brothers; but Mr. Arthur Barnes may justly assume the distinction of champion vaulter of the world.

A grand midday performance also took place that day, February 22, at two o'clock, by gas light, and there was another on the 26th. March 2 was a benefit night for Eaton Stone, and March 4 was one for Hernandez. That was the day Madame Isabelle's second son, William Henry, was baptized at St. Peter's, Liverpool. On March 5, 1853, they closed in Manchester, and the next day, Sunday, was spent traveling to Bury, where they opened on the 7th. Saturday, March 12, was the closing performance at the American Equestrian Circus at Bury, when there were upwards of two thousand spectators in attendance. The various acts of horsemanship were performed in first-rate style, and received the plaudits of the assembly.

On Sunday, March 13, 1853, they were off to Bolton, opening there the following night (*Bolton Chronicle*, May 3, 1853). The *Era* of March 20, 1853, referring to this Bolton gig, tells us that the American Circus had been crowded during the past week. Young Hernandez's riding had created quite a furor. The company consisted of the following artistes: Madame Pauline Newsome; Mdlle. Zamezou; Messrs. Stone, Newsome, Arthur Barnes, Ryland, Signor Zamezou; Knight; and the Brothers Hutchinson.

The American Circus closed in Bolton on the 19th, and the following day traveled to Preston, where they opened on March 21, 1853, at Chadwick's Orchard, for six days only. Ticket prices and availability, as well as prices, were identical to those of Manchester. Still on the bill were Hernandez, Pauline Newsome, Mdlle. Josephine Zamezou, Eaton Stone, Mr. Arthur Barnes, Jem Newsome, Signor Zamezou and his two talented sons, George Ryland, the Brothers Hutchinson, and George Knight, the Shaksperian jester. A grand midday performance took place on Tuesday, March 22, at two o'clock, by gas light. They closed at Preston on March 26, and the following day, Sunday, were on the move again, this time to Blackburn, where they opened on March 28.

The *Blackburn Standard* of March 30, 1853, has this:

> Positively the last four days. American Circus, New Market Place, Blackburn. Under the management of Hernandez and Stone. Wednesday, Thursday, Friday, and Saturday, March 30th and 31st, and April 1st and 2nd. First night of *Uncle Tom's Cabin*. Glorious success of the brilliant Hernandez. The daring Pauline Newsome. The unique and original Eaton Stone. The Paragon vaulter Arthur Barnes. The Eastern Magi Mr. G. Ryland. Signor Zamezou and his two wonderful sons. The eccentric scene act rider Mr. J. Newsome. The graceful equestrienne Mdlle. Josephine Zamezou. Clowns—Messrs. Knight and Russell. A combination of talent not to be surpassed in the world. By particular desire, the last day performance will take place on Thursday, March 31st, at 2 p.m., by gas-light.

They closed at Blackburn on April 2, and on the Sunday moved to Burnley, opening there on Monday, April 4, 1853. The *Blackburn Standard* of April 6, 1853, says: "American Circus. Messrs. Hernandez and Stone, with a talented equestrian troupe, are performing during the present week, in their large and splendid amphitheatre erected on the cricket ground, Burnley. This company is about the best that has visited this town for a long time; their daring and agility being truly astonishing." The *Preston Guardian* of April 9, 1853, says: "Burnley. American Circus. Messrs. Hernandez and Stone, with a splendid equestrian troupe, have been performing during the present week in the large and splendid amphitheatre erected on the cricket ground, Burnley, to large and respectable audiences. They daily parade the streets, having in the cavalcade no fewer than four caravans with two horses each; two ditto with four horses each; two phaetons and two horses; and a carriage drawn by six horses." The *Era* of April 10, 1853, reports

> Burnley. Hernandez and Stone's American Circus. This establishment has been exhibiting during the past week in this town to full and fashionable audiences. Madame Newsome and her two highly-trained horses are nightly hailed with rapturous plaudits, and the pantomimic equestrian scene by M.J. Newsome [her husband], representing the sailor in a storm, is a finished piece of riding. This talented couple are engaged at Vauxhall to open Whitmonday. On Tuesday the entertainments are under the patronage of Col. Sadlier and the officers of the 4th King's Own.

Their last night in Burnley seems to have been April 9, and then it was on to Bradford, where, we are told by the *Era* of April 10, 1853, that the American Circus, Messrs. Hernandez and Stone, were to open their portable establishment on the 18th inst., for six nights only. However, there was a change in plan, as explained by the *Bradford Observer* of April 14, which tells us: "Notice. American Circus, under the management of Hernandez and Stone, will open this day (Thursday) April 14th, in place of Monday the 18th, as previously advertised, when, in addition to the celebrated artistes already engaged, will appear Mr. W.O. Dale, the American champion vaulter and horseman! Morning performance on Tuesday, April 19th, 1853, at two o'clock, by gaslight. Open every evening at a quarter before seven." This change is confirmed by the *Era* of April 17, which tells us that the American Circus opened in Bradford on the 14th, and not on the 18th as previously announced. The *Era* gives us a lineup of the stars: Mr. W. O. Dale, the American vaulter and horseman; "Mr. A. Barnes, the champion vaulter (having thrown 91 somersaults at one trial)"; Signor Zamezou and his two sons; George Ryland, Jem Newsome, George Knight, the Shaksperian clown, and Henry Russell, equilibrist, with Madame Pauline Newsome and Mademoiselle Zamezou, who assisted the talented proprietors, Messrs. Hernandez and Stone, in furnishing an agreeable entertainment rarely given by "tenting" managers. A day performance took place on Tuesday, April 19, 1853.

Still in Bradford, April 21, 1853, was benefit night of Eaton Stone, the performance being under the patronage of the mayor, Mr. Samuel Smith, Esq. The following night Hernandez appealed to the town under the patronage of Captain Addison and the Bradford Troop of the 2nd West York Yeomanry Cavalry. They closed in Bradford on Saturday, April 23, and the Sunday was taken up traveling on to York, where they opened on April 25.

On May 1, 1853, the *Era* reported, "York. Hernandez and Stone's American Circus. This talented troupe have during this week been performing in this city to full and fashionable audiences. The vaulting of Messrs. Ragland [should say Ryland], O'Dale [sic] and Barnes [Hiram Franklin had left by then] has caused immense excitement. Mr. Barnes, having in three trials, thrown the extraordinary number of 247 somersaults. On Friday evening the entertainments were under the especial patronage of the Rt. Hon Lord Mayor and Lady Mayoress."

They seem to have spent only a week at York, in which case the next two weeks are a lacuna to history. The *Newcastle Courant* of May 13, 1853, tells us that the American Circus would open on May 16, 1853, near the Central Railway Station, Newcastle-on-Tyne, for a few days only. Arthur Barnes was on the list of performers, as was Bill Dale. A grand midday performance would take place Monday, Tuesday, and Wednesday, at two o'clock, by gas light. They extended in Newcastle until Saturday, May 21, 1853.

On Sat., June 11, 1853, the company was at Beverley (this from the *Hull Packet and East Riding Times* of June 10). On June 12, 1853, the *Era* reported the circus again, "Beverley. Hernandez and Stone's American Circus. This company have, during the last few days been performing in this town to crowded and fashionable audiences. The Brothers Elliot [sic; great friends and long time companions of Arthur Barnes], in their wonderful feats on the trapeze and [on] La Perche, have caused immense excitement, and Mr. G. Knight, the clown, after a short absence, has again joined the corps. Next week the company performs in Hull."

Sunday, June 12, 1853, was spent traveling to Hull. The *Hull Packet* of June 10, 1853, tells us that the American Circus, under the management of Hernandez and Stone, will open at the cricket ground, Anlaby Road, Hull, on June 13, 1853, for three days only — i.e., that Monday, then Tuesday the 14th and Wednesday the 15th. Morning performances at two o'clock (i.e., 2 p.m.). Evening entertainment at half past seven. Arthur Barnes and Bill Dale were on the bill. The stay at Hull is confirmed by the *Era* of June 12. Their last night in Hull was June 15, and then the Hull paper gives us the next few days of their tour — Driffield on the 16th and Bridlington on the 17th. Then we lose them for a week, before picking them up in Wakefield on June 27 and 28, 1853.

Incidentally, on June 27, 1853, Madame Isabelle's appeared at Mansfield (Arthur Barnes was no longer with them, of course). The *Nottinghamshire Guardian* of June 30, 1853, has this to say of that Mansfield gig: "Some parts of the performance were very well received, but others did not give much satisfaction." Hernandez and Stone (with Arthur Barnes) would appear at Mansfield 10 days later, but in the meantime they were in Barnsley on June 29 (*Sheffield and Rotherham Independent*, July 2, 1853), where they gave two of their performances "to large numbers of patrons, who were much gratified with the treat."

The same Sheffield and Rotherham paper, but of June 25, warns us that on June 30 the American Circus will be playing Rotherham on June 30, and then "will open at the Cattle Market, Sheffield, for three days only—July 1, July 2, and July 4." Arthur Barnes and Bill Dale are on the bill. "These distinguished performers made so favorable an impression on their last visit, that many will hail their return with pleasure." The *Era* of July 10 confirms their stay here, and also that this Sheffield gig marked the beginning of the summer season for Hernandez and Company's Circus. "This monstre equestrian establishment pitched their tent in Sheffield" and "remained over Monday, having two performances each day, all of which were highly successful, both as regarded entertainment and profit".

It must not be imagined that all circus folk were gentlemen. In fact, it could be a downright rough arena, as we have already seen. The *Derby Mercury* of July 13, 1853, tells us of a donnybrook that happened at Wirksworth, on July 2, when Madame Isabelle's was playing that town (Arthur Barnes was no longer with them, of course). Two men from the circus, Bill Keeling, alias Bill Boatman, the tentmaster (he paid the laborers their wages) beat the hell out of Bill Brady after an argument. Brady was very severely damaged.

On the 4th of July, 1853, the American Circus left Sheffield for Mansfield, where they played a morning and evening performance on Thursday, July 7 (*Nottinghamshire Guardian*, June 30, 1853). On July 8 and 9, 1853, they were in Newark (*Nottinghamshire Guardian*, July 14, 1853), to rave reviews. About 1700 people came both days.

We pick them up again in Cambridge, at Midsummer Common, on July 27 and 28, 1853.

> Hernandez and Stone's American Circus. This talented troupe have been performing in this town these last few days to crowded and fashionable audiences. The graceful equestrian feats of Young Hernandez, and the daring riding of Eaton Stone and the Wild Indian, have created quite a furore. On Wednesday [July 27, 1853] a vaulting match took place between Arthur Barnes and O. Dales [sic], the American and English vaulters, on which occasion Mr. Dale threw 69 and Mr. A. Barnes 82 somersaults. Next week the company proceed to Norwich en route for Drury Lane, where they appear on Oct. 3 [*Cambridge Chronicle*, July 30, 1853; *Era*, July 31, 1853].

Mme. Dale was another act at this time.

On August 4, 1853, from Norwich, Mr. Knight, of the troupe, wrote a letter published in the *Era* of August 7, in which he mentions that the troupe has clubbed together to raise some money for the troupe at Rosemary Branch Gardens, at Islington, who had just suffered a fire.

They left Norwich on Sunday, August 7, 1853, and the *Ipswich Journal* guides us through their next week: Southwold (August 8, 1853), Aldeburgh

(August 9, 1853), and then into Ipswich, where they played at Woodbridge Road on August 11 and 12, 1853. Barnes and Dale were still with the troupe. Then it was Bury St. Edmunds on the 13th. On Sunday, the 14th, they traveled to Colchester. The *Essex Standard* of Friday, August 12, 1853, tells us: "American Circus. The Colchester public will next week [i.e., the week beginning Monday, Aug. 15] have the opportunity of witnessing the performances of the celebrated American horsemen, Hernandez and Stone, who were last season quite the 'stars' of Astley's, and are now making the tour of the provinces." They closed in Colchester on the 20th, and, on Sunday, August 21, they moved on to Leamington, where they opened on the 22nd (*Era*, August 28, 1853). "Leamington. Hernandez and Stone's American Circus. This talented troupe have been performing in this fashionable town for the last few days to crowded audiences. The unparalleled achievements of Mr. Eaton Stone have astounded all beholders; his daring leaps and miraculous bounds when mounted on his Prairie Horse must be seen to be credited; and the daring riding of young Hernandez, as graceful and classical as the most fastidious lover of equestrianism could desire. Next week the company performs in Coventry."

They closed in Leamington on August 27, and on the Sunday it was off to Coventry, where they opened on the 29th, and closed on Sept 3. The *Era* of September 11, 1853, says: "Messrs. Hernandez and Stone, the great American equestrians, have announced their intention of visiting Worcester in a few days." On September 26, 1853, they were at Leicester, where "they gave one performance, not so well attended as it deserved" (*Era*, October 2, 1853). They went straight to Derby after Leicester (*Era*, October 2, 1853), opening there on Tuesday the 27th.

"This unrivalled troupe performed in this town [i.e., Derby] during the past week to overflowing audiences. The graceful equestrianism of Young Hernandez, the daring vaulting of Eaton Stone, and the talented performances of the Brothers Elliot, O. Dale [sic], G. Ryland, A. Barnes, and G. Knight (clown) have given universal satisfaction. Next week the company appear in Nottingham" (*Era*, October 2, 1853).

So, their final performance at Derby was on Saturday, October 1, 1853, and the following day they traveled to Nottingham, where the *Nottinghamshire Guardian* is our guide.

> Grand American Circus. The very justly celebrated Monster Equestrian Establishment, under the management of Hernandez and Stone, will enter Nottingham on Monday next [i.e., Oct. 3, 1853], at eleven o'clock, with their splendid stud of 40 horses and magnificent carriages, pass through the Market Place and public streets, and give two performances on each of the three first Goose-Fair days. The troupe consists of the most popular artistes in their peculiar different styles of grace, dignity, daring, and exquisite agility — Young Hernandez, the

very prince of equestrian perfection, forming the greatest attraction, and Eaton Stone, unexcelled in his most singular exploits, being a popular adjunct. Mr. W.O. Dale, the celebrated vaulter, and a graceful and admirable horseman, is also one of the company, and returns to us with an increase of skill to his former excellence, which rendered him a great favorite in this town. Mr. Arthur Barnes, the champion vaulter, whose truly wonderful somersault displays used in his former visits, to attract a great amount of interest, and who has thrown the extraordinary number of ninety-one, will also revisit us. Of the Brothers Elliott, in their astonishing feats, we must leave the admirers to judge. We cannot describe their unique performance. And then there is Knight, the very beau ideal of a Shaksperian clown—witty, quaint, clever, and what is best, original. The portable equestrian palace, as it is called, is capable of holding 3000 persons, and some idea of its size may be formed from the fact that Mr. H. Rutley, the much respected agent to the establishment, in his arrangements, was obliged to secure a portion of Mr. Martin's timber-yard, as the immense space where Franconi's building stood was not large enough to admit of the full extension of the tent.

They erected their circus in the vicinity of Tollhouse Hill. "One of the great features of attraction is the summersault throwing by Messrs. Barnes and Dale, the former, on Monday evening [i.e., opening night], throwing clearly, cleverly, and gracefully, 63, and W.O. Dale 52." During the week Mr. Dale was most successful in the amazing feat of throwing some extraordinary clear summersaults on horseback. On October 5 there was another trial of skill between the two somersault throwers, in which Mr. W. O. Dale threw 60 and Mr. Arthur Barnes 62. By desire, Messrs. Hernandez and Stone concluded to prolong their stay in Nottingham until the end of the week.

The *Era* of October 9, 1853, tells us that the circus was going to wrap up its summer tour at Nottingham on Saturday, October 8, after having played there a week.

> Nottingham. American Equestrian Establishment. One of the many sources of attraction for the pleasure seekers of the Nottingham Goose Fair is the large circus under the proprietorship of Hernandez and Stone. It is a marquee of circular form, and holds 3,000 persons. The performances are superior. The circus has been crowded to excess, and the performances went off with the greatest éclat, especially Hernandez and the daring exploits of Stone, the distinguished horseman of the Camanches [sic]. The ball-throwing of G. Ryland, of the extraordinary performances of the Bros Elliot, the comicalities of Mr. Knight, the Shaksperian jester. Repeated applause greeted these acts. Mr. W.O. Dale, the American vaulter, is highly admired.

However, as the *Era* tells us, "Hernandez and Stone prolong their stay in Nottingham till the end of the week," meaning their final night was October 15. On Sunday, October 9, in London, the Acrobat's brother Henry married Jane

Sophia Freeth at St. Barnabas, Homerton. On the 16th, the troupe left "Nottingham tomorrow for London (Drury Lane, 24th October)."

Obviously October 3, 1853, the original scheduled date for Drury Lane, had been put back to October 24. On October 23, 1853, the *Era* announced, "Drury Lane. Scheduled to appear on the 24th: Pauline Newsome (from Franconi's); Bros Elliot, gymnasts; Arthur Barnes, the champion vaulter of all the world, who has accomplished the unprecedented feat of throwing 91 somersaults in succession, his first appearance in London; W.O. Dale, the renowned American artiste." In that same issue appeared another announcement, which included the words "Arthur Barnes (The champion vaulter)."

The circus did, indeed, open at Drury Lane, on October 24, 1853. The *Theatrical Examiner* of October 29, 1853, says (in part): "And there, for a climax, is the champion vaulter of all the world, Arthur Barnes, who has accomplished the unprecedented feat of throwing ninety-one somersaults in succession; attended by that renowned Artiste, Mr. W.O. Dale, the thrower of eighty-one. From the great American Dale, by four somersaults only, the greater English Barnes snatched the crown! It will surely be worth the whole price of admission to see this American hero, mighty even in defeat, by the side of his mightier vanquisher, Arthur of old England." This verbiage was repeated, pretty much verbatim, in Henry Morley's book, *Journal of a London Playgoer from 1851 to 1856.*

The *Times* of November 16, 1853, mentioned in an ad: "Arthur Barnes, the champion vaulter of the world, who has accomplished the unprecedented feat of throwing 91 somersaults in succession. His first appearance in London."

There are a couple of quotes from the *Era* of October 30, 1853, covering this gig: "The victory of the vaulters was completed in throwing nearly 200 somersaults by O. Dale [sic] and Barnes, the European and American champions" (this quote runs in the form of an announcement also in the *Era* of November 6, 13, and 20, 1853). "The vaulting in the air and turning of innumerable somersaults by others of the performers are still more astonishing." There was a morning performance on the 9th of November, Lord Mayor's Day, when the children of the Duke of York's School, with their band, attended. Doors opened at 1:30, and the show began at 2:00. There were more morning performances on November 16 and November 23. The troupe had left Drury Lane by November 27, 1853, but returned to begin a series of special performances on December 17, 1853, and they continued to do that until January 1854.

Theatre Royal, Drury Lane, London. "E.T. Smith [the new owner/manager of Drury Lane] has engaged Hernandez (equestrian rider), Eaton Stone (Indian bare back rider), O. Dale [sic] (champion vaulter and equestrian),

Barnes, Stokes, George Rieland [should say Ryland], James Newsome, Master Leon [an equestrian, also known as Young Leon], The Elliot Brothers, Knight and Wild," for the Christmas and New Year season (*Era*, July 24, 1853).

The *Musical World*, of 1853, reviewed this act, in their section called "Dramatic." "The 'Great Acrobat Scene,' performed by the Brothers Elliott and Arthur Barnes, who is entitled to the distinction of being the champion vaulter of the world, constitutes one of the principal attractions of the performances."

Edward Tyrrel Smith (born 1803), son of an admiral, and one of the famous British circus men of the 19th century, became the lessee of the Marylebone Theatre in 1850, and in 1852 he moved to the Drury Lane Theatre which he bought and managed for 10 years.

Punch, vol. 25 (1853) says: "Arthur Barnes, 'the Champion of All the World," who throws ninety-one somersaults in succession, a living anatomical illustration of the truth that one good turn deserves another." *Punch*, as usual, thought they were being funny.

For the record: We can keep a reasonably close eye on Macarte's Monster American Circus as they toured throughout 1853, with, among other star attractions, John Samwell, Richard Hemming, that great clown, Tom Barry, and, of course, Marie Macarte, the equestrian enchantress. On May 24, 1853, they were in Taunton. One of the local militiamen attempted to obtain a sneak look through the canvas, but was spotted by a zealous circus hand, who stuck a knife in the soldier's head. This precipitated an armed invasion by the militia, who ripped the tent and the wagons to pieces. Not a good day for Macarte's. All the papers snapped that story up, as they did with all of Macarte's mishaps. St. Columb (unknown date), Hayle (June 21, 1853), Bideford (July 7, 1853), Barnstaple (July 8, 1853), Ilfracombe (July 9, 1853), Barnstaple again; (July 11, 1853), South Molton (July 12, 1853), Crediton (July 13, 1853), Exeter (July 14 and 15, 1853), Ottery St. Mary (July 16, 1853), Lyme Regis (July 18, 1853), Axminster (July 19, 1853), Chard (July 20, 1853), Yeovil (July 21, 1853), Crewkerne (July 22, 1853), Witney (August 7, 1853). On August 8, as they were making their grand entrée into Oxford, with John Samwell, as usual, driving the lead wagon with the band on it, they had just turned off High Street into Long Wall when Mr. Samwell's near fore-wheel got into the gutter, and the whole carriage spilled over. What a mess. The drummer boy was the only one injured. Loughborough (August 31, 1853), Rochdale (October 18, 1853), Bradford (November 16, 17, 18, and 19, 1853), Huddersfield (November 21 through December 17, 1853). On December 19, 1853, Macarte's Monster American Circus opened at Hull for the winter season.

In January 1854, Arthur Barnes was still performing at Drury Lane, with

Hernandez and Stone's. Late that month they all left London for Liverpool, where they played the Royal Amphitheatre on Great Charlotte Street, with Pablo Fanque's Equestrian Company as a double troupe from January 30, 1854, to the week beginning February 19, 1854 (*Era*, January 29, 1854).

The *Liverpool Mercury* of January 31, 1854, carried this ad:

> Hernandez, the great American star rider; Arthur Barnes, the English champion vaulter; the celebrated Brothers Elliott; and the Liverpool Bell Melodists, are performing with Pablo Fanque's, for this present Tuesday, the 31st instant, and four following days only. Day performances on Wednesdays and Saturdays, at two o'clock each day. Doors open in the evening at a quarter to seven; commence at half past seven. Admission: Dress Circle, 3s; side boxes, 2s 6d; pit, 1s 6d; gallery, 6d. Children under ten years of age admitted from the commencement at second price to boxes and pit.

On February 5, 1854, the *Era* reported, "Liverpool Amphitheatre. During the past week, in addition to the clever company [Pablo Fanque] which has for some weeks been delighting our good old town with their admirable performances, we have had the renowned Young Hernandez, Mr. Arthur Barnes (the great champion vaulter), The Bros Elliot, from the Theatre Royal, Drury Lane, who have elicited thunders of applause by their graceful and astonishing feats." Other acts were Little Ella, and Young Leon the "Fire King."

The circus did a guest day or two at Bolton at this time (*Bolton Chronicle*, February 11, 1854). On February 12 the *Era* referred to "Arthur Barnes, the greatest vaulter in the world." On Wednesday, February 8, 1854, the Earl of Sefton visited the circus. By the middle of February they were still at Liverpool, although some of the performers had left for Manchester, their next venue, including Little Ella, Hernandez, Leon, the Bros. Elliott, Arthur Barnes, and Tom Barry the clown.

Little Ella. Ella Zoyara was the epitome of female grace and beauty. She set thousands of hearts aflame, and was followed by love letters and proposals of marriage wherever she went. Her equestrian gymnastics were beyond belief. After a long run she married Sally Stickney, daughter of a clown. Sounds like a strange marriage, but Ella was, in actual fact, a man, a blond Creole boy named Olmar Kingsley, who had been reconfigured (so to speak) as Little Ella by Spencer Stokes, American showman.

On February 18, 1854, then, the American Equestrian Establishment closed in Liverpool, and the following day traveled to their next gig, at Fountain Street, Manchester, where they opened on Monday, the 20th. What's more, Mr. Newsome was now a partner, and the name of the outfit had officially become Hernandez, Stone and Newsome's Circus. Arthur Barnes didn't actually rejoin Hernandez and Stone in Manchester until February 27. For their stay here we rely on the *Era*, the *Bolton Chronicle*, and the *Manchester*

Courier. The circus did roaring business at Manchester, but on March 2 there was a fire, and on March 5, W. F. Wallett was introduced as guest artist. George Ryland, la Petite Anne, Mdlle. Adele Newsome, Pauline Newsome, Mdlle. Sidoni, Roxanne, the Zamezous, the Brothers Elliott, Jem Newsome, Josephine Zamezou, Young Hernandez, Eaton Stone, Tom Moseley (equestrian), and Arthur Barnes were the acts. The circus stayed at Manchester until April 28, 1854.

We pick them up again in Bradford, where they opened at the Fair Ground, on May 19, 1854, also playing there on the 20th and 22nd, a morning performance taking place each day. The *Bradford Observer* is our guide here, as well as the *Era*. Other acts mentioned at this time were: Monsieur Parisoni, (Richard) Dewhurst, and Mdlle. Rosalie. Arthur Barnes was still being mentioned, of course, as was the star attraction, "W.F. Wallett, M.A., the Jester of the Two Hemispheres ... the King of Clowns ... presented to H.M. the Queen ... July 11, 1844." The gig at Bradford was for three days only. Incidentally, on Tuesday, May 16, 1854, Pablo Fanque also opened at Bradford, near the railway station, Bridge Street.

From now until June 3, 1854, for Hernandez, Stone, and Newsome's American Equestrian Establishment, we have the distinct advantage of the *Era* and the *Sheffield and Rotherham Independent* to help us through. The first three gigs were Wakefield (May 23 and 24, 1854), Barnsley (May 25, 1854), and Doncaster (May 26, 1854), and then they performed at Rotherham twice on Saturday, May 27, to crowded attendances. On Sunday, the 28th, they remained in Rotherham, packing up, and in the early hours of Monday, the 29th, they traveled just down the road, entering Sheffield at 11 o'clock, and giving their unequaled entertainment in the Cattle Market, positively for two days only, two performances each day, at 2:00 and 7:30. Wallett, the Rex Jocundi, was the "principal star." Then came Pauline Newsome; Mdlle. Sidoni, the daring *ecuyere*; Mr. George Ryland; Eaton Stone; Mdlle. Rosalie; Mons. Parisoni; Master Eaton; Mr. Jem Newsome; the Brothers Elliott; "Mr. Arthur Barnes, the Champion Vaulter of the World"; the clown Dewhurst was also mentioned. Mr. H. Rutley was advance agent. The members of this monster equestrian establishment were very extensively patronised. Incidentally, Pablo Fanque was following them to Sheffield, for the ensuing Whitsuntide and fair.

For the American circus, after Sheffield, it was on to Chesterfield on Wednesday, May 31, 1854; Worksop, on Thursday, June 1, 1854; and Retford, Friday, June 2, 1854. Then, using the *Era*, as well as the *Nottinghamshire Guardian* of June 8, 1854, we learn that on Saturday, June 3, 1854, they entered Newark in procession and gave an entertainment in the afternoon and evening in a monster booth erected in a field on the London Road. The great attraction was the King of Clowns, Mr. W. F. Wallett, inimitable as usual, who kept the company in roars of laughter with his facetious remarks and well-selected hits of the day. The scenes in the circle were well executed, and the horses, which were in excellent condition and well trained, went through some novel and interesting performances satisfactory to the company present, "which we regret to say was not so numerous as was expected."

On Sunday, June 4, 1854, they were traveling to their next gig. The *Nottinghamshire Guardian* of June 8, 1854, tells us:

> Whitsuntide holidays. The equestrian troop of Messrs. Hernandez and Stone, with the immortal clown Wallett, entered en grand cortege into the town [of Nottingham], driving four, six, and eight in hand, cream coloured piebald horses and ponies; and one adventurous damsel in blue not only drove but rode tandem — that is to say she sat on the back of one milk white steed, driving another before her in blue ribbons. Their marquees were pitched in the new Market Place, on Burton Leys, where they performed, we believe, to large and admiring audiences on Monday and Tuesday [i.e., June 5 and 6, 1854].

After Nottingham, the vagueness of their schedule is only clarified a little by the *Era* of June 18, 1854, which tells us that Hernandez and Eaton Stone's American equestrian company are, at present, on a tour of the Potteries district. On June 26 and 27 they played Wolverhampton, both days being "only tolerably well attended" (*Era*, July 2, 1854). On July 6, they were in Worcester, where we pick up *Berrow's Worcester Journal* of July 1, 1854. They gave two performances there, at the Saracen's Head Bowling Green. Then it was on to Malvern on July 7, and to Cheltenham on July 8. On Sunday they were off to their next gig, at the Horse and Jockey, in Oxford, on July 10 and 11 (*Jackson's*, July 8, 1854). On the 12th they were in Wallingford, and in Reading on the 13th.

The next day they took the train from Reading to Portsmouth, finally getting to the south coast. The *Hampshire Telegraph* tells us they entered the town at 11 o'clock, and that they played at Lake Lane (Landport, Portsmouth) on Monday and Tuesday, August 14 and 15, 1854, under the patronage of Lord A. Russell and the Officers Depot 1st Battalion Rifle Brigade. Performances at 2:00 and 7:30 each day. "Mr. Arthur Barnes, the Champion Vaulter of the World" is mentioned in the ad. See also Item 415, Madden Playbill Collection, Portsmouth Library. On August 16, 1854, they played Gosport. That was the day Alfred Cooke, the equestrian, died of cholera in Lambeth. He was 32.

We find them next in Bristol. On Monday and Tuesday, September 4 and 5, 1854, Hernandez, Stone, and Newsome's American Equestrian Establishment (from the Theatre Royal, Drury Lane, London), played at the Full Moon Field, Bristol (two days only). They entered the city of Bristol at 11 o'clock on the Monday, "forming a magnificent procession with their beautiful horses and handsome American carriages, which are not equalled by any other establishment in the kingdom." Morning performances were at two o'clock (i.e., in the afternoon), and evening entertainment was at half past seven. Mr. H. Rutley was agent in advance of the establishment. Select seats were two shillings; second seats were a shilling; and promenade was sixpence. The performers included Young Hernandez, Pauline Newsome, Mdlle. Sidoni, George Ryland, Eaton Stone, Mdlle. Rosalie (the equestrienne), Mr. Jem Newsome, the Brothers Elliott, "Mr. Arthur Barnes, the champion vaulter of the world." All this from the *Bristol Mercury* of September 2, 1854.

The *Flying Post* is our next guide, for Hernandez, Stone & Newsome's American Equestrian Establishment's three-day gig in Exeter. They entered town in a magnificent procession at 11 o'clock, and, at the building on Paris Street gave two performances each day, at 2:00 and 7:30, on Wednesday, Thursday, and Friday, September 13, 14, and 15, 1854. Mr. Arthur Barnes, the Champion Vaulter of the World, was still on the bill. The performances were good and were very much admired.

On September 23, 1854, at the Town Hall in Torquay, one J. Hack, Esq., traveling with the troupe, was charged with passing base coin. No one appeared in court to press the charge, and the case was dismissed.

The *Era* will be our guide now for the next few months. On Monday, October 9, the troupe opened in a splendid new building near the Octagon, at Union Street, Union Docks, Plymouth, and that night Arthur Barnes threw a new world record, of 94 somersaults. Their stay at Plymouth is also covered by the *Plymouth and Devonport Weekly Journal*. The day they came to Plymouth, Hengler's, who had opened there on October 2, for a 12-night run, was still playing there, at the Theatre Royal.

Hernandez, Stone and Newsome's Circus was nightly crowded. On October 24, 1854, the performances were under the patronage of Lord Hilton. On October 30, Wallett joined them for six nights. On November 7, Maj. Gen. Eden patronized the circus, and on November 9, Baronet Yarde-Buller did the same. By late November the circus was still there but business was dropping off. It was rumored that Wallett was coming back. Harry Brown, the clown, took his benefit on Friday evening, November 24, and had a bumper, every part of the spacious amphitheater being inconveniently crowded. Jem Newsome had his benefit on November 27, under the patronage of Charles Trelawny, Esq., and the gentlemen of the hunt, and Eaton Stone took his benefit on the night of Friday, December 1, under the patronage of the Freemasons.

The *Era* of December 3, 1854, announced that Monday, December 4, would begin the last week of the circus at Plymouth, and that they had received great support despite the economic slump. The paper then announced that Jersey was to be their next gig, but this was corrected in the December 10 issue of the magazine. Another famous clown is added to the list of players here — Tom Swann, the grotesque. On December 4 Hercules the French strongman made his first appearance, and this astounding act gave the circus a much-wanted boost. However, business was so unpredictable, on-again, off-again. Bill Barlow, the lion-horseman, left England in December, bound for Australia, where he would perform for years.

On December 22, 1854, Hernandez and Harry Brown (the clown) took a one-night trip over to Hengler's, which had opened at Queen Street, Exeter, on October 23, and Hernandez took a benefit there.

The *Era* of December 31, 1854, tells us: "Plymouth. The American Circus. This place of amusement has continued to have a good run of business. Yesterday (Saturday) night was to be the last of the season. The Christmas treat was entitled *Jeanette and Jeannot, or The Vagaries of Pierrot*. The piece was well got up and the seriously laughable extravaganza has excited the risible faculties of crowded houses. In accordance with a re-engagement, the French Hercules has been exhibiting his wonderful feats of strength."

The *Era* (still our guide for the next few months) of January 7, 1855, says: "Plymouth. American Circus. It is rather difficult to say whether this is to be the last week of the season, the 'last week' having been announced so often; but we expect it will be, the company being wanted to join those that are in Bath. The houses this week have been very fair."

So, while part of Hernandez and Stone's Circus was finishing up at Plymouth, the rest were setting up at Bath. It is difficult to say which place Arthur Barnes was at during this period — Plymouth or Bath. January 13 was the last day at Plymouth, and the entire American Circus were all together at Bath the week beginning Monday, January 15, 1855. However, quick cash always being of paramount importance for a proprietor, usually to be able to pay hard-pressing creditors or performers who would otherwise quit, Young Hernandez himself, as a solo act, opened in Dublin that night at Bell's American Circus (i.e., Richard Bell, Madame Isabelle's husband), at the Music Hall on Lower Abbey Street. He played for 12 nights, leaving Dublin on the 27th. It was at Bath that Hernandez, Stone, and Newsome sold their circus to Mr. E. T. Smith. Mr. Smith carried the tour on, with Eaton Stone managing the day-to-day affairs, but it was now called "E.T. Smith's Leviathan Equestrian Company, Originally Hernandez and Stone's." Jem Newsome and Hernandez stayed with them, as did Arthur Barnes, but they were already preparing to break away; Hernandez and Newsome were already forming their own circus.

The *Era* of January 28, 1855, tells us that Smith's new circus was on the eve of quitting Bath, when they would resume their equestrian performances in the Philharmonic Hall, in Manchester. But first they went to Birmingham, where, in February 1855, Arthur Barnes threw 95 somersaults for a new world record. We know that from an article in the March 3, 1855, edition of the *Manchester Times*, a paper which, with the *Era*, will show us the way now until the end of March.

On Saturday, February 24, 1855, E. T. Smith opened his Circus Royal, in conjunction with Pablo Fanque's troupe, to a crowded house at the newly renovated Philharmonic Hall, on Fountain Street, Manchester. They had quite a cast list opening night: Eaton Stone (who was also the manager); Pablo Fanque on his horses Albert and Beda (this was Pablo's first appearance in Manchester in four years); the Brothers Hemming (the great gymnastic clowns); Mr. Barnes, the champion vaulter of Europe; the celebrated Brothers Elliott; Harry Brown (the Shaksperian jester); and Mr. George Ryland, the Chinese juggler.

In the Philharmonic Hall ad for Smith's Circus Royal in the *Manchester Times* of February 28, 1855, Arthur Barnes does not appear in an otherwise very extensive and detailed list of the performers. That is because February 24 was his one and only night with Smith's in Manchester. Jem Newsome and Hernandez had finally broken away, formed a new cirque, at that time provisionally called Hernandez and Newsome's Circus, and had booked the Theatre Royal, to go head to head with Mr. Smith in Manchester.

The *Manchester Times* of February 28, 1855, ran an ad, "Theatre Royal, Manchester. Last night of the pantomime. This evening (Wednesday), February 28, 1855, for the benefit of Mr. Chambers [the treasurer of the theatre]. Tomorrow (Thursday) [i.e., March 1] will be produced a new equestrian spectacle entitled *Schamyl* [*The Prophet of the Caucasus*], after which a variety of entertainments in the Magic Ring, in which will appear Madame Pauline Newsome, Mademoiselle Rosalie, Mr. J. Newsome, the Brothers Elliott, Mr. A. Barnes, and Hernandez. Grotesque, Mr. T. Swann." The same day's paper, predicting for the morrow's advent of Newsome's at the Theatre Royal, says: "All this should bring good houses, in spite of bad weather and a whig [sic] ministry." At this time, Harry Walker was vaulting in Melbourne.

Actually, Hernandez & Newsome's were a day later in opening, as is borne out by the March 3, 1855, edition of the *Manchester Times*, which reported that last evening [i.e., March 2, 1855] "the equestrian company including the young Hernandez, with Mr. and Madame Newsome, commenced their engagement in the Theatre Royal." It goes on to say that "added to these clever performers we have also that extraordinary thrower of somersaults, Mr. A. Barnes, who, we understand, threw the other evening at Birmingham, the almost unbelievable number of 95." That same edition (March 3) of the *Manchester Times*, as well as the one on March 7, ran an ad, which says: "Theatre Royal, Manchester. Every evening, till further notice, the new equestrian spectacle *Schamyl*, after which a variety of entertainments in The Magic Ring, in which will appear Madame Pauline Newsome, Mademoiselle Rosalie, Mr. J. Newsome, Mr. A. Barnes, and Hernandez. Grotesque, Mr. T. Swann."

The *Manchester Times* of March 7, 1855, says: "Theatre Royal. The equestrian drama entitled *Schamyl*, with the gymnastic and other performances of the circle, including those of Hernandez, and Mr. and Mrs. Newsome, continue at the theatre. We hear that the old favorite piece, *Mazeppa*, is in preparation, and may be expected in a few days." The ad for the Theatre Royal, on March 7, lists Mr. A. Barnes on the bill.

The grand equestrian spectacle *Mazeppa* was finally produced on the evening of Saturday, March 10, 1855, and the show was concluded with new entertainments in the Magic Ring, in which appeared the celebrated troupe of Hernandez and Newsome. The performances of Friday evening, March 16, being for the benefit of the great and renowned Hernandez, commenced with *Mazeppa*, and, as usual, concluded with the scenes in the Magic Ring, by the first equestrian artistes of the day. For this night only, Mr. Harry Connor appeared for the first time these five years in conjunction with the Brothers Elliott and Arthur Barnes, in their extraordinary performances.

The following night, Saturday, March 17, 1855, was probably Arthur Barnes's last night with this cirque in Manchester. He isn't named individually after March 16, and he surely would have been if he had stayed longer, so it is likely that he took his leave of Manchester on Sunday the 18th, and went to Denmark. We know he was in Copenhagen by May, performing with Tom Hutchinson's summer circus in Copenhagen, and we don't pick him up anywhere else in the intervening two months, so our guess might be a pretty safe one.

Meanwhile, on the night of March 22, 1855, when a benefit was given for Jem and Pauline Newsome, the operatic drama *Rob Roy* was performed for the first time that season, with H. J. Wallack as Rob Roy, after which, of course, all new scenes in the Magic Circle. The *Manchester Times* of March 24, 1855, reviewed *Rob Roy*. The night of March 23, they were going to perform *Timour the Tartar*, one of the old melodramatic favorites, but *Rob Roy* had been so successful that they stuck with that instead, also playing it the following night. On Monday, the 26th, they performed *Mazeppa*; on the 27th it was *The Battle of Alma*; on the 28th, *Rob Roy* again; and on the 29th, *Guy Mannering*. Attendance was poor at the Theatre Royal, and despite changes, it got no better. Hernandez & Newsome's last night there was March 31, 1855, at which they produced *Guy Mannering*. Then it was on to the Theatre Royal, Sheffield. E. T. Smith's company, with Eaton Stone still managing, would outlast them in Manchester.

For the record, on April 1, 1855, a Sunday, Jem Newsome left Manchester, bound for Oldham and a five-night gig in conjunction with Pablo Fanque. The joint circus played in Oldham from April 2 to April 6, 1855. On April 4, Hernandez appeared with E. T. Smith's Drury Lane Equestrian Company in Manchester, and on April 14 that cirque came over to Sheffield and, for the first ever time, joined with the Newsome-Fanque combo, to open there that night, for a run that lasted until the 18th. A month later, on May 14, 1855, the same giant combo opened in Huddersfield. The cast included Eaton Stone, Richard Hemming (the incomparable horseman), Henri Hemino (i.e., Harry Hemming), George Ryland, Mons. Zamezou and pupil, Roussell du Nord, Mdlle. Jenny Hemino, Mdlle. Zamezou, Harry Brown (the clown), James Hemming, Mons. Parisoni, and Mr. Nelson. Then the giant combo split up into its original two components. Newsome-Fanque played Holmfirth (May 21, 1855), Meltham (May 23, 1855), and Honley (May 24, 1855). In the meantime, E. T. Smith's Drury Lane Company opened at Sheffield for the Whitsun holidays. They would stay there until the last day of May. Incidentally, on May 16, 1855, Lavater Lee arrived in the United States.

The *Era* of June 3, 1855, tells us that the Royal Tivoli Gardens in Copenhagen opened its doors on Sunday, May 27, 1855. The weather was anything but serene. Harry Connor was there, as was John Milton Hengler. "The pantomime company, under Herr A. Price's direction, is an improvement worthy of notice on last year." It then says that Mdlle. Petoletti [sic] made a lively Columbine. It is certainly tempting to think that this Mdlle. Petoletti might be Alexine, Arthur Barnes's wife, but it could be his daughter, Alexine Caroline, who had just turned three. The same paper goes on to say "Copenhagen. The Victoria Rotundo. Unless witnessed, no just idea can be formed of the surprising and wonderful feats displayed by Messrs. Hutchinson (proprietors), Mr. A. Barnes (champion vaulter), Brothers Elliott (la perche), and George Thompson, the graceful bottle equilibrist. We feel confident, when they are once seen, nothing can prevent them from being classed, by every judge, at the head of their profession, which they certainly are." While Barnes and the Elliotts continued on at the Tivoli, the Brothers Hutchinson took a troupe over to Sweden for a short visit.

The *Era* of July 8, 1855, says: "Royal Tivoli Gardens [Copenhagen]. The talented Mr. A. Barnes and the Brothers Elliott, who have been added to the general company, together with Mr. Conner [sic] and sons ... are becoming great favorites, and deservedly." The King of Denmark was a patron on June 6. The August 26, 1855, *Era* says, of the Tivoli Gardens, "Messrs. Elliott have concluded their engagement, and also Mr. Barnes, they have left for England." However, this is an undated report from the *Era*'s Danish correspondent, so we have no idea precisely when Arthur Barnes returned home. The said Danish correspondent, in another article in the *Era* of August 26, says: "After giving five performances in the Victoria Pavilion, the Brothers Hutchinson left for Hobro," presumably sans Barnes and the Elliott Brothers. The report also tells us that Tom Hutchinson was planning to retire after that summer.

E. T. Smith's Drury Lane Company were in Wolverhampton from June 18 to the end of the month, and, on July 3, 1855, billed as "Hernandez and Stone's Circus, Under the Proprietorship of Mr. E.T. Smith," they opened at Worcester. On July 7, 1855, they left Worcester, and on the 9th were in Oxford. But the internal dissensions within this cirque were so great that something had to give, and in August 1855 Arthur Nelson, the famous clown, took over the management of E. T. Smith's Royal Circus. They were in Maidstone by this time, and they continued to gig, on August 20, 1855, opening at Canterbury. By the end of the month they were in Margate, where they remained until September 3, when they went to Ramsgate.

It looks as if Arthur Barnes's next date, after coming back from Copenhagen, was with William Cooke's Circus at Astley's New Royal Arts Amphitheatre, London, on September 17, 1855. The *Era* of September 16, 1855, says: "On Monday, Sept. 17, last 6 nights of 'Mazeppa and the Wild Horse.' After which, the acts in the arena introducing Mr. Arthur Barnes, the Champion Vaulter, who has accomplished the daring feat of throwing 95 somersaults in succession. He will be assisted by the Bros Elliot and an entire troupe of premier voltigeurs." The *Morning Post* of September 17 confirmed that Barnes opened at Astley's that evening, but then they ran exactly the same ad every day for the rest of the week. Barnes was still at Astley's for the week beginning Monday, September 24, 1855, as testified to in the above newspapers (all the ads, in all the papers for this second week, refer to him merely as "The Champion Vaulter"— no name, as do the ads in the succeeding week). The *Morning Chronicle* of September 25, 1855, reviewed the previous night's performance, which was the debut of the great spectacle *The Fall of Sebastopol*, written by J. H. Stocqueler. In the *Era* of September 30 Arthur Barnes is referred to as "The Champion Vaulter" again. The Astley's ads from October 6 onward refer to "a variety of other entertainments," and the weeks after that "with other entertainments." However, notwithstanding the diminution of his prominence in the press, Arthur Barnes was still definitely still at Astley's.

Something interesting here. The New Royal Surrey Theatre (lessees: Richard Shepperd and Mr. Creswick) had opened in London for the season on September 17, 1855, with Shakspere's *Henry IV*. The show concluded with *Sam Patch, the Yankee in France*, starring American comedian, J. H. McVicker. From September 21 to the 24th, the theater was closed on account of John Shepperd, Richard's brother, having been accidentally shot by Mr. Creswick. The *Era* of September 30, 1855, tells us that opening at the Surrey on Monday,

October 1, 1855, and running for the week, was a Parisian drama in three acts, entitled *The Flower Girl*, or *The Convict Marquis*. Supported by Mr. J. H. Rickards, C. A. Calvert, Vollaire, Morgan, Norman, and Widdicomb; Miss Marriott; Miss E. Sanders; and Mrs. Woollidge. This was followed by an original American drama called *Emigration*, or *Home in the West*, written specifically for Mr. M'Vicker. Finally, there was presented the ballet *Perequillo*, or *Terror in a Tub*, supported by Madame Auriole, Mr. Flexmore, Mr. A. Barnes, and a numerous Corps de Ballet. However, this "Mr. A. Barnes" is not Arthur Barnes. Arthur Barnes remained at Astley's. The *Daily News* of October 3 and 4, 1855 (and other dates too), ran a small ad: "Surrey. This evening. *The Flower Girl*, Messrs. C.A. Calvert, Rickards, Miss Marriott and Miss Emily Sanders; *Emigration*— Mr. M'Vicker — and *Perequillo*; Messrs. Flexmore and A. Barnes; Madame Auriole. Doors open at 6." Portions of this show were changed, but Barnes, Flexmore, and Mme. Auriole made their last appearance (in the ballet, *The Spanish Dancers*, or *Two Lovers Too Many*) on Saturday, October 27, 1855. This mysterious "Mr. A. Barnes" appears quite often in ads of this period.

As a matter of incidence, Young Hernandez left for New York on the *Ericsson* on October 19, 1855, along with George Ryland and Richard Hemming. The *Era* of November 19, 1855, referring to Monday night, November 12, at Astley's, says: "and the somersaults of Mr. Arthur Barnes, who turned sixty with an ease and dexterity which was really astonishing." Clementine Soullier, the equestrienne, who had come to England in April 1851, from Paris, was now the main attraction of this cirque. Chatteris Jackson and Jem Thorne were the clowns performing with them.

On Weds., November 14, 1855, they threw a benefit at the Strand Theatre for Mr. Edward Stirling, of the Theatre Royal, Drury Lane. Tom Matthews (John Thomas Matthews; 1805 — 89) and Mr. Flexmore, the great clowns, took part, as did Mr. A. Barnes, Mdlle. Auriol, and the Strand Ballet Company, all of whom took part in the act called the *Dancing Scotchman* (*Era*, November 11, 1855). Richard Flexmore Geatter, an agile, inventive clown with a notoriously hoarse voice and risqué delivery, and Mdlle. Francisca Christophera Auriol had married in 1849. Flexmore died in Lambeth on August 20, 1860, from strain of work, and his widow died in 1862, aged 33. Again, this "Mr. A. Barnes" is not Arthur Barnes, who was still at Astley's on December 17, as testified to by a playbill of that date, which lists "Mr. Arthur Barnes, equestrian." On December 20, 1855, Edward Murray had his benefit at the Strand Theatre. A Mr. Barnes performed at it. Again, not our man. Meanwhile, in Boston, George Ryland was performing at the National, with Colonel Joseph Cushing's New York Circus, along with Hernandez, Rose Madigan, Joe Pentland, and Felix Carlo.

Meanwhile, back in the slum of Masons Place, whence the Acrobat had sprung, things were happening, as things always happen, even in a squalid byway. Henry Barns, the old man, had been blinded in a foundry accident and couldn't work any more, poor bugger. He would continue to live in the brick tenement at No. 25, which would always remain the family home, so to speak. Mary Ann and Jane, the Acrobat's sisters, continued to live with the aging parents, as did Richard. Henry, the Acrobat's elder brother, still grinding away in the foundry, had begun to produce a family at various houses in Masons Place.

America

In 1855, Isaac Van Amburgh, the American showman and circus man, was in Europe recruiting talent for a company he worked for. This company, Raymond & Co., was owned by Chauncey R. Weeks (born 1812), of Carmel, New York, and Hyatt Frost, and they were, somewhat unsurprisingly, in the circus business to make money. The name Raymond comes from James Raymond who, a few years earlier, had been the leading animal show impresario in the United States. Chauncey Weeks was Raymond's son-in-law. They had two American circuses, Van Amburgh's and Driesbach's, and they sent Van Amburgh over to Europe to stock both with the world's best acts for the 1856 U.S. season. The two circus men, Van Amburgh and Driesbach, would open as one big circus in Cincinnati in April, then take both circuses separately on the road for a summer tour. Van Amburgh made a deal with the great British circus proprietor, William Cooke. Cooke was about to present a series of shows at Astley's that did not really require Arthur Barnes and several other acts, so a lend-lease sort of deal was cut with Van Amburgh, whereby Henry Cooke would take a small party out to play with the Van Amburgh-Driesbach outfit for the summer. Arthur Barnes was one of them.

Herr Jacob Driesbach, born on November 2, 1807, in Sharon, New York, was not a German at all, although everyone thought he was. It was his grandfather, who had come over to the United States, who was the German. Jacob, indeed never left the States. In the meantime he became a lion tamer, like Van Amburgh, and worked with Cooke's in the 1830s, as well as other big circuses. By the 1850s he was primarily an animal presenter.

On February 22, 1856, Michael McCarthy (i.e., John Macarte) died at his home in Ipswich. He was 29. That month, Arthur Barnes left Astley's, prepared to go to the United States as part of the group known as the Cooke Family, led by Henry Cooke and his two sons, John Henry Cooke and Louis Cooke. The troupe also included Eaton Stone, the Jameson Family (otherwise known as the Zamezous), the Worrells, Harry Crouette (a clown, really Henry Crowhurst, aged 23, from Lambeth originally) and Den Stone (clown), Mlle. Zamezou (the rider, who burst 45 balloons at full speed), the Francisco Brothers (gymnasts from Paris), and others. Arthur Barnes left Cowes on March 12, 1856, on the U.S. mail steamer *Fulton*, Captain James Wotton commanding, and after a tedious journey of 17 days arrived in New York in the morning of March 29, 1856, bringing the second edition of the London *Times* of March 12. Arthur Barnes, traveling in the forward cabin, is listed on the ship's manifest as 28, an artist, from England, bound for the United States. The *Cincinnati Daily Commercial* of March 22, 1856, mentions their voyage.

Meanwhile, on March 24, 1856, while Arthur Barnes was mid-Atlantic, Harry Connor opened at John Byrne's Mammoth Concert Hall and City Tavern, on Capel Street, in Dublin. *Freeman's Journal* of March 20 advertises him as the "world-famed Professor O'Connor and his extraordinary sons." This Dublin paper tells us that "Professor O'Connor" is engaged direct from Astley's, and will introduce his incomparable feat of throwing 60 somersaults from a spring board, for which he was presented with a large and handsome gold medal by Mr. W. Batty and a silver snuffbox by Mr. Wm. Cooke. Harry was still there on May 19, still with the name O'Connor.

The *Cincinnati Daily Commercial* mentions the American circus again on March 29, and on April 5 Arthur Barnes is mentioned as the gymnast from England, the 100-somersault man. He is also one of the troupe advertised in the same paper of April 8. The wonderful old church of St. Peter's, in Liverpool, is gone now, has been gone for decades, and is now a kitsch shopping mall, but on April 8, 1856, the baptism took place there of Sarah Louisa, the youngest daughter of Arthur Barnes's old employer, Edwin Hughes.

The combined Van Amburgh-Driesbach show opened in Cincinnati on Monday, April 14, 1856, the same day Mlle. Rosalie died in Cheltenham as the result of injuries after falling off her horse. The American ring was carpeted instead of the old fashioned method of filling it with sawdust and tanbark. Prices were 50 cents for a reserved box seat, and general admission (where one stood) was a quarter. These prices were considered astonishingly high (*Cincinnati Daily Commercial*, April 14, 1856), but despite that, at least 6,000 people attended (according to the same paper of April 15, 1856). They played through the 26th of the month, and then got ready for the summer tour, as two separate circuses. It was Driesbach's that Arthur Barnes went with. Van Amburgh's followed a different itinerary, and consisted of the Cookes, the Franciscos, Le Jeune Louis (the most classical equestrian of the age), Frank Carpenter (the daring bareback rider), Den Stone and Harry Croueste (the clowns).

The Driesbach circus was actually known as Herr Driesbach's Grand Consolidated Circus and Menagerie. It was owned by Chauncey R. Weeks and Ira W. Gregory. The manager was B. Kipp, and the agent was G. I. Eaton. For the tour, we are indebted, with certain reservations, to Stuart Thayer's book, *Annals of the American Circus*.

The *Scioto Daily Gazette* (Ohio) of April 19, 1856 says, "We learn from the *Zanesville Aurora* that Herr Driesbach and his menagerie will visit that city about the first of May. Wonder if the elephant will make its appearance in our city [i.e., Chillicothe] this summer." The same paper of April 29, 1856, says: "Herr Driesbach, the 'Lion King,' got married two or three years ago, and became a farmer in Ohio. The other day, he visited — at Zanesville, where they have been wintered — his pet animals, which had not seen him for more than two years and (with one exception) they appeared to recognize him; and those which had been his especial favorites became jealous of the caresses he bestowed upon the others." They did, indeed, open the tour in Zanesville on May 1, one of several American circus troupes zigzagging the country. Indeed, two of those other circuses were featuring Madame Isabelle and Lavater Lee.

Their next gig was Mt. Vernon, Ohio, on May 5, 1856. That was the Monday Levi North's Circus left Milwaukee on its summer tour, a circus that comprised Tony Pastor, the comedian, James McFarland, the tightrope walker, and Mr. Tinkham, "the greatest double somerset thrower in the world." Then, for Driesbach's, it was on to Belleville, Ohio (May 6, 1856), Mansfield, Ohio (May 7, 1856), and Gallion, Ohio (May 8, 1856). On that day, at 8:00 in the morning Southampton time, Alexine and her daughter Alexine, left on the *Fulton*, bound for New York. For the acrobatic husband it was on to Bucyrus, Ohio (May 9, 1856), and Tiffin, Ohio (May 10, 1856).

That day, May 10, 1856, a Saturday, as Van Amburgh's was traveling from Brownsville to Newark, Hannibal the elephant's keeper fell in a fit from his horse. The whole menagerie immediately came to a halt, and some members of the company went forward to pick up the man. But the elephant would not allow any person to approach the senseless form of his keeper. Taking him up with his trunk, softly, he went to place him back on his horse, but finding that the man was senseless, he laid him on the ground, and kept watch over him. Many members of the menagerie tried to soothe the faithful elephant, who had now become furious at what he thought was the death of his master, but to no purpose, and there the man lay, watched by the sagacious animal. After the man had been lying in this condition for some time, a physician, who had been sent for, arrived, and yet the elephant would allow no one to approach. At length, the keeper became so far conscious as to command the elephant to let the physician come near. The animal was docile and obedient in a moment, and the keeper was properly cared for — Hannibal all the while expressing the utmost anxiety for the sick man. The papers all over the country loved that one.

For Driesbach's it was on to Fremont, Ohio (May 12, 1856), Maumee, Ohio (May 13, 1856), and Toledo (May 14, 1856). Then it was over into Michigan, for Blissfield (May 15, 1856), Adrian (May 16, 1856), Tecumseh (May 17, 1856), and Ypsilanti (May 20, 1856). Only the previous day, the lady who performed the feat of walking up the wire at Myers' Circus, then in Woonsocket, was blown off by a gust of wind, falling 30 feet, and fracturing three ribs. That day, and the following day, Van Amburgh's part of the circus opened in Cleveland. They had to turn away 2,000 persons that first night. For Driesbach's it was on to Dearborn, Michigan (May 21, 1856), and then to Detroit, where they played Cass Park for two nights, May 22 and 23, 1856. At 4:30, on May 21, the Acrobat's wife and child arrived in New York from Southampton, on the *Fulton*. Also on board was the notorious James Gordon Bennett, proprietor of the *New York Herald*, with dispatches from Paris. On the following morning the passengers were discharged into New York. The Acrobat's wife is listed in the manifest as Madame Barnes, aged 30, living in England, born in Denmark. In tow is Alexine Barnes, aged 3, born in England. The *Herald* printed a list of the passengers, including "Madame Barnes and child." It is obvious that they were there to join Arthur Barnes, but, as for their movements in the United States, this remains a mystery.

Then it was on to Mt. Clements (May 24, 1856), St. Clair (May 26, 1856), and Port Huron (May 27, 1856). A nine-year-old lad living in Port Huron at that time was Thomas Alva Edison. For the cirque, it was on to Romeo (May 28, 1856), Pontiac (May 29, 1856), Milford (May 30, 1856), Howell (May 31, 1856), Ann Arbor (June 2, 1856), Dexter (June 3, 1856), Jackson (June 4, 1856), Albion (June 5, 1856), Marshall (June 5, 1856), Battle Creek (June 7, 1856), and Kalamazoo (June 9, 1856).

Then on into Indiana: First the town of Goshen on June 12. The *Goshen Democrat*, Indiana, of May 28, 1856, advertised the coming of Driesbach's, and tells of European and American stars, and goes on to say, "Arthur Barnes. The champion vaulter and 100 somerset man. No other gymnast has ever approached this extraordinary phenomenon of the 19th century." There's also a bill, from Kewanee, Illinois, advertising Driesbach's, and its European and American stars, and the name Arthur Barnes is in big lettering. It reiterates, word for word, the Goshen blurb.

The roster for this circus, culled from the *Goshen Democrat*, lists Arthur Barnes as an acrobat. Other acts were Herr Driesbach, the lion tamer; the riders Sophia Worrell, Irene Worrell, Jennie Worrell, and Charles Walters; the acrobats The Jamieson Family; William Worrell and Tom Burgess, the clowns; Davis and Howard, perch act; Prof. Robjohn, airship (which was actually a cigar-shaped balloon with a carriage underneath). Goshen was one of the many towns visited during this tour, and this is one of the many examples of local newspaper blurb. The *Michigan Argus* of May 30, 1856, printed in Ann Arbor, tells of Arthur Barnes on page three.

From Goshen it was on to South Bend (June 13, 1856), back over into Michigan for the gig at the town of Niles on June 14, then back into Indiana, for the performance at La Porte. The June 28, 1856, issue of the *New York*

Clipper tells us, "Professor and [sic] Arthur Barnes give specimens of the English style of riding." This quote refers to La Porte, Indiana, where Driesbach's played on June 16, 1856.

Then on to Valparaiso, Indiana (June 17, 1856), and on into Illinois, for gigs at Joliet (June 20, 1856), Wilmington (June 21, 1856), Morris (June 23, 1856), Ottawa (June 24, 1856), LaSalle (June 25, 1856), and, on July 2, 1856, Chicago. On July 1, 1856, Bill Dale opened with Madigan & Co.'s Great National Circus in Cleveland. Dale had left Liverpool with Wallett, and returned to the United States on February 22, 1855. He was with the Crescent City Circus, and the *Mississippian* of February 26, 1856, reports on that establishment's southern tour of the United States. He is referred to as W. O. Dale, the company's principal equestrian, the finest rider of the age, and the 100-Somerset Man. So, Arthur Barnes was not the only one being thus billed. Hiram Franklin was appearing with Rowe's Circus in San Francisco in March 1857. Joseph A. Rowe and James Hernandez were the equestrian stars.

On July 7, 1856, Driesbach's played Waukegan, and then it was into Wisconsin, where they played Kenosha on July 8, only four days after a German with the unlikely name of John Reynolds had had his head blown off by a cannon during the Fourth of July celebrations. For Driesbach's, it was on to Racine on the 9th. That very day, in Racine, King Strang, the renegade Mormon prophet, died, not as a result of seeing the circus, but from shots he had received two weeks before on Beaver Island. Arthur Barnes then played Milwaukee on the 10th and 11th. From June 23, 1856, the *Milwaukee Sentinel* had been running an ad for the upcoming attraction, and now it was here. The ad ran:

> Herr Driesbach & Co's Great Colossal Consolidated Circus and Menagerie. The most extensive traveling exhibition of the age. A double troupe! of equestrians, acrobats & voltigeurs, and a collection of rare and beautiful animals, selected by special agents to Europe, Asia, Africa, and America, among which may be found the only living giraffe in America, will exhibit at Milwaukee on Thursday and Friday, July 10 and 11 at 2:30 and 7:30 p.m. Admittance to the whole exhibition under one mammoth canvass [sic], Boxes 50 cents, children 25 cents, Pit 25 cents. Among the artists of the equestrian and gymnastic departments are the following unexampled array of the first of their profession: M'lle Zamezou, late premiere equestrienne from the Cirque Nationale, Paris; Eaton Stone, the great champion bare-back rider; W.H. Stout, the brilliant four and six horse equestrian; B. Stevens, the daring and classic principal horseman; Arthur Barnes, the great English vaulter and 100 somerset man; the Jamieson family, whose Antipodean and Grecian feats have never been approached by any other artists; C. Walters, the daring gymnast and dashing equestrian; W. Davis, the extraordinary Perche performer; the Juvenile Graces, Irene, Sophia, and Jennie, three beautiful disciples of the goddess Terpsichore; Mr. W. Worrell, emphatically the

clown of the age, the most original wit and humorist in the country; T. Burgess, the famous Western jester; and a complete troupe of voltigeurs, dramatists, and pantomimists. The brilliant cortege will parade town upon the morning of the day of the exhibition, preceded by Herr Niebuhr's Military Band. The world renowned lion tamer, Herr Driesbach, will close each performance by entering the cages, and performing with his trained lions, tigers, and leopards. During the month the company will exhibit in most of the principal places of Wisconsin.

On July 14, 1856, they played in Oconomowoc, on the 15th in Watertown, on the 16th in Horicon, on the 17th in Waupun, on the 18th in Fond du Lac, and on the 19th in Berlin, Wisconsin. On July 22 it was in Ripon, and on July 23 in Kingston, still in Wisconsin. On July 24 they played Beaver Dam, and on the 26th performed in the state capital of Madison. Still in Wisconsin, they played Janesville on July 29 and Beloit on the 30th. On July 31, they were back in Illinois, at Belvidere, and on August 6, 1856, they played Galena.

The next day they played Dubuque, Iowa, very close by, and then into another neighboring town on the 8th, Platteville, Wisconsin. On August 9 they played Potosi, Wisconsin, and on the 12th, Tipton, Iowa. They were in Davenport on August 15 (*Davenport Daily Gazette* of August 2, 1856, and every other day until the event), and Fairfield, Iowa, on the 23rd. Still in Iowa, they played Mt. Pleasant (August 25, 1856), New London (August 26, 1856), and Burlington on the 27th. On August 27, 1856, the Royal Mail Steamship *Canada* left Boston Harbor, bound for Halifax, leaving there the next day bound for Liverpool, with 86 passengers on board, including "Mrs. Barnes and child." They pulled into the Mersey on September 6. One does not know if this was Alexine and her daughter, but another explanation offers itself shortly.

Driesbach's Circus was back in Illinois on September 1, 1856, at Greenbush, in the southeast corner of Warren County. After Greenbush, they traveled the 20 miles south to Macomb, in McDonough County, for the September 2 gig. Then it was on to Augusta, Hancock County, for the performance of September 3; then Quincy (September 5, 1856), the next town of any significance on the banks of the Mississippi south of Keokuk, Iowa; then down the river all the way to Belleville for the night of the 6th. On the Sunday they made the short hop from Belleville over to St. Louis, where they opened on September 8, 1856. There were a lot of people living in St. Louis at that time, most of whom went to see the show over its six-day run there. There was a family named Grant, just moved into their farm named Hardscrabble, the husband being a fairly recently retired Army captain, and the wife, Julia, just having had a daughter. One likes to think they were among the audience one of those nights. It would have done the captain good to take a break from his worries, how he was going to support his family, how he was going to shuck off a drinking problem, what the future held for him.

The circus closed in St. Louis on September 13th, 1856, and on the 16th was playing in Peoria, Illinois. On the 20th, they were in Kewanee, still in Illinois. There is a bill from Kewanee advertising Driesbach's and its European and American stars, and the name Arthur Barnes is in big lettering. It says "The champion vaulter and 100 somerset man. No other gymnast has ever approached this phenomenon of the 19th century." After Kewanee, they made their way back through Peoria, to Bloomington, Illinois, where they played on September 30, 1856.

On September 22, 1856, while the circus was making its way to Bloomington, Welch & Lent's combined circus was playing at Buffalo, New York, just before heading out to Cleveland, Ohio. Hiram Franklin threw "57 somersets in succession, with a grace that appeared to be effortless" (*Daily Cleveland Herald*, of September 23, 1856, copying from the Buffalo *Republic*).

Arthur Barnes next performed in Decatur, Illinois, on October 2, 1856 (see the regular ad in the *Illinois State Chronicle* of that date), then they crossed into Indiana, playing the town of Lafayette, on the bend of the Wabash, on October 9. From there they made their way up the Wabash, back to the Illinois line to the major Indiana town of Terre Haute, for the October 16 gig. On the 21st and 22nd of October, 1856, they played the state capital of Illinois. It's fascinating to think that during their two-day run in Springfield, the entire citizenry of that town must have turned out to see them. One of the citizens, by nature more curious than most, was a lawyer, then only four years or so away from the presidency of the United States. The immense backward and forward traveling between states was grueling, to say the least. Better planning would have yielded less gruel.

And less gruel they got. On October 24 they were in Jacksonville, Illinois, and the following day in Winchester, same state. On October 28 they played Carrollton, on Thursday the 30th in Alton, Illinois (see the *Alton Weekly Courier* of October 23, 1856, for the usual big ad. They even ran the ad again on November 6, when it was all over), and then on November 3 they returned to their headquarters in St. Louis, just in time to see James Buchanan become 15th president of the United States. Meanwhile, back in England, on that day, November 3, 1856, Chatteris Jackson, the clown, opened with Hengler's in Chester. On December 20, Hengler's would open in Bradford. Jem Frowde was with Hengler's at this time. Driesbach's were in St. Louis for an eleven-day stay, leaving there on the 13th. On November 29, 1856, they opened in Cincinnati, joining together with Van Amburgh's in Cincinnati for a combined winter show. The animals were wintered in the building opposite the Police Court on 9th Street.

The winter show closed in Cincinnati on January 3, 1857, and Chauncey Weeks sold his interest in Raymond & Co. to Hyatt Frost. Madame Celeste, while playing on stage in the pantomime at the Adelphi, in London, on February 20, 1857, was seized with a severe illness. She would not emerge until April 14. On March 26, 1857, Tom Barry, the clown, died after a lingering illness. Only the night before, they had held a benefit for old Tom at Astley's.

On April 15 the Cunard Royal Mail steamship *Asia* left New York bound for Liverpool, with 124 passengers, under the command of Capt. Edward G. Lott. On board were a "Mr. and Mrs. Barnes and child, New York." After encountering adverse easterly winds nearly the entire voyage, the *Asia* arrived off Holyhead at 12:45 p.m., on April 27, and docked in Liverpool on Tuesday, April 28.

One does not know when Arthur Barnes returned to England, so this mention of "Mr. and Mrs. Barnes and child, New York" may be the Barnes family, although the term "New York" is somewhat off-putting. However, if it is them, or if the earlier reference to "Mrs. Barnes and child" on the *Canada* is relevant, then the daughter did not die in the United States. But then again, neither reference may be relevant, in which case the girl may well have died in the United States. We never pick her up again, ever, not for certain we don't (however, more possible sightings will be presented shortly), and she was dead by 1877 (when the Acrobat named another of his daughters Alexine), and almost certainly by 1871 (she does not appear in the census of that year, and, unfortunately, we do not find the family at all in the 1861 census). She is also not in the Acrobat's will. She did not die in England or Wales, that's for sure, so, if she did make it back to England during or after the Acrobat's American tour, then she probably died in Europe in the late 50s or sometime in the 60s, best bets Copenhagen, Paris, or Spain.

The Hengler Years

On May 11, 1857, Arthur Barnes began a long on-again, off-again association with Hengler's Grand Cirque Variete, which lasted until 1864. On that day he opened with Hengler's, at Dale Street, Liverpool. For his stay with Hengler's in that great city, we are grateful to the *Era* and to the *Liverpool Mercury*. The *Mercury* of May 4, 1857, says: "Mr. Arthur Barnes, the great English champion vaulter of the world, having just arrived from the United States, where he totally eclipsed all competitors, has been engaged by Mr. C. Hengler for a limited period, and will have the honour of making his first appearance in the course of a few days." Over the next few weeks, the *Mercury* repeatedly advertised "Mr. Arthur Barnes, the great English champion vaulter of the world." Already playing with Hengler's when Arthur Barnes arrived were the Bedouin Arabs.

Howes and Cushing's Great United States Circus was fitted out in New York expressly to travel in England, left New York on March 25, 1857, aboard the chartered packet *Southampton*, and arrived in Liverpool on April 24, 1857. They went straight into performance at Liverpool, on the site of the late Islington Market, on April 30, and would wrap up there on May 16, 1857, before moving on to St. Helens on the 18th to begin a grinding tour of the provinces. On Monday, May 11, the same night Arthur Barnes opened with Hengler's, the star attraction for that last week with Howes and Cushing's also opened at the American circus, James Robinson, the champion trick rider of America. Rose Madigan, the equestrienne, was performing with Howes and Cushing's at this time, as were George Batchelder, the vaulter, Jim Myers, the clown, and Joe Pentland. By July, the Bedouin Arabs would also be with them.

The *Era* of May 17, 1857, tells us, of Hengler's, "The circus enjoys a well-earned celebrity, were it for nothing but the opportunity afforded the public of witnessing the incredible feats of the Bedouin Arabs, whose performances are little short of miraculous. The gymnastic exertions of these acrobats are unsurpassed by any artiste, and their feats of strength and agility are as novel as they are amazing. A re-engagement of one week more has been effected. Mr. Arthur Barnes, 'The Champion Vaulter,' has also met with great success." On May 16, 1857, at Drury Lane, an equestrian group opened for a short engagement there. It consisted of Mr. Wallett, Miss Ella, Mr. Swann, and Mr. Newsome.

The *Era* of May 24, 1857, tells us that Hengler's were still at Liverpool, doing *The Rigs of Mr. Briggs*. It says, "Mr. Arthur Barnes, the champion vaulter, and Mme. Cariot, the graceful, daring equestrienne, are still attached to the company," and it goes on to tell us that on Monday, May 25, Herr Hengler, the tightrope dancer, will be added, and John Milton Hengler, on his way from America. "Business continues excellent."

The *Liverpool Mercury* of May 29, 1857, calls Arthur Barnes "the champion of summersault throwing." He also appears billed in the *Mercury* ads of June 1 and June 3, June 5 and June 22. The *Mercury* of June 24, 1857, informs us that "The great somersault champion, Mr. Arthur Barnes, assisted by the entire corps des artistes, will appear in an extraordinary performance entitled *Le Grande Voltege* [sic]." The spelling mistake was corrected by the June 26 edition.

Throughout June the circus was still at Dale Street, and Arthur Barnes was still with them. The circus performed nightly and daily, but after June the day performances were continued only on Wednesdays and Saturdays. In mid-June, Wallett the clown and the Delavantis (John and George, acrobats and clowns) joined the circus as star attractions. In the meantime, on July 1, 1857, the day the troupe appeared at the zoological gardens for the Licensed Victuallers' Annual Soiree and Ball, Harry Connor was awarded a silver snuffbox by William Cooke (then lessee at Astley's) for doing 80 somersaults.

The *Illustrated London News* ran an ad in July 1857, which says

> Hengler's Grand Cirque Variete, Liverpool. Enthusiastic and brilliant reception of the Prince of Tightrope Artistes, Young Hengler, in consequence of which he will go through his unrivalled performance every evening next week in conjunction with the greatest equestrians in Europe, and the champion of Summersault throwers, Mr. Arthur Barnes. Monday next (July 6), the last night but eight of the season, is fixed for the complimentary benefit of Mr. Charles Hengler, the proprietor, and which will take place under the patronage of the leading professional and mercantile gentlemen of Liverpool.

On that very day, July 6, Howes and Cushing's American Circus opened in Nottingham, where they would also play the next day before moving on to Loughborough, Leicester, Rugby, and Northampton on successive nights.

Mr. Powell took his benefit at Hengler's on July 7, 1857, and July 13, 14, and 15 were the last three days at Dale Street before the vacation. The theater would be redecorated, ready for September. They closed at Dale Street on July 15, 1857, and took to the road.

On July 17 and 18, 1857, Hengler's (with Arthur Barnes) played in Chester (*Cheshire Observer and General Advertiser*, July 11, 1857). They gave two performances each day, at two and seven o'clock. Their entry into the city on the 17th was described by the paper on the 18th. The expectation of seeing the company with their splendid stud of horses drew together a large crowd of people in the main thoroughfares of the city, and shortly after one o'clock their wishes were gratified by the appearance of the procession. The cavalcade was headed by a carriage, conveying an excellent band of musicians, who played a variety of popular airs in their progress through the streets. The procession was formed of a number of profusely decorated carriages and vans, having upon their ends and sides paintings illustrative of scenes in the circus, chariot driving and gymnastic feats; the carriages were drawn, some by four, and others by six and eight horses, and one vehicle had eight pretty little ponies harnessed to it. The rear was brought up by a richly gilt and handsomely ornamented car, drawn by four white steeds carrying bells on their collars. The performances in the evening, which took place in a commodious pavilion erected at the Linen Hall, were well attended and met with great and deserved success. The entertainment, which included all the usual circus feats of horsemanship, vaulting, leaping, etc., were enlivened by the jokes of the clowns, of whom there were three attached to Mr. Hengler's company. "As it is the intention of the exhibitors to proceed to Wrexham on Monday, we would advise all who wish to witness an excellent entertainment not to miss the opportunity of visiting the circus, at either of the performances given this day."

The attendance on the first evening was the best, it falling off on the second night. On July 19, 1857, a Sunday, Hengler's Mammoth Circus and Great Equestrian Exhibition traveled to Wrexham, opening there on July 20. This from the *Wrexham and Denbigh Weekly Advertiser* of July 25, 1857: "Hengler's celebrated troupe of artistes visited Wrexham on Monday night last, and drew a very large company. Their marquee, which is a large and beautiful one, was erected in the field adjoining the Cock Inn on the Holt Road." The article goes on to say that it was "very nearly filled, there not being less than 1000 persons present we should say." In addition to the ordinary equestrian feats and extraordinary vaulting, there were some wonderful feats done on the tightrope and a perpendicular pole. Young Hengler's performances on the former were certainly the most daring and clever which the reporter ever witnessed, and in his opinion fully justified the high encomiums which had been passed on Hernandez by the press, both in this country and in America. Young Hengler walked the rope without a pole or anything to balance himself with as much ease and grace as an ordinary person would upon the flag pavement of High Street. He then leaped through a hoop twice at a bound to the utter amazement and astonishment of the company, which greeted the feat with a hearty burst of applause. As a coup de grace to the wonderful performance he effected a summersault with as much ease and certainty as most persons would on terra firma. "The effort must be seen to be appreciated, for some of them are almost incredible." Another gentleman, whose name the reporter did not learn, literally ran up a perpendicular pole some nine or ten yards in height like a monkey, and with as much agility. The pole was balanced by another person, and the daring climber, when upon the top, actually swung on it, first by one leg and then by one arm. This feat was concluded by a rapid descent down the pole head foremost, to the consternation of all the old maids and timid bachelors in the company, who expected that death would have been the result. "We need hardly say that their fears were quite groundless in this respect." Altogether, the performances were of the very first class in this department of gymnastics, and the equestrianism was equally as good. The only thing to regret was that from some cause there were no ladies in the company, which certainly in the eyes of the gentlemen, to a certain extent, diminished the attraction. In other respects the entertainment was perfect.

The day Hengler's was playing Wrexham, Wallett was giving a miscellaneous entertainment at the Trent Bridge Cricket Ground in Nottingham. Despite a gloomy day which brought out fewer people than anticipated, those who came were privileged to see the highlight of the entertainments, Signora Delavanti ascending, with considerable ease and fearlessness, an inclined rope of considerable altitude. Wallett would repeat his entertainments there on August 3, 1857.

We now rely principally on the *Era* for a while. For Hengler's, reckoned to be the best English company traveling at that time, after Wrexham it was through Wales to Cardiff, where they played from August 12 until August 15, 1857, hard on the heels of Tom Thumb, who had recently been playing there at the Town Hall Assembly Rooms. Then on to Gloucester on the 18th, and Cheltenham on the 19th, where they gave two well-attended performances, one in the afternoon and one in the evening. It was Evesham on August 20, 1857, Upton-on-Severn on the 21st, and Malvern, Worcestershire, on the 22nd. On Monday, August 24, 1857, they opened in their elegant tent at Worcester, and also played there on Tuesday the 25th. Worcester, at the Saracen's Head, Bowling Green, was well attended (*Berrow's Worcester Journal*, August 29, 1857). On Wednesday, August 26, 1857, they were at Stourport, and on the 27th at Stourbridge. On August 31, 1857, they pitched their tent at Wellington, in Shropshire. "Mr. A. Barnes" gets another mention in the *Era* of August 30, 1857. On the standard Hengler's poster from this period are billed J. M. Hengler, the prince of tightrope artistes; Mr. W. Powell, the great Caledonian horseman; Mr. J. Bridges, the graceful leaping act equestrian; Mr. Arthur Barnes, the champion somersault thrower of England; Mr. J. Powell and Mr. A. Bridges, the inimitable character act riders; Mr. Ogeani, the wonderful equilibrist; MM. Bibb and Edwardes, Parisian grotesques and gymnasts; M. Lusillian, the daring; MM. Revolti, Delinski, Richards, etc., etc.;

wit, humor, and philosophy dispensed in the most precise manner by the inimitable jester, James Frowde.

On Friday, September 11, 1857, Hengler's Circus visited Grantham. The day was unfavourable (*Nottinghamshire Guardian*, September 17, 1857). Then it was on to Horncastle and Louth. In the meantime, on September 9, 1857, while performing at the Theatre Royal, Liverpool, Madame Celeste was suddenly taken ill again.

The Wrexham paper of September 12, 1857, ran a cute story entitled "A pretty pony." It goes:

> In a field on the road leading from Wrexham to Bersham may be seen a pony which, in regard to size and colour, is quite a curiosity. He stands about thirty-six inches high, and is a beautiful piebald, a chestnut and white. We are informed that this miniature horse belongs to Mr. Hengler's circus, and being in a delicate state of health when the company was in Wrexham a few weeks ago, he has been left to rusticate for a few months in the green pastures, in order to recruit his strength, and enable him to perform with more vigor the serio-comic part which falls to his lot in the equestrian drama of life. The little fellow is very docile and sociable, and spends a good deal of his time by the gate fraternizing with the passers by; his habits leading him to prefer the company he meets with at this point to the monotonous intercourse of the two cows who appear to be his only companions, and who pass the day in grazing and chewing their cuds. In consideration of his diminutive size and proportionately small appetite our little hero is boarded and lodged for 2s a week.

The *Derby Mercury* of September 23, 1857, carried this remarkable notice, from a "watchman of the Church of England," dated September 19, 1857:

> Hengler's Circus. All ministers of the Christian religion, Sunday School teachers and others, who remember the demoralization caused by the prolonged stay of this circus in the Town of Derby, about two years ago, are earnestly invited to memorialize the chief magistrate, and other authorities of the Borough on the subject, in order, if possible, to prevent a recurrence of such evils; and considering the awful judgments which have fallen upon British India, and the present sufferings [of] our countrymen, it is hoped that all those who fear the wrath of God, and sympathize with their afflicted brethren in the East, will, by way of humiliation, abstain from giving their money and patronage to such vain amusements.

Hengler's may or may not have had Derby on their schedule for that year, but, if they did, they never played there. However, the Anglican vigilante's wrath seems not to have been directed at the more diminutive specimens of *homo circensis*, as General Tom Thumb played there on October 5.

After the summer tour with Hengler, Arthur Barnes disappears off the face of the map for a while. Hengler's opened at Dale Street for their winter season on October 12, 1857, but, although Barnes was with them in December (*Era*, December 20, 1857), he was not with them at the grand reopening.

The *Era* of November 8, 1857, has this: "Howes and Cushing's American Circus. The proprietors of the above circus have taken a large plot of land at the corners of Portland Street and David Street [in Manchester], where they are erecting a commodious cirque. They stay here a fortnight, and have two performances daily. Mr. Arthur Barnes, the vaulter, is announced as being engaged, and also the Bedouin Arabs." They opened in Manchester on Monday, November 9, for two weeks (*Manchester Times*, November 14, 1857), and gave two performances each day, having 220 men and horses, the largest establishment in the world. "Mr. Arthur Burnes [sic], the greatest vaulter in either hemisphere, and who challenges the world for an equal." On November 30, James Robinson, the great trick rider of America, appeared. Howes and Cushing's extended their stay, and closed in Manchester on Saturday, December 5. Then it was off to Dublin.

Freeman's Journal, of Dublin, on December 9, 1857, has a large ad for The Great United States Circus, "the largest establishment in the world, numbering upwards of 200 men and horses!." It opened in Dublin on December 7, 1857, for 15 days only, "in their new, beautiful, and novel building in the Rotunda Garden, capable of seating 4000 persons comfortably, and so admirably arranged that every visitor has a clear, unobstructed view of the performances of this extensive and unequalled troupe," which included Arthur Barnes, the champion vaulter. Others on the bill were James Robinson, the wonder of the world; Miss Rose Madigan, the American prima donna equestrienne; Mr. Davis Richards, the prairie rider; Messrs. Holland and Murray, the greatest gymnastics of the day; George Bachelder, the greatest leaper and somersault act thrower; Messrs. H. Madigan, J. Madigan, Armstrong, Rosston, and 20 others, represent the native American talent; Jim Myers and Joe Pentland, the jesters of the circus; and the two educated mules, Pete and Barney, as well as North American Indians and the Bedouin Arabs.

Arthur Barnes left Dublin while Howes and Cushing's were still playing. He opened with Hengler's at Dale Street, Liverpool, on December 14, 1857. The *Liverpool Mercury* of that date says, "Mr. Arthur Barnes, the greatest somersault thrower in the world, for the first time this season, will execute his astounding acts of vaulting." His fellow acts were Chatteris Jackson, the clown; James Bridges, the tightrope artist; Jem Frowde (occasionally billed, in a moment of publicity exuberance, as "Don Jemmyfrowderene"); John Milton Hengler; Madame Clementine Quaglieni and Mdlle. Josephine Quaglieni (daughters of circus owner Antonio Quaglieni; Clementine was born in Constantinople in 1840, and Josephine in Germany in 1841); Leopold et Boutelier, the grotesques; Little Bibb; Funny Franks, the clown; and Petit Romeo (i.e., Romeo Quaglieni, son of Antonio; born in Brescia in 1845) doing his somersaults on horseback. The *Era* of December 20 tells us, "Mr. Arthur Barnes, the champion somersault thrower, made his first appearance this last week [December 14; at Hengler's], and was well received." On November 21, Wallett began a week's stint with Hengler's, a stint that was extended into early January 1858. On December 22 the Siamese ambassadors were among the audience (*Era*, December 27, 1857). The featured spectacle was *Jack the Giant Killer*.

In early January 1858, Liverpool offered both William Cooke's Circus, at the Amphitheatre (with the Brothers Hutchinson as the stars) and Hengler's, with Wallett and Arthur Barnes proving great attractions. Mr. Barnes's last night with Hengler's at Liverpool was January 9, 1858, and the following day, Sunday, he traveled down to Birmingham by train, to rejoin Howes and Cushing's Great United States Circus, which had opened for a short winter season in the new and splendid circular and commodious brick building especially erected for the purpose on Moor Street, on December 26, 1857, with James Robinson and the Bedouin Arabs as stars.

On January 18, 1858, a part of Howes & Cushing's in Birmingham left for Manchester. However, the main part of the company, including Arthur Barnes for a while, remained in Birmingham. Also arriving in Manchester was a part of William Cooke's company from Liverpool, and, with the Howes & Cushing splinter, they formed a double company in Manchester, opening that night, the 18th. At that time, in Liverpool, Wallett left Hengler's and was replaced by the Bedouin Arabs, who had come from Howes & Cushing's in Birmingham. Wallett would move with Pablo Fanque down to Bristol toward the end of January.

That January there were also circuses in Glasgow and Plymouth. The Cirque Napoleon was in Wolverhampton, under the management of Mons. Hogini, and occasionally featuring a moonlighting Pablo Fanque on his mare Beda. The Cirque Napoleon would wrap up there on March 6, 1858, after mixed fortunes. Mr. Emidy's circus had been playing in Norwich for some time, while Ginnett's had been in Cardiff since November 1857, featuring John Samwell and Monsieur Polaski. At that stage, Mr. Ginnett was building a circus in Bath (or rather, Mr. G. Ball, the local builder and carpenter, was), capable of holding 2,000 persons, and Ginnett would take up residence there on February 1, 1858.

So, Arthur Barnes, with Burnell Runnells, the American trick rider, opened with Howes and Cushing's in Birmingham on Monday, January 11, 1858. For Arthur Barnes's brief stay here we rely primarily on the *Birmingham Daily Post*, at least up until their last mention of Mr. Barnes on January 13,

1858, but there is this, from the *Era* of Sunday, January 24, 1858, reflecting on the week just gone:

> United States Circus. Messrs. Howes and Cushing have made considerable and highly interesting alterations in their programme, the principal stars who have appeared this week being Mademoiselle Clementine Quaglieni, a youthful artiste as lovely in person as graceful in performance, and the famous Hengler, of tightrope celebrity, whose ability as a first-class performer are [sic] unquestioned. Barnes, also, the Star Vaulter, throws innumerable somersaults, apparently without effort, whilst Cooke and Jackson, the new clowns, who are both clever in their way, excite roars of laughter. Frank Pastor is announced to appear in the ensuing week.

That Arthur Barnes was still in Birmingham for the week beginning January 18 is proved by the *Era* of January 17, which, although it doesn't mention Arthur Barnes, tells us that Mdlle. Quaglieni will be appearing this coming week, i.e., the week beginning January 18, the week we know from the *Era* that Arthur Barnes was performing with her. So, he was still with Howes and Cushing's as late as Saturday, January 23, 1858. He may have remained in Birmingham after January 23, but his last possible day there would have been February 20, 1859, as we shall see. The dual Cooke's-Howes & Cushing's Circus closed somewhat unexpectedly in Manchester on January 30, 1858, and two days later, on February 1, 1858, moved into their newly and specially erected temporary space in Leeds, with their intelligent mules, Pete and Barney.

February 27, 1858, was the Birmingham branch of Howes & Cushing's last night there for a few weeks. On the following day, Sunday, they moved up to Manchester, opening there on the 29th. On March 15, 1859, they moved back down to Birmingham.

Sanger's Royal Amphitheatre had left Aberdeen on January 12, 1858, bound for Lindsay Street, Dundee, their circus featuring Young Hernandez on the *corde volante*. We next pick up Arthur Barnes opening with Sanger's there, on February 22, 1858. For the next week we have the great pleasure of being conducted by the *Dundee Courier*. That first night with Sanger's, Arthur Barnes turned 55 somersaults. He was engaged for six nights, but extended his run. On the 27th of February, the clown Billy Seal came to the end of his run with Macarte & Clarke's in Newcastle, and two days later opened with Sanger's, in Dundee. The paper of March 3, 1858, says: "The Circus. During the period this place of amusement has been open in Dundee (now upwards of two months) it has been conducted in a manner that does credit alike to the Messrs. Sanger and to all the parties connected with it." It goes on tell us that on March 1, 1858, "Mr. Arthur Barnes threw the astonishing number of seventy-one somersaults, thus establishing his claim to be accounted the greatest somersault thrower in the world." On Thursday evening, March 4, he performed there in a benefit for Messrs. J. and G. Sanger. While Sanger's would stay in Dundee, it looks as if this, March 4, was Arthur Barnes's last night there. Where he went, we don't know, but it was probably back to London. Sanger's wrapped up in Dundee in April 1858.

Things were going on with other circuses, of course, in the first quarter of 1858. Since late 1857, J. H. Emidy's Continental Cirque had been playing Norwich, but on February 15, 1858, they opened in Ipswich, with Pitney Weston, the clown, as the star attraction. On March 8, 1858, Arthur Nelson, the clown, made his first appearance with Emidy's, in Ipswich. On April 6 and 7, Emidy's, who now had Billy Seal, the clown, left Ipswich bound for the stock fair at Woodbridge.

On March 14, 1858, in Liverpool, Jem Frowde's wife, Elizabeth, died of typhus. She was 24. By now Tim Elliott, of the Brothers Elliott, had settled in a house on Drury Lane with his family, which was still growing, and had taken the King's Head, on Duke Street, making his debut there as a publican on April 24, 1858.

Back on December 28, 1857, Harry Brown, the clown, had opened his own Cirque Unique at Swansea, and would be there until March 1858, featuring, aside from himself, Miss Moseley and thirteen-year-old equestrian wonder Alfred Clarke. The week beginning April 18, 1858, Mr. Brown's circus performed two nights in Newport, Monmouthshire. On June 5, 1858, Brown's Royal Equestrian Establishment played Bromyard, and on June 16, 1858, played Deddington.

In 1858, E. T. Smith bought the Royal Panopticon of Arts and Sciences, in Leicester Square. The Royal Panopticon had opened in 1852 as a place of popular instruction and as a home for the sciences and music, but had failed. When Mr. Smith bought it, it was lying empty. He changed the name to The Alhambra and ran it as a circus from February 7, 1858, until 1860, and as a place of popular entertainment until 1862.

In January 1858, Hayes' Equestrian Circus was in Derby. There were originally three performing Hayes Brothers, Manchester natives, performing since the early 1850s. In 1857, they formed their own circus, or rather two of them did — Bob and Bill. On March 22, 1858, the Brothers Hayes opened their Cirque Variete at Wrexham, with the daring somersault rider, Young Felix, as the main attraction.

On February 20, 1858, Bell's Monster Circus opened in Kilmarnock for a twelve-day run, while Hengler's was still in Liverpool. Bell & Co. opened in Belfast on March 22, and on Easter Monday, 1858, they opened in Dublin. The weather that Monday was awful in Dublin too, preventing Mr. Bell from opening that night. He had had a good run the week before, despite lousy weather, but this Monday was a washout. However, he was able to reopen on the Tuesday.

On February 8, 1858, William Cooke's opened in Edinburgh; Harry Walker was with them. On April 3, they wrapped up there, and on April 5 and 6, appeared in York. On the 8th they arrived in Leeds, but were prevented from doing a grand entrée into the town on account of the heavy snow and sleet. On April 12 they were in Bradford, and on the 13th in Halifax. On April 14, 1858, William Cooke's Monstre Troupe of over 200 men and horses entered Huddersfield, and on April 17 they were in Oldham. On April 26, 1858, they were in Macclesfield, and the next day in Congleton.

Madame Newsome's circus was playing Plymouth, and on March 8, 1858, would move to Exeter to take up residence in a building especially constructed for them. Bill Mitchell (alias Felix Revolti), the clown, was one of their stars there over the Easter holidays, and he and Tom Swann made a great pair. The Newsomes' production of *Cinderella* was decidedly successful. On April 21, Madame Blanche, from the Cirque Napoleon in Paris, joined Newsome's.

Pablo Fanque had two circuses going in January and February 1858 — one at Birmingham and the other at Bristol. The reason for this was that Pablo wanted to go head-to-head with Howes and Cushing's in Birmingham, but he also wanted to establish a circus in Bristol. So, while reserving his main strength for Birmingham, he sent down a rather weak detachment to Bristol, but that mistake cost him dear in that port, and he closed there on March 20, 1858. Meanwhile, at Pablo's circus in Birmingham, Frank Pastor ended his run on March 3; on March 27, 1858, Jim Myers' engagement there came to an end, and he was succeeded by clown Jim Doughty, and on March 29, Astley's clown Harry Crouste, joined them. On April 10, Pablo left Birmingham and opened in Manchester on the 13th, to a rather slender audience. He had had a lot to contend with, running a show in Birmingham and one in Bristol, and also being embattled by Howes and Cushing's in the former town, but, largely thanks to the stupendous efforts of his tireless agent, Tom Sheffield, the end result in Birmingham was not all bad.

On March 25, 1858, we find Arthur Barnes vaulting against Conrad (i.e., Harry Connor) and Henderson at the Royal Britannia, Hoxton, in London, as part of a benefit for Mr. Henderson (London *Standard*, of that date).

A few general circus notes: On April 26, 1858, Hernandez, the great equestrian, pulled into Sydney Harbor on the *Leveret*, out of San Francisco. On Easter Monday, Wild's Colossal Establishment opened in Blackburn, and on May 20, 1858, they entered Preston. The biggest name in show business in 1858, anywhere in the world, was the American singer, Jenny Lind, the Swedish Nightingale. There was nothing to stop ruthless promoters cashing in on her name, for example, "Jenny Lind," in huge letters, and then in small letters, "unfortunately cannot be present, as she is abroad," or some such scurrilous wording. Wild's had a midget horse named Jenny Lind, and he promoted it for all it was worth, i.e., the name Jenny Lind was in enormous letters, while the fact that said attraction was equine rather than, say, human, was in script to match the animal's size.

After a successful and protracted season at Liverpool, Hengler decided to go on a tour of the provinces. In fact the proposed tour never came off. What they (or some of them, anyway, including Arthur Barnes) did was go to Copenhagen. The *Era* of Sunday, May 2, gives a notice: "Copenhagen — Summer. Engagements 1858. Mdlles. Christine, Agnes, Clara Morgan, N. Milano, Mr. John Milton Hengler, Mr. A. Barnes, and troupe of acrobats, and all persons engaged, are requested to be in London not later than Tuesday, May 4, as they must sail in company with the secretary on May 5. Tivoli opens for season on May 10. By order of board of Directors, J.W. Anson, sole agent."

The *Era* of June 27, 1858, tells us, "Copenhagen. Tivoli Gardens. Tivoli and Summer season mean the same in Copenhagen. The direction have done well in appointing J.W. Anson (London) as their agent. First, we have three old friends: Madame Culine, the celebrated rope-dancer and ascensionist [Louisa Jeffries, she had married Clifford Culine, the showman, and she was later known as Mrs. Louisa Edwards]; Mr. Arthur Barnes, the champion vaulter; and the Vestris of the tightrope, Mr. John Milton Hengler." Later in the same article it says, "The Pantomime Company includes Messrs. Volkersen (Pierrot), Luin (Harlequin), Bosholm, Hesse and Mdlle. Pettiletti [sic] (Columbine)." Again, as with a similar mention in 1855, it's certainly tempting to think that this Mdlle. Pettiletti was the Acrobat's wife or daughter. Even more tempting, as a matter of fact.

On, or around, August 2, 1858, Arthur Barnes left Copenhagen with John Milton Hengler, bound for Paris, where they played the Cirque de l'Imperatrice and the Cirque Napoleon. We pick up echoes of them in various newspapers, such as the *Glasgow Herald* of September 8, 1858, and *Freeman's Journal* (Dublin) of August 27, 1858. The appropriately circular Cirque de l'Imperatrice had been built in the Champs-Elysees by Jacques Hittorf, who, in 1852, had also built the Cirque Napoleon (later called Cirque d'Hiver). That Hengler was at the Cirque de l'Imperatrice in 1858, we know from the *Gazette Musical de Paris*, vol. 25 (1858).

After John Milton Hengler returned to England, on the front page of the *Era* of August 22, 1858, appeared an ad:

> Herr Hengler, the renowned tightrope artiste, begs to inform directors of theatres, circuses, etc, that he just returned from a highly successful tour through Portugal, Spain, and France, where he had the honour of appearing before Pedro

V, Queen Isabella, and (recently at the Hippodrome, Paris) before the Emperor Napoleon, the Duke of Brunswick and all the nobility of the various courts, and that he is now ready to take engagements, and that he will reply to any communications addressed to: No. 8, St. George's Terrace, Cheltenham, Glos, where he is residing for a short time prior to returning to the Continent.

It goes without saying that Arthur Barnes also appeared in front of the aforementioned personages. It must be assumed that he stayed on the Continent while Hengler was in England. There is, extant, a small, wooden hand mirror, that had belonged to the Acrobat. On the back it says "A. Barns. Madrid. 1859." But there's some older writing as well. It clearly says "Madrid" and then a date, but the date's too obscure to read now.

Meanwhile, Cooke's Circus was touring England, as was Astley's. Harry Connor was in Dublin. Newsome's opened at Cheltenham on September 20, with the Infant Wells also aboard as an attraction. Newsome's would be succeeded in Cheltenham on October 8 by Howes and Cushing's, who were on a major tour. Charles Hengler's Circus played Leicester on September 23 and 25, to good audiences, and on the 26th played Loughborough. They would reopen at Dale Street, Liverpool, on October 16, 1858. Sanger's Circus played the Goose Fair at Nottingham on October 4 and 5. And Charles Dickens was moving around the country like clockwork, giving readings. Like Dr. Mark and his team of traveling midgets, Dickens could be seen anywhere and everywhere.

For the record: On January 9, 1858, Macarte & Clarke's Circus (Marie Macarte and George Clarke; they had married in Kent in August 1856, six months after Madame Macarte's first husband, Michael McCarthy, died) wrapped up in Edinburgh, after a very successful visit. On the 11th, they would open in Newcastle for a long stay, with Madame Macarte as the star and Billy Seal, the clown, as a main feature. During their run they would add James Cooke and Mademoiselle Virginie. On March 19, 1858, Macarte & Clarke's closed in Newcastle, and on April 3, 1858, they arrived in Belfast, calling themselves the Champs Elysees Cirque. The following day, Monday, the wind was so strong it blew down their tent, and defied puny mortals to reerect it. However, the wind abated somewhat on the Tuesday, and erection was achieved. However, they couldn't sustain the erection, the wind being so strong that night, while on the Wednesday the rains were so torrential that the cirque decided to quit Belfast for other towns in northern Ireland. On October 18, 1858, Macarte & Clarke's Magic Ring opened in Dublin. The cast at that time included Le Petit Adrian, Alfred Moffatt, Alfred Nelson, Mr. Hemming, the Quaglienis, and Billy Seal, the clown. Then it was on to Ipswich, where they wintered. November 23 was Edward Platt's benefit night. For this special occasion, the clown decided on something really special for the audience, a real killer act. He got up on to the gallery, took a flying leap toward the center of the ring, executing three somersaults in mid-air as he descended the 22 feet onto a quilt and mattress held by 10 men true and strong. It would have been all right if he'd made the triple, but he only managed two and half and landed on his head. He never moved again.

For the record: Wallett had played with Howes and Cushing's at Manchester in March, 1858; with Ginnett's at Bath later that month; then, to round out March he was a week with Sanger's in Dundee. In early April he was appearing in Hull, with the Delavantis, in some theatrical pieces, leaving there on April 17, 1858, bound for Nottingham, where they opened for the week on the 19th, to very indifferent houses. But Wallett could no longer resist the idea of being a proprietor again, and so put together another circus, the Great Equestrian Company, and, hiring a groom named Good, from Barton, Yorkshire, to drive him, toured it throughout the summer of 1858. The troupe included Burnell Runnells, the great American rider; Master Frederic Runnells; the Delavantis; Carlos and Henrico, the acrobats; James Cooke, from Astley's; Kate Clements, the fairy equestrienne; Chatteris Jackson; Footit the clown; the Bedouin Arabs; and Mr. Pearson, the rider. This move, by Wallett, to own a circus again, was not altogether a good one, the country having become somewhat surfeited with circuses. Attendance throughout England anyway (as opposed to, say Scotland, perhaps), was noticeably falling off, and, with this in mind we find that Astley's (under the new lessee, William Cooke) had also put together a touring troupe, kicking off in Wolverhampton on May 10. As we shall see, sometimes, these two touring circuses played the same town only a few days apart. Something had to give, and it did; Wallett moved back to London for a lengthy stay at the Alhambra, and Astley's moved north. In addition to all this, on June 21, Howes and Cushing's began a lengthy tour of the provinces, but, fortunately, they confined their activities to Scotland and the north of England.

Wallett's itinerary was: Coventry (May 3, 1858), Rugby (May 4, 1858; the boys of this famous school took a half holiday to watch the circus), Northampton (May 5 and 6, 1858), Daventry (May 7, 1858), Leamington (May 8, 1858), Warwick (May 10, 1858), Stratford (May 11, 1858), Redditch (May 12, 1858; this gig replaced the scheduled Evesham), Worcester (May 13 and 14, 1858), Malvern (May 15, 1858), Hereford (May 17, 1858), Abergavenny (May 18, 1858), Brecon (May 19, 1858), Merthyr Tydfil (May 20, 1858), Aberdare (May 21, 1858), Newbridge (May 22, 1858), Swansea (May 24 and 25, 1858), Neath (May 26, 1858), Bridgend (May 27, 1858), Cowbridge (May 28, 1858), Cardiff (May 29, 1858), Newport (May 31, 1858), Pontypool (June 1, 1858), Chepstow (June 2, 1858), Monmouth (June 3, 1858), Ross-on-Wye (June 4, 1858), Gloucester (June 5, 1858), Tewkesbury (June 7, 1858), Cheltenham (June 8 and 9, 1858), Stroud (June 10, 1858), Cirencester (June 11, 1858), Malmesbury (June 12, 1858; this gig replaced the scheduled Swindon), Trowbridge (June 14, 1858), Devizes (June 15, 1858), Bath (June 16, 1858), Bristol (June 17 and 18, 1858), and Chippenham (June 19, 1858). On June 21, 1858, they opened at the Royal Alhambra Palace, in Leicester Square. This beat touring, especially in towns that were being besieged by circuses, and Wallett remained in London for the rest of the year. On July 19, 1858, Tom Thumb opened with them for a short while before going on to Europe, and then to a retirement.

For the record: Astley's 1858 summer tour looks like this: Wolverhampton (May 10, 1858), Stourbridge (May 11, 1858), Bromsgrove (May 12, 1858), Droitwich (May 13, 1858), Stourport (May 14, 1858), Kidderminster (May 15, 1858), Bewdley (May 17, 1858), Tenbury (May 18, 1858), Leominster (May 19, 1858), Hereford (May 20, 1858), Ross-on-Wye (May 21, 1858), Monmouth (May 22, 1858), Chepstow (May 23, 1858), Newport (May 25, 1858), Pontypool (May 26, 1858), Tredegar (May 27, 1858), Merthyr Tydfil (May 28, 1858), Aberdare (May 29, 1858), Newbridge (May 31, 1858), Cardiff (June 1, 1858), Cowbridge (June 2, 1858), Bridgend (June 7, 1858; this date was put back from the 3rd), Aberavon (June 8, 1858; this date was put back from the 4th), Neath (June 9, 1858; this date was put back from the 5th), Swansea (June 10, 1858), Llanelli (June 11, 1858), and Kidwelly (June 12, 1858). Then there is a gap before we pick them up again: Shrewsbury (June 29 and 30, 1858), Oswestry (July 1, 1858), Wrexham (July 2, 1858), Denbigh (July 3, 1858), Llanrwst (July 5, 1858), Bethesda (July 6, 1858), Carnarvon (July 7, 1858), Beaumaris (July 8, 1858), Llangefni (July 9, 1858), Holyhead (July 10, 1858), Bangor (July 12, 1858), Llandudno (July 13, 1858), Abergele (July 14, 1858), Rhyl (July 15, 1858), Holywell (July 16, 1858), Mold (July 17, 1858), Chester (July 19–23, 1858), New Brighton (July 24, 1858), Birkenhead (July 26, 1858), Parkgate (July 27, 1858), Runcorn (July 28, 1858), Northwich (July 29, 1858), and Altrincham (July 30, 1858).

For the record: After Birmingham, Howes and Cushing's had gone down to London, to play the Royal Alhambra Palace, in Leicester Square. On May 14, 1858, they gave a command performance for the Queen, and then, on June 19, 1858, wrapped up at the Alhambra. On the 21st, Wallett's Equestrian Company, taking a break from touring the country, took over at the Alhambra. Howes & Cushing's then embarked on a monster 1858 summer tour, which looked like this: Coventry (June 21, 1858), Nuneaton (June 22, 1858), Leicester (June 23, 1858), Ashby-de-la-Zouch (June 24, 1858), Derby (June 25, 1858), Nottingham (June 26, 1858), Sheffield (June 28, 1858), Doncaster (June 29, 1858), Barnsley (June 30, 1858), Huddersfield (July 1, 1858), Halifax (July 2, 1858), Wakefield (July 3, 1858), York (July 5, 1858), Harrogate (July 6, 1858),

Ripon (July 7, 1858), Thirsk (July 8, 1858), Northallerton (July 9, 1858), Richmond (July 10, 1858), Barnard Castle (July 12, 1858), Bishop Auckland (July 13, 1858), Darlington (July 14, 1858), Stockton (July 15, 1858), Hartlepool (July 16, 1858), Durham (July 17, 1858), Sunderland (July 19, 1858), South Shields (July 20, 1858), Newcastle (July 21 and 22, 1858), Morpeth (July 23, 1858), Alnwick (July 24, 1858), Berwick (July 26, 1858), Kelso (July 27, 1858), Jedburgh (July 28, 1858), Hawick (July 29, 1858), Melrose (July 30, 1858), Peebles (July 31, 1858), Edinburgh (August 2, 3, and 4, 1858), Dunfermline (August 5, 1858), Kirkcaldy (August 6, 1858), Cupar, Fife (August 7, 1858), St. Andrews (August 9, 1858), Dundee (August 10 and 11, 1858), Arbroath (August 12, 1858), Montrose (August 13, 1858), Forfar (August 14, 1858), Perth (August 16, 1858), Kinross (August 17, 1858), Alloa (August 18, 1858), Stirling (August 19, 1858), Falkirk (August 20, 1858), Linlithgow (August 21, 1858), Airdrie (August 23, 1858), Glasgow (August 24, et seq.), Lancaster (September 20, 1858), Preston (September 22, 1858), Blackburn (September 23, 1858), Chorley (September 24, 1858), Chester (September 28, 1858), Cheltenham (October 8, 1858), Banbury (October 12, 1858), and Oxford (October 13, 1858). On November 8, 1858, they returned to their London home base, the Royal Alhambra Palace, in Leicester Square.

Arthur Barnes and John Milton Hengler, fresh from Paris, re-joined Hengler's on February 21, 1859, at Dale Street, Liverpool, where we again pick up the *Liverpool Mercury* as a guide. That paper, of Saturday, February 19, 1859, ran an ad which tells us: "On Monday next, the 21st instant, first appearance of Mr. Arthur Barnes, the champion vaulter; also first appearance of Mons. Oriel, the celebrated Clown Grotesque." The *Mercury* of February 21, 1859, says, in another ad: "This (Monday) evening, the 21st instant, first appearance of Mr. Arthur Barnes, the champion vaulter."

The *Mercury* of February 22, 1859, reviewed the cirque on Arthur Barnes's opening night there: "In order to render his cirque still more attractive, Mr. Hengler has made further additions to his company. Last evening, that extraordinary vaulter, Mr. Arthur Barnes, renowned as the champion of the art which he professes, appeared in the circle, and was enthusiastically received. He went through a variety of surprising feats, all of which justified the high anticipations formed of his performances, and the world-wide fame he has acquired as an artiste." The paper of February 22 says, in an ad: "This (Tuesday) evening, the 22nd instant, second appearance of Mr. Arthur Barnes, the champion vaulter," and the one of February 23 says "This (Wednesday) evening, the 23rd instant, third appearance of Mr. Arthur Barnes, the champion vaulter." The *Mercury* of February 24, says, "This (Thursday) evening, the 24th instant, fourth appearance of Mr. Arthur Barnes, the champion vaulter," and the edition of February 25, says: "This (Friday) evening, the

25th instant, fifth appearance of Mr. Arthur Barnes, the champion vaulter." Arthur Barnes was a big name, very big, so why not plug him for all it was worth.

On February 26, 1859, Hengler's held a grand fashionable morning performance, by the kind permission of the mayor, William Preston, Esq., and upwards of 700 pupils from St. Ann's National School and St. John's School attended. The *Era* of February 27, 1859, lets us know that "Mr. Arthur Barnes, the champion vaulter, has also been added to the company, which now contains some really celebrated and clever performers." March 3 was the benefit night of William Powell, the great English horseman, and March 4 was Jem Frowde's benefit night. On March 7, 1859, St. *George and the Dragon* was produced for the first time by this cirque, and Barnes was in it.

On March 5, 1859, Charles Hengler wrote a letter to the *Mercury*, which they published on the 8th. Someone had been spreading a rumor that one of the Hengler troupe had got drunk at the Altcar coursing meeting and, for wagers, had jumped over a brook, several times "selling" and falling in. Hengler took objection to this, and said that "equestrian and gymnastic professionals are really not in the habit of visiting either coursing meetings or races." He adds that he is "fully aware that many in this town would gladly crush us, if possible annihilate us."

On March 11, 1859, "Mr. Arthur Barnes, the champion vaulter" threw 62 successive somersaults. A grand morning performance was given on Saturday, March 12, at which, by special invitation of Mr. Hengler, the children of Lady Sefton's School, West Derby, and also the children of St. Simon's schools, numbering altogether upwards of 600, attended. In addition to the grand spectacle of St. *George and the Dragon*, which was repeated at every performance, the scenes in the circle were of a very choice description.

The cast of St. *George and the Dragon* were: John Milton Hengler (as St. George), Messrs. Powell, Russelli, Clarke, Cooke, Hogini, and Wild (as the champion Knights), Mrs. Beacham (as the Enchantress), Mrs. C. Hengler (as Princess Satra of Egypt), Mr. Rivolti (as the King of Egypt), Mr. Frowde (as Tom of Coventry, a tinker, afterward Squire to St. George), and M. Bibb (as Sycorrae). Felix Revolti (sic; this is William Mitchell, clown, born about 1829) was the equestrian director of Hengler's. The night of March 14, 1859, was a special fashionable night, under distinguished patronage, being a complimentary benefit to Mr. Charles Hengler. It was also the first night of the gymnastic brothers Charlie and Steve Ethair, fresh from four years with the Cirque Vienna and at Berlin. The *Mercury* of the following morning (i.e., March 15, 1859) reviewed it: "Hengler's Cirque Variete. Last evening, the respected proprietor of this popular place of entertainment took his benefit," and, despite bad weather, the crowds flocked in. Miss Emily Jane Wells performed as Joan of Arc for the first time (she had opened with Hengler's on February 14, her first appearance before a Liverpool audience). Mr. Hengler himself introduced the new mare Victoria, and the Ethairs got raves. Mr. Powell impersonated Falstaff, Shylock, and Richard III. Mr. Bibb was excellent in his globe ascent, as was M. Oriel in his bottle equilibriums. "Nor was the reception of Barnes, the vaulter, a whit the less enthusiastic."

Emily Jane Wells was born in 1840, in Ashby-de-la-Zouch, Leicestershire, daughter of circus man John Wells. In 1861, in Scarborough, she married clown and vaulter James Barnes.

Each daily edition of the *Liverpool Mercury* between March 14 and 19, 1859, and again between March 21 and 23, says: "Mr. Arthur Barnes, the champion vaulter, is still retained, and elicits unmitigated applause from every beholder." The *Era* of March 20, tells us, "Mr. Arthur Barnes, the champion vaulter, is still under engagement, as also are the Brothers Ethair and Mr. John Milton Hengler."

The *Liverpool Mercury* of March 21, 22, and 23, 1859, tell us that Barnes was still retained. However, the same paper, of March 24, and subsequent editions, although it tells us Hengler's would be closing on April 1 (a fact confirmed by the same paper of March 29 and April 1), does not mention Arthur Barnes, which means his last night at Hengler's was March 23, 1859. Therefore, he wasn't there when John Clark broke his leg during his act on March 31, 1859, and he wasn't with Hengler's when they went to Sheffield on April 4. He was in Glasgow.

On Monday, April 4, 1859, Arthur Barnes opened in Glasgow with Macarte and Clarke's Magic Ring, in time to take part in a benefit there for Pablo Fanque. The *Glasgow Herald* of April 2, 1859, tells us that that Saturday (i.e., April 2) was the last performance at Macarte & Clarke's Magic Ring of W. F. Wallet and of the great Arab vaulter, Hassan (this is Aron Hassan, born in 1837, a real Moroccan Arab; i.e., his right name was not, say, Fred Jenkins, and he was not from Bermondsey. When he left Macarte & Clarke, he headed straight down to Sheffield, to open with Hengler's, and, shortly thereafter, married a French girl named Irene, who would become Madame Hassan). The ad (repeated daily thereafter) then goes on to say, "On Monday, April 4, the last night but four of this, the Greatest Equestrian Company in the World, remaining in Glasgow, as the Proprietors have arranged with Edmund Glover, Esq., to give thirteen representations in the Theatre Royal, Greenock, commencing on Monday, April 11. On Monday evening, April 4, the performance will be for the benefit of the renowned Pablo Fanque, upon which occasion Mr. Arthur Barnes, the greatest somersault thrower in the world, will have the honour of making his first appearance." The ad then goes on to tell us that Mr. Fanque's famous mare, Beda, had failed to appear, and that he had been training a new mare, Fleur de Marie, who would make her first appearance tonight.

"On Tuesday, April 5, the last night but three, the performances will be for the benefit of Mr. A. Henry, manager. Mr. Arthur Barnes will make his second appearance, and Mr. Henry will introduce his performing dogs" (*Glasgow Herald*, April 2, 1859). That night's performance was under the distinguished presence and patronage of Col. Brooke and the officers of the 2nd Battalion, 12th Regiment.

On the Wednesday, April 6, 1859, the night of Arthur Barnes's third appearance in Glasgow, he took part in a benefit for Charles Watson, the lyrical jester. On Thursday, there was no performance, but on Friday night, April 8, the circus held a benefit for Mr. W. B. Seal, the great clown. It was also the "fourth appearance of Mr. Arthur Barnes." On Saturday, April 9, 1859, in Glasgow, the last morning performance took place, in which Mr. Arthur Barnes appeared, and that Saturday evening the last performance of the season, the entire troupe of artists, and Mr. Arthur Barnes for the last time.

On April 8, 1859, Arthur Barnes's old friend, Jack Russilli, performed his last gig, in Penzance, with Mr. Emidy's Circus. On April 14, at the Globe Inn, he died, aged 41, and was buried two days later. About five years before, he had fallen badly and dislocated both collar bones. Then he got consumption, which led to a heart problem. On May 1, 1859, Boswell the clown died of a heart attack at the Cirque Napoleon, in Paris.

We learn from the *Era* and various London papers that a week after Howes and Cushing's left the Royal Alhambra Palace, at Leicester Square, there was a week's interval, and then on May 9, 1859, Tom M'Collum's Great Anglo-Saxon Circus opened there. The *Daily News* of May 10 reviewed opening night. "Among the most notable features in yesterday evening's performances was Master Connor's dancing and somersaulting on the elastic bar, the 'Trial of Skill' on the springboard by the champion vaulters, Messrs. Barnes and Connor, and the dancing and pantomime of Madame Blanche. The riding of Ella was also loudly applauded." Jackson, Doughty, and Lockhart were the clowns. During the run there, there were two performances daily, at two o'clock and eight o'clock. The *Era* of May 15, 1859, mentions "the acrobatic evolutions of the champion vaulters, Messrs. Barnes and Connor, in their trial of skill on the spring-board."

On June 8, 1859, the Ethiopian clown, Mr. W. B. Donaldson, the prince of fun, wit, and humor, made his debut with M'Collum's. On Whitmonday they produced the fairy spectacle, *Cinderella*. On June 20, Joe Brown, of the Christy Minstrels, came over to perform with them for the week.

The *Standard* (London) of July 18, 1859, tells us that M'Collum's Great

Anglo-Saxon Circus had its closing night in the cool and well-ventilated Alhambra on July 16, 1859. "A better circus than Mr. McCollum's has not been seen in London." "Messrs. Barnes and Connor proved themselves the kings of vaulting; they threw fifty summersaults in succession with such astonishing ease and rapidity that, like the man in one of Ben Gaultier's ballads, it was difficult to tell which was head and which was heel." Master Romeo was the equestrian acrobat, and the clowns were Jackson, Doughty, and Crouestre. However, the *Standard* was wrong about M'Collum's closing. This is the reason: James Henry Frowde had been born at Portsea in 1831. His mother was Charles Hengler's sister. When he was 15, Jem went to see Hengler's Circus in Portsmouth, and decided to become a clown, joining Hengler's in 1847. In June 1859 Hengler's returned to Liverpool, and Jem broke away from the main circus, forming his own Cirque Modele, which opened at Duke Street, Sheffield, on July 11, 1859. Leading up to the opening, he had rather prematurely booked M'Collum's outfit to open on that very day, but the deal fell through. The Great Anglo-Saxon Circus remained at the Alhambra, booking acts such as Omer, the great rider, and Harry Twist, the clown. About October, still there, they quietly changed their name to M'Collum's Grand Cirque Classique, and Mr. M'Collum would remain the lessee of the Alhambra well into 1860.

Jem Frowde did open on his appointed date, however, and by August 6, 1859, the *Sheffield and Rotherham Independent* was able to report that the company was continuing to draw tolerably good houses. Mr. Frowde had succeeded in engaging more talent, in the persons of Joseph Melillo, the equestrian, and his wife, Madame Caroline Melillo, as well as Mdlle. Anna Zweiker, who performed the usual feats of horsemanship with remarkable grace, and who were all very well received. Mr. Melillo and his horse Kaiser nightly received well-earned applause. Mr. Frowde's droll grimaces and clever gymnastics also added a good deal of mirth to the entertainment. Mr. Frowde's uncle, John Henderson, also joined the outfit, on the slack wire, along with Mr. Hemming and John Milton Hengler, who was also the acting manager. The band appeared to delight in putting forth all their strength, which contrasted rather oddly sometimes with their number, and making too much noise.

One assumes that Arthur Barnes was with M'Collum's until Saturday, August 6, 1859. The *Era* of August 7, 1859, tells us that "Barnes, the champion vaulter" was to join Frowde's Cirque Modele on August 8, 1859, the same day Steve Ethair married Oceana Sprake, sister-in-law of Clarissa Cooke, William Cooke's niece. This opening night for Arthur Barnes is confirmed by the *Sheffield and Rotherham Independent* of August 6, and the *Era* of August 14, which says, "Mr. Arthur Barnes, the champion vaulter, has been enthusiastically received, and Ella has created quite a furore." The same Sheffield paper said,

"Mr. J. Frowde has much pleasure in announcing that he has engaged Mr. Arthur Barnes, the champion vaulter and summersault thrower of the world, who will make his appearance on Monday. This gentleman has thrown the extraordinary number of ninety-four summersaults in succession at one trial, and has defeated all competitors in England, on the Continent, and the United States of America."

Jem Frowde gave up ownership of the circus to his uncle, and the new Henderson's Cirque Varieté opened in Chester (without Arthur Barnes) on September 24, 1859, with Jem being relegated to the role of principal clown, and with most of the troupe staying on.

On Wednesday, September 21, 1859, Barnes had left Frowde's and Sheffield, bound once again for the warmer climes of Madrid, but this time with the Circo Price. James Price, an Englishman, had founded Price's Circus in Copenhagen in 1795, the first permanent circus in that city. Tom Price, the somersaultist, and a relative of James Price's, later co-owned Price & North's Circus, which he took to Madrid in 1855 and changed the name to Circo Price. He later opened up circuses in Barcelona and other major Spanish towns. From 1859 to the end of November 1860, Arthur Barnes has to be in Madrid, at least part of the time. The rest of the time was at the Cirque Napoleon, in Paris (as we shall soon see). There is absolutely no mention of him in the British press.

Incidentally, on December 5, 1859, the Brothers Hayes' Imperial Circus opened in Nottingham, featuring Hassan, the Arab Chief.

Arthur Barnes was in Europe for over a year, and Sanger's was there scouting talent, picking Mr. Barnes and bringing him back to Edinburgh, which is the place we next pick him up in the British press, and also where we pick up the Edinburgh paper, the *Caledonian Mercury*. Monday, December 3, 1860, and during the week, was the "first appearance of Mr. Arthur Barnes, from the Cirque Napoleon, Paris, the greatest somersault thrower in the world" at Nicolson Street, Edinburgh, with Sanger's Circus and Hippodrome ("Lord" George Sanger was one of the great circus owners), who were wintering there at the Royal Alhambra, which was owned by Peter Paterson. The paper of December 4, 1860, carries an ad for Sanger's Circus and Hippodrome, mentioning "the immense success of Mr. Arthur Barnes, the greatest somersault thrower in the world." The same paper of December 7 and 8, 1860, ran an ad which said: "Notice extraordinary. The great features of the circus this week are the performances of Arthur Barnes, the champion vaulter of the world, and Hubert Meers, the flying acrobat." On Friday and Saturday, December 7 and 8, 1860,

> and every night till further notice, Grand Vaulting Act, headed by Mr. Arthur Barnes, who has achieved the unprecedented feat of turning ninety-five consecu-

tive Somersaults. Ninth night of the terrific trapeze feats of young Meers. Open every evening at seven o'clock. Wonderful novelties every night by a great treble company and the largest stud of horses in the world. There will also be new scenes in the circle, and new jokes and witticisms by Mr. Henry Brown, "The Modern Touchstone," who has been re-engaged. The whole of the company, numbering 70 performers, nightly appear in their various equestrian and gymnastic feats."

There was also a performance every Saturday at two o'clock. Admission: front boxes, 2s; side boxes, 1s 6d; pit and promenade, 1s; gallery, 6d. Half price at nine o'clock to pit and boxes only.

The *Era* of December 9, 1860, says

Edinburgh. Sanger's Circus. This place of amusement continues to be well-patronized. The performance of the Brothers Talliot [they were with Sanger's from 1854 to 1862] on pendant ropes, ornamented with huge rings, are, to use a hackneyed phrase, truly wonderful. Then we have Mr. Arthur Barnes, the Champion Vaulter; he possesses the almost unheard of talent of being able (and apparently with the greatest of ease) to turn no less than 60 somersaults without stopping. He even gives a little one in, but this time it is a forward throw. The latter feat is considered marvelous, the reversing the spring after so long a time being extremely difficult of accomplishment.

The *Era* of December 16, 1860 tells us, "The talents of the Meers family [this family revolved around Little Meers, right name Hubert William Meers, an equestrian clown from Birmingham], Mr. Arthur Barnes, and Mr. H. Brown [Harry Brown, the clown] seem quite sufficient to draw full houses to this favorite place of amusement."

The *Caledonian Mercury* of December 10 (a Monday), 1860, runs the same ad, basically, with "the immense success of Mr. Arthur Barnes, the Champion Vaulter of the World." The night of December 12, 1860 was Grand Military Night, and was under the patronage of Major Tremayne and the officers of Her Majesty's 13th Light Dragoons and the officers of the 78th Highlanders, on which occasion the splendid band of the 13th Light Dragoons attended and played several military marches and choice morceaux of the day. Again, the paper refers to the "immense success of Mr. Arthur Barnes." Saturday, December 15's day performance was under the patronage of James Moncrieff, M.P., the lord advocate, and Adam Black, Esq., M.P. The *Era* of December 23, 1860, tells us, "Edinburgh. Sanger's. The marvelous somersault throwing of Mr. A. Barnes, the Champion Vaulter, still proves very attractive, as is also the great trapeze of Young Meers." At Christmas, Sanger's did *Harlequin Blue Beard*, and Barnes was still there then.

Meanwhile, in Birmingham, Mr. G. W. Cassidy kindly gave his Grecian Amphitheatre over for the night of December 13, 1860, for the benefit of the unfortunate Tom Hutchinson, of the Hutchinson Brothers, who had gone blind. Tom would gamely set up as a professor of gymnastics in a house near the Free Trade Hall in Manchester. As a matter of incidence, but equally of import, especially to the principal of the story, a few weeks later, on January 7, 1861, one of Sanger's lions got a man named Smith, at Astley's, in London.

The *Caledonian Mercury*, of January 18 and 19, 1861, in an ad, says: "Sanger's Great Circus. Positively the last two nights of the season." The ads tell us that the Friday and Saturday were both benefit nights for Mr. A. Barnes, the Champion Vaulter of the World, and Mr. J. Wilson, the daring bareback rider. Saturday was Great prize night! By particular desire, a final midday performance was given at two o'clock [on Saturday], concluding with the pantomime."

During the course of Sanger's run in Edinburgh, thousands and thousands came to see the show. Anyone living in the capital would have attended, sooner or later. A lad who had just had his tenth birthday was Robert Lewis Balfour Stevenson, whose rather chronically sickly state was compensated for by a vehement curiosity, especially for institutions as bizarre as the cirque.

The *Era* of January 20, 1861, tells us: "Manchester. Sanger's Royal Circus, Portland Street, is progressing rapidly under the supervision of Mr. George Knight, their agent, and will be opened on Monday [i.e., Jan. 21]. The interior presents a richly decorated arena." It goes on to say that 30 horses have already arrived, and that "the company announced include Master Meers, Mr. A. Barnes, A. Powell [Anthony Powell, the equestrian], Henry Brown (the clown), and a host of others." The host of others included Mr. Chadwick, Mr. Griffiths, Mr. Footit (clown, right name Edward Haigh, then 18 years old, and already a drunk; he was related to Crockett, the lion-tamer, and would die in 1921); Mr. Edward Kerwin, a young Lancashire fellow, equestrian and elephant trainer; M. Hodgini & Pupils (Hodgini was really a Birmingham lad named Hodges), Mme. V. Powell, Mmlle. Josephine, and Miss Caroline. The *Era* of January 27, 1861, mentions a company that includes A. Powell, Mr. Wilson, Mr. A. Barnes, Mr. H. Brown, Mr. Chadwick, Mr. Griffiths, Mr. Footit, Mr. Kerwin, M. Hodgini & Pupils, Mme. V. Powell, Mlle. Josephine, and Miss Caroline. The *Era* of February 3, 1861, tells us that Sanger's was still at Manchester, and "The vaulting act is good, being headed by Mr. A. Barnes, who is so well-known as the champion somersault thrower it can not fail to be great."

The *Manchester Times* of February 9, 1861, says: "Then there is that renowned gentleman, Arthur Barnes—quite a Napoleon in his way, for turning himself head over heels, and the world upside down; twisting, turning, and flying, but always alighting on his feet at the end of his rowley powley."

The *Era* of February 17, 1861, mentions "the vaulting of Arthur Barnes," still with Sanger's in Manchester. A note on little Bob Chadwick, the great grotesque clown, who will become very important to this story. A Manchester lad, he was 22 at this time, and could do 50 somersaults, feet tied or otherwise, it made no difference. Not long before, in Manchester, he had married Isabella Baines, and they had a son, just born, Tom.

There were at this time several performers using the name Barnes. This may be accounted for by the simple fact that Barnes was a fairly common name, or it may be that some of them were trying to cash in on the Acrobat's fame. The most well known of these other Barneses was a pantaloon (clown) named Old Barnes. Born in 1810, William Augustus Barnes would end his own life in 1868. The *Era* of February 10, 1861, tells us, "Leeds. Pablo Fanque. Among the rest Mr. Barnes and Mr. Pymer make clever clowns." Jim Pymer, the famous Shaksperian clown from Bristol, was nine years older than Arthur Barnes, and wrote *The Clown's Scrap Book*. The reference to Mr. Barnes is to Old Barnes, rather than the Acrobat (who was then with Sanger's in Manchester), despite the fact that Arthur Barnes and Tom Barry had occasionally been clowns for Hernandez and Stone back in 1853. There's a reference later in the year, the *Era* of November 24, 1861, which tells us "Worcester: Classic Hippodrome. Messrs. Auriol [Jean-Baptiste Auriol, known as Young Auriol, also a great somersaulter, and father-in-law of Richard Flexmore, the pantomimic clown] and Barnes are a pair of funny fellows, brimful of wit, which they serve out very plentifully." Also, in the *Era* of September 29, 1861, we find a reference, at Rotherham, with Pablo Fanque's Circus, to James Barnes and his wife, Miss Wells, who had an act called "La Tranca" (The Bar). James Barnes was a clown and dog trainer, who died in 1888. His wife was the former Emily Jane Wells, who would die in Nottingham in 1911. A little later, 1864, an Ethiopian comedian, vocalist and dancer named Will Barnes would be playing in Preston, Lancsashire.

On February 16, 1861, Arthur Barnes left Sanger's and two days later joined Hengler's Grand Cirque Variete, at Dale Street, Liverpool. The *Liverpool Mercury* is our guide here. On February 13, the paper began advertising his coming. "John Milton Hengler begs most respectfully to announce to his many patrons and the public generally that his benefit is announced for Monday next, February 18, on which occasion the Champion Vaulter of the World, Arthur Barnes, will appear." At that stage they were doing the grand equestrian spectacle, *The Lion's Heart of England, or The Brave Scot and His Faithful Steed*. Others with Hengler's at this time were Funny Franks, Little Bibb, Bill Samwell, and John H. Cooke. The paper of Monday, the 18th, advertises, "The first night of Arthur Barnes, the world's champion vaulter." The papers of February 20, 21, and 22 all say, "In addition to the star company of male and female artistes, Arthur Barnes, the champion somersault thrower, will appear every evening." On February 23, a Saturday, Hengler's last day performance but one took place, at 2:30. Monday, the 25th, was benefit night for the circus manager, Felix Revolti. Talking about that night, the *Mercury* ad that morning predicts that "Arthur Barnes will throw a miraculous number of somersaults." Barnes is not mentioned henceforth, which may well mean he was gone. However, it is hard to believe that his last night was a Monday, rather than a Saturday, so, the chances are, if he did leave Liverpool about this time, it was at the end of that week, after the Saturday performance of March 2. If this is the case, we don't know where he was for the whole month of March 1861. On March 16, 1861, Hengler's opened for a short season at Sheffield, with, among others, Little Bibb, Funny Franks, Felix Revolti, John Milton Hengler, John Henry Cooke, Steve Ethair, and Alfred Clarke. "Gymnasts of great celebrity" were advertised, but not Arthur Barnes by name. He would have been billed if he had been with them, a star of his magnitude.

On February 24, 1861, in Havana, Dick Sands died of congestion of the brain. He left a fortune. It was the second time Dick had died. In August 1852, while walking a ceiling upside down in Wolcott, New York, the ceiling collapsed. "His neck had been broken by the fall, and death ensued immediately," cried the papers. However, it was a hoax, that first "death." The second one, although more mundane, was real.

Arthur Barnes was reengaged by Sanger's on April 1, 1861, which was the day strongman Herr Maus opened his circus in Leicester (the German "tower of strength" was now a proprietor). The *Era* of April 7, 1861, tells us, "Manchester. Sanger's. The hippodromatic hemisphere has been enlivened this week by the engagement of Mr. W.F. Wallett, Mr. Davis Richards [an American bareback rider, 'The Wild Horseman'], and Mr. Arthur Barnes." So, Barnes and Wallett were finally playing together again. Not for long. Sanger's summer tour began on April 15, at Altrincham. Barnes wasn't with them, neither was he with Pablo Fanque on his summer tour. He and Harry Connor were in London.

April 7, 1861, was the night of the 1861 British census. So far, we have been unable to find Arthur Barnes and his wife in this census, and it is unlikely that we ever will. We know Barnes was playing with Sanger's on Saturday, April 6, and that on the 15th he was in London. So, on the 7th, he should still have been in Manchester, along with Bob Chadwick, John Griffiths, the Zamezous, George Knight, Davis Richards, Anthony Powell, and Edward Kerwin. But he wasn't; so he must have been on the train with his wife, heading down to London, and therefore slipped through the census taker's net.

On April 8, 1861, the clown Harry Crouesté came over from Doncaster and opened with Hengler's in Sheffield, and a week later the great American performer, Dan Castello, made his English bow with them. On May 2, 1861, James Hernandez opened in Calcutta. He would die on July 10, 1861, in Singapore, leaving behind an English wife, Sarah, and a six-year-old son, George, in Lambeth. On May 13, 1861, Hengler's opened their summer tour at Chester. In late May, Hayes' Circus, still going, was playing in Preston.

Music Halls

Now, for the first time, we find Arthur Barnes playing music halls in London. The trend was going that way, music halls putting on circus-type events mixed with more legitimate variety acts, charging more, and paying bigger money to performers. While the fine evenings of early summer would tempt the Metropolitan amusement seekers out into the suburbs and make the Gardens of Cremorne, Highbury, the Royal Pavilion Gardens of North Woolwich, and Rosherville Gardens, at Gravesend, the attractive points of pleasant excursions in search of cool, fresh air and agreeable recreation, there were many to whom a light entertainment, making less demands upon the time, if not upon the purse of the general public, would always be found alluring in the course of a street stroll in the prolonged twilights of June. In this way the music halls of the metropolis, with their admirable system of ventilation and their capacity for quenching the physical thirst, as well as satisfying the mental appetite, inclined rather to enjoy little relishes at this season than a more substantial repast, came in for a large share of summer patronage, and a visit to each of them as they fell in one's way would be found a pleasant mode of turning a leisure evening to account, when it was not convenient to run into late trains and late hours.

There were the Oxford (at 6 Oxford Street), the Canterbury (on the south side of the Thames), Weston's (in Holborn), Wilton's (in Whitechapel), Islington Philharmonic Hall (also called the Islington Music Hall; opposite the Angel), the South London Music Hall (on the London Road, near the Elephant and Castle), and Frampton's (at the Lord Nelson, Euston Square). There were also the Marylebone Music Hall (at High Street, Marylebone), the London Pavilion Music Hall (at Tichborne Street, Haymarket), the Middlesex New Music Hall (Drury Lane; proprietor Mr. E. Winder), Deacon's Music Hall (adjoining the Sir Hugh Myddleton, opposite Sadler's Wells), the Bedford (in Camden Town), the Lansdowne (on Islington Green), and the London Eldorado Grand Music Hall (at 5 Leicester Square). It wasn't just the Metropolis that had music halls; provincial towns too were discovering the benefits of the institution. Middlesbrough had the Canterbury Music Hall, Bradford had Uncle Tom's New Music Hall. In addition to all this, in 1861, E. T. Smith got involved in another circus, the Cremorne, in Cremorne Gardens, and ran it, as one of the few major permanent London circuses, until 1869.

On April 15, 1861, Arthur Barnes opened with Harry Connor at the Royal Alhambra Palace, another one of the great music halls in London. "First appearance of Mr. Arthur Barnes and Henry Connor, who will throw upwards of 50 somersaults each" (*Morning Post*, April 15, 1861). Others engaged were Charles Woodman, the two-voiced vocalist; John Henderson, the great performer on the slack wire, and Mr. William Tanner and his performing dogs. Sam Collins was also there (more on Mr. Collins later). Saturday, April 27, 1861, was Barnes & Connor's last night at the Alhambra (*Morning Chronicle*, April 29, 1861).

In May Arthur Barnes and Harry Connor were at the Knightsbridge Music Hall, located at the Sun Tavern, proprietor Edwin Williams. "The Knightsbridge Music Hall enjoys a large amount of patronage in this district, and well merits the support it has received. Mr. J.G. Forde, Mr. Sam Collins, and Mr. W.G. Ross are the comic vocalists; Messrs. Arthur Barnes and Henry Connor throw somersaults with wonderful quickness and precision; the New York Minstrels [ten in number] give their characteristic entertainment" (*Era*, May 19 and 26, June 16, July 14 and 21, 1861). That article goes on to tell us that there is an exceedingly agreeable variety imparted to the amusements of the evening. Doors opened at seven, performances commenced at half past. Sam Collins was appearing at the South London Music Hall as well.

Newsome's Alhambra Circus came direct from Reading and opened at Oxford on June 24, 1861, somewhat in defiance of the town council. The building they performed in, located at Cowley Road, St. Clement's, was built by John Dover, a local builder. Doors opened at 7:30, performances started at 8:00, and, from the very beginning, the crowds justified Jem Newsome's defiance. The July 6, 1861, edition of *Jackson's* tells us some of the acts who were appearing with Newsome's then: Jem and Pauline Newsome themselves, of course; Miss Emma Newsome; Adele Newsome (daughter of Jem and Pauline); Miss Marie Newsome; Miss Lizzy Keys (equestrienne, born 1849, Dundee, she was Jem Newsome's niece); Master Andrew Ducrow (born in 1853, in Berlin, he was Jem's nephew); Billy Matthews (he had 21 surviving children, most of whom were in the circus); Mr. John Harrison Pearson (equestrian acrobat, born in Carlisle as John Henry Pearson, son of a hotel keeper; he was known as Nancy, for reasons obvious to his colleagues); Joe Bradshaw, the flying horseman, a Manchester lad, considered an equal of Hernandez (Bradshaw was not the only one using the epithet "the Flying Horseman"; Young Dockerill was being billed in a like manner with Howes & Cushing's); Madame Laurette on the tightrope; the Brothers Pentland on the double trapeze. Tom Swann, Tom Matthews, and Harry Brown were the three capital clowns. On Monday July 15, 1861, Newsome presented a tribe of "real Bedouin Arabs, from Morocco," 10 in number, headed by their chief, Aron

Hassan, the most wonderful tumblers in the world. The other nine Arabs were Mahomen Ben Said, Molay Abdullah, Ali Ben Said (born 1828, Morocco), Ahye Abon, Braheim, Ali Ben Braheim, Ahye Aussaiene, Mondy Benahi, Amadi Ben Mahomed. It was all part of the fun. That day, July 15, 1861, a rival circus came to town, Bell's Hippodrome, and set up in the Horse and Jockey Field, St. Giles's. This competitor fared badly, as Newsome's was playing to packed houses. Meanwhile, Herr Maus's circus opened at Rotherham on July 5, 1861, and Charles Watson, the clown, died on July 13, 1861, of consumption, aged 30.

Jackson's of Saturday, August 10, 1861, tells us, of Newsome's Circus at Oxford, that the performances at this popular place of entertainment appeared to be as attractive as ever, for the circus was well filled every night. The graceful dancing of the Arab bride, Madame Hassan, on the tightrope, was an attractive feature, and the wonderful feats of her husband, Aron Hassan, on the revolving globe, and the performances of young Ducrow on horseback, were very successful. The pantomime of *Mother Goose* afforded considerable amusement, and was cleverly managed. "The Queen's Jester, the celebrated Wallett, and Barnes, the renowned tumbler, are engaged for a few nights next week" (actually six nights, from August 12 to August 17; then reengaged for another six nights, August 19 to August 24). The same paper, a week later, informs us that this popular place of entertainment had been well attended during the week, and the two new additions to the company (Mr. Wallett, the celebrated jester, and Mr. Barnes, the far-famed summersault thrower) had drawn forth loud and well-deserved applause by their clever performances. Wallett's witticisms gave great zest to the evening's amusements, "and the extraordinary number of summersaults thrown by Barnes, without cessation, excite much admiration. On the evening of our visit, he turned himself over sixty one times without stopping, but he can go on even further than this, as he has been known to do it ninety-five times!." The *Era* of August 18, 1861, says, "W. F. Wallett, the famous jester, with the other clowns, Messrs. Barnes, Matthews, and Swann, have nightly kept the audience in a roar of laughter. Barnes, the great American [sic] somersault thrower, quite astonished all present." This has to mean that Barnes the pantaloon and Arthur Barnes were finally appearing on the same bill. The fact that Arthur Barnes is referred to as American means nothing. It was either deliberate by the promo men, or a mistake based on Barnes having done the United States a few years before.

Newsome's were due to leave Oxford after the August 24 performance and move on to Cambridge. The *Era* of August 25, 1861, says:

> Cambridge. Newsome's Equestrian Company are about paying us a visit for a short season, a large building now in course of erection by Mr. Harmston, archi-

tect to the establishment, on the Bell Bowling Green, Newmarket Road. From what we have heard of the exploits at Oxford, where the company have been performing since June the 24th, there must be some attraction and merit in the company; for we find by the bills the names of W.F. Wallett, Henry Brown, Tom Swann, and Tom Matthews, clowns; and for equestrians, Madame and Mr. Newsome, and their talented family, young Ducrow, Mr. Bradshaw, Aron Hassan (the Arab chief) and his new made wife ["new made" in that he had married her that year]; Mr. Pearson, and the Little Wonder, Miss Lizzy Keys; also the well known Barnes, the somersault thrower, and the extraordinary exploits of the Pentland Brothers.

However, the move to Cambridge was delayed.

It was natural for the great boxers of the day to tour with a circus here and there, even to have their own cirque. For example, in 1861 and 1862, Jem Mace was touring with Pablo Fanque's Circus, and Tom Sayers with Howes and Cushing's. Jem's experience with Pablo included not getting paid and bringing a lawsuit against the circus proprietor. However, this didn't stop the Swaffham Gypsy setting up his own equestrian company, Jem Mace's Circus. However, Jem didn't do a very good job of his new career, and the troupe died a quick death.

On September 2, 1861, Steve Ethair was performing at the Alhambra in London. That same night, in Leicester, where the Bedouin Arabs were performing with Stevens' Circus, young Jemmy Stevens, eldest son of the proprietor, met with a tragic accident. After doing very well on the horses, and throwing somersaults with the Arabs, he got dressed as a monkey for the next act, a farce. While climbing the pole in the center of the ring, his dress caught fire, and he was badly burned, despite his father and Dan Cook, the clown, rushing to his aid and whipping his clothes off. He died the next day, poor little bastard. He was 13.

On September 3, the great Blondin appeared on the tightrope at the Alhambra in Edinburgh, on his Scottish tour. The next day he was in Dundee, performing at the shipyard, 40 feet up, to the accompaniment of the local band whipped to a frenzy by its leader Bill Hall. On September 5, Tom Sayers, the champion boxer, exhibited with young Brooks at Howes and Cushing's Circus in Weymouth. On the 6th, Blondin was back in Edinburgh, at the Experimental Gardens. On September 7, 1861, the same day Blondin was playing to a packed house in Glasgow, Newsome's was still at Oxford, crammed nightly, but Arthur Barnes was no longer there. The following week Tom Sayers, still with Howes & Cushing's, was in Brighton. On the 10th, while Sanger's Circus was in Uxbridge, Jem Mace gratified the audience at Rochdale, there to see Pablo Fanque's Circus, when the former boxing champ took on "The Wolf." Newsome's was rescheduled to open in Cambridge on the 16th, but finally closed in Oxford on Friday, September 20, 1864, when Harry Brown took his benefit. On the 23rd and 24th, Jem Mace, still with Pablo's Cirque, played Sheffield, and on the 25th of September, Tom Sayers was in Canterbury.

The *Hampshire Telegraph and Sussex Chronicle* of Saturday, October 26, 1861, says,

> South of England New Music Hall, St. Mary Street, Portsmouth. Proprietor Mr. W. Brown. Unparallelled attractions!! Grand concentration of talent!!." They tell us that on Monday next, October 28th, 1861, will be "the first appearance of Mr. A. Barnes, champion vaulter of the world, late of the Emperor of Russia's Circus, St. Petersburg. Patronized by his majesty the king of Denmark and the king of Sweden. This extraordinary gentleman has been presented with a gold medal by Mr. Pablo Fanque, equestrian manager, for having thrown the great number of sixty six somersaults in one trial. Mr. Barnes has also been presented with a silver snuff box lined with gold, and a magnificent diamond pin, by W. Cooke, Esq., proprietor of the Great Colossal Establishment, for having thrown the extraordinary number of ninety-one somersaults at one trial — the greatest number ever performed by an artiste anywhere in the world. Also, first appearance of Mr. Hemmings [sic], celebrated vaulter.

Arthur Barnes was reengaged at Portsmouth for the following two weeks, and while he was there, Bob Chadwick was performing in Liverpool, with Hengler's.

Arthur Barnes left Portsmouth on November 16 and joined Sanger's again, this time at Boar Lane, Leeds, for the Christmas season of 1861. The Boar Lane circus building, erected by Pablo Fanque at the beginning of 1854, was 100 feet long, 72 feet wide, and had stabling for 32 horses. The December 29, 1861, issue of the *Era* tells us, "One gentleman, for instance (Mr. Arthur Barnes) throws 63 clean somersaults without stopping." On December 28, one of the camels gave birth, a rare occurrence in England at that time. Sanger's would stay in Leeds for a few more months, but Arthur Barnes left them around the New Year of 1862, to head south.

There's another cryptic reference in most of the late December 1861 and the January 1862 editions of the *Era*. It's in connection with Drury Lane, under the management of E. T. Smith, for the Christmas 1861 holiday panto, *The Witches' Glen and Waterfall*. Two of the "ignes fatui" were Mmlles. Barnes and A. Barnes, i.e., two ladies. We don't know who they are. Arthur Barnes was playing at Leeds for Christmas, not at Drury Lane, but the two ignes fatui could be Miss Pettoletti and her daughter, the Alexine Catherine Barns born in 1852 in Bath.

As 1862 opened Hengler's was playing Liverpool, featuring the Brothers Ridley, while William Cooke's Circus, now under the direction of William

Cooke, Jr., was playing in Rochester and Chatham. Maus's Circus was in Leicester, at the old Stevens Circus building at Belgrave Gate, but it wasn't a very lucrative stay there, and he wrapped up on March 8. Ginnett's Monstre Circus was in Bradford the week beginning January 12, 1862. Jee & Orford's newly formed circus had opened at Derby on November 27, 1861, but it was all done on the cheap. They didn't even place an ad in the *Derby Mercury*, and were not even covered in the news by that otherwise comprehensive paper. They were at Grantham the week beginning January 6, 1862, for at least two weeks, with Bill Orford the clown giving a good account of himself with this rather small troupe. This cirque must have folded after that, because the name drops off the planet.

On January 5, 1862, the Alhambra Circus opened in Brighton, under the direction of Madame Macarte. Her company included the Wells Family, Mr. Moffatt, and Mr. Barnes (*Era*, January 12, 1862). We don't know which Saturday Mr. Barnes left Madame Macarte, whether it was January 10 or January 17, but it was one of those two. The New Exhibition Circus, under the direction of the Brothers Pinder and Mr. Swallow, played Dundee the week beginning January 13, 1862. The Sardinian Circus, under the direction of Mons. Antonio Quaglieni (born Brescia, in 1815), had been in Britain since 1857, often being billed as the Cirque Royal de Sardaigne. They had been in Bristol since Christmas 1861 and were featuring Romeo and Luigi, the somersaultists, and John Samwell, while Les Frères Quaglieni appeared on the flying trapeze. They wrapped up in Bristol on January 20, and on January 22, opened at Manchester. By Monday, January 20, 1862, at least, Arthur Barnes was opening with Hogini's Equestrian Palace, which had been in Cork since the Christmas 1861 entertainments. The *Era* of January 26, 1862, tells us that on Friday morning, the performances were under the patronage, and honoured by the presence of, Sir John Arnott, M.P., and a large party. Mr. Hogini has added considerably to the attractions of his Circus. "Mdlle Smicht is a most daring, graceful, and clever Equestrian, and Mr. A. Barnes the most astonishing somersault thrower we ever saw. The house is crowded nightly." Although press notices are vague, it certainly looks as if Arthur Barnes was with Hogini's until Saturday, February 15, 1862.

Arthur Barnes was back with Sanger's in Manchester, for the week beginning February 17, 1862, the same day Quaglieni's opened at Nottingham with Jem Elliotte, the comic tumbling clown, as a star attraction. The *Era* of February 16, 1862, says, "Manchester. Royal Alhambra Circus. Portland Street. Next week the proprietor [Mr. T. B. Burton] presents an entirely new company, including Mr. J. Wilson [and] Mr. Arthur Barnes, the celebrated vaulter." Wallett was there too. It's possible, although unlikely, that the two had made up their differences by now. Barnes was still at Manchester in

March. The *Era* of February 23 confirms that "the champion somersault thrower, Arthur Barnes" was now with Sanger's. The *Era* of March 2 mentions "The great vaulter Arthur Barnes," and the same periodical for March 9 says, "Mr. Barnes, the Champion Vaulter." The *Era* of March 16 says, "Arthur Barnes, the Champion Vaulter, who throws somersaults varying from 60 to 80 at one attempt." Carl Stonette was also on the bill. On March 17, 1862, Sanger's opened in Sheffield.

It may or may not be that Arthur Barnes was with Sanger's in Sheffield for that first week, beginning Monday, March 17, 1862, but it is most likely. The following Monday, March 24, 1862, the day William Wallett, the clown, married the composer Henry Farmer's sister, Arthur Barnes opened at the Surrey Music Hall, in Westbar, Sheffield. The *Sheffield and Rotherham Independent* of that date says, "This evening, Surrey Music Hall. Manager Mr. M. Donnelly. Great Novelty!! Engagement of Mr. Arthur Barnes, the champion vaulter of the world, whose extraordinary feat of throwing one hundred somersaults in succession [this is mere blurb] is pronounced to be unparalleled." Robert Chadwick was also on the bill, as was the singer Mrs. Frankford; the dancers Brothers Travis; the comic Mr. R. Templeton; the dog man Mr. R. Harrison. It was also the last week of Mr. F. O'Flanagan, the Irish comedian. Barnes was due to play there until the evening of April 4, but he and Chadwick were reengaged for a few nights. Those few nights turned into a few weeks, and they were still there on the night of April 18, their last night but one. Jenny Lind did a one-night stand at the Music Hall in Sheffield on the 27th, and Sanger's played there on March 31 and April 1.

In early April 1862, Jack Heenan, the Benicia Boy, the heavyweight champion pugilist of America, arrived from the United States with a fat purse, but, apparently no intention of fighting Mace, Sayers, or anyone else, ever again. He was, he said, merely in the United Kingdom to fulfill a six-month circus tour obligation with Howes and Cushing's Equestrian Troupe. Jem Mace, the British champion, was ready to fight Heenan for the championship of the world, even put up £1000, but the Boy was not interested. So, Jem joined Ginnett's Circus for their 1862 summer tour: Gloucester (April 4, 1862), Stroud (April 5, 1862), Wootton-under-Edge (April 7, 1862), Bristol (April 8, 1862), Bath (April 9, 1862), Chippenham (April 10, 1862), Swindon (April 11, 1862), Faringdon (April 12, 1862), Oxford (April 14, 1862), Abingdon (April 15, 1862), Henley (April 17, 1862), Reading (April 18, 1862), Portsmouth (May 19 and 20, 1862).

As for Hengler's Circus, they opened in Glasgow on April 7, 1862, still featuring Anthony Bridges and clowns James Franks, John Clarke, and Little Bibb, but with the addition of John Henderson and John Henry Cooke.

Arthur Barnes left Sheffield on April 19, 1862. He was living in London by now, with his wife. He and Chadwick opened at Wilton's Magnificent Music Hall, on Monday, April 21, 1862, for the Easter shows (*Era*, April 20, 1862). Architected by Jacob Maggs and built by Thomas Ennott in 1850 as one of the leading music halls in London, with John and Ellen Wilton as lessees, Wilton's was to be found at the Prince of Denmark Public House, 1 Grace's Alley, Wellclose Square, Leman Street, Whitechapel. Some years later it was renovated, so as to be able to seat 1,500, and the new hall opened on March 28, 1858. The main hall was mainly covered with mirrors, and light was provided by a chandelier. The Wiltons remained lessees until 1869. The building is still there.

Business kept getting better and better for Quaglieni's troupe in Nottingham, and, had they cared to, they could have extended their stay there beyond their last night, April 26, but they had a commitment to open at the Cremorne Gardens in London on May 1. On his way out, Signor Quaglieni was stung by the town of Nottingham for quarterly rates (property tax). They would be replaced there on May 10 by Herr Maus's circus.

The *Era* of April 27, 1862, still has Arthur Barnes at Wilton's, and the same magazine of May 4, 1862, says:

> Another new "sensation" in the acrobatic and nerve-shaking line is "the champion vaulter of the world," Mr. Arthur Barnes, who throws sixty somersaults in less than as many seconds, and the beautiful precision in which this feat is accomplished certainly gives the performer a right to the somewhat high-sounding title he has assumed, for we question if any one would be found handy enough to enter the lists with him. He is assisted by Mons. Chadwick, also a good tumbler, and a clever performer on stilts, and the Etoile family make up the evening's diversions belonging to the drawing-room element.

Barnes and Chadwick were at Wilton's certainly until May 15 (for example, the *Era* of May 11, 1862, has them still there). On June 9, 1862, they were at Crystal Palace, for the Whitmonday performances, and on June 23, they opened at the Leeds Amphitheatre. The *Era* of June 29 tells us, "Arthur Barnes and R. Chadwick, the celebrated vaulters, and the former well-known for his great feat of throwing 100 consecutive somersaults, have appeared every evening during the week, together with Stafford Barker, the admired tenor, and the other old favorites, whose names were duly recorded last week [they weren't, actually]." This 100 mentioned above was simply picked up from the promo men. Barnes still hadn't done the ton. If this gig was advertised locally, it certainly wasn't in the *Leeds Mercury*.

By May 1862, Jem Mace had left Ginnett's, and was putting his own circus together. However, this didn't work out, and Jem went back on the road with Ginnett. The rest of Ginnett's tour included: Exeter (June), St. Columb (June

24), Liskeard (July 8), Devonport (July 9), Weymouth (July 30). At Weymouth, Tom King, the great pugilist, was announced, but for some reason didn't appear. Incidentally, Howes' American Circus played Swansea on May 31, 1862.

Barnes and Chadwick, now a traveling team, left Leeds on July 11, 1862. The *Era* of July 6, 1862, says, "Leeds. Amphitheatre. Messrs. Chadwick and Arthur Barnes, the vaulters, conclude a successful engagement here this week." In the old days Barnes had teamed with Harry Connor, and to some extent with Bill Dale. His new partner was Bob Chadwick. A partner of equal, or almost equal, talent was very important to the spectacle presented. The pair could get the crowd going as they vaulted against each other in head to head competition. Sometimes one would win, sometimes the other. The outcome was undoubtedly arranged beforehand, in a manner similar to the "fixes" of today's professional wrestling. After all, the circus was a business, not a sport. These fixes had the effect not only of producing an uncertainty as to the outcome of a world-class and thrilling contest, but also of creating an atmosphere of side-betting that was fast and furious. It's a safe bet that the Acrobat profited enormously from these competitions.

The town of Leicester was bemoaning "Where are the circuses? We have now at our command a most convenient and central spot for anything of this kind near the Railway Station, and the above question is continually asked."

On July 28, 1862, the day Newsome's Circus opened in Cambridge, featuring Harry Brown, the great clown, Barnes and Chadwick were at the Pavilion Gardens, North Woolwich, owned by Charles Bishop, late of Cremorne and Surrey Gardens. This from the *Era* of August 3: "First appearance of Barnes, the champion vaulter." On Wednesday, July 30, at the Crystal Palace, James Glaisher, a fellow of the Royal Society, with 16 men, made an ascent in Coxwell's Mammoth Balloon at precisely four o'clock. They would go five miles up. Before they rose, however, at three o'clock in the balloon enclosure, "Mr. Barnes and Mr. Chadwick (both of whom are celebrated for the great number of consecutive somersaults they have thrown)" engaged in a great vaulting contest. We rely for this tidbit on that day's (and the previous day's) *Standard* and *Morning Post*. "The almost incredible number of sixty-eight consecutive somersaults were recently thrown by Mr. Barnes," the champion sauteur of the world.

The *Era* of August 10 says, "Second week of Barnes and Chadwick, the champion vaulters" at North Woolwich. The *Era* of August 17 and 24, 1862, say the same thing, so it's somewhat difficult to say exactly when the two vaulters left North Woolwich.

Howes' American Circus played Hull on July 31, 1862, with, among other performers, Wallett, the clown, and the great American pugilist John C.

Heenan. That very day, Jean-Francois Gravelet — Blondin — the Hero Of Niagara, appeared at the Crystal Palace (he had made his debut there on June 1), on the low tightrope. On Friday, the Great Fountains, and the whole series of cascades and waterworks, were exhibited. Blondin appeared in Ipswich on August 26, 1862, prior to his departure for Russia. August 13, 1862, was Hengler's last night in Glasgow, and then, on the 16th, they opened in Greenock.

On Monday, September 15, 1862, Mr. Arthur Barnes (the champion summersault thrower) with Mr. Robt. Chadwick (the clown) made his first appearance at the New St. George's Hall, Scarborough, "and his feats have the theme of admiration of all the frequenters of this successful hall" (*Era*, September 14 and 21, 1862). Their last night in Scarborough was Saturday, September 27, 1862, as testified by the fact that the *Era* of September 28 has them still there as of the 27th, "nightly received with approval."

On Monday, September 29, 1862, Barnes and Chadwick opened at the Mechanics Large Hall in Hull, as part of the Springthorpe's Waxworks and Promenade Concerts series. The place was jammed that whole week, and people had to be turned away. They left there on Saturday, October 6 (*Era*, October 5, 1862). As for Hengler's, they closed in Greenock on October 19 and the following day reopened in Liverpool, where they stayed for the rest of the year. Pinder & Swallow's New Exhibition Circus played October 21, 1862, in Sunderland, featuring Billy Seal, the clown.

By late September, Jem Mace was taking another shot at circus proprietorship and was playing Ipswich. On October 20 he was in King's Lynn, featuring, aside from himself, Jim Myers, the clown, and his wife. But Mr. Mace had a problem, certainly in his native county of Norfolk. The magistrates there, frowning on pugilism, as did many other counties, had forbidden him even to spar publicly, the penalty being arrest. So, to the great disappointment of the crowds, the whole attraction of Jem Mace was nullified, and he lost big money repeatedly.

The *Nottinghamshire Guardian* of October 31, 1862, says: "Newsome's Alhambra Circus. The attractions at this popular place of amusement [i.e., the handsome and commodious building on Mansfield Road, in Nottingham] have been increased this week by the appearance of several of the bright, particular stars of the day, including Mr. Barnes, the champion vaulter, and several equestrians of surpassing ability." This means Barnes opened in Nottingham with Newsome on Monday, October 27, 1862. At that time Quaglieni's were playing in Cardiff, and Herr Maus's outfit was in Gloucester. On November 3, 1862, Ginnett's opened in Birmingham for the winter season.

For the record: Bell's Hippodrome, under the direction of Richard Bell, was in Belfast from 1861 and into the New Year of 1862. On February 28, 1862, Mons. Clevori was performing on a primitive type of trapeze, 45 feet up, when he fell. He didn't die, but he was in an awful state. On March 5, Mr. Bell threw a benefit for the poor bastard. That would fix him up, set Mons. Clevori back on the road to a deliriously happy life—and it did. On March 7, Mr. Bell treated 70 advanced, but unhappy, lunatics from the local asylum. They loved the show—they were now happy lunatics—and then left. But a demon escaped, lodged itself in the cat cage, and wouldn't leave for the rest of the year. On June 9, 1862, Bell's opened in Dublin for several weeks, with that bloody fool Clevori doing his same old act. On July 15, at Kingstown, as Bell's were parading through the town, one Tom Kelly got too close to the puma cage. Two of the big cats got him bad, ripped his arm off. If it hadn't been for Tom Batty (the lion tamer with the troupe, and William Batty's nephew) and a local constable, Tom would have had to have more than his arm amputated. Mr. Kelly, a shoemaker, at one fell swoop, found himself no longer able to earn his living. Mr. Bell was kind enough to pay him 30 shillings, set the fellow right. Good old Bell. Those were the days when a shilling was worth—well, a shilling. On August 13, in Kerry, as they were parading through the town, one Cournane got too close to the puma cage. One of the big cats got him, and was about to rip him to pieces when Mr. Batty, aided by a young man named Eugene Browne, intervened with whips and things and succeeded in getting the critter off its unfortunate victim. Aside from a cut shoulder and hand, Mr. Cournane was alright, if a bit shook up. By November, Bell's was in Liverpool, beginning their winter season there. One night, one of the lion tamers, a 23-year-old Munsterman named Tom McCarthy passed too close to the cage, and a lioness reached out and ripped his arm off. Mr. Batty intervened before the big cat could go all the way, and the man was whipped to the hospital, where what remained of his arm was amputated. Sounds like a joke, doesn't it? Going to Bell's could cost you an arm and a leg. On the other hand, Mr. Moffatt, the elephant man, kept his charges under control, in and out of the ring. There's more to come, in January 1872, on the awfully unlucky Mr. McCarthy.

For the record: Tom Sayers, the boxing champion, had purchased the three touring companies owned by Howes and Cushing, as well as that of Jim Myers, and formed them into the Mammoth Hippodrome, otherwise known as The Champion Circus, the biggest circus in the world. On January 6, 1862, they were going to pitch their "royal tent" at Dale Street, Liverpool, which had been Hengler's premises, and thousands turned up for the big event, only to find the corporation had seized the land amid a dispute about who owned it. Police stood by to quell riots. Tom tried to get the city to change its mind, and let them play there, but to no avail. Losing money every minute, he finally worked out a deal to take a vacant lot of land at the Derby Arms Hotel, near the zoo, on West Derby Road, to play there on January 10 and 11, 1862. But that was a poor option; Liverpool had done to Tom what the Benicia Boy had failed to do to him in the ring. This company, featuring the horsemen Jim and John Powell, the clown Bill Mitchell (when Bill got sick in April and May, Alec Harrison stood in), and Howes & Cushing's old mules Pete and Barney (for which Tom had paid 180 guineas), visited Accrington (January 16, 1862), Halifax (January 22, 1862), Barnsley (January 27, 1862), Sheffield (January 28, 1862), Rotherham (January 29, 1862), Doncaster (January 30, 1862), Goole (January 31, 1862), Selby (February 1, 1862), Hull (February 5 and 6, 1862), York (February 10, 1862), Masham (February 15, 1862), Pateley Bridge (February 17, 1862), Grassington (February 18, 1862), Settle (February 19, 1862), Skipton (February 20, 1862), Colne (February 21, 1862), Cross Hills (February 22, 1862), Keighley (February 24, 1862), Bingley (February 25, 1862), Shipley (February 26, 1862), Otley (February 27, 1862), Wetherby (February 28, 1862), Kirkstall (February 29, 1862), Retford (March 10, 1862), Newark (March 11, 1862), Southwell (March 12, 1862), Nottingham (March 13, 1862), Bingham (March 14, 1862), Ely (April 2, 1862), Mildenhall (April 3, 1862), Newmarket (April 4, 1862), Bury St. Edmunds (April 5, 1862), Brandon (April 7, 1862), Swaffham (April 8, 1862), Poplar (May 17 and 19, 1862), Dalston (May 20 and 21, 1862), Tottenham (May 22, 1862), Holloway (May 23, 1862), Chalk Farm (May 24 and 26, 1862), Hammersmith (May 27 and 28, 1862), Richmond (May 29, 1862), Kingston (May 30, 1862), Clapham (May 31, 1862), Bath (July 7 and 8, 1862), Bristol (July 9 and 10, 1862), Gloucester (July 11, 1862), Chepstow (July 12, 1862), Newport (July 14, 1862), Cardiff (July 15, 1862), Newbridge (July 16, 1862), Merthyr Tydfil (July 17, 1862), Tredegar (July 18, 1862), Pontypool (July 19, 1862), Swansea (August 1, 1862), Bangor (August 30, 1862), Llandudno (September 1, 1862), Rhyl (September 2, 1862), Holywell (September 3, 1862), Mold (September 4, 1862), York (September 27 and 29, 1862), Malton (September 30, 1862), Pickering (October 1, 1862), Thorne (October 17, 1862; Tom passed through the Thorne toll-bar without paying, and the town fathers came after him), Tickhill (October 18, 1862), Sheffield (October 20, 1862), Chesterfield (October 21, 1862), Ripley (October 22, 1862), Derby (October 23, 1862), Leicester (October 24, 1862), Rugby (October 25, 1862), Northampton (October 27, 1862). On November 6, amid false rumors of an Australian tour, the circus, including Pete and Barney, was sold piecemeal at the Welsh Harp Hotel in Hendon. For 20 guineas, Mr. Batty bought Wallace, the cream-colored carriage horse, and for 7 guineas he got Yankee. Van Hare, the impresario, bought Tike for 6 guineas and Emma for 20. Jemmy Welsh, Tom Sayers' second in many of his fights, bought the brown ring horse Jem for 14 guineas. A new rumor was now spreading that Tom Sayers and John C. Heenan were going to merge with Howes & Cushing to form a truly monstre equestrian company.

For the record: Sanger's, after leaving Sheffield after their April 1, 1862, performance, featuring Crockett, the lion king, the Bedouin Arabs, and Ajax (the elephant bought from William Cooke's circus for £500), played Rotherham (April 2, 1862), Doncaster (April 3, 1862), Thorne (April 4, 1862), Goole (April 5, 1862), Hull (April 8, 1862), Malton (April 16, 1862), York (April 17, 1862), Knaresborough (April 19, 1862), Harrogate (April 21, 1862), Boroughbridge (April 22, 1862), Ripon (April 23, 1862), Richmond (April 24, 1862), Barnard Castle (April 25, 1862), Darlington (April 26, 1862), Middlesbrough (April 28, 1862), Sunderland (May 10, 1862), South Shields (May 12, 1862), North Shields (May 13, 1862), Newcastle (May 14 and 15, 1862), Edinburgh (May 31, June 2, 3, and 4, 1862), St. Andrews (June 13), Dundee (June 14 and 16, 1862), Arbroath (June 17, 1862), Montrose (June 18, 1862), Brechin (June 19, 1862), Forfar (June 20, 1862), Coupar Angus (June 21, 1862), Airdrie (July 4, 1862), Lancaster (July 21, 1862), St. Helens (July 28, 1862), Chester (July 31), Kidderminster (August 8, 1862), Worcester (August 9, 1862), Bristol (August 18 and 19, 1862), Trowbridge (August 23, 1862), Winchester (August 30, 1862), Southampton (September 1 and 2, 1862), Fareham (September 3, 1862), Gosport (September 4, 1862), Portsmouth (September 5 and 6, 1862), Northampton (October 20), Redditch (October 25), Derby (October 28), Redditch (November 1, 1862), Birmingham (November 4, 1862), Greatbridge (November 5, 1862), West Bromwich (November 6, 1862), Smethwick (November 7, 1862), Walsall (November 8, 1862). Their new winter quarters were being built in Sheffield, on the Victoria Road near the Victoria Railway Station, and Sanger's Great International Circus opened there, with Arthur Barnes as a star, on Monday, November 17, 1862.

We rely on the *Sheffield and Rotherham Independent* to tell us that that opening night, commencing at 7:30, was under the patronage of John Brown, the mayor, and was a benefit for the distressed in Lancashire (the evening's take was £48, and Mr. Sanger added £2 out of his own pocket). "The vaulting we have never seen surpassed; and the manner in which Mr. A. Barnes and his compeers vaulted over six chargers, side by side, turning somersaults in their aerial flights, certainly entitles them to rank among the first vaulters in the world." This is very interesting, in that it is one of the few indications we have that Arthur Barnes performed in events other than straight still-vaulting. The paper goes on to say that the company "is rich in clowns, and 'Mr. Funny Footit,' fool though he is, almost rivals Mr. Barnes in vaulting." Opening night was a triumphant success, with a crowded house, and a complete settlement of the question as to the stability of the building. On Saturday, November 22, the first day performance took place, at 2:30, to a somewhat slender audience (from now on there would be a day performance every Tuesday and Saturday; however, the week beginning Monday, the 24th, was Fair

Week, so there was a morning and evening show every day). That first week, precisely 17,159 persons stopped by to see the show. Tuesday, the 25th, was the actual Fair Day in Sheffield, and the two performances were very successful. About midday, the company made a grand procession, in full dress, through the town, some of them being on horseback, others in carriages, others again on camels, and the remainder on the elephant. The procession was evidently intended to represent an Oriental cavalcade, and included a caravan containing three lions. A second caravan had a large lion on the top, with a lady occupying a seat beside the animal. The novel procession attracted vast numbers of spectators. Just at the evening performance on Fair Day, 3,370 persons came to the circus. Fair Day in Sheffield brought out its lunatics too, as, of course, it always does. Down the road, at the Royal Lyceum Theatre that evening, they were playing *Peep o' Day*. One of the crowd, Jim Graham, wouldn't stop clapping. This really annoyed the people sitting around him. Then Jim kept getting up and going in and out of the theater, which annoyed them even more. Finally he met Constable Brown, the cop on pit duty, and slashed him across the forehead with a knife, and then stabbed him repeatedly. Jim's rather egregious behavior was terminated by onlookers, and he was thrown into jail.

On December 1, 1862, Monsieur Goldkette, the great Parisian rider, opened in Sheffield with Sanger's. They were now concluding the show with *The Rigs of Mr. Briggs*. December 5 was a grand fashionable box night, under the patronage of W. Butcher, Esq., the town regent. Mr. Crockett and his lions made their debut with Sanger's on Monday, December 8, as did Madame Rosalie, from the Cirque Napoleon, in Paris, but that was two days after Arthur Barnes and Bob Chadwick's last night with Sanger's, Saturday, December 6, 1862. They had also given a day performance that Saturday, at half past two. That was the night the *Marvels of Peru* opened in Sheffield, at the Surrey Music Hall, for one week only.

The *Era* of December 28, 1862, gives us a nice look at Turnham's Grand Concert Hall on Edgeware Road. Built on the site of the White Lion pub (which dated from 1524), it was rebuilt as Turnham's Grand Concert Music Hall in 1836, rebuilt in 1862, and opened its doors on December 23, 1862, with a successful (treble the normal price) opening night. Capacious and comfortable, the building was then the largest of its kind in London, hexagonal in shape; one of the sides formed the stage, and a spacious balcony ran around the five other sides. The hall, lighted by 12 chandeliers hanging from the ceiling, was 80 feet long and 50 feet high. Those artistes John Turnham hired included "The Champion Vaulter of the World, Mr. Arthur Barnes and his clown, Mr. Chadwick." The whole of the company assembled on the stage at 7:30, and sang the national anthem. Then the acts performed, and "Mr.

Arthur Barnes then made his bow, and with his partner, Chadwick, entertained the audience for about a quarter of an hour, the first named throwing no fewer than fifty-six consecutive somersaults in the interim." In 1864, Turnham's would become the Metropolitan Music Hall.

On December 26, 1862, Barnes and Chadwick, while they were playing Turnham's at night, opened at the Crystal Palace during the day. This had been predicted by the *Era* of December 21, 1862, which, talking about performers who would be playing the Crystal Palace over Christmas, mentions "the great Arthur Barnes, the Champion Vaulter" and "Mr. Chadwick, the grotesque." The *Daily News* of December 27 reviewed the opening performance. "Mr. Arthur Barnes went through some clever gymnastic performances, assisted by Mr. Chadwick, the grotesque clown." They were still there on Saturday, December 27, 1862, as advertised in the *Morning Post* of that day, as well as the *Standard* (also of that day), and also on the 29th, 30th, and 31st (*Morning Post* of those dates). This dual role played by Arthur Barnes—at the Crystal Palace by day and Turnham's by night—continued at Turnham's until at least February 13, 1863, and at the Crystal Palace until at least Easter of 1863.

The London *Morning Post* of January 1, 1863, says,

> Crystal Palace. Great Christmas revels, Juvenile fete, and gigantic holiday fancy fair, this day (Thursday). Parisian illuminations (by Messrs. Defries). Entire place comfortably warmed by 50 miles of hot-water pipes. All approaches under cover. Wet or dry, equally agreeable. The largest decorated Christmas tree, 100 feet high. Blondin's farewell performances. Continuous amusements from twelve o'clock, under the direction of Mr. Nelson Lee. The Bianchi family; Unsworth, "or any other man"; Comic Songs and dances by Miss Kate Harley; Miss Lizzie Watson; Mr. Wm Randall, Messrs. Uriah and Edgar Parry; the champion sauteur of the world, Mr. Arthur Barnes and Mr. Chadwick, the Parisian grotesque; concluding with a comic Christmas pantomime entitled *Harlequin, or the Good Fairy of the Invisible Grotto*; the whole of the characters (11 in number) in elegant costumes, with songs, parodies, and burlesque dances, by Mr. E. Marshall.

The same ad appeared in the *Morning Post* of January 2, 1863, except that it pertained to that day (Friday), as it did in the London *Daily News* and *The Standard*. It also appeared in the *Morning Post* (again, pertaining to the relevant day) of Saturday, January 3; and Monday, January 5. The last one did warn us that Blondin's last performance would be on Thursday (January 8, 1863). It also advertised Don Jose Manuel, the Brazilian wire-walker, and the Etoile family. The *Morning Post* of Thursday, January 8, said, "Blondin's farewell performance. Positively his last appearance at the Palace. He will give his marvellous low rope performance this day (Thursday) at three."

The *Morning Post* of Saturday, January 10, 1863, says,

Crystal Palace. Varied holiday attractions, this day. Programme: Part One, commencing one o'clock: Overture, by orchestral band; Mr. William Randall, comic songs; Mr. Arthur Barnes, champion vaulter; Mr. Chadwick, Parisian grotesque; Mr. Levy, cornet solo; Messrs. Uriah and Edgar Parry. Interval for promenade. Part Two. Three o'clock. Leotard [this is Jules Leotard, the French aerialist who invented the flying trapeze act. He had made his debut at the Alhambra on May 20, 1861, and was paid £180 per week]. Interval for promenade. Part Three. Four o'clock. The Toy Symphony, by orchestral band; the Etoile Family, gymnastic entertainment; Don Jose Manuel, the Brazilian wire-walker; Master Eugene, the Ethiopian prima donna; Unsworth, "or any other man"; Mr. E. Marshall's comic pantomime. Great organ performance and illuminated promenade.

The *Era* of Sunday, January 11, 1863, advertised this: Turnham's Grand Concert Hall. Edgeware Road. Sole proprietor Mr. John Turnham. Every evening at seven. Operatic selections. Great success of John Burnett's *Mountain Sylph*, with full band and chorus. Vocal and instrumental solos. Comic talent: Mackney, Sam Collins, Mr. and Mrs. Brennan; West ("or any other man") and Taylor; Arthur Barnes (Champion Vaulter of the World); Chadwick (the Parisian Grotesque); and Mdlle. Cerito (the great Transformation Dancer). Admission sixpence and one shilling. Musical director and manager, Mr. Charles Greville. This ad was repeated in *The Standard* of Thursday, January 15 and Friday, January 16, 1863. In the latter, E. Loder's *Night Dancers* had been added. The following day Barnes and Chadwick moonlighted (so to speak) at the Crystal Palace.

The *Morning Post* of January 17 tells us of the Crystal Palace, this day (Saturday). All the amusements as follows: 1:00: Orchestral band in center transept; 1:15: Mr. Chadwick, Stiltonian gymnast; 1:30: Mr. Arthur Barnes, champion vaulter; 1:45: Master Eugene, premiere danseuse; 2:00: Don Jose, Brazilian wire-walker. Interval for promenade. 3:15: Orchestral band; 3:30: Madame Elise Adams, tightrope artiste, with Chadwick as grotesque; 3:45: the Etoile Family, gymnasts; 4:00: Master Eugene, Ethiopian prima donna; 4:15: Unsworth, "or any other man"; 4:30: Marshall's pantomime. Cornet solos by Mr. Levy at intervals. Organ performance during illuminated promenade, with Palace fully lighted; also Defries' Great Prismatic Mirror. Mrs. Adams got a separate ad: "Madame Elise Adams on the tightrope will repeat her graceful performances, and introduce new feats, concluding with her extraordinary pirouette on the rope." Admission to the Palace was half a crown, with children and parties of 12 getting in for a shilling.

On Monday, January 19, 1863, Barnes and Chadwick were still at Turnham's, as the *Era* of Sunday, January 18, and those of January 25, February 1, and February 8, tell us. There were a couple of new acts at Turnham's that week, but basically it was the lineup of the week before. Barnes and Chadwick were certainly at Turnham's until February 20, but it's doubtful after that; they no longer appear in the ads after February 15.

On or around February 25, 1863, Arthur Barnes must have been with his wife (whether she was traveling with him or not), as nine months after that their daughter, Annie, would be born. We don't pick him up in the London theaters the week beginning February 22, 1863.

The week beginning February 22, 1863, Les Frères Conrad were playing the Alhambra. Pinder's were in Dundee, featuring Wallett and Aron Hassan, but, on occasion, Wallett appeared at the Theatre Royal, Dundee, by permission of the Pinders. He was doing *Raphael's Dream*, a representation of Grecian statues. He was not packing them in. Hogini's Circus was in Cork, and Quaglieni's was at Bath. On March 2, 1863, Hengler's wrapped up in Liverpool, and on March 7 opened in Edinburgh. Newsome's Circus was presenting *Cinderella* at Leicester, with Lizzie Keys in the title role, and Miss Newsome as the Prince. At the same packed houses, the Pentland Brothers were doing their thing on the globe. Charles Adams and Tom Swann were the clowns, and Wallett would be with them the next week, coming from Scotland. The *Marvels of Peru* were at the People's Concert Hall in Manchester, sharing the bill with our old friend, Stafford Barker, the tenor. Myers' Circus had arrived in Norwich, and on March 2 were in Nottingham. On March 9, Pablo Fanque's Circus opened at Bolton. But, no Arthur Barnes. On March 9, 1863, Herr Maus's Circus opened at Cardiff, and on March 30, in Bradford, Jem Mace's new circus began its tenting season.

On Smallbrook Street, Birmingham, in April 1862 (the year before), James Day, the famous owner of the Crystal Palace, in London, laid the foundation stone for a building he planned to call the Crystal Palace Music Hall. It opened on September 19 of that year, as the Crystal Palace Concert Hall, which he touted as the most splendid hall in Europe. Designed by architected Thomas Naden and built by William Matthews, it was 135 feet long, 62 feet wide, and 49 feet high. The stage was designed by George Langley of the Theatre Royal, Drury Lane. On March 5, 1863, the Brothers Elliott were playing there, i.e., Tim and Harry. We know this not from any ad (they simply weren't billed), but from an article in the *Birmingham Daily Post* of March 6, reviewing the charity performance given the night before. Thus, the famous Brothers Elliott, who should have been billed, weren't. One would expect, therefore, that the Brothers Elliott had played all that week, i.e., the week ending Saturday, March 7. However, again, they're not billed in any of the daily editions of the *Post* that week. Then, beginning on Monday, March 9, the paper advertised "those extraordinary acrobatic artistes, *The Four Marvels of Peru*, the greatest wonders of the world." These were, in reality, the Ridgway Family,

Charles Ridgway and his sons Tom, George, and John. An article in the *Post* of March 14, 1862, says: "The Brothers Elliot [sic] have given place to 'The Marvels of Peru'—a very clever company of acrobats." *The Marvels of Peru* are advertised every day until Saturday, April 4, when they drop out of print. Then, the *Era* of April 5, 1863, tells us that Barns [sic] and Chadwick (champion vaulters and acrobatic artistes) are scheduled for the Easter entertainments at the Crystal Palace. What they meant, of course, was not the famous Crystal Palace in London but Day's Crystal Palace Concert Hall in Birmingham. Enormous engagements for the Easter Holidays. On Easter Monday, April 6, Messrs. Barnes and Chadwick opened there for the week, the champion vaulters and celebrated acrobatic artistes (*Birmingham Daily Post*, April 8, 1863, et seq.). There was a morning performance on Easter Monday and Tuesday. Barnes and Chadwick remained with Day the next week, and the next. The week beginning Monday, April 27, marked their last six nights there, and they wrapped up on Saturday, May 2.

The May 30, 1863, *Penny Illustrated* says this: "Upwards of 36,000 holiday folks visited the [Crystal] Palace on Whitmonday [i.e., May 25, 1863], partly attracted by the unequalled beauty of the place, and partly by the round of amusements specially provided for the occasion." This time, this is the real Crystal Palace, in London. "These amusements comprised some extraordinary performances by M. Silvani, the great leaper; Mr. Arthur Barnes, the champion sauteur; Mackney, the inimitable; the Elliott Brothers." This was all performed until, and including, Friday, May 29, 1863. A lot of newspapers covered this article, verbatim.

Various editions of the *Era* in 1863 show us an ad placed by managing agents George Webb and Harry Montague, which gives a list ("the Excelsior List") of their performers under contract. Arthur Barnes and Chadwick (champion vaulters, from the Crystal Palace), Steve Ethair, George Hutchinson, the Elliott family, the Brothers Conrad, the Delavantis, John Henderson, Jim Thorne, among others. All the Great Stars Appearing!! Webb & Montague, International, Musical, and Equestrian Star Agency, 3 Snow Hill, London, EC.

The *Hampshire Telegraph* of August 22 and 29, 1863, tells us, via an ad: "South of England Music Hall, St. Mary Street, Portsmouth. Proprietor, Mr. W. Brown. On Monday next, August the 24th, 1863, and during the week, first appearance of Mr. Arthur Barnes, Champion Vaulter of the World, late of the Emperor of Russia's Cirque, St. Petersburg; Cirque Napoleon, Paris; and the Crystal Palace; Mr. Robert Chadwick, the great tumbling clown and chair performer, from Renze's Cirque, Vienna." August 27 was a grand special night, under distinguished patronage. They also played there from Monday, August 31, to Saturday, wrapping up there on September 5.

On September 5, 1863, the Inman steamer *City of London* left New York, under the command of Capt. P. C. Petrie, on its regular shuttle run to Liverpool, carrying 48 bags of mail for Britain, as well as 34 cabin passengers and 125 steerage. On the 9th they were off Cape Race, and on the 15th at Queenstown, in Ireland. On the 16th, they arrived in Liverpool, but with only 33 cabin passengers. The missing man was George Clarke, Madame Macarte's husband. He had fallen into the stoke hole, thus contributing more to the transatlantic passage than he could ever have dreamed.

On Monday, October 19, 1863, Arthur Barnes opened in Leicester. The *Leicester Chronicle* of Saturday, October 17, 1863, is revealing:

> Pablo Fanque's Great Circus (late Newsome's). Queen Street, Leicester. Great success of the new company. Crowded! Crowded nightly! Acknowledged by the press to be the best company since the days of [Andrew] Ducrow. Pablo Fanque's beautiful stud of horses, the admiration of every beholder. This truly classical performance may be witnessed by every sect and denomination. Young and old can view it without a blush. There will be morning performances each Wednesday and Saturday, at 2.30 [i.e., in the afternoon], equal in every respect to the night representations. Children half price. Evening performance at half past seven. The splendid brass band will play several favorite airs during the representations. Half price at nine o'clock. Monster engagement of Arthur Barnes, the champion vaulter, who has accomplished the daring feat of throwing 95 sommersaults at the Crystal Palace, and at the Hippodrome, Paris.

The same paper of Saturday, October 24, 1863, says: "Go and see Arthur Barnes, the great somersault thrower." Also on the bill were the Brothers Ridley and clowns Mitchell, Camille, Stonette, and Egan.

The *Leicester Chronicle* of Sat., October 31, 1863, says, about Pablo Fanque's Circus, "We observe that there is to be a change in the programme next week, and that Mr. Arthur Barnes, the somersault thrower makes his last appearance, prior to performing at the Crystal Palace." So, his last night in Leicester was October 31, a Saturday, the great night for the working classes. That night was not as crowded as usual, but still not bad; at the gallery end considerable numbers had to be turned away. Arthur Barnes's act would be replaced the following week by the Brothers Ridley, and, despite really winter weather that week, the houses remained good.

The day after he left, the *Era* wrote: "Arthur Barnes is not a whit less attractive than when he first appeared, throwing about sixty somersaults every night." Bob Chadwick and his family went to Paris, where they would have two more daughters. Talking of families, the Acrobat was ready to begin one again. He and Alexiné had two children, not counting their first one from 1852. On October 25, 1863, the first, Annie, was born, at 8 Great May's Buildings, London (now in the area of May's Court, which runs between St. Martin's Lane and 11 Bedfordbury). She was baptized at St. Martin-in-the-Fields on November 14, 1863, by the curate Frederick B. Dickinson.

Emidy's Circus was due to have opened on October 24, 1863, in Aberdeen, but the building wasn't ready, and the event had to be postponed for a week. They finally opened to an overflowing house. Quaglieni's Circus was playing in Cardiff that October and November. On October 28, 1863, Hengler's wrapped up in Glasgow, and on November 2 opened in Liverpool. By late November, their star clowns were James Franks, Tom Barry, and Little Bibb. In late October 1863, Newsome's Alhambra Circus was playing Manchester, featuring Jim Doughty and Harry Crouéste, the clowns, and Fred Felix (still known as Mileson back then). Wallett opened with them for a week on November 2, 1863. In October 1863, Pinder's was building their new circus in South Shields. On November 7, 1863, after playing Gloucester for a fortnight to good houses, Herr Maus's Circus opened for a short season at Cheltenham. The town of Derby was lamenting that, with the circus being so popular there, and with trade now good in the place, wouldn't it be nice if an equestrian company saw fit to present a Christmas entertainment. And they were right. In late October-early November, 1863, Cooke's Alhambra Circus was still in Plymouth. Myers' American Circus was also playing Liverpool by the middle of November 1863. On November 21, 1863, Crouéste's International Circus opened for the winter season at Northampton, featuring Louis Tourniaire and his wife, Jim Furr, and the Infant Perks. This was Edwin Crouéste's circus, Edwin being brother of the clown Harry Crouéste.

The *Era* and the *Hampshire Advertiser* are our guides now. On November 9, 1863, Ginnett's Grand New Drawing Room Circus, designed by John Bostock, opened on Oxford Street in Southampton, in a well gas-lit commodious and nicely fitted wooden structure specially erected for the purpose, and designed to be Fred Ginnett's winter quarters. Arthur Barnes opened with them on November 16, for the week. Fred Ginnett and his brother George were the stars, or at least two of them, the others including Mr. Barnes (for one week only, however), Mr. Pastor, Mr. Lloyd, Saddi d'Jalma, the acrobat, and Jim Pymer, the clown.

"The somersault throwing of Mr. Barnes causes great astonishment, upwards of sixty somersaults being thrown by him each evening." Also starring was Mons. Clevori, the same lad who had taken the big fall at Bell's the year before in Belfast. Clevori was actually a Southampton boy. Friday, November 20, was a grand fashionable box night under the mayor, G. S. Brinton, Esq., the proceeds (£20, as it turned out) going to the Royal South Hants. Infirmary. On Saturday, November 21, they held a grand morning performance. The *Advertiser* of November 21, has this to say:

Ginnett's Circus. There is perhaps no class of entertainment more popular with a Southampton audience than equestrian performances; it is therefore no matter of surprise that the circus is filled nightly to overflowing. The company consists of some of the most expert equestrians and acrobats in the profession. Mr. Arthur Barnes causes no little astonishment and enthusiasm by his clever somersault throwing which sometimes exceed seventy in number. The bare-backed riding of Mr. Lloyd produces bursts of applause. Saddi d'Jalma, one of the most extraordinary contortionists in the world, goes through his wonderful performances with great spirit. Mr. Hutchinson officiates as master of the ring; he is also the general manager, and is indefatigable in his exertions.

Ginnett's would stay on at Southampton into 1864, but on Sunday, November 22, 1863, Arthur Barnes took the train up to Manchester, for a gig with Sanger's.

On October 31, 1863, to a full house of 3000 persons, Sanger's opened their Monstre Hippodrome and Imperial Circus in Manchester, which had been designed by George Sanger and George Knight, and built by Mr. Matthews, of Sheffield. The dome, decorated by Richard Anderton, of Manchester, was in 24 compartments, each 43 feet high, the whole colored to appear as one ethereal dome of celestial light by being studded by a constellation radiating to the center, and giving it great altitude. It was supported by 24 pillars, which were decorated with 50 crystal chandeliers supplied by Messrs. Defries & Son, and large figures diverging from the dome to the promenade. The ceiling was decorated with Messrs. White & Son's immense paintings representing female figures from ancient mythology, while around the promenade were paintings of a rural character. Frank Pastor was the star on opening night, and other featured acts were Anthony Powell, John and Alfred Clarke, Mr. Kerwin, the Brothers Pentland, Little Ella, Mons. Plege, Griffiths and Footit, the clowns, the Boorn Family, and Miss Caroline Sanger. Mr. James Twigg was the ringmaster. On November 23, 1863, Arthur Barnes opened with Sanger's in Manchester. The *Era* of November 29, 1863, says this:

> Sanger's Hippodrome [Portland Street, Manchester]. The programme presented this week to the numerous audiences has been entirely changed, and, in addition to the large company, we have Arthur Barnes (the champion vaulter) and the Brothers Ridley. To specify the many feats on the programme would require too much space, and we can only record the general excellence of the company, including amongst the members Frank Pastor, Anthony Powell, E. Kerwin (with his trained elephant, Ajax), Alfred Burgess, Alfred Clarke, George Boorn, Little Ella, Caroline, the Brothers Pentland, and the Clowns, Herbert Williams, Foottit, Griffiths, and John Clarke. Mr. George Knight (the acting manager) and Mr. James Twigg (the equestrian director) also deserve complimentary notice at our hands.

December 1, 1863 was under the patronage of Sir Humphrey de Trafford, Bart., and December 4 under that of Lt. Col. C. Adams and the officers of the 49th Regiment.

There is a tantalizing ad in the *Era* of December 13, 1863, "Pinders' Circus, South Shields. Wanted, through the indisposition of Mdme Hassan, a first class female equestrian. All stars liberally treated with. Arthur Barnes will please write." What could it be that made Pinder place such an urgent ad for Arthur Barnes in the *Era*? It certainly seems to have nothing to do with Madame Hassan's indisposition. Separate issue. Bill and George Pinder had opened a circus in Dundee, and after a tour of Scotland and England in 1863, decided to build a large building for their "International Circus," opposite the railway station in South Shields. They opened on time, on November 28, 1863, to a packed house. Aron and Irene Hassan (the female Blondin) were both performing with Pinder's when that circus opened, but Arthur Barnes is not mentioned. That's because he was performing with Sanger's, in Manchester. It may well be that the Pinders were trying to contact him on December 13, to see if they could snag him. Whatever the truth was, it seems as if Arthur Barnes did not appear at Pinder's until November 1864. Incidentally, George Pinder married Dick Bell's daughter, Emma.

Just at that time, in Manchester, Jem Newsome was having problems with his Maori act at the Alhambra Circus. The New Zealand chiefs walked off the set, so to speak, when Jem couldn't pay them. Jim Doughty, the clown, Joe Hogini, and Harry Crouste, all stayed. It had only been on November 20, at the Free-Trade Hall (in Manchester) that Jenny Lind had sung a principal part in *Elijah*. She had been so past her best, was so awful, that the management apologized to the audience.

Mr. Strange, of the Crystal Palace, entered into an agreement with Messrs. Sanger, the well-known circus proprietors, to carry out the arrangements of the Great Tournament and Christmas Fete at the Mammoth Royal Agricultural Hall, in Islington. Two special trains were engaged to convey the horses, camels, paraphernalia, etc., from Manchester to London. So, it really looks as if Arthur Barnes came direct from Sanger's in Manchester to play the Royal Agricultural Hall. He opened there on December 26, 1863, with Strange and Pulleyn's Roman Amphitheatre and Sports of the Arena (also called the Grand Equestrian Entertainment), appearing at half past two and half past seven. This outfit had been advertising for talent certainly from November 15, 1863, onward, for the Christmas season. The *Era* editions throughout January 1864 presented the same ad, "Mr. Arthur Barnes, the Champion Vaulter, who has accomplished the unprecedented feat of throwing nearly 100 consecutive somersaults!!." This ad would run, basically unchanged, in these papers and others, throughout his stint there.

That Boxing Day (December 26, 1863), the day Arthur Barnes opened at the Royal Agricultural Hall, they put on a Great French Challenge Vaulting Act, wherein 30 of the champion vaulters and gymnasts competed. That was only one of the splendid acts presented as a complete entertainment on a scale hitherto unstamped in Britain — immense assemblages of metropolitan, provincial, continental, and colonial artistes in every class of amusement; 350 performers and nearly 100 horses, as well as 50 suits of brass and steel armor; chariot races, steeplechases, Roman races on barebacked steeds, daring and graceful acts of equestrianism, English clowns, Parisian grotesques, Italian pierrots, Chinese drolls, and much, much more. All conducted in a hippodrome 300 feet long and 150 wide, accommodating 10,000 persons, with a promenade able to take 16,000.

Frank Pastor, the premier horseman of America, was here, (he married Blondin's daughter); Mr. John Henderson, eminent professor of the corde elastique, from Le Folie Dramatique, Paris, and also Equestrian Director; Mr. Arthur Barnes, the champion vaulter; the Delavantis, performers on the horizontal bar; Henri Franconi, founder of the Hippodrome in Paris (or, at least, the brother of the founder), was appearing on his palfrey Chanticleer; Les Frères Conrad, William and Richard, sons of Harry Connor, appearing on the double corde tension; Joe Jee (one of the "Musical Jees," a family clown act); the Infant Perks (one of the Perks riding family); Langlois, the great Indian juggler; Bill Jee (Joe's son), the loftiest living leaper; Messrs. Holloway, Wencart, Harry Welby, and Jem Thorne, the clowns; Valentina, Seline and Augusta; Mr. J. W. Hird, conductor of the band; James Crockett, the lion king (a Welshman, born in 1820, son of the Nottinghamshire giantess, Miss Cross. He married the sister of George Sanger, the circus owner; indeed, Crockett was the former band leader at Sanger's); Mmlle. Caroline; John Powell; Mackett and Parish (W. Mackett and William Parish, equestrians. Mr. Parish, born in London in 1844, apprenticed with Richard Bell as an equestrian at the age of five, and later inherited the Circo Price in Madrid, after marrying Price's adopted daughter, Matilde De Fassi, in Liverpool in 1867). Prices were: Reserved numbered stalls — 3/-. Reserved seats — 2/-. 1st Class promenade — 1/-. Balcony — 6d. The reading and refreshment rooms, with every comfort, were open. It was a leap into the future for the circus business.

The *Era* of January 10, 1864, says: "There has been, too, some wonderful vaulting by the most celebrated among English and French somersault throwers, headed by Mr. Arthur Barnes who, on the evening we visited the Hall, turned himself over no fewer than sixty-three times consecutively." The *Era* of January 24, 1864, reviewed the show: "We should say a word for the vaulters, especially Mr. Arthur Barnes, who accomplished between sixty and seventy consecutive somersaults."

In 1865 *Routledge's Every Boy's Annual* was published, written by Edmund Routledge. The chapter headed "At a Circus" contains the following, relating to the author's January 27, 1864, visit to the Royal Agricultural Hall: "The attendants now cleared away the sides of the small circus, and the whole arena was henceforward devoted to the display of the different sights. We were soon treated to some capital vaulting, in which a Mr. Barnes, the champion vaulter of the world, turned head over heels 61 times without stopping!"

On February 7, 1864, the ads changed from the one of late 1863 to individual performers' ads: The *Era* of February 7, 1864, ran a little ad saying, "Royal Agricultural Hall. Great French vaulting act, headed by Mr. Arthur Barnes, the champion vaulter of the world." The same magazine for February 14 words it slightly differently, "Royal Agricultural Hall. Mr. Arthur Barnes, the champion vaulter, who has accomplished the unprecedented feat of throwing nearly 100 consecutive somersaults!!" (i.e., back to the ad of 1863). *French vaulting* was a term coined by Mr. Batty, at Astley's, in 1852, to make still-vaulting sound a little more attractive. Although the term was, indeed, more pleasant, it never caught on.

The *Manchester Times* of February 13, 1864, ran a quip: "Change of name. The champion vaulter of the Agricultural Hall, Islington, Mr. Arthur Barnes, has turned a Somerset." They were trying to be funny, but it does show, by assuming that the readership would understand it, how widespread Arthur Barnes's fame was. The *Era* of February 14, 1864, says: "Mr. Barnes, upon his springboard, turns no end of somersaults, and quite puts in the shade anything ever seen before in the jumping line." In early 1864, John Reeves was injured by one of Mr. Crockett's lions, and the circus world had a whip round for the unfortunate man. Arthur Barnes contributed 10 shillings, as did Mons. Franconi. Strange & Pulleyn contributed 10 guineas, Seth Howes and Messrs. Sanger contributed 5 guineas each, Charles Hengler, Frank Pastor, and Mr. Henderson 2 guineas each. Mr. Crockett donated a quid. Bill and Joe Jee both put in 5 bob, while the Brothers Conrad put in a guinea. It all came to 61 pounds and 13 shillings.

Strange & Pulleyn quit Islington on February 20, but this was only a temporary hiatus, while renovations were being done. They reopened under John Henderson on February 29, with Strange & Pulleyn still the lessees. During the recess, the interior had been entirely remodeled, forming a vast amphitheatre and cirque, 20 feet larger in diameter than the Cirque Napoleon in Paris. The *Daily News* of March 1, 1864, had this to say:

> Agricultural Hall. A very short recess has served to clear away all traces of Messr. Strange & Pulleyn's gigantic hippodrome, and to erect a light and capacious amphitheatre for pure circus performances, which was opened last night by

Mr. John Henderson. Most of the leading members of the old company are retained by the new manager, and what the entertainments lose in display they gain in compactness. The circus is well lighted, and the seats are well arranged in the usual circus form. The program contains a great variety of gymnastic and equestrian tricks, all of them good, and some of them novel — the bare-backed riding of Mr. John Powell being particularly graceful, daring, and perfect. Master Perks on his pet pony is still a pleasing attraction, and Mr. Henderson, in addition to his labours as manager, goes through his exceedingly clever balancing performance on a swinging wire. Mr. Arthur Barnes heads the vaulters; the clowns are still amusingly personated by Messrs. Thorne, Ghee [sic], and the Brothers Conrad; the horses are spirited and well trained; the dresses and the ring discipline are good; and the band is effective. The new season, we believe, will only last six weeks, and there is every prospect of its being successful.

The *Era* of March 6, 1864, says: "The second part opens with some clever summersault throwing, in which Mr. Arthur Barnes, the Champion Vaulter of the World, peculiarly distinguished himself by flinging sixty summersaults in succession." Sometime in the middle of March, the circus went on hiatus, reopening on March 19, 1864.

About this time, the Hayes Brothers were in Bolton, but later that spring became Manley & Hayes, touring Wales and England. On March 14, William Wallett, the clown, opened with Pinder's at South Shields.

The *Era* of March 27, 1864, mentions "Arthur Barnes, the champion vaulter" at the Great National Circus, run by John Henderson, at the Royal Agricultural Hall, Islington. The *Standard* of March 28, 1864, describes Barnes as a wonderful vaulter. Arthur Barnes was still being advertised there in the papers of Thursday, March 31, but not thereafter. However, the Royal Agricultural Hall was still there, and so was the circus. It's just that they cut back tremendously on their advertising, and it therefore has to be assumed that Mr. Barnes was still with them until his next gig, at Nicolson Street, Edinburgh, with Hengler's Grand Cirque Variete. This ad from the *Caledonian Mercury* of April 11, 1864: "Important engagement of Arthur Barnes, the greatest vaulter in the world, from the Cirque, St. Petersburg; Cirque Napoleon, Paris; Cirque, Madrid; who has thrown 95 somersaults at one swing at the Crystal Palace, London; will appear this evening [i.e., in Edinburgh], for six nights only." The performance of April 15 was under the distinguished patronage of Lord William Kennedy. On Saturday, the 16th, there was a morning performance as well. The *Era* of April 17, 1864, tells us, "Among other novelties here [i.e., Edinburgh] is the engagement of Mr. Barnes, the Champion Vaulter, who has been known to throw the extraordinary number of 95 somersaults at one swing." Barnes stayed on in Edinburgh for the next week. The night of the 20th was under the patronage of the Lord Provost and Lord Abercromby. Friday, April 22, was a grand fashionable box night, for the benefit of Little Bibb, clown and gymnast. It was also the first night of a new entertainment by the celebrated Lee Family. Arthur Barnes, Champion vaulter, is billed, as are Eugene of the Trapeze, and Bibb in his globe ascent. "And, for the last time this season, John Henry Cooke in his grand part of Sambo in *Where's Your Ticket.*" Arthur Barnes stayed on yet another week. Friday the 29th was Charles Hengler's benefit night. Those present that evening included the Duke of Roxburgh, the Marquess of Bowmont [sic], the Earl of Haddington, Lord Elphinstone, Lord Binning, and Sir Hew Dalrymple, Bart. Arthur Barnes ended his run with Hengler's, at Edinburgh, on April 30, 1864.

Hengler's was going to wrap up in Edinburgh on May 4, due to go over to Belfast, to open on the 7th at the new building that had been erected for them (to lease for the season) on Victoria Street, close to the gate of George's Market. However, on that very May 4, the Belfast building caught fire and was totally destroyed. It had been made entirely of wood, and the roof was of felt.

The Hengler Company, which was going to play there, was an all-star cast (not Arthur Barnes, however)— Emily Cooke, Rosina Cooke, Harry Welby, Anthony Bridges, Lavater Lee and family, William Powell, Monsieur Franconi, the Brothers Carlo, James Franks, Felix Revolti, Herbert B. Williams, Mdlle. Cardoni, M. Lehman, and Little Bibb, among others. The pet pony of the stud (some of the horses already being there) was the only casualty. A great deal of circus property also went up in flames. Some of the performers had already arrived from Edinburgh, and they lost their costumes. The building was not insured. So, suddenly with nowhere to go in Belfast, Hengler stayed on in Edinburgh, on May 7 giving a grand day performance there. Their last night in Edinburgh was Monday, May 23, 1864.

On May 13, 1864, Billy Seal, the clown, died in Newcastle. Arthur Barnes was presumably at the old place in St. Luke's, Finsbury, at St. Barnabas's Church, on May 15, 1864, for the baptism, of his nephew, Arthur Frederick, son of Henry and Jane. The baby had been born at 19 Masons Place. This lad would die a lunatic in Dartford, in 1932. As all the London papers tell us, the Acrobat was certainly back at the Crystal Palace on Monday, May 16, for five days only at the Whitsun holidays. However, he extended his run there to include Monday, May 23 and Tuesday, May 24. Incidentally, Barlow's Circus Royal was performing in Glasgow in May 1864, featuring Tom Samwell and Madame Rosalie.

On May 28, 1864, a new building, 120 feet long, 100 wide, and 70 feet in height, was ready for the unquenchable Mr. Hengler in Belfast. Arthur Barnes was not one of the company. That opening night was absolutely packed. After five weeks, their last night in Belfast was July 13, and they moved on to Glasgow, where they opened on July 16. Arthur Barnes never appeared with them during their run in Belfast.

For the record: Pinder's opened at Accrington on July 4, 1864, with the promising young John Pinder, William Hogini doing somersaults on horseback. Salt & Jennings, the gymnasts, were with them then, as were the clowns Wallett and Barnes (this is not the Acrobat). The following day they were playing Blackburn. Ginnett's closed at Southampton, and at Easter were playing at Bristol, featuring Tom King, the pugilist, who had beaten Jack Heenan for the world championship. On July 4, 1864, Sanger's played Leamington, and on July 13, 1864, they opened in Cambridge. On July 2, 1864, Quaglieni's Circus wrapped up in Cheltenham. Later that month they began a three-month stint in Swansea. In early July 1864, Samwell's Circus, then playing Scotland, left Coatbridge for gigs in Wishaw, Lanark, Hamilton, etc. On July 16, 1864, Newsome's Circus ended a lengthy stay in Dublin. The Brothers Sedgwick had been their gymnastic attraction. Newsome's then moved on to Greenock. On that very day, July 16, 1864, Hengler's opened in Glasgow.

On October 9, 1864, Arthur Barnes's younger brother Richard married Fanny Ashworth at St. Mark's, Shoreditch. One assumes Arthur was at the wedding, but, professionally, we don't pick the Acrobat up until late that year, when Mr. Barnes (the champion vaulter) opened in Cardiff on November 7, 1864, at the New Amphitheatre Music Hall, with Wallett (*Era*, November 6, 1864). Interestingly, also on the bill were Mr. James Barnes and his wife Emily Jane. Jem Thorne was there too, as were Mons. Rochez and his performing dogs, as well as the Brothers Ridley, and Mr. Devon, the ventriloquist. Arthur Barnes's last performance at Cardiff was on Saturday, November 12, 1864.

On Monday, November 14, 1864, he opened with Pinder's Circus, at their large building opposite the railway station, in South Shields. "This week we have had appearing Mr. Arthur Barnes, who has attracted considerable attention by his vaulting" (*Era*, November 27, 1864). Appearing with him were Bill Mitchell, John Griffiths, and Jim Pymer, the clowns, as well as the Hogini family. There is no evidence that Arthur Barnes had ever appeared with Pinder's before. Now, it looks as if he did two weeks with them, i.e., until Saturday the 26th, because Jim Pymer ran an ad in the *Era* of November 20, saying that he was at liberty as from Monday, the 28th of November.

The *Times* from December 27, 1864, until January 13, 1865, advertised the Christmas Holyday Amusements at the Crystal Palace, acts "impossible to describe in advertisement" that included "Barnes, the [great] Champion Vaulter, in his 60 somersaults." These amusements ran from 10:00 in the morning until 6:00 at night, and others included: Le Petit Blondin, the juvenile rope dancer; Jean Bond and his wonderful dog; Herr Willio, the great German contortionist; Mr. Jackson Haines, the champion American skater;

Silvester, the charmed monster; and Les Frères Cavallini, the Italian clowns and gymnasts. Meanwhile, the Brothers Ridley went up to Edinburgh, to the Theatre Royal, to play sprites in the comic pantomime, *Little Tommy Tucker*.

Just to bring a tinge of dramatic sadness to the narrative, in late 1864, Jem Guest, the old clown, died in Birmingham. Also that year, Hiram Franklin was lost aboard a ship in 1864, off the coast of South Africa.

With the *Era* and *Morning Post* as our guides, we learn that Arthur Barnes was still at the Crystal Palace in the first week of 1865, as he was for the week beginning Monday, January 9. Nelson Lee was the master of ceremonies. Arthur Barnes closed there on January 13, 1865.

On January 30, 1865, Arthur Barnes had a new gig, at the City of London Theatre (sole lessee: Mr. Nelson Lee). The *Era* of January 29, 1865, says: "Engagement of the wondrous Barnes, the champion vaulter, and Thorne, the grotesque. On Monday, January 30, and until further notice, the *King of the Golden Valley, or Harlequin Little Blue Boy*. Harlequin, Mons. Schmidt; Columbine, Signora Teresita; Pantaloon, the veteran Morelli; Sprites, Louis and Eugene French; Clown and a Half, the great little Huline and son; also will appear, the champion Barnes, aided by Thorne, and a bevy of talent. Concluding with *The White Gipsy*. Stage manager, Mr. F. Marchant."

The *Era* of February 5, 1865, says, "Astounding success of that Champion Vaulter, Barnes," and the same magazine of February 12, 1865, says: "Another week of enormous success." It goes on to say, "That Champion Vaulter Barnes elicits thunders of applause by his truly exciting performances." The *Era* of February 19, 1865, says: "Signal triumph of Barnes, that champion vaulter, and last week of his engagement, during which period he has accomplished the astounding feat of throwing upwards of 1000 somersaults." The *Era* of March 5, 1865, tells us:

> Mr. Arthur Barnes, the champion vaulter, has just concluded an engagement here [i.e., Feb. 25, 1865]. During his stay in the theatre, a wager was laid that he would not throw one thousand somersaults in eighteen nights. Mr. Barnes, however, not only completed the Herculean task, but threw twenty-one in addition, and was presented by the owner with a handsome silver cup bearing the following inscription — Presented to Mr. Arthur Barnes, the champion vaulter, for the talent displayed by him in throwing one thousand and twenty-one somersaults in eighteen nights at the City of London Theatre.

It may be that he didn't gig again for a few months after concluding at the City of London, as we can't seem to find notice of him.

On April 5, 1865, Newsome's Grand Circus opened in York. It was a star-studded lineup: the Brothers Ridley, Jem Newsome and his wife, and son Tom Newsome, the Brothers Francisco, Lizzie Keys, Mons. Zamezou, and Charles and Andrew Ducrow, grandsons of the great Andrew Ducrow.

A couple of obituaries: On June 4, 1865, George Knight, former clown, and many years manager of Sanger's circus, died at the age of 43. Crockett, the lion tamer, died in Cincinnati on July 6, 1865.

This from the *Glasgow Herald* of June 29, 1865:

> Price's Spanish Circo (from Madrid and Lisbon), Glasgow, this evening (Thursday), Mr. Price respectfully intimates as being positively the last night but two of the Queen's Jester, Mr. W.F. Wallett, that gentleman having to appear in Manchester on Monday next; the highly successful equestrian pantomime spectacle *The Bandit of the Mountains of Calabria*, with other novel and brilliant equestrian and gymnastic scenes. A grand mid-day performance on Saturday next, July 1, at 2.30. Tomorrow evening (Friday) a special extra-brilliant routine of entertainments being for the benefit of Mr. W.F. Wallett, and the last night but one of his engagement. On Monday next [i.e., July 2], the first appearance of the champion vaulter of the world, Mr. Arthur Barnes; the great clown from Astley's, Mr. James Thorne; the celebrated grotesque, Mr. Harry Hemmings [sic]," [etc.].

That Monday duly arrived. From the same paper: "Glasgow Green. This evening." Price's Spanish Circo. "Mr. Arthur Barnes, champion vaulter of the world" got top billing. Also on the bill, as before mentioned: Mr. James Thorne; Harry Hemming, the admitted Grimaldi of this age, and inimitable grotesque dancer, also late of Astley's Amphitheatre; Le Grande Oriel, the French comique, from the Paris cirques; and Herr Bernard Dieter, the Continental contortionist. It was also the first time in Glasgow of the Spanish equestrienne Senorita Lina Schwartz's leaping act on a barebacked horse. Mr. Frank Pastor, the renowned American rider, was reengaged. Two grand midday performances to take place on Saturday next, commencing at one and half past three. The same ad ran in the *Glasgow Herald* for the next several days. The *Era* summed up: "Mr. Arthur Barnes, who throws somersaults in marvellous numbers, and with a rapidity perfectly wonderful."

Then to Nicolson Street, Edinburgh, with Price's, where the *Caledonian Mercury* of September 11, 1865, said "Open this evening. Commencing at 7.45. First appearance of Mr. Arthur Barnes, the champion vaulter of the world." Again, a grand midday performance, on Saturday the 16th, at 2:30. Arthur Barnes left Edinburgh on September 23.

On Saturday, November 4, 1865, Arthur Barnes, while waiting for the Cirque Hippodrome to open at the Agricultural Hall, in Islington, opened with Sanger's Monstre Hippodrome, at Portland Street in Manchester. Mr. Footit and the Brothers Carlos were also on the bill. Sanger's closed in Manchester on Saturday, December 16, 1865. While Arthur Barnes was playing Manchester, they buried poor old Tom Sayers the champion pugilist, in London, on November 15, 1865. Isaac Van Amburgh died in Philadelphia on November 29, 1865.

For Christmas 1865 Barnes was with the Cirque Hippodrome, at the Royal Agricultural Hall, Islington, vaulting against Fred Felix. Fred Felix, primarily a clown, was born Frederick Mileson, on February 4, 1824, in Sunderland. He would still be performing into his 90s, and died in Blackpool in 1920. His daughter Florence married the midget strongman Joe Wrigley, alias Abex.

All the *Era* editions throughout December say: "Islington. Royal Agricultural Hall. Great Christmas Entertainments. Cirque Hippodrome and Grand Historical Tournament." It tells us that 100 horses were to be introduced, as well as 250 suits of real armor, and 500 performers, and that it was the largest hall in Europe. Performers with the cirque included: Herr Gerard Goldschmid, the great German rider; Mr. John Bridges (the first man ever to do a somersault on the tightrope), with his horse Kepitoke; Mr. Frank Clifton, slack rope performer (best remembered as a clown and gymnast) and pupil of the great Hiram Franklin; Arthur Barnes, the champion vaulter of the world; Thomas Samwell, British horseman (this was the younger brother of John and Bill Samwell; he was born in 1835, in Kent); Mme. Amelia Bridges (wife of John Bridges); Mmlle. Bruloff, the bareback rider; and Herr Otto Motty, the equestrian juggler. The prices were: Reserved seats—3/-; 1st Class—2/-; 2nd Class—1/-; Promenades—6d.

The big cirque opened with a day performance on Boxing Day, the only day performance given in London on that day. They then did an evening performance at 7:30. The *Penny Illustrated* of January 6, 1866, describes the event of New Year's Day at the Royal Agricultural Hall, Islington: "Then Mr. Arthur Barnes, the champion vaulter, turned heels over head about 56 consecutive times." In all the London papers of January 14, 1866, and for the week following, Barnes had his own little ad, taken out by the establishment, which says, "Agricultural Hall. Marvelous vaulting by Barnes, Ginnett ['Gentleman' George Ginnett, of the famous circus family, he was known primarily as an equestrian; he was brother of Madame Macarte] and a full corps of accomplished gymnasts." *The Era* of January 21 also has this to say: "and the Champion, Mr. Arthur Barnes, afterwards takes his place on the spring board, and performs a series of those startling evolutions for which he has become so famous." The *Era* of January 28 says: "The vaulting act by Mr. Arthur Barnes, Mr. George Ginnett, and the company, we are told, averages fifty-five continuous somersaults every evening, and Mr. Ginnett's 'high-spring' of twenty-two feet is also a very notable exploit in its way."

On February 19, 1866, Arthur Barnes opened with Sanger's Hippodromatic Circus, in Dundee, where we rely on the *Dundee Courier*. "During the week Mr. Arthur Barnes, who has previously appeared in Dundee, has been astonishing the visitors to the circus by his astonishing feats in somersault throwing. Last evening Mr. Barnes threw upwards of fifty somersaults without halting, a feat which we believe no one but himself could perform." Also on the bill were Mr. Powell, the Pickwickian actor; Messrs. Footit, Carlos, and Kerwyn, and Miss Rosa Mayne.

The *Era* of February 25, 1866, says: "The performances here [i.e., Sanger's, in Dundee] have undergone a considerable change this week, the spectacle of *Blue Beard* having been withdrawn after a successful run, and one or two farces have been substituted in its place. Airec has also gone, and in his place we have Barnes, the champion vaulter, whose performances are of a most astonishing description."

The *Courier* announced on February 24, 1866, that Arthur Barnes was engaged for six nights more, and the same paper of Monday, February 26, 1866, said: "Sangers' Hippodramatic Circus. On Saturday evening [i.e., Feb. 24], besides a change in the ring performances, there was produced for the first time in Dundee a grand spectacular drama of *Richard Plantagenet, or the Days of Wat Tyler*. The part of the former was taken by Mr. Webster Vernon and of the latter by Mr. James Holloway." It goes on to say, "It will be seen that the great somersault thrower, Mr. Arthur Barnes, whose achievements are only accomplished by himself, and whose marvellous exhibitions of skill have won him the heartiest reception in Dundee, as well as in other large towns, has been re-engaged for five nights longer."

Friday March 2, and Saturday March 3, 1866, were both benefit nights for Arthur Barnes. Ads in the *Courier* for both days said, "This being the last opportunity the public will have of witnessing the extraordinary feats of this Gymnastic Wonder." The same Dundee paper, this time from March 5, 1866, said: "Sanger's Hippodramatic Circus. This place of amusement was crowded on Saturday evening, when the performances were for the benefit of Mr. Arthur Barnes, the great vaulter." That night was Barnes's last night in Dundee.

From the *Bristol Mercury* of May 19, 1866, we learn that Sanger's Grand Hippodrome was playing at the Newfoundland Gardens, Newfoundland Street, Bristol, for two nights only — Whitmonday and Whittuesday, May 21 and 22. There were 50 performers, including "the greatest company of vaulters in the world," among them "the greatest of all performers that ever appeared in this country, Mr. Arthur Barnes, the public and the press have, and must again, in one voice exclaim — he is the greatest of all performers." That same paper refers to him as "that great gymnast from the Crystal Palace, Barnes."

Retirement

After Bristol, that was it. It was all over. Arthur Barnes went to live at 36 Baker Street, Sparkhill, Birmingham, bought the street, and became a landlord. It was all over for his father too; the old man, blind and spent, died in Finsbury in the latter part of 1866. The Acrobat's brother Richard and his wife, Fanny, moved into 25 Masons Place from Charles Street. This enabled Fanny to look after the old mum, but it also afforded Richard all-too-easy access to the inferno across the alleyway, and he would make the deadly crossing of those cobblestones every morning and night until he too was spent.

In 1866, Bill Dale died, penniless, so it is said, in an institution in Cleveland. Alfred Moffatt, the equestrian and tightrope walker turned elephant trainer, met a sticky end in Morat, Switzerland, on June 28, 1866, while with Bell's Cirque American. Palm, the elephant, got him in his trunk, threw him 20 feet in the air, and caught him on his tusks on the way down, then stomped him to death. Poverty and pleurisy got John Henderson in Ipswich, on May 10, 1867, aged 45. Jim Wild, the equestrian clown, laughed his last on May 31, 1867, aged 56, in the Lunatic Asylum in Birmingham.

For years now, Arthur Barnes had been the famous Acrobat — the rich relative. His extended family, most of whom he would have been rather surprised to find were his relations in the first place, all named their children Arthur, or Alexine (if it was a girl) whenever they could, in the vague hope that he might throw something their way that was more than just a somerset. Neighbors and friends were doing the same thing. Pretty much any girl in Birmingham or London with the name Alexine was named with a brass ring in mind. It was one of the prices the Acrobat paid for fame.

When Harry Connor drew up his will, on July 23, 1867, he named Arthur Barnes of Lawley Hill, near Birmingham, as one of his trustees. We might assume this to be the Acrobat, but it may not be. The other trustee was one Edward Barnes Crichton, of London, absolutely no connection to the Acrobat. In 1878, Harry Connor amended these two gents out of the will. The Lawley Hill in question must be the one near Wellington in Shropshire. This remains incomprehensible.

Edwin Hughes, one of Arthur Barnes's early employers, went to his reward in Lower Norwood, on December 7, 1867 (well, let's hope that Lower Norwood was not his ultimate lodging place). Charles Hengler was one of the executors of his will. Davis Richards, the American equestrian, was killed in 1867 while performing a double somersault on horseback in St. Petersburg, Russia; he was 38. Charles John Kean, the celebrated actor, died in London, on January 22, 1868, aged 57. Mr. Batty, the great circus proprietor, came to the end of his long and glorious career in London, on February 7, 1868, after which Astley's was sold to Sanger's. Adolph Maus, the strongman, lifted his final weight in Norwich on April 25, 1869, only two months after his wife Louisa. In St. Helier, Jersey, Henry Cornwall, the old circus proprietor, went to a better place on June 29, 1869, that is, if there is a better place than St. Helier. A week or two after his death, his great horse, Tony, was sold off on the auction block. Jim Cooke, the old circus proprietor, set out on his last tour, a tour into the great unknown, on September 5, 1869.

The Acrobat was a witness to the wedding of Mary Williams and Joseph Terry at Christ Church, Sparkbrook, on April 17, 1870. We have his signature from this document. He was now Arthur Barns again, very private citizen. Joseph Terry was the brother of Emily Terry, who a couple of years later would marry the Acrobat's first cousin, Arthur William Barns.

Rosina Julia Etheridge, better known as Rose Ethair, was transformed into a spirit on April 26, 1870. She wasn't even 30; Monsieur Leotard, the gymnast, somersaulted into the ether in August 1870, age 28; and Madame Isabelle, aged only 40, left Lambeth, on October 11, 1870, for the destination so much sung about in hymn books.

In the 1871 census Arthur Barns is listed as an owner of houses. He was living with his wife Alexine and daughter Annie. Soon after this census was taken, Pablo Fanque died on May 4, 1871, in Stockport. Peter Stevens, the circus proprietor, got off the rollercoaster of life on January 1, 1872, and Nelson Lee, the pantomime writer, followed suit the next day, aged 65, in Dalston. Old Tom M'Collum, the circus proprietor, died on March 22, 1872, in Lambeth; not so old, only 44. Arthur Barns, now described as a gentleman, had a second child, Jessie, baptized at Christ Church, Sparkbrook, on September 25, 1872, the same year the Acrobat's old mum died at 25 Masons Place, worn out. Bill Samwell died in 1873, and that year, the *Birmingham Daily Post* of October 11 said, "Barns. On the 7th inst., at Spark Hill, aged 44 years, Alexine Wilhelmina, the dearly beloved wife of Arthur Barns; deeply regretted." She was buried at Marston Chapel, in Hall Green, Yardley, on October 11, 1873. On October 28, 1873, in Wyoming, John C. Heenan, the Benicia Boy, was knocked out for good. On August 6, 1874, Mrs. Cooke, William Cooke's wife, died. In 1875, the old circus proprietor, Jem Ryan, perished in poverty in Paris, aged 76.

The Acrobat married again, on November 10, 1875, at Marston Church, to Catherine Edgington, the little girl who had seen him perform at Stratford-upon-Avon all those years before. She was grown up now and was Edward Hewitt's servant on Stratford Road, in nearby Bordesley. On the marriage certificate, Arthur Barns is listed as a gentleman and widower. Witnesses to the marriage were Eliza Edgington, the bride's youngest sister, and Benjamin Matthews, a neighbor from Stratford St., Sparkbrook. R. Jones officiated.

Jessie, the Acrobat's daughter, died young, being buried at Marston Chapel on February 28, 1876. E. T. Smith, the great circus proprietor, died in Kennington, on November 26, 1877. That was the year Herr Driesbach passed over to the great animal menagerie in the sky. The Acrobat and his new wife, Catherine Edgington, had a child, Alexine Mary Barns, baptized on December 16, 1877, at Marston Chapel. In 1877, at 25 Masons Place, the Acrobat's sister Mary Ann died, unmarried, aged 48, and Richard, the youngest brother, was fired from the foundry because he could no longer sweat hard enough. He moved into 7 Masons Place, reduced to laboring for a mean living.

The most grotesque circus death in the 1870s was perhaps Tom McCarthy, the fellow who, if you remember, had had his arm ripped off by a lion while working for Bell's Circus in Liverpool in 1862. On the night of January 3, 1872, while Manders' Menagerie was playing Bolton, Mr. Macarte (as he was being billed), who had replaced Maccomo at Manders,' and who was dressed as a Roman gladiator, was in the cage with five lions, in front of a packed crowd, when the cats got him and almost ripped his head off, right in front of the audience. However, managing to keep his head under most trying circumstances, Mr. Macarte fought back gamely with his sword. But the lions got him again, tearing off his only arm and taking a massive chunk out of his thigh. The other lads had almost got him out of there when the cats grabbed poor old Macarte again, and dragged him back in their den, and began to make a meal of him. Those were the days when a human on the menu was a rare treat for any performer. Blood everywhere, as they tossed the unfortunate Irishman all over the cage, devouring him piecemeal. Not a good day for Mr. McCarthy, not good at all. His colleagues finally managed to extricate him and whip him off to the hospital. His famous last words were, "I'm done for." All this for a salary of £4 a week, including perks, and a widow left behind.

On March 6, 1879, in a railway carriage at Caledonian Station, Glasgow, Bill Mitchell, the clown, alias Felix Revolti, breathed his last. On April 10, 1879, Little Ella is meant to have passed on in the United States. In 1880, three of our old circus friends died — Tom Ridgway, one of the old *Marvels of Peru*, in St. Thomas's Hospital, Lambeth, on August 25; John Griffiths, the clown, on Sept 8, aged 61; and Charles Adams, the clown, on December 19. On the plus side of life, Arthur Henry Barns, the Acrobat's last child, was born on May 23, 1880, at 36 Baker Street (his birth was registered on June 4, 1880, by registrar George Stafford, and he was baptized on June 23, 1880, at Christ Church, Sparkbrook). Back to the minus side of life, John Wells, the old circus owner, died on September 18, 1880, and Richard Barns, the Acrobat's brother, came to the end of his earthly existence at 7 Masons Place in early 1881, a man, like so many men, spent, but not so spent that he couldn't continue to reproduce to the very end the tragically wasted life that he so ably represented. He was 42.

The 1881 census for 36 Baker Street nominates Arthur Barnes, 52, retired artiste, with his wife and their three children. Not far away, on Fox Street, Yardley, Harry and Susannah Russell (Russilli) had come to live, before moving on to Ipswich in the 1880s. Dick Bell, the old circus proprietor died, in September 1881, in Kimberley, South Africa; John Samwell died in 1882, Anthony Powell on September 7, 1882, Tom Jameson on April 9, 1885, and Frank Pastor, the American, in June 1885. Tom Hutchinson, the blind gymnastics instructor and former member of the Brothers Hutchinson, mercifully passed on in 1885, in Barnet, Hertsfordshire.

William Cooke, the great proprietor, died on May 6, 1886, in Brixton, and Levi North vaulted into the sky on July 6, 1886. On March 11, 1887, Arthur Barnes's brother, Henry, died, a spent man. John Henry Pearson, the one known as Nancy, made his exit on July 1, 1887. Harry Connor died on August 1, 1887, at 6 Keogh Road, Water Lane, in Stratford, Essex, and was buried in Ilford on the 6th. When Harry died, the *Era* of August 13, 1887, gave him an obit, which said, among other things, "Later on [i.e., after 1857], while under an engagement with Mr. Edward Hughes, the well-known circus proprietor, he threw 97 successive somersaults in a contest, but was beaten by his partner, Mr. Arthur Barnes, who threw one hundred." Now, this gem is fraught with inaccuracies. First, it was Edwin Hughes, not Edward Hughes. Second, Barnes and Connor were partners in the 1840s, not after 1857. Third, Hughes retired in 1847. Fourth, this is the only record of 100 somersaults being thrown by anyone prior to 1881. Incidentally, Hannahbella, Harry's widow, would die in 1911, the same year as young Steve Ethair (Steve Ethardo; he was 75). Charles Hengler, the great circus proprietor, died on September 28, 1887, in London. Bob Chadwick is reported to have passed away on July 26, 1889, at the Paris Hippodrome, aged 49.

On September 26, 1888, the *Liverpool Citizen* ran a piece by Milward, to do with recollections of Hengler's Circus. Arthur Barns was tracked down, and described as the owner of considerable house property in Birmingham. Also in that edition was a letter to the editor, entitled "Hengler's Circus in Dale-Street." There's a paragraph about Arthur Barnes, to wit: "Arthur Barnes, the champion somersault-thrower — turning fifty odd consecutive somersaults, and a reverse one at the finish — was engaged occasionally." On

July 3, 1888, Mrs. Dillon, the actress, died, and on October 8 of that year, so did James Barnes.

There is a provocative ad in the July 3, 1889, *Birmingham Daily Post*: "To let, furnished for two months, small country residence situate in its own grounds of nearly four acres, close to the village of Knowle, Warwickshire. Address: Copenhagen Cottage, Baker Street, Sparkhill." How many people on Baker Street would name their house Copenhagen Cottage?

Joe Jee died on October 4, 1890, in Lambeth, 11 days before his 52nd birthday; he was buried in Tooting two days later. They buried the old acrobat Lavater Lee in Norwood Cemetery on March 21, 1891. On the night of April 5, 1891, the census was taken in Britain: Arthur Barnes, retired artiste, aged 62, was still head of household at 36 Baker Street, and living there with Catherine, Annie, and young Arthur. On June 10, 1891, the clown, Harry Crouestè, expired of pneumonia in West Bromwich, leaving a wife and five young children totally unprovided for. Later in 1891 old Steve Ethair, father of the Ethair family, died in Sheffield, aged 74. Wallett, the clown, formerly Arthur Barnes's employer, passed away amid his usual much fanfare, on March 13, 1892. Acrobat-turned-pawnbroker Moses J. Lipman was eternally transformed in 1892, in Cincinnati, so they say. On July 12, 1892, old Signor Quaglieni breathed his last in Brescia, Italy, where he had retired in 1870. It is rumored that Madame Marie Macarte, who had retired in the United States in the 1860s, died on September 3, 1892. James Washington "Jim" Myers, the American circus owner, left Bristol on December 1, 1892, aged 69, for a better place. In 1897, James Furr, the clown, was sent on his mission to entertain new audiences in the celestial sphere. Blondin, the Hero of Niagara, died in bed on February 22, 1897, in London, and Thomas Edwin Cooke, brother of Mr. William Cooke, died in the United States in 1897.

Arthur Barns, gentleman, drew up his will on December 28, 1898, in front of two Birmingham solicitors— F. Swinson and L. Broughton Chatwin, and the question arises: How much money did the Acrobat make? We don't have any idea, really, except that by his own admission he was well paid (see Honeyman's book. But, as an example, in 1848 Young Auriol, the famous clown, was making the French equivalent of £10 a week, and in 1842, £20 a week. However, in 1860 he was making £144 every three months. That doesn't include side money and perks. Auriol was a top liner, although not quite in the same league as Barnes. Earlier, in 1848, Mlle. Palmyre Anato was earning the French equivalent of £720 a year, and could make even more overseas. In 1851 she reportedly made £2,000 a year. Tom Barry, the clown, was making £10 a week in the 1850s, and in September 1857, Pablo Fanque took on the well-known clown, Arthur Nelson, at £7 a week. In 1860 Wallett hired the tumbler Assam ben Mahomet for £6 a week, for a six-month contract; James

Crockett, the great lion tamer, was making £20 a week in 1863; and James Wilson, the aerialist, was making £1,000 a year in the 1870s and 1880s. It's likely Arthur Barnes was making £200 every three months, or £800 a year, which was a lot of money in those days. His event, somersaulting, was a natural for sidebets, and he probably made a stack of money on those. Certainly he was frugal, so it's very likely that he cleared £1,000 a year, including his earnings from sidebets. And there was no income tax in those days. In a 22-year career, and if you half what you think he made, he may well have retired with a nest egg of £10,000.

Jim Pymer, the clown, died on December 29, 1898. Jem Frowde, the circus proprietor, advanced to a new state of infinite consciousness on August 28, 1899, in Gloucester, while Harry Russell (Russilli) followed the same route that year from Ipswich, and William Powell, Arthur Barnes's first employer, did likewise in 1900. The 1901 census for 36 Baker Street lists Arthur Barnes, 72, retired artist, with his wife and three children. Living next door, at No. 38, were the Dewis family, including the son, Walter. Bill Fenner, the old vaulter, died in 1901, in Birmingham, his long-time home, and Harry Brown, the clown died in April 1902, in Brighton, his long-time home. Pauline Newsome died in 1904 (Jem would die in 1912). On June 20, 1904, in Sparkhill, the acrobat's daughter, Alexine Mary, married Walter Dewis. Unfortunately, she would die in London giving birth to her only child, Harvey Walter Dewis, and was buried in Norwood Cemetery on June 23, 1906. George Pinder, the circus proprietor, took his last gasp on January 19, 1906.

Arthur Barns died on July 1, 1908. There's absolutely no obituary on him, either in the local press, or in *The Era Almanac*. He was buried at Marston Chapel, in the same grave as his first wife and Jessie, on July 4, 1908. The Rev. W. R. Probert officiated. Marston Chapel is now called Church of the Ascension. The church records list the burial as entry #109.

Arthur Barnes's will was proved on November 16, 1908, in Worcester. Wills are notoriously difficult to interpret at the best of times, wrapped up as they are in legalese and stuff hidden by trusts, and so forth. His widow, Catherine, and their son Arthur Henry were the executors and trustees. He left all his jewelry, furniture and other household effects to Catherine, as well as £20. He left all his real and personal estate to his trustees, upon trust that Catherine would, during her life, receive the rents, profits and incomes thereof. After Catherine's death (which would be 1929) the trustees (Arthur Henry, the son, was the only one by that stage) were to sell his five freehold houses Numbers 20, 22, 24, 26 and 28 Baker Street, with the yards, gardens and appurtenances thereto belonging, and also all his leasehold (which included, perhaps among others, Nos. 34 and 36 Baker Street) and personal estate, and divide the proceeds of the whole lot equally among his three children, Arthur Henry, Annie, and Alexine Mary (who actually predeceased her father; however, her son would get that share in 1927, when he came of age). He left £819 in cash. All the rest was tied up.

Annie, the Acrobat's eldest surviving daughter, never married. She continued to live with her stepmother, Catherine Edgington Barns, until that lady died in 1929 (buried August 1, 1929, with the Acrobat). Annie thereupon moved next door, into No. 34 Baker Street, and lived there until she died in 1935. She was buried with her father on February 9, 1935. The monumental inscription says: "In affectionate remembrance of Alexine Wilhelmine, the beloved wife of Arthur Barns, of Copenhagen, who departed this life Octbr. 7th, 1873, aged 44 years. Also of Arthur Barns, who died July 1st, 1908, aged 80 years. Also of Catherine, widow of the above, who died July 27th, 1929, aged 88 years. Also of Annie Barns, daughter of the above, who died February 6th, 1935, aged 71 years."

That leaves the son, Arthur Henry Barns. He never, ever talked about his father, which gives one a clue as to how he got on with the Acrobat. Arthur Henry married twice, and died in 1970, having had five children, including the mother of this author.

Bibliography

Primary Sources

All newspapers are British, except where otherwise stated.

Alton Weekly Courier (Illinois), Oct. 23, 1856.
Belfast News-Letter, Nov. 22, 1831.
Berrow's Worcester Journal, July 1, 1854.
Birmingham Daily Post, Jan. 1858 (various editions); March 6, 1863; March 9, 1863, et seq.; March 14, 1863, et seq.; April 5, 1863; April 8, 1863, et seq.; Oct. 11, 1873; July 3, 1889.
Blackburn Standard, March 30, 1853; April 6, 1853.
Bolton Chronicle, May 3, 1853; Feb. 11, 1854, et seq.
Boston Daily Atlas (Massachusetts), Dec. 20, 1841; July 16, 1851.
Bradford Observer, Nov. 8, 1838; Jan. 7, 1847; June 1847 (various editions); May 24, 1849; June 14, 1849; July 5, 1849; May 23, 1850; April 14, 1853; May 1854 (various editions).
Brighton Patriot, Oct. 4, 1836; Oct. 11, 1836; March 19, 1839.
Bristol Mercury, Nov. 1837 (various editions); Dec. 14, 1839; Oct. 10, 1840; Jan. 4, 11, 18, and 25, 1845; Nov. 22, 1845; Nov. and Dec. 1850 (various editions); Jan. and Feb. 1851 (various editions); July 19, 1851, et seq.; Aug. 1851 (various editions); Oct. 18, 1851; March, April, and May 1852 (various editions); Sept. 2, 1854; May 19, 1866.
Bury and Norwich Post, Oct. 23, 1850.
Caledonian Mercury, Nov. 8, 1838; Dec. 3, 4, 7, and 8, 1860; Dec. 10, 1860, et seq.; Jan. 18 and 19, 1861; April 11, 1864; Sept. 11, 1865.
Cambridge Chronicle, Aug. 21, 1852; July 30, 1853.
Cheshire Observer and General Advertiser, July 11, 1857.
Cincinnati Daily Commercial (Ohio), March 22, 1856; March 29, 1856; April 5, 8, 14, and 15, 1856.
Cleveland Herald (Ohio), Oct. 5, 1846; July 30, 1847; Sept. 23, 1856.
Cork Advertiser, Aug. 1839 (various editions).
Daily Commercial Bulletin (St. Louis, Missouri), Dec. 1, 1838.
Daily News, May 10, 1859; Dec. 27, 1862, et seq.; Jan. 2, 1863, et seq.; March 1, 1864.
Davenport Daily Gazette (Iowa), Aug. 2, 1856.
Derby Mercury, April 3, 1839; Oct. 29, 1845; Nov. 5, 1845; Dec. 31, 1845; Jan. 7 ans 21, 1846; May 22, 1850; Sept. 15, 1852; July 13, 1853; Sept. 23, 1857.
Dover Gazette and Strafford Advertiser (New Hampshire), Sept. 16, 1848.
Dundee Courier, Aug. 11, 1846; Feb. 1858 (various editions); Feb. 1866 (various editions); March 5, 1866.
The Emancipator (New York), Dec. 29, 1847.
The Era, March 9, 1845; Sept. 21, 1845; March 7, 1847; April and May 1847 (various editions); Oct. and Nov. 1847 (various editions); Feb. 13, 1848; April 16, 1848; May 14, 1848; Nov. 5, 1848; Jan. 7, 21, and 28, 1849; Oct. 7 and 14, 1849; Nov. and Dec. 1849 (various editions); Jan. and Feb. 1850 (various editions); March and April 1850 (var-

ious editions); May 5, 1850, et seq.; June (various editions); July 7 and 14, 1850; Aug. 4 and 18, 1850; Sept. 1, 1850, et seq.; Oct. 1850 (various editions); Nov. 3 and 17, 1850; Dec. 15, 1850; Feb. 9, 1851, et seq.; March and April 1851 (various editions); May 4, 1851; May 11, 1851, et seq.; June 1, 1851, et seq.; July and Aug. 1851 (various editions); Sept. 1851 (various editions); Oct. 5, 1851, et seq.; Nov. 2, 1851, et seq.; Dec. 1851 (various editions); Jan. and Feb. 1852; March, April, May, and June 1852 (various editions); July 4, 1852, et seq.; Aug. 1852 (various editions); Sept. 12, 19, and 26, 1852; Oct. 1852 (various editions); Dec. 26, 1852; Jan. 9, 1853, et seq.; Feb. 6 and 27, 1853; March 20, 1853; April 10 and 17, 1853; May 1, 1853; June 12, 1853; July 24 and 31, 1853; Aug. 7 and 28, 1853; Sept. 11, 1853; Oct. 2, 9, 23, and 30, 1853; Nov. 6, 13, and 20, 1853; Jan. 29, 1854; Feb. 5, 1854, et seq.; May and June 1854 (various editions); July 2, 1854; Oct. and Nov. 1854 (various editions); Dec. 3, 1854, et seq.; Dec. 31, 1854; Jan. 7, 1854, et seq.; Jan. 28, 1855; June 3, 1855; July 8, 1855; Aug. 26, 1855; Sept. 16 and 30, 1855; Nov. 11 and 19, 1855; May 17, 1857; May 24, 1857; Aug. and Sept. 1857 (various editions); Nov. 8, 1857; Dec. 20 and 27, 1857; Jan. 17 and 24, 1858; May 2, 1858; June 27, 1858; Aug. 22, 1858; Feb. 27, 1859; March 20, 1859; May 1859 (various editions); Aug. 7 and 14, 1859; Dec. 9, 16, and 23, 1860; Jan. 20 and 27, 1861; Feb. 3 and 10, 1861; April 7, 1861; May 19 and 26, 1861; June 16, 1861; July 14 and 21, 1861; Aug. 25, 1861; Sept. 29, 1861; Nov. 24, 1861; Dec. 29, 1861; Jan. 1862 (various editions); Feb. 16 and 23, 1862; March 9 and 16, 1862; April 27, 1862; May 4 and 11, 1862; June 29, 1862; July 6, 1862; Aug. 3, 10, 17, and 24, 1862; Sept. 14, 21, and 28, 1862; Oct. 5, 1862; Dec. 21 and 28, 1862; Jan. 11, 18, and 25, 1863; Feb. 1, 8, and 15, 1863; Nov. 1863 (various editions); Dec. 13, 1863; Jan. 1864 (various editions); Feb. 7 and 14, 1864; March 6 and 27, 1864; April 17, 1864; Nov. 6, 20, and 27, 1864; Jan. 1865 (various editions); Feb. 5, 12, and 19, 1865; March 5, 1865; Dec. 1865 (various editions); Feb. 25, 1866

Essex Standard, Jan. 19, 1849; Aug. 30, 1850; Sept. 6, 1850; July 30, 1852, et seq.; Aug. 12, 1853

Freeman's Journal and Daily Advertiser, ; June 25, 1839; May 30, 1842; March 20, 1856; Dec. 9, 1857; Aug. 27, 1858

Gazette Musicale de Paris (France), 1858 (vol. 25).

Glasgow Herald, Sept. 8, 1858; April 2, 3, and 4, 1859; May 3, 1864; June 29, 1865; July 2, 1865.

Goshen Democrat (Indiana), May 28, 1856.

Hampshire Advertiser and Salisbury Guardian, ; June and July 1845 (various editions); Nov. 29, 1845; May 22 and 29, 1852; Nov. 1863 (various editions).

Hampshire Telegraph and Sussex Chronicle, ; June and July 1845 (various editions); July 13, 1850; June 5, 1852; Aug. 1854 (various editions); Oct. 26, 1861; Aug. 22 and 29, 1863.

Hull Packet and East Riding Times, Oct. 21, 1845; Sept.—Nov. 1846 (various editions); Nov. 19, 1847, et seq.; June 10, 1853.

Illinois State Chronicle (Illinois), Oct. 2, 1856.

Illustrated London News, July 1857.

Ipswich Journal, Sept. 1850 (various editions); Aug. 1853 (various editions).

Jackson's Oxford Journal, April 26, 1845; May 31, 1845; June 7, 1845; June 29, 1850; May 8 and 15, 1852; July 8, 1854; July 6, 1861; Aug. 10 and 17, 1861.

Lancaster Gazette, Jan. 27, 1827; Sept. 11, 1847.

Leeds Intelligencer, March 25, 1848; July 7, 1849.

Leeds Mercury, July 11, 1846; Aug. 8 and 15, 1846; Nov. 21, 1846; March 13 and 18, 1848; Feb., March, and April 1850 (various editions).

Leicester Chronicle, Jan. 20, 1827; ; May 24, 1845; Jan. and Feb. 1846 (various editions); Feb. 10, 1849; March 10, 1849; Sept. 1852 (various editions); Oct. 17, 24, and 31, 1863.

Liverpool Albion, Dec. 27, 1852.

Bibliography 215

Liverpool Citizen, Sept. 26, 1888.
Liverpool Mercury, Nov. 1, 1839; March 8, 1844; March 19, 1847; Dec. 17 and 28, 1852; Jan. 25 and 28, 1853; Feb. 4 and 8, 1853; Jan. 31, 1854; May 4 and 29, 1857; June 1, 3, 5, 22, 24, and 26, 1857; Dec. 14, 1857; Feb. 19, 22, 24, and 25, 1859; March 8, 14, 15, 16, 17, 18, and 19, 1859; Marcgh 21, 22, 23, 24, and 29, 1859; April 1, 1859; Feb. 13, 20, 21, 22, and 25, 1861.
Lloyd's London Weekly Newspaper, Feb. and March 1844 (various editions); May 12 and 19, 1844; Nov. 10, 1844; Dec. 8, 1844.
Madden Playbill Collection. Portsmouth Library. Item 415.
Manchester Times, March 29, 1834; April 9 and 16, 1847; Oct. and Nov. 1847 (various editions); Sept. 1, 1849; Nov. and Dec. 1849 (various editions); Jan. and Feb. 1850 (various editions); Feb. and March 1853 (various editions); Feb. 1854 (various editions); Feb. 28, 1855; March 3, 1855; March 7, 1855, et seq.; March 24, 1855; Nov. 14, 1857; Feb. 9, 1861; Feb. 13, 1864.
Milwaukee Sentinel (Wisconsin), June 23, 1856, et seq.
The Mississippian (Mississippi), Feb. 26, 1856.
Morning Chronicle, Sept. 25, 1855; April 29, 1861.
Morning Post, Sept. 17, 1855, et seq.; Sept. 24, 1855, et seq.; April 15, 1861; July 30, 1862; Dec. 27, 1862, et seq.; Jan. 1, 1863, et seq.; Jan. 8, 10, and 17, 1863; Jan. 1865 (various editions).
Musical World (annual), 1853.
Natchez Semi-Weekly Courier (Mississippi), July 1848.
New York Clipper (New York), June 28, 1856.
New York Herald (New York), Dec. 4 and 10, 1840; Oct. 14 and 21, 1843; Dec. 15, 1843; March 1 and 8, 1844; Sept. 6, 1844; May 22, 1856
Newcastle Courant, Oct 10, 1845; May 13, 1853.
Nottinghamshire Guardian, March 29, 1849; April 5, 12, 19, and 26, 1849; May 30, 1850; Sept. 23, 1852; June 30, 1853; July 14, 1853; Oct. 1853 (various editions); June 8, 1854; Sept. 17, 1857; Oct. 31, 1862.
Penny Illustrated, May 30, 1863, Jan. 6, 1866.
Pittsburgh Manufacturer (Pennsylvania), Aug. 8, 1835.
Plymouth and Devonport Weekly Journal, Oct. 1854 (various editions).
Portsmouth Herald, June and July 1845 (various editions).
Preston Guardian, ; May 18, 1844; Oct. 31, 1846; May 15, 1847; June 5, 1847; April 9, 1853; May 7, 1864.
Punch, 1853 (vol. 25).
Royal Cornwall Gazette, Aug. 29, 1851; Sept. 12, 1851.
St. Louis-Globe Democrat (Missouri), Dec. 26, 1883.
Scioto Daily Gazette (Ohio), Aug. 26, 1852; April 19 and 29, 1856.
Sheffield and Rotherham Independent, Nov. 27, 1847; Jan. 15, 1848; May 25, 1850; Sept. 25, 1852; Jun 25, 1853; July 2, 1853; May and June 1854 (various editions); Aug. 6, 1859; March 24, 1862; Nov. 1862 (various editions).
Standard, June 7, 1845; April 27, 1850; March 25, 1858; July 18, 1859; Dec. 27, 1862, et seq.; Jan. 2, 1863, et seq.; Jan. 15 and 16, 1863; March 28, 1864.
The State (South Carolina), Oct. 18, 1896.
Theatrical Examiner, Oct. 29, 1853.
The Times, Nov. 16, 1853; Dec. 27, et seq.
Trewman's Exeter Flying Post, Aug. 7 and 21, 1851; Nov. 1851 (various editions); March 8, 1852; Sept. 1854 (various editions).
Wrexham and Denbigh Weekly Advertiser, July 25, 1857; Sept. 12, 1857.
York Herald, July 5, 1845; Oct. 25, 1845; Oct. 31, 1846.

Secondary Sources

Bemrose, Paul. *Circus Genius: A Tribute to Philip Astley, 1842–1814.* Newcastle-under-Lyme: Priory, 1992.
Boase, Frederic. *Modern English Biography.* Truro: Netherton & Worth, 1892.
Bratton, Jacqueline S., and Ann Featherstone. *The Victorian Clown.* Cambridge: Cambridge University Press, 2006.
Broadbent, R.J. *Annals of the Liverpool Stage.* Liverpool: Edward Howell, 1908.
Circus Friends Association Archives. Scrapbook 609, p. 47.
Dictionary of National Biography. Entry for Arthur Barnes.
Frost, Thomas. *Circus Life and Circus Celebrities.* London: Tinsley Bros, 1875.
_____. *The Old Showmen, and the Old London Fairs.* London: Tinsley Bros, 1875.
Hare, Van. *Fifty Years of a Showman's Life, or The Life and Travels of Van Hare.* London: W.H. Allen, 1888.
Honeyman, William C. *Strathspey Players, Past and Present.* Edinburgh: Larg & Sons, 1922.
Manning-Saunders, Ruth. *The English Circus.* London: Laurie, 1952.
Morley, Henry. *The Journal of a London Playgoer from 1851 to 1856.* London: George Routledge & Sons, 1891.
Paterson, Peter. *Glimpses of Real Life: Theatrical and Bohemian.* Edinburgh: Nimmo, 1864.
Routledge, Edmund. *Routledge's Every Boy's Annual.* London: George Routledge & Sons, 1865.
Sherwood, Robert Edmund. *Recollections of an Old Circus Clown.* Indianapolis: Bobbs-Merrill, 1926.
Speaight, George. *History of the Circus.* London: Tantivy Press, 1980.
Thayer, Stuart. *Annals of the American Circus.* Manchester, MI: Rymack Print Co., 1976.
Turner, John. *Victorian Arena: The Performers: A Dictionary of British Circus Biography.* Formby: Lingdale's Press, 1995 and 2000; 2 vols.
Wallett, W.F. *The Public Life of W.F. Wallett, the Queen's Jester.* England: Bemrose & Sons, 1870.
Wild, Samuel. *The Original, Complete and Only Authentic Story of Old Wild's.* London: Vicker's, 1888.

Index

Abdullah 47
Aberavon 89, 163
Abercromby, Lord 199–200
Aberdare 162–163
Aberdeen 42, 98, 157, 194
Aberdeenshire 99
Aberford 65
Abergavenny 89, 162
Abergavenny, the Earl of 109
Abergele 83, 100, 163
Aberlour 99
Abex *see* Wrigley, Joe
Abingdon 69, 100, 106, 112, 115, 181
Accrington 101, 186, 201
The Acrobats of Albion 17
An Act of Fancy 18
Act of the Menage 79, 85, 103
Adams, Charles 14, 37–38, 40–41, 44, 49, 103–105, 191, 208
Adams, Elise 190
Adams, Lt. Col. C. 195–196
Adams, Mary 37
Addingham 65
Addison, Capt. 124
Adelphi (Liverpool) 48
Adelphi (London) 149
Adelphi (Sheffield) 49
Adrian, Eliza 33
Adrian, Henry (Le Petit Adrian) 33, 38, 62, 64, 101–102, 161
Adrian, Mich. 144
The Aerial Phenomenon 49
The Aerial Puck 85
The Aeronautic Hero 121
The Afghanistan War 68
Ahmad 47
Ahye Abon 177
Ahye Aussaiene 177
The Air Diver of Venice 9, 16
Airdrie 82, 164, 187
Airec 205
Ajax (elephant) 187, 195
Albert (horse) 136
Albert, Prince 20, 44, 49
Albion, Mich. 145
Albrighton 88
Alcester 116
Aldeburgh 46, 74, 126–127

Alexander the Great into the City of Babylon 104
Alexandria, Egypt 95
Alfreton 32
Alhambra (Edinburgh) 178
Alhambra (London) 158, 162–164, 167–169, 176, 178
Alhambra (London) 190–191
Alhambra Circus 180, 184, 194, 196
Ali Ben Braheim 177
Ali Ben Said 177
Alice, Princess 44
Alloa 82, 99, 164
Allonby 82
Alnwick 64, 81, 99
The Alpine Springer 80
Alston 99
Altcar 165
Alton 106
Alton, Ill. 148
The Alton Weekly Courier 148
Altrincham 163, 173
Alyth 82, 99
Amadi Ben Mohamed 177
The Amateurs of Bath 104
Amelie, Mademoiselle 60, 86
The American Apollo 49
The American Brothers 19–20, 43, 52
The American Circus 118–119, 121, 123–128, 132–135
Amherst, J.H. 25
Amlwch 83, 100
Amphi Arabs 49
Amphitheatre (Birmingham) 27
Amphitheatre (Bristol) 33
Amphitheatre (Hull) 43
Amphitheatre (Leicester) 36
Amphitheatre (Liverpool) 50
Amphitheatre (London) 4, 8
Amphitheatre (New York) 10, 12
Anato, Palmyre 210
The Andalusian; or Cheval Conqueror 79
Anderson, Sir Charles 68
Anderton, Richard 195
Andover 69, 96, 106
Angel (Islington) 175

Anglesey 83
Anglican Church (Copenhagen) 51
Anlaby Road, Hull 125
Ann Arbor, Mich. 145
Annals of the American Circus 143
Annan 82, 99
Anne, La Petite 132
Anson, J.W. 160
Anstruther 82
The Antipodean Brothers 19, 38
The Antipodean Professors 14, 24
The Antipodean Vaulter 14
The Antipodean Wonders 49
Apollo on the Steeds of the Muses 121
Appleby 82
The Arab and His Steed; or The Pearl of the Euphrates 48, 52–53
Arbroath 82, 99, 164, 187
Arizona 43
Armitage, Elkanah 44
Armstrong, Mr. 155
Arnott, Sir John 180
Arthur, Colonel 57
Arthur, King 94
Artillery 64
Arundel 70, 115
Ashbourne 32, 68
Ashburton 91
Ashby-de-la-Zouche 68, 163
Ashford 71, 108
Ashton 61
Ashton Road, Manchester 62
Ashton-under-Lyne 27
Ashworth, Fanny 201
Asia (ship) 149
Aspatria 99
Assam Ben Mahomet 210
Assembly Rooms, Bristol 26
Astley, John 4
Astley, Philip 4
Astley's Circus 6–8, 11, 13, 15–16, 19, 21, 23–26, 29, 41–43, 48–49, 52, 54–55, 58, 68, 74, 76, 85–86, 97, 105, 116–117, 127, 139–140, 142–

217

Index

143, 149, 151, 159, 161–163, 198, 203, 207
Aston Juxta 5
At a Circus 198
Athenaeum (Manchester) 62
Atherstone 77
Atlantic Ocean 8, 83, 143
Attlee, Clement 107
Attlee, Henry 107
Auchterarder 82
Auchtermuchty 82, 99
Augusta, Ill. 147
Auriol, Jean-Baptiste 50, 172, 210
Auriole, Mme 140
Australia 135, 186
The Automaton Polander 118
Aveton Gifford 91
Aviemore 99
Avon, River 91
Axminster 46, 130
Aylesbury 83, 117
Aylsham 75
Aymar, John 14
Ayr 82, 99
Ayton 81, 99

Babington Lane, Derby 33–35
Babworth Hall 68
Bachelder, George *see* Batchelder
Baines, Isabella 172
Baker, the attitudinarian 64
Baker, Benjamin 95
Baker, Fanny 95
Baker, Sarah 95
Baker Street, Sparkhill 206, 208, 210–212
Bakewell 68
Ball, G. 156
Balls Bridge 111
Balls Head Hotel, Loughborough 113
Bamber Bridge 45
Bampton 95, 101
Banbury 13, 69, 164
The Bandit of the Mountains of Calabria 203
Banff 98
Bangor 21, 83, 100, 163, 186
Banham, William 86
Banks, D.W. 63
Bannister, the stud groom 58
Barcelona 169
Baripper 84
Barker, Stafford 182, 191
Barking 47
Barlow, Bill 33, 37, 79–81, 85–86, 102, 105, 135
Barlow, Jim 82
Barlow's Circus 200
Barnard Castle 82, 99, 164, 187

Barnes (not the Acrobat) 201
Barnes, A. 140
Barnes, A. (a lady) 179
Barnes, Arthur 3–6, 8–9, 11–17, 18, 20, 22–28, 31–32, 34–35, 37–41, 43, 45–52, 54, 56, 59–63, 66–70, 74, 76, 78–81, 86–91, 93, 96, 103, 105, 107, 109–110, 114, 117–143, 145–146, 149–151, 153–161, 164–173, 175–184, 187–196–207, 209–212
Barnes, Arthur (baby in Lichfield) 78
Barnes, Arthur (solicitor) 78
Barnes, Emily Jane 201
Barnes, Henry 5
Barnes, James 172, 201, 210
Barnes, Jim (Old Barnes) 43, 172
Barnes, Madame *see* Barns, Alexine Wilhelmine
Barnes, Mademoiselle 179
Barnes, Old *see* Barnes, Jim
Barnes, Samuel 5
Barnes, Thomas 78
Barnes, W.A. 43
Barnes, Will 172
Barnes, William Augustus 172
Barnesconi, Signor 23
Barnet 209
Barns, Alexine Caroline 94, 103, 107, 138, 144, 147, 149, 160, 179
Barns, Alexine Mary 208, 211–212
Barns, Alexine Wilhelmine 51, 86–87, 94, 107, 138, 147, 160, 179, 207, 212
Barns, Annie 191, 193–194, 207, 212
Barns, Arthur Frederick 200
Barns, Arthur Henry 208–212
Barns, Arthur William 207
Barns, Catherine 69, 207–208, 210–212
Barns, Fanny 201, 206
Barns, Harriet 51
Barns, Henry (the Acrobat's brother) 5, 9, 27, 128–129, 141, 200, 209
Barns, Henry (the Acrobat's father) 5, 9, 141, 206
Barns, Jane (the Acrobat's mother) 5, 9, 207
Barns, Jane (the Acrobat's sister) 5, 9, 27, 141, 200
Barns, Jessie 207–208, 211
Barns, Mary Ann 27
Barns, Mary Ann 5, 9, 27, 141, 208

Barns, Richard 5, 9, 27, 141, 201, 206, 208–209
Barns, Thomas 5, 9, 27, 51, 87
Barnsley 66, 100, 125, 132, 163, 186
Barnstaple 10, 94, 116, 130
Barry, Tom 23, 29, 42, 130–131, 149, 172, 194, 210
Bartholomew Fair 107
Barton 162
Basinghall Street, Leeds 118
Basingstoke 106
Bassett, N.F. 93
Batchelder, George 150, 155
Bateson, John 34–35
Bateson, Selina 34–35
Bath 22, 37, 90, 96, 101–104, 107, 116, 135, 162–163, 179, 181, 186, 191
Bath Registry Office 107
Bathgate 82, 99
Battle 71, 108
Battle Creek, Mich. 145
The Battle of Alma 137
Battle of Waterloo 69–70, 73, 78, 87
The Battle of Waterloo (Glorious) 25–26, 35, 63, 65–67
Batty, Tom 185
Batty, William 6, 8–10, 14–15, 23–24, 30, 49–50, 68, 76, 87, 106, 143, 185–186, 198, 207
Batty's Circus 7–9, 11, 14, 17, 19, 25, 46, 48, 52–53, 94
Bawtry 100
Beacham, Henrietta 22
Beacham, Richard 22
Beaminster 90
Beattie, Madame 86
Beattie, Mons. 86
Beaufort, the Duke of 103
Beauly 98–99
Beaumaris 100, 163
Beaver Dam, Wisc. 147
Beaver Island 146
Beccles 75, 111
Beckett, Sir Thomas 68
Beda (horse) 43, 44, 48–49, 52–53, 136, 156, 167
Bedale 82
Bedford 114
Bedford, the Duke and Duchess of 44
Bedford Music Hall 175
Bedfordbury, London 194
The Bedouin Arabs 47–48, 150, 155–156, 162, 176, 178, 187
Belfast 87, 158, 161, 184–185, 194, 200–201
The Belfast News-Letter 6

Index

Belford 81
Belgrave Gate, Leicester 180
Bell, Emma 117, 196
Bell, Isabelle *see* Isabelle, Madame
Bell, Richard 60, 83, 117–118, 120–121, 135, 184–185, 196–197, 209
Bell, William Henry 122
Bell Bowling Green, Cambridge 178
Belleville, Ill. 147
Belleville, Oh. 144
Bell's Circus 135, 158, 177, 184–185, 194, 206, 208
Beloit, Wisc. 147
Belper 66
Belvidere, Ill. 147
Bemrose & Sons (publisher) 50
Ben Mohamed 47, 48
Bennett, James Gordon 145
Beresford Street, Woolwich 16
Berkshire 96
Berlin 165, 176
Berlin, Wisc. 147
Bermondsey Hotel, Bradford 64
Berrow's Worcester Journal 133, 153
Bersham 154
Berwick-upon-Tweed 81, 99, 164
Bessey's Wharf, Yarmouth 29
Bethesda 83, 163
Beverley 41, 125
Bewdley 88, 163
Bianchi family 189
Bibb, Little 153, 156, 165–166, 172–173, 181, 194, 200
Bicester 100
Bideford 94, 108, 130
Bidford-on-Avon 68–69
Biggar 82
Biggleswade 114
Bignold, Samuel 52–53
Billericay 72
Bilston 78
Bingham 186
Bingley 100, 186
Bingley Hall (or House), Birmingham 78, 86, 121
Binning, Lord 200
Birchall Street, Deritend 5
Birkenhead 163
Birmingham 5, 8, 13–14, 19, 23, 27–28, 33, 35, 42, 78, 83, 86–87, 102, 114, 121, 135–137, 156–157, 159, 163, 170–171, 184, 187, 191, 202, 206, 210–211

The Birmingham Daily Post 156, 191–192, 207, 210
Birstal 100
Bishop, Charles 183
Bishop Auckland 81, 100, 164
Bishop's Stortford 46, 76
Biss, River 96
Black, Adam 170
Black Bess (horse) 58
Black Diamond (horse) 67
Black Raven (horse) 97
Blackburn 43, 88, 123, 159, 164, 201
The Blackburn Standard 123
Blackpool 204
Blairgowrie 82, 99
Blanche, Madame 159, 167
Blandford Forum 96
The Blighted Troth 61
Blissfield, Mich. 144
Blondin 178, 184, 189, 196–197, 210
Bloomington, Ill. 148
Blue Beard 205
Blue Bell (pony) 103
Blutherrups (dog) 18
Blyth 99
Boar Lane, Leeds 63–64, 179
Boatman, Bill 126
Bocking 72
Bodmin 46, 84, 94
Bognor Regis 70
Bolivar (elephant) 21
Bolton 38, 123, 131, 191, 199, 208
The Bolton Chronicle 123, 131
Bonaker, Billy 7, 9
Bond, Jean 201
Bonny Black Bess (horse) 58
Boorn, George 195
Bordesley 208
Boroughbridge 20, 82, 187
Borrow, George 112
Bosholm, Mr. 160
Bostock, John 194
Boston 10, 43, 147
Boswell, James Clements 38, 62, 79–81, 86, 88, 102, 167
Boswell, Rebecca 80, 86
The Bottle 48
The Bottle Imp Pedestrian 121
The Bounding Athletae 10
The Bounding Ball 6
The Bounding Salamander 9
Boutelier 155
Bowery 10, 49
Bowery Amphitheatre 12
Bowery Theatre 10, 24
Bowman the clown 38, 45, 49
Bowmont, Marquess of 200
Brackley 100
Bradbury, Charles 111

Bradford 8, 38, 45, 58, 59, 64–65, 118, 124, 130, 132, 148, 159, 175, 180, 191
The Bradford Observer 7, 42, 45, 58–59, 64–66, 124, 132
Bradford-on-Avon 96
Bradshaw, Joe 176, 178
Brady, Bill 126
Braheim 177
Brain, River 72
Braintree 46, 52, 72, 76, 109
Brampton 100
Brandon 110–111, 186
Brechin 82, 99, 187
Breckland 110
Brecon 89, 162
Brennan, Mr. and Mrs. 190
Brentford 109, 114
Brescia 180, 210
Brewood 88, 114
Bridge of Allan 82
Bridge of Avon 99
Bridge Street, Bradford 132
Bridgeman, John 68
Bridgeman, Orlando 68
Bridgend 89, 162–163
Bridges, Amelia 204
Bridges, Anthony 153, 181, 200
Bridges, James 155
Bridges, John B. 6, 60, 86, 153, 204
Bridgwater 44, 83, 90, 110, 116
Bridlington 82, 125
Bridport 90, 116
The Brigand Chief 48
Briggs, Mr. (agent) 36
Briggs, W. 55
Brighouse 45
Brighton 7, 20, 71, 94, 96, 108, 114, 178, 180, 211
The Brighton Patriot 7–8
Brinton, G.S. 194
Bristol 9, 20, 23–26, 33, 40, 48, 52, 68, 78–79, 83, 85–86, 90, 103–105, 115–116, 133–134, 156, 159, 163, 172, 180, 181, 186–187, 201, 206, 210
The Bristol Mercury 7, 9, 23–26, 33, 37, 78–81, 89–90, 95, 103, 134, 205
Bristol Royal Infirmary and General Hospital 26, 85
Britannia Inn (Deritend) 5
Brixham 44
Brixton 91, 209
Broad Street, Birmingham 78, 86
Broad Street, Oxford 106
Broad Street, Portsmouth 31
Broadway Circus 12
Bromley 71

Index

Bromsgrove 88, 100, 163
Bromyard 88, 158
Brooke, Col. 167
Brooks the pugilist 178
Broomhall Street, Sheffield 114
Broseley Way 88
Broughty Ferry 99
Brown, Aaron Nutt 101
Brown, Constable 188
Brown, Harry 33, 52–53, 86, 108, 134–135, 138, 158, 170–171, 176, 178–179, 183, 211
Brown, Joe 167
Brown, John 41–42, 187
Brown, Miss 26, 45, 49, 86
Brown, W. 179, 192
Browne, Eugene 185
Brown's Circus 158
Brown's Mammoth Circus 6
Brownsville, Oh. 144
Bruce, Sir Hervey and Lady 56–57
Bruloff, Mademoiselle 204
Brunswick, the Duke of 161
Bruton 95
Bryngwran 83
Buchanan, James 148
Buck the clown 84
Buckie 98
Buckley, Jem 33
Bucyrus, Oh. 144
Buffalo, N.Y. 148
The Buffalo Republic 148
Bullock, Dickie 94
Bungay 74–75, 111
the Bure (Yarmouth) 29
Burford 101
Burgess, Alfred 195
Burgess, Tom 145, 147
Burke, Deaf 43
Burkham, Master 50
Burlington, Ia. 147
Burnett, John 190
Burnham, Master 44–45
Burnham Market 75
Burnham Westgate 75
Burnham-on-Sea 90, 110
Burnley 31, 45, 59–60, 91, 101, 123–124
Burton 100
Burton Leys 133
Burton-on-Trent 68, 83, 113
Bury 122
The Bury and Norwich Post 76
Bury St Edmunds 22, 54, 76, 110, 127, 186
Bush, H. 25
Butcher, W. 188
Butler, Mr. 38
Buxton 114
Byrne, J.C. 62
Byrne, John 143

Cabin Croft, Leyland 45
Calcutta 174
Caledonian Mercury 7, 169–170, 199, 203
Caledonian Station, Glasgow 208
Callington 46, 84, 92
Calmady, Charles and Mrs. 102
Calne 96
Calvert, C.A. 140
Camborne 84, 93, 108
Cambridge 22, 31, 76, 110, 126, 177–178, 183, 201
The Cambridge Chronicle 110, 126
Cambridgeshire 76–77
Camden Town 175
Camelford 46, 84, 94
Camelot 94
Camille the clown 193
Campden 101
Canada (ship) 147, 149
Canterbury 14, 21, 46, 71, 109, 139, 179
Canterbury (music hall, London) 175
Canterbury Music Hall (Middlesbrough) 175
Capel Street, Dublin 143
Cardiff 89, 153, 162–163, 186, 191, 194, 201
Cardigan, the Earl of 98
Cardoni, Mademoiselle 200
Cariot, Madame 151
Carlisle 82, 99, 176
Carlo, Felix 10, 140
Carlo Brothers 200
Carlorini *see* Carterini
Carlos, Mr. 205
Carlos & Henrico 162
Carmarthen 89
Carmel, N.Y. 142
Carnarvon 100, 163
Carnarvonshire 83
Carolina, Mademoiselle 16
Caroline, Mademoiselle 117, 197
Caroline, Miss 171
Carpenter, Frank 143
Carrollton, Ill. 148
Carter, James 14, 16, 44
Carterini, Signor 23
Carver, Thomas 55, 57
Casorti Troup 51
Cass Park, Detroit 145
Cassidy, G.W. 170
Castello, Dan 174
Casterini *see* Carterini
Castle Bailey, Colchester 72–73
Castle Douglas 99
Castle Eden 99
Castle (Colchester) 109–110

Cattle Market (Sheffield) 132
Caulfield, Mr. 25
Cavallini, Les Frères 202
Celeste, Madame 149, 154
The Centaur Horseman 41, 44–45
Central Railway Station (Newcastle) 125
Cerito, Mademoiselle 190
Chadwick, Isabella 172
Chadwick, Robert 171–173, 179, 181–184, 188–193, 209
Chadwick, Tom 172
Chadwick's Orchard, Preston 19, 38
Chalk Farm 186
Chamberlin, Robert 53
Chambers the theatre treasurer 136
Champion Circus 185
Champs-Elysees 90, 160
Champs Elysees Cirque 161
Chandos-Pole, E.S. 36
Chanticleer (horse) 197
Chard 97, 130
Charles I 76
Charles Street, Finsbury 9, 206
Charlton the clown 25
Chatham 19, 31, 180
Chatham Circus 12
Chatteris 77
Chatwin, L. Broughton 210
Chelmsford 20, 21, 46, 72, 196, 109
Cheltenham 19, 23, 89, 101–102, 116–117, 133, 153, 161–164, 194, 201
Chepstow 89, 162–163, 186
Cherry Tree Yard, Market Harborough 30
Chertsey 115
Cheshire 50
The Cheshire Observer and General Advertiser 151
Chester 83, 100, 148, 151–152, 163–164, 169, 174, 187
Chesterfield 32, 42, 66, 114, 132, 186
Chicago 146
Chichester 70, 107, 115
Chifney, Sam 16
Chillicothe, Oh. 144
The Chinese Juggler 136
The Chinese Junk; or, The Maid of Pekin 87
Chinese Law 16
The Chinese Vaulters 7
The Chinese Sea Junk; and Feast of Lanterns 62
Chippenham 30, 90, 163, 181
Chipping Barnet 114
Chipping Norton 27, 69, 115

Index

Chorley 43, 164
Christ Church, Sparkbrook 207, 209
Christchurch 96
Christian Street, Liverpool 48
Christy Minstrels 167
Church of Our Lady, Copenhagen 51
Church of the Ascension, Hall Green 211
Church Stretton 88
Churchstow 91
Cincinnati 10, 142–143, 148, 210
The Cincinnati Daily Commercial 143
Cinderella 191
Cinderella, or The Little Glass Slipper 63–64, 85, 159, 167, 191
Circassian Flower Girl 17–18
Circassian Maid 18
Circo Price 169, 197, 203
Circus (Bristol) 90
Circus Friends Association 37
Circus Life and Circus Celebrities 50
Circus People on the Stroll 11
Circus Royal (E.T. Smith & Pablo Fanque) 136
Circus Royal, Bristol 79
Circus Royal, Hull 40
Cirencester 90, 105, 163
Cirque de l'Imperatrice 160
Cirque d'Hiver 160
Cirque Hippodrome 203–204
Cirque Modele 168
Cirque Napoleon 156, 159–160, 167, 169, 188, 192, 198–199
Cirque National, Paris 146
Cirque Olympique 24
Cirque Unique 158
Cirque Vienna 165
City of London National Theatre 23
City of London Theatre 202
City of London (ship) 193
City Royal Amphitheatre Manchester 43
Clapham 109, 186
Clara, Madame 160
Clark, John 166
Clarke, Alfred 158, 173, 195
Clarke, George 161, 193
Clarke, John 108, 165, 181, 195
Clarke & Palmer's Circus 108, 112
Clementi, Madame 86
Clements, Kate 162
Clements, Mr. (bandleader) 58
Cleopatra's Needle 95

Clerkenwell 111
Clevedon 90, 110, 116
Cleveland Herald 41, 46
Cleveland, Oh. 145, 146, 148, 206
Clevori, Mons. 184–185, 194
Clifford, John 16–17
Clifton, Frank 204
Clifton, Lady 56
Clifton, Sir Juckes Granville Juckes 56–57
The Clown and His Granny of Eighty on Horseback 79
The Clown's Scrap Book 172
Coatbridge 201
Cock Inn (Wrexham) 152
Cockermouth 82, 99
Coggeshall 46, 72, 109
Coggeshall Gang 72
Colchester 21, 46, 54, 72–73, 109–110, 127
Coldstream 99
Cole, Mary Ann 38
Cole, W.H. 38
Cole, W.W. 38
Coleford 89
Collins, Sam 176, 190
Colne 186
Colosseum, London 47
Colquitt Street, Liverpool 118
Colyton 90
Common Hard, Portsmouth 30
Concert Hall (Liverpool) 118
Congleton 159
Connor, Hannahbella (wife) 15, 209
Connor, Hannahbella (daughter) 102
Connor, Harry 3, 15–18, 24–26, 32, 35, 37–38, 40–41, 48–50, 52, 56, 60–63, 68, 79–81, 86, 88, 102–103, 137–138, 143, 151, 159, 161, 167–168, 173, 176, 183, 197, 206, 209
Connor, Master 167
Connor, Richard 197
Connor, William 197
Conquest, Clara 61
Conrad *see* Connor, Harry
Conrad, Les Frères 191–192, 197–199
Conrad Brothers 191–192, 197–199
Constable, Sir Clifford and Lady 49
Constantinople 155
Conway 83, 100
Cook, Dan 178
Cooke, Albert 37
Cooke, Alfred 25, 38, 40, 62–

64, 67, 79–80, 86, 88, 91–92, 97–98, 103, 104, 133
Cooke, Alfred Eugene Godolphin 85, 97, 104
Cooke, Clarissa 37, 80, 85–86, 168
Cooke, Ellen 38
Cooke, Emily 62, 80, 85–86, 92, 94, 97, 103, 200
Cooke, George 49, 60
Cooke, Harry Welby Cooke 38
Cooke, Henry 37–38, 79–80, 85–86, 102–103, 142
Cooke, James 161–162
Cooke, James Thorpe 31, 37, 42, 52, 65, 81–82, 98–100, 102, 104, 108, 207
Cooke, John 48, 66–67, 88
Cooke, John Henry (Master John) 38, 62, 79–80, 85–86, 103–104, 142, 172–173, 181, 200
Cooke, John William 37–38, 103
Cooke, Kate 38, 62, 67, 76–77, 85–86, 88, 92, 103
Cooke, Louis 142
Cooke, Mary 37
Cooke, Mary Ann 38
Cooke, Mr. 165
Cooke, Rebecca 37
Cooke, Rosina 86, 200
Cooke, Susannah 22, 74, 79–81, 86, 94, 207
Cooke, Tertius John 87
Cooke, Thomas 37, 41, 43
Cooke, Thomas Edwin 37, 210
Cooke, Thomas Potter "T.P." 15
Cooke, Thomas Taplin 37
Cooke, William Henry 3, 22–23, 27, 29, 31, 33, 37–38, 46, 48, 50, 52, 62–70, 72–80, 85–90, 91, 93–94, 96–98, 102–103, 105–110, 112–113, 142–143, 151, 156, 159, 162, 168, 179, 209–210
Cooke, William, Jr. 180
Cooke Family 142–143
Cooke the clown 157
Cooke's Circus 10, 16, 23–24, 27–28, 31, 33, 37–38, 40–44, 46–47, 48, 50, 52, 62–63, 65–116, 122, 139, 156, 157, 159, 161, 179, 187, 194
Copenhagen 51, 137–139, 149, 160, 169, 212
Copenhagen Cottage, Sparkhill 210
Corelli, Mons. 102
Cork 180, 191
The Cork Advertiser 9

Index

Corn Laws 39
Corn Market Street, Oxford 30
Cornwall 20
Cornwall, Henry 10, 20, 207
Cornwall, Mary Ann 20
Cornwall's Circus 10, 20
The Corporal of the 41st; or Tom Late for Drill 18
Coryton, Colonel Commander 102
Cotswolds 27
Cotterell, Miss 86
Coupar Angus 82, 99, 187
Cournane, Mr. 185
Courteau, Louis 60, 116–117, 121
Coventry 34, 68, 114, 127, 162–163
Cowbridge 89, 162–163
Cowbridge Fair 89
Cowes 142
Cowley Road, Oxford 176
Cowper the poet 112
Coxwell's Mammoth Balloon 183
La Cracovienne 85
Craigellachie 99
Cranmore 95
Crediton 84, 97, 130
Cremorne 60, 94, 175
Cremorne Gardens 89, 175, 182–183
Crescent City Circus 146
Creswick, Mr. 139
Crewkerne 97, 130
Cribb, Tom 17, 18
Crichton, Edward Barnes 206
Cricket Ground (Derby) 113
Cricket Ground (Leicester) 113
Crickhowell 89
Crockett, James 171, 187–188, 193, 197–198, 211
Cromer 75, 112
Cross Hills 186
Cross, Miss (the giantess) 197
Crouesté, Edwin 194
Crouesté, Harry 83, 142–143, 159, 168, 173, 194, 196, 210
Crouesté's Circus 194
Crowhurst *see* Crouesté
Croydon 71, 109
Cruickshank's Illustrations 48
Crystal Palace 89–90, 182–184, 189–193, 196, 199–202, 205
Crystal Palace Music Hall, Birmingham 191–192
Culine, Clifford and Madame 160
Cullen 98
Cullompton 44, 97
Cunard 149

Cupar, Fife 82, 99, 164
Cupid in a Soot Bag 17
Currie 99
Cushing's Circus 140

The Daily Atlas (Boston newspaper) 10, 90–91
The Daily Cleveland Herald 148
The Daily Commercial Bulletin (St. Louis, Mo.) 8
The Daily News 167, 189, 198–199
Dalbeattie 99
Dale, Madame 126
Dale, William Owen 3, 10–12, 27, 33–35, 43, 46, 124–126, 127–129, 146, 183, 206
Dale Street, Liverpool 150–151, 155, 161, 164, 172, 185, 209
Dalkeith 81, 99
Dalrymple, Sir Hew 200
Dalston 186, 207
Daly, Joseph 38
The Dames of Athens 85
The Dancing Scotchman 140
Danske Volkekirke, Der 51
Darby, Susannah 50
Darby, William *see* Fanque, Pablo
Darby's Royal Tenting Company 42
Darley Street, Bradford 58
Darlington 81, 99–100, 164, 187
Dart, River 91
Dartford 109, 200
Dartmoor 97
Dartmouth 91, 116
Davenport, Ia. 147
The Davenport Daily Gazette 147
Daventry 114, 162
David Street, Manchester 155
Davis, Leon 26
Davis, W. 145–146
Davousie, Moses 47
Dawlish 91, 116
Day, James 191–192
Deacon's Music Hall 175
Deadwood Dick 94
Deal 71, 108
Dearborn, Mich. 145
Decatur, Ill. 148
Deddington 158
Deer, River 94
De Fassi, Matilde 197
Defries, Messrs. 189, 195
Defries' Great Prismatic Mirror 190
Dejean's Circus 50, 117

Delavanti, George 151, 162, 192, 197
Delavanti, John 151, 162, 192, 197
Delavanti, Signora 153, 162, 192, 197
Delinski, Mons. 153
Demaine & Johnson (carpenters) 58
The Demon Rider 44
Denbigh 83, 163
Denbighshire 83
Denmark 3, 51, 137–139, 145, 179
Denmark, the King of 138, 179
Derby 32–34, 36, 43, 66, 83, 113, 117, 127, 154, 158, 163, 180, 186–187, 194
Derby, the Earl of 97
Derby and Chaddesden Troop 35
Derby Arms Hotel 185
The Derby Mercury 8, 32–36, 66–67, 113, 126, 154, 180
Derby Race Fund 36
Derby Road, Nottingham 86, 96
Derbyshire 68
Deritend 5
Derwent, River 114
De Trafford, Sir Humphrey 195–196
Detroit 145
Devizes 96, 116, 163
Devon 38, 94
Devon the ventroloquist 201
Devonport 98, 183
Dewhurst, Richard 14, 25, 132
Dewis, Alexine Mary 211
Dewis, Harvey Walter 211
Dewis, Walter 211
Dewsbury 39
Dexter, Mich. 145
Dick Turpin's Ride; or, The Death of Black Bess 58
Dickens, Charles 161
Dickinson, Frederick B. 194
Dieter, Bernard 203
Dillon, Charles 14, 61
Dillon, Clara 61, 210
Dingwall 98
Diss 110
Dixon, Dr. Fred 70
Dock Green, Hull 40
Dockerill, Young 176
Dodridge 91
Dog and Gun (Leicester public house) 55
Don Jose Manuel 189–190
Don Juan the Libertine on Horseback 15, 104

Index

Donaldson, W.B. 167
Doncaster 82, 132, 163, 173, 186–187
Donnelly, M. 181
Donnybrook Fair, Dublin 23, 111
Dorchester 90
Dorking 107
Doughty, Jim 83–84, 104–105, 107, 159, 167–168, 194, 196
Douglas, Capt. 73
Doulting 95
Douro, the Marchioness of 44
Dover 14, 71, 108, 115
Dover, John 176
The Dover Gazette and Strafford Advertiser 46
Downham Market 76, 112
Dragoons 64
Driesbach, Jacob 142, 144–145, 147, 208
Driesbach's Circus 142–143, 145–148
Driffield 20, 82, 125
Droitwich 19, 163
Droxford 33
Drury Lane 33–34, 121, 126, 129–131, 133, 140, 158, 175, 179, 191
Dublin 9–10, 15, 23, 37, 87, 111, 135, 143, 155, 158, 160–161, 185, 201
Dubuque, Ia. 147
Ducrow, Andrew 33, 42, 52, 56, 83, 86, 193, 202
Ducrow, Charles 202
Ducrow, Master Andrew 176–178, 202
Ducrow's Circus 14
Dudley 78, 83, 88, 100
Dufftown 99
Duke of York's School 129
Duke Street, London 158
Duke Street, Sheffield 168
Dulwich 109
Dumfries 82, 99
Dumos, Caroline 24
Dumos, Master 24
Dumos, Mme. 23–24, 26
Dumos, Mons. 23–24
Dun, River 96
Dunbar 81, 99
Dundee 40, 52, 76, 82, 98–99, 157–158, 162, 164, 176, 178, 180, 187, 191, 196, 204–205
The Dundee Courier 40, 157, 204–205
Dunfermline 82, 164
Dunmow 21, 46, 76
Dunning 82
Duns 99
Durham 99–100, 164

Easingwold 82
East Anglia 46, 110
East Dereham 76, 112
East Grinstead 107
East Retford 68
Eastbourne 71
The Eastern Magi 123
Eaton, G.I. 143
Eaton, Master 132
Ebbesen, T.B. 51
The Ebony Wonder 86
Eden, Maj. Gen. 134
Edgbaston 33
Edgeware Road 188, 190
Edgington, Catherine *see* Barns, Catherine
Edgington, William 69
Edinburgh 7, 11, 14, 40, 42, 52, 65, 81–82, 97, 116, 159, 161, 164, 169–171, 178, 187, 191, 199–200, 202–203
Edison, Thomas Alva 145
Edwards, Louisa 160
Edwards, Mons. 153
Egan the clown 193
Egerton, Col. 98
Egerton, Mr. (manager) 47, 49
Egyptian Museum (Liverpool) 118
The Elastique Sauteurs 37, 45
Elephant and Castle 175
11th Hussars 73, 98
The Elfin Sprites 79
Elgin 98
Elijah 196
Elizabeth, Queen 34, 36
Ella 131, 150, 167, 195, 208
Elliott, Henry 17–18, 24–26, 60, 191
Elliott, Master 40
Elliott, Mr. 38, 92
Elliott, Timothy 17–18, 24–26, 35, 60, 89, 158, 191
Elliott Brothers 17, 18, 24, 25, 26, 50, 81–82, 89, 116, 125, 127–131, 134, 136–139, 158, 166, 191–192
Elliotte, Jem 180
Ellis, Rev. B.J. 51
Ellon 98
Elphinstone, Lord 200
Elson, S. 55
Ely 31, 77, 110–111
The Emancipator (N.Y. newspaper) 49
Emery, Mr. (actor) 48
Emidy, J.H. 111, 158
Emidy, Mrs. 111
Emidy's Circus 111, 156, 158, 167, 194
Emigration, or Home in the West 140

Emma (horse) 186
Emperor of Russia's Circus 179, 192
The Enchantress 165
The English Wrestlers 50
Ennott, Thomas 182
era 190, 192–194, 196–199, 201–205, 209
The Era 15–16, 23, 27, 31–32, 37–38, 42–43, 47, 50, 52–53, 61–63, 65, 67, 69–72, 74–80, 86–88, 91, 94, 96–97, 103, 106, 108–110, 112–114, 118, 121–136, 138–140, 150, 153, 155–157, 160, 165–168, 170–173, 176–177, 179–184, 188–189
The Era Almanac 211
Ericsson (ship) 140
Erme, River 91
Errol 82, 99
Essex 42, 46–47, 72, 76, 83, 209
Essex and Colchester Hospital 54
The Essex Standard 54, 72, 109, 127
Ethair, Charles 60, 115, 165–166
Ethair, Rose 60, 86, 115, 207
Ethair, Steve 60, 79–80, 85–86, 115, 168, 173, 178, 192, 209–210
Ethair, William 79–80, 86, 115
Etheridge, Steve *see* Ethair, Steve
Etoile family 182, 189–190
Eugene, Master, trapeze artist 190, 200
Europe, Asia, Africa and America 18
Euston, London 175
Evans, David 89
Evercreech 95
Evesham 101, 116, 153, 162
The Excelsior List 192
Exeter 22, 38, 44, 83–84, 90–91, 102, 105, 116, 130, 134–135, 159, 182
Exmouth 84, 90
Experimental Gardens (Edinburgh) 178
Eye, Suffolk 110

Fair Field, Southampton 31, 106
Fair Ground, Bradford 132
Fair Meadow (Peterborough) 112
Fairfield, Ia. 147
Fairy Gnomes of the Golden Caves 23
Fakenham 75

224 Index

Fal, River 93
Falkirk 82, 99, 164
The Fall of Sebastopol 139
Falmouth 20, 46, 84, 93
Falstaff 17, 122, 166
Fanny, Mademoiselle 116
Fanque, Pablo 3, 19, 20, 31, 38–45, 47–50, 52, 54, 60, 83, 86, 131, 136, 138, 156, 159, 166, 172–173, 178–179, 193, 207, 210
Fanque, Pablo Jun. 49–50
Fanque, Susannah 42, 50
Fanque's Circus 19–20, 38–39, 42, 44–45, 49–50, 52–53, 87, 89, 97, 131, 136, 172, 178–179, 191, 193
Fareham 30, 70, 107, 187
Faringdon 181, 105
Farmer, Henry 181
Farnham 106
Farnsfield 93
Farrer, Capt. and Mrs. 103
Farrington 101
Fassi, Matilde de 197
The Fat Boy 85
Faversham 46, 71, 109
Felix, Fred 194, 204
Felix, Young 158
Feltham 95
Felton 81
Fenner, Bill 52, 86, 211
Fenner, Mary 52
Fennerophilus 52
The Fens 76
Ferguson, Col. 70
Filey 81
Finsbury 9, 11, 27, 200, 206
The Fire King 131
1st Battalion Rifle Brigade 133
Fishkill, N.Y. 13
Fitzmartin, Bill 103
Fitzsimmons, Arthur 93
Fitzsimmons, Billy 93
Fitzsimmons, Bob 93
Fitzsimmons, James 92–93
Fitzsimmons, James, Jr. 93
Fitzsimmons, Jane 93
Fitzsimmons, John 93
Fitzsimmons, Mary 93
Flaming Vulture 95
The Flaxen-headed Cowboy 56
Fleur de Marie (horse) 167
Flexmore, Richard 140, 172
Flint 83, 100
The Flower Girl; or, The Convict Marquis 140
The Flying Cord 16
The Flying Gymnasiast 16
The Flying Horseman 176
The Flying Man 19, 119

The Flying Post 90–91, 92, 97, 103, 134
Fochabers 98
Le Folie Dramatique 197
Folkestone 71, 108
Fond du Lac, Wisc. 147
Footit the clown 162, 171, 187, 195, 205
Forde, J.G. 176
Fordingbridge 96
Foresters, Ancient Order of 45
Forfar 82, 99, 164, 187
Forres 98
Forth Bridge 95
49th Regiment 195–196
Fountain Street, Manchester 131, 136
The Four Marvels of Peru see Marvels of Peru
Four Persian Acrobats 10
4th Dragoon Guards 62
4th King's Own 124
The Fox Hunt 27
Fox Street, Yardley 209
Frampton's Music Hall 175
France 160
Francisco Brothers 85, 142–143, 202
Franconi, Bastien 60, 86
Franconi, Henri 60, 86, 116, 197–198, 200
Franconi, Madame 116
Franconi's Circus 24, 38, 48, 52, 60–61, 76, 83, 86–87, 89, 94, 96–98, 102, 104, 106, 108, 112, 117–118, 128–129
Frankford, Mrs. 181
Franklin, Hiram W. 3, 41, 49, 51–52, 87, 90–91, 116, 119–121, 125, 146, 148, 202, 204
Franks, James, "Funny Franks" 156, 172–173, 181, 194, 200
Fraserburgh 98
Fraustinia, Madame 25
Frederick VIII of Denmark 3
Frederiksberg 51
Freeman's Journal and Daily Advertiser 9, 10, 143, 155, 160
Freemasons 36, 134
Freeth, Jane Sophia 9, 129, 200
Freeth, Sarah 9
Free-Trade Hall, Manchester 60–61, 63, 87, 171, 196
Fremont, Oh. 144
French, Eugene 202
French, Louis 202
Les Frères Cavallini 202
Les Frères Conrad (*see also* Conrad) 191, 197
Les Frères Quaglieni 180
Fridaythorpe 82

Frome 44, 94–96, 116
Frome Bob 94–95
Frome Market 94
Frost, Hyatt 142, 148
Frost, Thomas 50
Frowde, Elizabeth 158
Frowde, Georgianna 22
Frowde, James 154
Frowde, James Henry "Jem" 22, 102, 148, 155, 158, 165, 168–169, 211
Frowde's Circus 168
Full Moon Field, Bristol 105, 133
Fulton (ship) 142, 144, 145
Fulwood 48
Furr, James 17, 18, 194, 210

Gabriel, S.B. 79
Gainsborough 32, 68
Galashiels 82
Galena, Ill. 147
Gallagher the ventriloquist 63
Garrood, John 75
Garstang 45, 47
Gatehouse 99
Gaulier, Ben 168
Gazette Musicale de Paris 160
Gee, Joe *see* Jee
General Tom Thumb 25–26, 112, 153–154, 163
George Knight's Circus 105
George Street, Finsbury 27
Germany 155
Gibbs, Mary Ann 78–79
Ginnett, Ann 42
Ginnett, Fred 194
Ginnett, George 42, 194, 204
Ginnett, John 42, 83, 156, 182
Ginnett, Mary Elizabeth 83
Ginnett's Circus 20, 42, 83, 85–87, 91, 93, 108, 156, 162, 180–184, 194–195, 201
Girvan 99
Glaisher, James 183
Glasgow 15, 38, 97, 104, 156, 164, 166–167, 178, 181, 184, 194, 200–201, 203
The Glasgow Herald 8, 11, 160, 166–167, 203
Glastonbury 44
Glimpses of Real Life; Theatrical and Bohemian 11
Globe Inn (Penzance) 167
Globe Inn (Portsmouth) 31
Globe Lane, Chatham 19
Glorious Battle of Waterloo see Battle of Waterloo
Glossop Road 48
Gloucester 19, 33, 89, 105, 116, 153, 162, 181, 184, 186, 194, 211

Gloucestershire 117, 161
Glover, Edmund 166
Godalming 107
Godiva and Peeping Tom of Coventry see *Lady Godiva*
Golden Ball Inn, Poulton 47
Goldkette, Mons 188
Goldney, G. 25
Goldschmid, Gerard 204
Good the groom 162
Goole 82, 186-187
Gore Langton, W.H. 104
Goshen, Ind. 145
The Goshen Democrat 145
Gosport 133, 187
Goswell Road, Finsbury 9
Grace's Alley, Whitechapel 182
Graham, Jim 188
The Grand Greek Entree 42
Grand National Hippodrome 87
Le Grand Voltege 151
Grant, Captain 64
Grant, Daniel 44
Grant, Julia 147
Grant, Ulysses S. 147
Grantham 113, 154, 180
Grantown 99
Grassington 186
Gravelet, Jean-Francois see Blondin
Gravesend 74, 88, 109, 175
Great Bridge 88, 187
Great Charlotte Street, Liverpool 131
Great Coggeshall 72
Great Dunmow 76
Great Exhibition 89-90, 105
Great Fountains 184
Great May's Buildings, London 193-194
Great National Circus 199
Great North Road 65
Great United States Circus 155-157
Great Yarmouth 75, 111
Greatbridge see Great Bridge
Grecian Amphitheatre (Birmingham) 170
The Greek Warrior 18
Green, Mr. 37
Green Street, Deritend 5
Greenbush, Ill. 147
Greenock 82, 166, 184, 201
Greenstreet, Eliza 109
Greenstreet, John J. 109
Greenstreet, Sydney Hughes 109
Greenstreet, William 109
Greenwich 14-15, 21, 109
Gregory, Ira W. 143
Greville, Charles 190

Griffiths, John 19, 38, 52, 171, 173, 195, 201, 208
Grimaldi of the Arena 104
Grimsby 41
The Grove (Bristol) 25
Guernsey 29
Guest, Elizabeth 35
Guest, Jem 30, 35, 87, 202
Guildford 107
Guildhall (York) 41
Guisborough 81
Guy Mannering 137
The Gymnical Nonsuchs 33

Haberfield, Lady 90, 104
Haberfield, Sir John Kerle 25, 80, 90, 104
Hack, J. 134
Haddington 81, 99
Haddington, the Earl of 200
Hadleigh 46, 52, 110
Haggerstown, London 51
Haigh, Edward see Footit the clown
Haines, Jackson 201
Halesworth 74, 110-111
Halifax 38, 45, 118-119, 159, 163, 186
Halifax, N.S. 147
Hall, Bill 178
Hall Green 207
Halstead 52, 76, 109
Haltwhistle 100
Hamilton 82, 201
Hamlet 73, 88
Hammersmith 14, 186
Hampshire 30, 33, 96
The Hampshire Advertiser and Salisbury Guardian 30, 32, 106, 194-195
The Hampshire Independent 107
The Hampshire Telegraph and Sussex Chronicle 30, 70, 107, 133, 179, 192
Hancock County, Ill. 147
Hanham, Frederick 107
Hanley 105, 114
Hannibal (elephant) 144
Harding, J. (high sheriff) 25
Hardscrabble 147
Hardy, Thomas 90
Hare, Van 48, 186
Harewood, the Earl of 64
Harlequin 160
Harlequin Blue Beard 170
Harlequin, or the Good Fairy of the Invisible Grotto 189
Harley, Kate 189
Harmston the architect 177-178
Harpur-Crewe, Sir John 36

Harrington (U.S. performer) 49
Harrison, Alec 186
Harrison, Bill 101
Harrison, R. 181
Harrogate 20, 65, 82, 163, 187
Harrow 114
Hartlepool 20, 99, 164
Harwich 21, 73
Harwood, James 58
Hassan, Aron 166, 169, 176-178, 191
Hassan, Madame Irene 166, 177-178, 196
Hassan Ben Abdallah 47
Hastings 21, 31, 71, 108
Hatfield 114
Hatherleigh 46
Havana 173
Havant 70
Haverfordwest 89
Haverhill 52
Hawarden 83
Hawick 82, 164
Haydon Bridge 100
Hayes, Bill 158
Hayes, Bob 158
Hayes Brothers Circus 158, 174, 169, 199
Hayle 46, 93, 130
Haymarket, London 175
Haywood, James 66
Headford Street, Sheffield 114
Heenan, John C. 181, 183-184, 186, 201, 207
Helmsley 82
Helston 46, 84, 93
Hemino, Henri see Hemming, Harry
Hemming, E. 61
Hemming, Hannah 33
Hemming, Harry Wilson 33, 37, 138, 203
hemming, James 138
Hemming, James John 33
Hemming, Jane 33
Hemming, Master 33
hemming, Mr. 79, 161, 168, 179
Hemming, Professor 33
Hemming, Richard 28, 33, 37, 41, 56, 79-80, 86, 130, 138, 140
Hemming, Sarah 33
Hemming, Susan 33
Hemming, William Edward 33
Hemming Brothers 136
Henderson, Agnes 22
Henderson, John 14-19, 22, 159, 168, 176, 181, 192, 197-199, 206
Henderson's Circus 169
Hendon 186

Index

Hendric, Signor 105
Hengler, Agnes 22
Hengler, Alfred Hugh 6, 14, 22
Hengler, Charles 6, 17, 21–22, 52, 150–151, 161, 165–166, 168, 198, 200, 206–207, 209
Hengler, Edward Henry 17, 19, 21–22, 52–53
Hengler, Elizabeth Anne "Eliza" 14, 22
Hengler, Georgianna 22
Hengler, Henrietta 22
Hengler, Henry Michael 21–22
Hengler, John Michael *see* Hengler, John Milton
Hengler, John Milton 15–18, 22, 73, 88, 102, 138, 151–153, 155, 157, 160–161, 164–166, 168, 172–173, 157
Hengler, Mary Ann Frances 22
Hengler, Michael 21
Hengler, Susanna Jane 22
Hengler's Circus 50, 65–66, 76, 85, 100–103, 105, 108, 110, 114–115, 134–135, 148, 150–151, 153–156, 158, 160, 164–165, 168, 172–174, 179, 181, 184–185, 191, 194, 199–201, 209
Hengler's Fireworks 21
Henley-in-Arden 100
Henley-on-Thames 115, 117, 181
Henry, Mr. A. 167
Henry IV 139
Hercules 135
Here We Are Again: Recollections of an Old Circus Clown 46
Hereford 88, 114, 162–163
Hernandez, James 3, 43, 60–61, 67–68, 71, 75, 87–88, 94, 98, 102, 109, 116–117, 119, 121–129, 131–135, 137–138, 140, 146, 152, 157, 159, 174, 176
Hernandez & Newsome's Circus 136–137
Hernandez & Stone's Circus 3, 109, 120, 131, 139, 172
Herne Bay 71
The Hero of Niagara 184
Hertford 46
Hertfordshire 209
Hesse, Mr. 160
Heveningham 111
Hewitt, Edward 208
Hexham 100
Hicken, Edward 27
High Street, Chatham 31
High Street, Dorking 107
High Street, Marylebone 175

High Street, Newmarket 76–77
High Street, Oxford 30, 106, 130
High Street, Portsmouth 31
High Street, Wrexham 152
Highbury Gardens 175
Higher Brockhampton 90
Hilton, Lord 134
Hinckley 77
Hinne, Pauline 24
Hippodrome (Paris) 161, 193, 197
Hird, J.W. 197
History of the Circus 34
Hitchin 114
Hittorf, Jacques 160
Hobro 139
Hodge, Lt. Col. 62
Hodges *see* Hogini
Hodgini *see* Hogini
Hogini, Joe 156, 165, 171, 196, 201
Hogini, William 201
Hogini's Circus 180, 191
Holborn 175
Holland the gymnast 155
Holloway, James 186, 197, 205
Holmes (Derby) 113
Holmfirth 100, 138
Holsworthy 94
Holt 75, 112
Holt, Dick 101
Holt Road, Wrexham 152
Holyhead 83, 100, 149, 163
Holyoake the vaulter 14
Holywell 83, 100, 163, 186
Holywell Street, Oxford 30, 106
Homerton 129
Honeyman, William C. 12, 210
Honiton 83, 90
Honley 138
Horicon, Wisc. 147
Horncastle 154
Horse and Jockey (Oxford) 133
Horse and Jockey Club, St Giles's 177
Horsforth 100
Horsham 107–108
Hoste, Col. Sir George 18
Houdini 64
Houghton-le-Spring 81
Houndwell (Southampton) 106
Howard of the Perch Act 145
Howard Street, Shrewsbury 32
Howden 82, 101
Howe, Lord and Lady 44
Howell, Mich. 145
Howes, Seth 198
Howes & Cushing's Circus

150, 155–157, 159, 161–164, 167, 176, 178, 181, 185–186
Howes' Circus 46
Howes's American Circus 183
Hoxton 159
Huddersfield 35, 42, 59, 86–87, 117, 130, 138, 159, 163
Hughes, Cattie 42
Hughes, Edwin 17, 23–38, 40, 42–44, 46–47, 80, 114, 143, 206, 209
Hughes, Ellen 38
Hughes, Fred 80
Hughes, Master 35
Hughes, Sarah Ann 26, 34–35
Hughes, Sarah Louisa 143
Hughes, William 114
Hughes's Circus 23–26, 29–37, 40–42, 44
Huline, Mons. 202
Hull 40–41, 43, 45, 47–49, 54, 73, 101–102, 125, 130, 162, 183–184, 186
The Hull Packet and East Riding Times 32, 40, 48, 125
Hulse, Mrs. 53
Hume, Mr. 27
Le Hungarien 103
Hungerford 96
Hunslet 100
The Hunting Boy of Bohemia 40
Huntingdonshire 77
Huntly 99
Hurd, Bob 94–95
Hussein 47
Hutchinson, Arthur 61
Hutchinson, Edward 61
Hutchinson, George 192
Hutchinson, Mr. 195
Hutchinson, Thomas Proctor 61, 137, 139, 171, 209
Hutchinson Brothers 61, 122–123, 138–139, 156, 171, 209
Hythe 71, 108

Idle 45
Ilford 209
Ilfracombe 94, 130
Illinois 8, 145–148
The Illinois State Chronicle 148
The Illustrated London News 151
Ilsley 100
The Inca of Peru 6–7
Independent Order of Odd Fellows 41
Indiana 145–146, 148
The Infant Prodigy 16
Infant Wells 161
Infantry Barracks, Leeds 59
Inman Company 193

Index

Inveraray 99
Invergordon 98
Inverness 98–99
Iowa 147
Ipswich 21, 37, 46, 50, 52, 54, 73–74, 103, 105, 110, 127, 142, 158, 161, 184, 206, 209
The Ipswich Journal 73–74, 126
Ireland 86, 193
Irvine 82
Isabella, the Queen of Spain 3, 161
Isabelle, Madame 25, 60, 83, 117–122, 125, 126, 135, 144, 207
Isle of Wight 108
Islington 17, 27, 33, 126, 196–199, 203–204
Islington Green 175
Islington Market, Liverpool 150
Islington Music Hall 175
The Italian Bandit 18
Italy 210

Jack the Giant Killer 156
Jackson, Chatteris 27, 37, 66, 79, 81, 140, 148, 155, 157, 162, 167–168
Jackson, Edmund 85–86, 88, 98, 102–105, 107
Jackson, Madame 86
Jackson, Mich. 145
Jackson's Oxford Journal 27, 30, 69, 105, 133, 176–177
Jacksonville, Ill. 148
James, Frederick 15–16, 56, 58
Jameson, Professor Tom *see* Zamezou, Signor
Jamieson *see* Zamezou
Janesville, Wisc. 147
Jeanette, or the Vagaries of Pierrot 135
Jedburgh 82, 164
Jee, Bill 197–198
Jee, Janie 111
Jee, Joe 82, 111, 197–199, 210
Jee & Orford's Circus 180
Jeffries, Louisa 160
Jem (horse) 186
Jenny Lind (horse) 160
Jersey 14, 20, 207
Le Jeune Louis 143
Jim Crow (pony) 18
Jim Crow and his Granny 15
The Jingling Jumpers 18
Joan of Arc 166
Johnny Gilpin 26
Joliet, Ill. 146
Jones, Joseph 49
Jones, R. 208

Jones, Rymer 63
Josephine, Mademoiselle 104, 171
Journal of a London Playgoer 129
Jullien, the orchestra leader 101, 118
Juvenile Refuge and School of Industry, Manchester 63

The Kaffir War 104
Kaiser (horse) 168
Kalamazoo, Mich. 145
Kean, Charles John 207
Keeling, Bill 126
Keighley 100, 186
Kelly, Tom 185
Kelso 82, 164
Kemp the artist 53
Kemp the vaulter 14
Kendal 100
Kenilworth Castle 34, 36
Kennedy, Lord William 199
Kennet Valley 96
Kennington 208
Kenosha, Wisc. 146
Kensington 87, 94
Kent 14, 71, 161, 204
Kent, the Duchess of 20
Keogh Road, Stratford, Essex 209
Keokuk, Ia. 147
Kepitoke (horse) 204
Kerry 185
Kerwin, Edward 171, 173, 195, 205
Kestler, Mr. 37
Keswick 82, 99
Kettering 100
Kew 33
Kewanee, Ill. 145, 148
Keys, Lizzie 176, 178, 191, 202
Kidderminster 88, 100, 163, 187
Kidwelly 163
Kilmarnock 82, 99, 158
Kimberley 209
King, Miss 17
King, Tom 183, 201
King Charles Croft, Leeds 38, 42, 50
The King of Egypt 165
King of the Golden Valley; or, Harlequin Little Blue Boy 202
The King's Gardener; or Nipped in the Bud 49
King's Head (Duke Street, London) 158
King's Head Inn (Bungay) 74
King's Lynn 16, 75–76, 112, 184
Kingsbridge 91
Kingsley, Olmar 131

Kingsmead Terrace, Bath 103, 107
Kingston 109, 186
Kingston, Wisc. 147
Kingstown 185
Kington 69, 88
Kinross 82, 164
Kipp, B. 143
Kirkby Lonsdale 100
Kirkby Stephen 82
Kirkbymoorside 82
Kirkcaldy 82, 164
Kirkcudbright 99
Kirkham 45
Kirkstall 186
Kirriemuir 82, 99
Kite, William 19
Kitley Hill 91
Klare, Mons. 86
Knaresborough 20, 82, 187
Knight, George 86, 105, 108–109, 116, 119, 122–128, 130, 171, 173, 195, 203
Knight's Circus 105, 108–109
Knightsbridge Music Hall 176
Knott Mill, Manchester 43
Knowle 210
Kobke, Johanne Laurenze 51

La Petite Anne 132
La Petite Emily *see* Cooke, Emily
La Porte, Ind. 145–146
Lady Godiva and Peeping Tom of Coventry 62, 64, 80
Lady Sefton's School, West Derby 165
Lafayette, Ind. 148
Lake Lane, Landport 133
Lamb, Sir Charles 21
Lambeth 22, 24, 33, 52, 117, 133, 140, 142, 174, 207–208, 210
Lanark 82, 201
Lancashire 19, 50, 91, 171–172, 187
Lancaster 164, 187
The Lancaster Gazette 47
Land, Mr. (pianist) 36
Landport, Portsmouth 30, 70, 101, 133
Langdon Hall 102
Langley, George 191
Langlois the juggler 197
Langport 90, 110
Langton, Mrs. 104
Lansdown, Bath 103, 107
Lansdowne Music Hall 175
Larg & Sons (publisher) 12
LaSalle, Ill. 146
The Last of the Mohicans 85
Launceston 20, 46, 84, 94, 116

228 Index

Laurena, Mademoiselle 38
Laurencekirk 99
Laurette, Madame 176
Lavenham 76
Lawder 82
Lawley Hill 206
Laxfield 111
Le Jeune Louis 143
Le Petit Blondin 201
Leamington 68, 100, 127, 162, 201
The Leaper of Streamers 79
The Leaper of the Rialto 121
Lecture Hall, Manningtree 73
Ledbury 89, 114
Lee, Lavater 7, 9–10, 16, 25, 52, 138, 144, 200, 210
Lee, Nelson Richard 33, 63, 80–81, 189, 202, 207
Lee, Tom 14, 16, 52
Leeds 7, 31, 34, 38–39, 42, 50, 59, 63–65, 98, 102, 117–118, 157–159, 172, 179, 182–183
Leeds Amphitheatre 182–183
The Leeds Intelligencer 50, 59
The Leeds Mercury 38–39, 42, 50, 63, 182
Leek 114
Lehman, Madame 86
Lehman the strongman 81, 86, 200
Leicester 36–37, 54–55, 77, 83, 101, 11, 113, 117, 127, 151, 161, 163, 173, 180, 183, 186, 191, 193
The Leicester Chronicle 17, 29, 36, 55, 113, 193
Leicester Square 158, 163, 164, 167–168, 175
Leicester Town Council 37
Leicestershire 77, 113
Leigh-on-Sea 83
Leman Street, Whitechapel 182
Lemon, River 91
Lemon Street, Truro 92–93
Lenton the clown 102
Leominster 88, 163
Leon, Master 130
Leonard, Mons. 27
Leopold et Boutelier 155
Leotard, Jules 190, 207
Leroux, Camille 38
Le Tort, Mons. 102–103
Leven 82
Leveret (ship) 159
Levy the cornetist 190
Lewes 71, 108
Lewis, John 95
Lewis the clown 26, 102
Lewisham 114
Leyland 44–45

Licensed Victualler's Annual Soiree and Ball 151
Lichfield 77–78, 100
Lincoln 67, 83
Lincoln, Abraham 3, 148
Lincolnshire 77, 101
Lind, Jenny 159–160, 181, 196
Lindsay Street, Dundee 157
Linen Hall, Chester 152
Linlithgow 82, 99, 164
Linton 76, 81, 99
The Lion's Heart of England; or, The Brave Scot 172
Lipman, Moses J. 13, 19, 25, 27, 210
Lisbon 37, 203
Liskeard 46, 84, 92, 183
Lisson Grove 14
Little Coggeshall 72
Little Ella 131, 195, 208
The Little Grenadier 14, 18
The Little Horticulturist 17
The Little Jockey 16
Little Red Riding Hood 63
Liverpool 25, 27, 29, 33, 48–50, 52, 80–81, 83, 86, 114, 117–119, 121–122, 131, 143, 146–147, 149, 150–151, 154–156, 158, 160–161, 164–166, 168, 172–173, 179, 184–186, 191, 193–194, 208–209
The Liverpool Albion 117
Liverpool Amphitheatre 121
Liverpool Bell Melodists 131
The Liverpool Citizen 209
The Liverpool Mercury 9, 13, 42, 117–121, 131, 150–151, 155, 164–166, 172–173
Livingston, R.P. 44
Llandeilo 89
Llandovery 89
Llandudno 163, 186
Llanelli 89, 163
Llanerchymedd 83, 100
Llangefni 83, 100, 163
Llangolen 83
Llanrwst 83, 163
Lloyd the equestrian 194
Lloyd's London Weekly Newspaper 14, 16–17, 19, 21, 37
Lockhart the clown 167
Loder, E. 190
Lomas, Mrs. 53
Lomas the clown 45, 53
Lombard Street, Portsmouth 31
London 4, 7, 9–11, 13, 18–19, 21–24, 26, 33, 41–44, 47–50, 54, 58, 60, 64–65, 68, 74–76, 85–87, 89–90, 95, 116, 121, 128–129, 131, 133, 139–140, 149, 158, 160, 162–164, 167–168, 173, 175, 178, 181–182, 191–192, 194, 196–197, 200, 203–204, 206–207, 209–211
London Eldorado Grand Music Hall 175
London Pavilion Music Hall 175
London Road 175
London Road, Newark 132
London Street, Greenwich 14
Long Island, N.Y. 6, 8
Long Wall, Oxford 106, 130
Lord Mayor's Walk, York 20
Lord Nelson (public house) 175
Lord Nelson Street, Liverpool 118
Lostwithiel 46, 92
Lott, Edward G. 149
Loughborough 113, 130, 151, 161
Loughran the clown 6
Louis XVI 22
Louis, Le Jeune 143
Louth 154
Lower Abbey Street, Dublin 86, 135
Lower Norwood 206
Lowestoft 75, 111
Lowestoft Road 110–111
Lubin and Annette 18
Lucy Neal (song) 41
Ludlow 88
Ludovic, Herr 49
Luigi 180
Lusillian, Mons. 153
Luton 114
Lydney 89
Lyme Regis 90, 116, 130

Macarte, John 102, 142
Macarte, Madame Marie 42, 52, 83–84, 101, 130, 161, 180, 193, 204, 210
Macarte, Mr. 208
Macarte & Bell's Circus 83–84, 101–102, 103, 105–106, 115
Macarte & Clarke's Circus 157, 161, 166
Macarte's Circus 130
Macclesfield 19, 114, 159
Maccomo 208
Mace, Jem 76, 111, 178–179, 181–182, 184, 191
Mace's Circus 178, 191
Mackanaw, Ill. 8
Mackett, W. 197
Mackintosh, Mr. 117, 121
Mackney, Mr. 190, 192
Macomb, Ill. 147

Index

Madame Newsome's Circus 159
Madden Playbill Collection 133
Madigan, H. 155
Madigan, J. 155
Madigan, Rose 140, 150, 155
Madigan's Circus 146
Madison, Wisc. 147
Madrid 161, 169, 197, 199, 203
Magdalen Bridge, Oxford 30
Magdalen Street, Oxford 106
Maggs, Jacob 182
Maggs, Will 94–95
The Magic Barrel 85
The Magic Ladder 14, 79
Mahomen Ben Said 177
Maidstone 20, 71, 109, 139
Maldon 72, 109
Malling 109
Malmesbury 90, 163
Malton 82, 186–187
Malvern 114, 116, 133, 153, 162
Mammoth Hippodrome 185
Manchester 15, 25, 27, 31, 44, 47–48, 60–63, 87–87, 89, 121, 131–132, 135, 137–138, 155, 156–159, 162, 171–173, 176, 180, 194–196, 203
The Manchester Courier 131–132
The Manchester Times 6, 42–44, 47, 60–63, 121, 136–137, 155, 171, 198
Manchester Unity 41
Manders' Menagerie 208
Manley & Hayes' Circus 199
Manningtree 21, 73
Mansfield 32, 68, 87, 114, 125–126
Mansfield Road, Nottingham 184
Maoris 196
Marchant, F. 202
Marden, River 96
Margaret Roothing (town) 21
Margate 46, 71, 74, 109, 139
Marie Antoinette 22
Mark, Dr. 161
Market Deeping 77, 100
Market Harborough 20, 29, 100
Market Place, Nottingham 127, 133
Market Street, Leicester 54, 55
Marlborough 96
Marriott, Miss. 140
Marshall, E. 189–190
Marshall, Mich. 145
Marston Chapel 207–208, 211
Mart Yard, Gainsborough 32

Martin the timber yard man 128
Marvels of Peru 188, 191, 208
Marylebone 175
Marylebone Music Hall 175
Maryport 82, 99
Masaniello 16
Masham 82, 186
Masons Place, Finsbury 9, 11, 27, 141, 200, 206–209
Masotta, Paul 10, 19, 24–26, 32
The Masquerader on Horseback 85
Massachusetts 43
Matlock 68
Matthews, Benjamin 208
Matthews, Billy 176
Matthews, Tom 74, 140, 176
Matthews, William (architect) 191, 195
Mauchline 99
Maumee, Oh. 144
Maus, Friedrich Adolf 25, 32, 34, 36–37, 40, 42, 76, 86, 173, 177, 191, 194, 207
Maus, Joanna Louisa 42, 207
Maus's Circus 180, 182, 184, 191, 194
Maybole 99
Mayne, Rosa 205
Maynooth 86
Maze, Peter 25
Mazeppa, or the Wild Horse of Tartary 14, 53, 58, 64, 74, 76, 80, 98, 137, 139
McCarter, James 45
McCarthy, Dan 83
McCarthy, Michael (alias John) 83
McCarthy, Michael 142, 161
McCarthy, Tom 185, 208
McDonough County, Ill. 147
McFarland, James *see* McFarland, Tom
McFarland, Tom 3, 10, 11, 12, 39, 41, 46, 49–50, 111, 144
M'Collum, Tom 102, 167–168, 207
M'Collum's Circus 167–168
McVicker, J.H. 139
Mechanics' Institution (Derby) 36
Mechanics' Institution (Manchester) 63
Mechanics Large Hall, Hull 184
Meers, Hubert William "Little" 170
The Meeting of the Waters 63
Melbourne 136
Melillo, Caroline 168
Melillo, Joseph 168

Melksham 96
Melrose 82, 164
Meltham 138
Melton Mowbray 77, 83, 113
Menai Bridge 83
The Mendips 95
The Merry Corporal 17
Mersey, River 147
Merthyr Tydfil 89, 162–163, 186
Methven 82
Metropolitan Music Hall 189
Michigan 144–145
The Michigan Argus 145
Middlesbrough 99, 175, 187
Middlesex New Music Hall 175
Middleton 99
Middleton-in-Teesdale 82
Middlewich 100
Midsummer Common, Cambridge 22, 110, 126
A Midsummer Night's Dream 80
Milano, N. 160
Mildenhall 16, 186
Miles, Philip William Skinner 24–25
Mileson, Florence 204
Mileson, Fred 194, 204
Milford, Mich. 145
Milner, Prof. 86
The Milwaukee Sentinel 146
Milwaukee 146
Minchinhampton 90
Minehead 95
Mississippi River 147
The Mississippian (newspaper) 146, 215
Mr. Merryman 30, 81
Mr. Pickwick 85–86
Mr. Sam Weller 85
Mr. Twist 88
Mitchell, William *see* Revolti, Felix
Modbury 91
Moffatt, Alfred 161, 180, 185, 206
Mohammed Ben al-Hagghe 60
Molay Abdullah 177
Mold 83, 163, 186
Moncreiff, James 170
Mondy Benahi 177
The Monkey Man 9
Monmouth 89, 162–163
Monmouthshire 158
Monopologue on Horseback 79
Montague, Harry 192
Montague, Susan 103
Montgomery, Lady 21

Index

Montrose 82, 99, 164, 187
Montrose, the Duke and Duchess of 44
Moor Street, Birmingham 156
Morat, Switzerland 206
Morayshire 99
Morelli, Mons. 202
Moreton 101
Morgan, Agnes 160
Morgan, Christine 160
Morgan, Mr. 140
Morley, Countess of 91
Morley, Henry 129
Morning Chronicle 4, 139, 176
The Morning Post 60, 139, 176, 183, 189–190, 202
Morocco 48, 166, 176–177
Morpeth 81, 99, 164
Morris, Ill. 146
Morris the acrobat 7
Morton, Mr. 102, 117, 121
Moseley, Miss 158
Moseley, Tom 6, 20, 43, 56, 86, 132
Mother Goose 177
Motty, Otto 204
Mount Clements, Mich. 145
Mount Edgcumbe, the Earl and Countess of 103
Mount Pleasant, Ia. 147
Mount Street, Manchester 47, 121–122
Mount Vernon, Oh. 144
Mountain Sylph 190
Mousley, William Eaton 33
Munster 185
Murray, Edward 140
Murray the gymnast 155
Museum Street, Manchester 62
Music Hall, Dublin 86, 135
Music Hall, Sheffield 181
Musical Jees 197
The Musical World 130
Musselburgh 81, 99
Myers, James Washington 150, 155, 159, 184–185, 210
Myers' Circus 144, 191, 194

Naden, Thomas 191
Nairn 98–99
Nairnshire 99
Napoleon 4, 14, 18, 24, 35, 70, 171
Napoleon III 3, 161
Narberth 89
Narbro 51
Naseby 76
Natal 62
The Natchez Semi-Weekly Courier 51
National Baths 18

National Theatre, Boston 43
Neath 89, 162–163
Neath Fair 89
Nelson, Admiral 112
Nelson, Alfred 161
Nelson, Arthur 28–29, 116, 138–139, 158, 210
Nepalese princes 68
New Amphitheatre Music Hall (Cardiff) 201
New Brighton 163
New Exhibition Circus 180, 184
New Exhibition Hall, Birmingham 78
New Forest 96
New Hall, Leicester 36
New Hampshire 46
New London, Ia. 147
New Market Hall, Shrewsbury 32
New Market Place, Blackburn 123
New Marylebone Theatre 14
New Royal Surrey Theatre 139–140
New St. George's Hall, Scarborough 184
New York 10, 13, 37, 43, 49, 140, 142–143, 145, 148–150, 173
The New York Clipper 145–146
The New York Herald 10–11, 145
New York Minstrels 176
New Zealand 93, 196
Newark 67, 87, 126, 132, 186
Newark, Oh. 144
Newbridge 89, 162–163, 186
Newburgh 82
Newbury 96, 106
Newcastle 14, 24, 31, 65–66, 81, 99–101, 104, 108, 112, 157, 161, 164, 187, 200
The Newcastle Courant 31, 125
Newent 89
Newfoundland Gardens, Bristol 205
Newfoundland Street, Bristol 205
Newmarket 76–77, 110, 186
Newmarket Road, Cambridge 178
Newport 89, 100, 158, 162–163, 186
Newport, Isle of Wight 108
Newsome, Adele 132, 176, 191
Newsome, Emma 176
Newsome, Jem 10, 24, 25, 41, 50, 117–118, 122, 124, 130–131, 134–135, 137–138, 150, 176, 178, 184, 196, 202, 211
Newsome, Marie 176

Newsome, Pauline 24, 117, 121–124, 129, 132, 134, 136–137, 159, 176, 178, 202, 211
Newsome, Tom 202
Newsome & Fanque's Circus 138
Newsome's Circus 133, 161, 176–178, 183–184, 191, 193–194, 201–202
Newton Abbot 91
Newton Bushel 44, 91, 116
Newton Stewart 99
Niblo's Gardens 11
Nicolson Street, Edinburgh 169, 199, 203
Niebuhr, Herr 147
Night Dancers 190
A Night with Punch 79
Niles, Mich. 145
Nimmo (publisher) 11
Nimrod, the Fox Hunter 14
9th Street, Cincinnati 148
Noack, Joanna Louisa 42
Norfolk 16, 75–77, 110–112, 184
Norman, Mr. 140
Norreys, R. 62
North, Levi James 3, 7–11, 23, 25, 144, 209
The North American Indians 155
North River, Yarmouth 28, 29
North Shields 81, 99, 102, 187
North Street, Bristol 23, 33, 68, 78, 80, 103, 115
North Walsham 112
North Woolwich 183
Northallerton 100, 164
Northampton 30, 100, 114, 151, 162, 186–187
Northamptonshire 77
North's Circus 144
Northwich 100, 163
Norway 3
Norwich 19, 21, 54, 75, 102–103, 111–112, 126, 156, 158, 191, 207
Norwood 206, 210–211
Nottingham 27, 35, 55–56, 58, 67, 86, 94, 96–98, 101, 117, 127–129, 133, 151, 153, 161, 163, 169, 172, 180, 182, 184, 186, 191
Nottingham Goose Fair 128, 161
Nottinghamshire 93, 197
The Nottinghamshire Guardian 55, 56, 57, 67, 113, 125–128, 132–133, 154, 184
Nuneaton 68, 163
Nunn the strong man 10, 20

Index

Oakham 77
Oconomowoc, Wisc. 147
Octagon (Plymouth) 134
Odd Fellows 41
Oddfellows Literary Institution 59
O'Donnell, Master 40, 45
O'Donnell, Miss C. 17–18
O'Donnell, Mr. 49
O'Flanagan, F. 181
Oglou 35
Ohip 111, 143–144, 148
Okehampton 84, 97
Old Barnes *see* Barnes, Jim
Old Brompton 109
Old Cumnock 82
The Old English Gentleman 18
Old Giles's Wedding Day 18
Old Meldrum 99
Old Weller, the Prince of Whips 85
Oldham 34, 138, 159
Olio, or Masquerade 18
Oliver, Isabella *see* Isabelle, Madame
The Olympian Riders 17
The Olympic Ball Tosser 49
Olympic Circus 19, 48
Omer the equestrian 168
Ommanney, Adm. Sir John Acworth 102
Orford 74
Orford, Bill 180
Oriel, Mons 164, 166, 203
The Original Complete and Only Authentic Story of Old Wild's 41
Osborne the magistrate 92
Oscar I, King of Sweden and Norway 3
Oswestry 163
Otley 45–46, 65, 186
Ottawa, Ill. 146
Ottery St Mary 130
Oundle 100
Over 100
Oxford 30, 69, 105–106, 112, 130, 133, 139, 164, 176–179, 181
Oxford (music hall) 175
Oxford Fair 112
Oxford Road, Banbury 69
Oxford Street, London 175
Oxford Street, Southampton 194
Oxfordshire 27
Oyster Street, Portsmouth 31

Paddington, Pablo 16–18
Padstow 108
Page, Susanna 37
Paignton 105

Paine, Tom 110
Paisley 82
Palm (elephant) 206
Palmer, Alfred 33, 49
Pantomimist Hippodrome, Copenhagen 51
Paragon Street, Hull 41, 48
Parelli, Signor 118, 121
Paris 22, 24, 38, 47–48, 68, 86, 90, 117, 140, 142, 145–146, 149, 153, 159–160, 164, 167, 169, 188, 192–193, 197–199, 203
Paris Hippodrome 209
Paris Street, Exeter 134
Parish, Mr. (prop maker) 58
Parish, William 197
The Parisian Grotesque 190
The Parisian Masquerader 80
Parisoni, Mons. 132, 138
Parkgate 163
Partridge, Ann 42
Paston's Grammar School 112
Pastor, Frank 157, 159, 194–195, 197–198, 203, 209
Pastor, Tony 144
The Patagonian Samson 10
Pateley Bridge 186
Paterson, Peter 11, 169
Pavilion Gardens (North Woolwich) 183
Peace, Charlie 66
Peacock, John 39
Pearson, John Harrison 162, 176, 178, 209
Pedro, the V King of Portugal 3, 160–161
Peebles 82, 164
Peep o' Day 188
Peking 18
Pembroke 89
The Penny Illustrated 192, 204
Penrith 82, 99
Pentland, Joe 25, 49, 140, 150, 155
Pentland Brothers 176, 78, 191, 195
Pentonville 43
Penzance 46, 84, 93, 108, 167
Peoples Concert Hall, Manchester 191
Peoria, Ill. 148
La Perche 125
Perequillo, or Terror in a Tub 140
Perks, Infant 194, 197, 199
Perry, Edgar 189–190
Perry, Uriah 189–190
Pershore 116
Perth 82, 99, 164
Perth Road, Dundee 40

Pete and Barney (mules) 155, 157, 186
Peter Street, Manchester 121–122
Peterborough 77, 100, 111–112
Peterhead 98
Petersfield 106
Le Petit Blondin 201
Petit Romeo 156
La Petite Anne 132
La Petite Emily *see* Cooke, Emily
Petrie, Capt. P.C. 193
Pettoletti, Alexine Wilhelmine *see* Barns, Alexine Wilhelmine
Pettoletti, Johanne Laurenze 51
Pettoletti, Mademoiselle 138, 160
Pettoletti, Philip 51
Pettoletti's Circus 51
Petworth 107
Philadelphia 10, 102
Philharmonic Hall, Islington 175
Philharmonic Hall, Manchester 135–136
Pickering 82, 186
Pierrot 160
Pinder, Bill 196
Pinder, Emma 196
Pinder, George 196, 211
Pinder & Swallow's Circus 184
Pinder Brothers 180
Pinder's Circus 117, 191, 194, 196, 199, 201
Pittsburgh 6
The Pittsburgh Manufacturer 6
Platt, Edward 161–162
Plattville, Wisc. 147
Plege, Mons. 25, 195
Plymouth 71, 83–84, 91–92, 97–98, 102, 105, 116, 134–135, 156, 159, 194
The Plymouth and Devonport Weekly Journal 134
Poet Laureate 110
Polaski, Antoine 16
Polaski, Jean 10, 14, 16, 18, 56
Polaski, Mons. 65, 156
Police Court, Cincinnati 148
Pollard, Lt. Col. 119
Pollard, Mr. 30
Pontefract 20, 82
Pontiac, Mich. 145
Pontypool 89, 162, 186
Poole 96
Poplar 23, 186
Port Huron, Mich. 145

Index

Port William 99
Porter, Harriet 51
Portland Street, Manchester 155, 171, 180, 203
Portobello 81, 99
Portsea 30–31, 168
Portsmouth 20, 30–31, 46, 70, 84, 101, 107, 133, 168, 179, 181, 187, 192
The Portsmouth Herald 30
Portsmouth Library 133
Portsoy 98
Portugal 3, 160
Potosi, Wisc. 147
Potter, John 63
Potteries District 133
Poulton-le-Fylde 45, 47
Pound Houses (Fakenham) 75
Powell, Anthony 171, 173, 195, 209
Powell, Elizabeth Anne "Eliza" 14, 18, 22
Powell, Jim 153, 186
Powell, John 186, 199
Powell, Susanna Jane 22
Powell, V. 171
Powell, William 4, 14–18, 21–22, 151, 153, 165–166, 200, 205, 211
Powell, William Henry 22
Powell's Circus 14–20
The Prairie Horse 127
Preston 19–20, 38, 41, 44–45, 123, 159, 164, 172, 174
Preston, William 165
Preston Dispensary 41
The Preston Guardian 11, 19, 41, 44–45, 123–124
Price, A. 138
Price, Circo 169, 197
Price, James 169
Price, Tom 3, 6–9, 11–12, 17, 21, 169, 197, 203
Price & North's Circus 11, 12, 14, 20–21, 169
Price & Powell's Circus 14
Price's Circus 169
Pride of Birth 49
Prince (horse) 79
Prince Albert (horse) 118
Prince George (horse) 16
Prince of Denmark (public house) 182
The Prince of the Antipodes 45
Prince of Wales 44, 104
Prince's Street, Bristol 26
Princess Royal 44
Princess Satra of Egypt 165
Probert, W.R. 211
Proctor, Rosina 103
The Protean Artistes 26, 40

The Public Life of W.F. Wallett; the Queen's Jester 54
Puddletown 90
Pudsey 100
Punch 64, 80, 104, 130
Punch and Judy 81, 85, 87
Pwllheli 100
Pymer, Jim 172, 194, 201, 211
The Pyramidical Devices 85

Quaglieni, Antonio 155, 180, 182, 210
Quaglieni, Clementine 155, 157
Quaglieni, Josephine 155, 157
Quaglieni, Les Frères 180
Quaglieni, Romeo 156
Quaglienis Circus 161, 182, 191, 194, 201
Quay Gate, Portsmouth 30
Queen Elizabeth's Visit to Kenilworth Castle 34, 36
Queen Street, Exeter 38, 90, 135
Queen Street, Leicester 193
Queen Street, Oxford 105–106
Queen Street, Plymouth 92
Queen Street, Portsmouth 30
Queen's Theatre, Hull 47–48, 73, 102
Queen's Theatre, Manchester 25, 61
Queenstown 193
Quick & Mead's Circus 6
Quincy, Ill. 147

Race, Cape 193
Racine, Wisc. 146
Radbourn Hall 36
Rafael's Dream 191
Railway Station (Leicester) 183
Raines, Maj. 70
Raleigh, Sir Walter 34
Ramsden Street, Huddersfield 86–87
Ramsey 77
Ramsgate 46, 71, 108=109, 139
Randall, William 6, 33, 189–190
Raven (horse) 88, 91, 97, 104–105, 110
Raymond, James 142
Raymond and Agnes; or the Bleeding Nun of Lindenburg 17
Raymond & Co. 142, 148
Reading 69, 85–86, 100, 106, 115, 133, 176, 181
Rebecca, Mademoiselle 38, 62, 79–81, 85–86
The Red Man 64
The Red Man of the Far West 40, 41

Redditch 162, 187
Rede, L. 48
Redruth 20, 46, 84, 93, 108
Regent (dog) 104
Reid, Mr. (Truro) 92
Reigate 107
Renze's Cirque, Vienna 192
Retford 68, 87, 101, 132, 186
Revolti, Felix (William Mitchell) 153, 159, 165, 173, 186, 200–201, 208
Reynolds, John 146
Rhyl 83, 100, 163, 186
Ricardo, Mademoiselle 74
Richard III 17, 122, 166
Richard Plantagenet, or the Days of Wat Tyler 205
Richards, Davis 153, 155, 173, 207
Richards the strong man 49
Richardson, Elizabeth 35
Richer, Jean 21
Richmond 82, 99–100, 164, 187
Richmond, Surrey 109, 186
Rickards, J.H. 140
Ricketts, Col. 71
Ridgway, Charles 191–192
Ridgway, George 192
Ridgway, John 192
Ridgway, Tom 192, 208
Riding School (Halifax) 119
Riding School (Huddersfield) 59, 86–87
Ridley Brothers 179, 193, 195, 201, 202
Rifle Brigade 133
Rignold the theatre owner 73
The Rigs of Mr. Briggs 63, 64, 79–80, 85, 104–105, 151, 188
Ringwood 96
Ripley 68, 113–114, 186
Ripon 20, 82, 164, 187
Ripon, Wisc. 147
Risley 52
Rivers, Sir James 103
Rivolti, Felix see Revolti
Rob Roy 137
Robin Hood and Little John 62
Robinson, James 150, 155–156
Robinson, Mr. (horse dealer) 21
Robjohn, Prof. 145
Rochdale 19, 120, 130, 178
Rochester 109, 180
Rochez, Mons. 27, 201
Rockwell & Stone's Circus 11, 41, 49
Rockwell the clown 25
Rockwell's Circus 46, 51
The Roman Warriors 79, 104
Romeo 180
Romeo, Petit 156

Index 233

Romeo, Mich. 145
Romford 72, 109
Rosalie, Madame 188, 200
Rosalie, Mademoiselle 132, 134, 136–137, 143
Rosemary Branch Gardens, Islington 126
Rosina, Mademoiselle 57
Ross, T.B. 73
Ross, W.G. 176
Ross-on-Wye 89, 162–163
Rosston, Mr. 155
Rotherham 50, 66, 100, 114, 132, 172, 177, 186–187
Rothschild, Baron de 44
Rotunda Garden, Dublin 155
Routledge, Edmund 198
Routledge's Every Boys' Annual 198
Rowe, Joseph A. 146
Rowe's Circus 146
Roxburgh, the Duke of 200
Royal Agricultural Hall (Islington) 196–199, 203–204
Royal Alhambra Palace *see* Alhambra
Royal Amphitheatre (Hull) 48
Royal Amphitheatre (Liverpool) 25, 27, 117–118, 119–121, 131
Royal Amphitheatre (Norwich) 52
Royal Arena (Portsea) 31
Royal Britannia (Hoxton) 159
Royal Circus, Bristol 78
Royal City Amphitheatre (Manchester) 47
The Royal Cornwall Gazette 92–93
Royal Engineers 18
Royal Gardens (Vauxhall) 60
Royal Leamington Spa 68
Royal Leviathan Marquee 44
Royal Lyceum Theatre (London) 48
Royal Lyceum Theatre (Sheffield) 188
Royal Marines 102
Royal Olympic Arena of Arts 24
Royal Panopticon of Arts and Sciences 158
Royal Pavilion Circus (Brighton) 108, 114
Royal Scots Greys 71
Royal Society 183
Royal South Hants Infirmary 194
The Royal Stag Hunt 66
Royal Terrace Gardens, Gravesend 88
Royal the flautist 63
Royal Tivoli Gardens (Copenhagen) 138
Royal Western Yacht Club 102
Rugby 100, 114, 151, 162, 186
Rugeley 100, 114
Runcorn 163
Runnells, Burnell 116, 156, 162
Runnells, Frederic 162
Russell, Elizabeth 37
Russell, Harry 124, 209, 211
Russell, James 37
Russell, Lord A. 133
Russell, Madame 86
Russell, Mr. 122–123
Russell, Susanna 37, 209
Russell, William 86–87
Russelli, Mr. 56–165
Russelli Brothers 56–57
Russia 179, 184, 192, 199, 207
Russia, the Emperor of 3
Russilli, Harry 37, 86, 209, 211
Russilli, Jack 37, 58, 60, 62–63, 104, 167
Russilli, Madame 86
Russilli, Mr. 80, 85
Ruthin 83
Rutland 77
Rutley, H. 128, 132–133
Ryan, Jem 6–8, 13, 17, 23, 27, 102, 207
Ryan, Master 26
Ryan, Susan 102
Ryan's Circus 6–9, 14, 23
Rye 71, 108
Ryland, George 43–44, 52, 122–124, 127, 130, 132, 134, 136, 138, 140
Ryland, Madame 43–45
Ryton, River 68

Saddi d'Jalma 194–195
Sadler's Wells 175
Sadlier, Col. 124
Saffron Walden 76
St. Andrews 82, 99, 164, 187
St. Ann's National School, Liverpool 165
St. Asaph 83, 100
St Austell 46, 84, 92, 108
St. Barnabas, Finsbury 9, 129, 200
St. Clair, Mich. 145
St. Clement's, Oxford 176
St. Clement's, Toxteth Park 80
St. Columb 46, 84, 94, 108, 130, 182
St. Davy 108
St. George 37, 165
St. George and the Dragon 33, 57–58, 62–64, 85, 98, 103, 104, 108, 165
St. George's Field, York 41
St. George's Market, Belfast 200
St. George's Square, Portsea 31
St. George's Terrace, Cheltenham 161
St. Giles,' Oxford 30
St. Helens 150, 187
St. Helier 207
St. Ives 93
St. John Street, Lichfield 78
St. John's Masonic Lodge 36
St. John's School, Liverpool 165
St. John's, Deritend 5
St. Just 93
St. Louis, Mo. 8, 49, 147–148
The St. Louis Globe-Democrat 28
St. Luke's, Finsbury 9, 200
St. Mark's, Shoreditch 201
St. Martin-in-the-Fields 194
St. Martin's Lane, London 194
St. Martin's, Birmingham 5, 42
St. Mary Magdalene, Woolwich 117
St. Mary Street, Portsmouth 179, 192
St. Mary's, Shoreditch 51
St. Paul's, Islington 27
St. Peter's Street, Derby 32, 66–67
St. Peter's, Liverpool 122, 143
St. Petersburg 179, 192, 199, 207
St. Simon's Schools 165
St. Thomas Street, Portsmouth 31
St. Thomas's Hospital, Lambeth 208
Salame, Mons. 47
Salcombe Estuary 91
Salford 15, 44
Salisbury 20, 38, 69, 96
Salt & Jennings 201
Sam Patch; the Yankee in France 139
Sambo 200
Sampson's Cricket Ground, Sheffield 114
Samwell, John 10, 14, 16–18, 20, 35, 86, 88, 103, 130, 156, 180, 204, 209
Samwell, Thomas 200, 204
Samwell, William 16, 20, 35, 86, 88, 172, 204, 207
Samwell's Circus 16–17, 201
San Francisco 146, 159
Sanders, Emily 140
Sandgate 108
Sands, Maurice 25

Sands, Richard 8, 13–14, 19–20–22, 25, 43, 173
Sands & Van Amburgh's Circus 13–14, 19
Sands Circus 19, 25
Sands, Lent & Co.'s American Circus 43
Sandwich 71, 109
Sanger, Caroline 195
Sanger, George 3, 96, 158, 169, 187
Sanger, J. 158
Sanger's Circus 11, 157, 161–162, 169–173, 178–179–181, 187–188, 195–196, 198, 201, 203–205, 207
Saracen's Head Bowling Green, Worcester 133, 153
Sardinian Circus 180
Satra, Princess 165
"The Sawdust Circle" 28
Saxmundham 46, 74
Sayers, Tom 178–179, 181, 185–186, 203
Scarborough 81, 101, 184
Scarsdale, Lord 35
Schamyl, the Prophet of the Caucasus 136–137
Schmidt, Mons. 202
Schwartz, Lina 203
The Scioto Daily Gazette 111, 143
Scotland 36, 65, 98, 162, 178, 191, 196, 201
Seal, Billy 31, 52, 82, 157–158, 161, 167, 184, 200
Seaton House 20
2nd West York Yeomanry Cavalry 119, 124
Sedgwick Brothers 201
Sefton, the Earl of 119, 131
Selby 20, 82, 186
Selkirk 82
Settle 100, 186
Sevenoaks 21, 71, 109
78th Highlanders 170
77th Regiment 98
Severn, River 89
Seymour, M. 98
Shaftesbury 96
Shakespeare 54, 65
Sharon, N.Y. 142
Shaw the Lifeguardsman 70
Sheffield 9, 48–50, 61, 66, 114, 126, 132, 137–138, 163, 166, 168–169, 173, 179, 181, 186–188, 195, 210
Sheffield, Mr. (agent) 31
Sheffield, Tom 159
The Sheffield and Rotherham Independent 48–49, 66, 114, 125, 132, 168–169, 187

The Sheik Riders 105
Shelton 19
Shepherd, Rev. William 21
Shepperd, John 139
Shepperd, Richard 139
Shepton Mallet 44, 95
Sherborne 96
Sherburn 82
Sherwood, Robert Edmund 46
Sherwood Forest 68
Shifnal 88
Shillerett, Signor 118, 121
Ship Yard (Wigan) 60
Shipley 100, 186
Shoreditch 51, 84, 201
Shrewsbury 19, 32–33, 37, 88, 100, 163
Shropshire 206
Shylock 17, 122, 166
Siamese ambassadors 156
Sidi Ali 47
Sidmouth 84, 90, 116
Sidoni, Mademoiselle 132, 134
Silvani the sprite and leaper 84, 192
Silvester the charmed monster 202
Simpson, John 68
Simpson, Major 104
Sinclair, Charles 73
Singapore 174
Sir Gilpin Cabbage 17, 19
Sir Hugh Myddleton 175
Sir Roger de Coverley; or the Flitch of Bacon 16, 19
Sittingbourne 71, 109
16th Lancers 52
Skelley, George 174
Skelley, Sarah 174
Skelley, Tom *see* Hernandez, James
Skelton, John 110
Skipton 65, 100, 186
Smallbrook Street, Birmingham 191
Smethwick 187
Smicht, Mademoiselle 180
Smidt, Herr and Rose 83
Smith, Bill 4
Smith, Charlotte 9
Smith, Edward Tyrrel "E.T." 129, 135–137, 158, 175, 179, 208
Smith, Grayham 41
Smith, Samuel 124
Smith, Sarah 79
Smith, Sgt. 94–95
Smith, Spencer 9
Smith the vaulter 14
Smith's Circus 135–139
Snaith 82
Snow Hill, London 192

Somerset 94–95
Somerville, Lord 68
Somerville, Mr. 27
Somerville the Shakespearian lecturer 65
Soullier, Clementine 140
South Africa 202, 209
South Bend, Ind. 145
South Devon and East Cornwall Hospital 98
South London Music Hall 175–176
South Molton 94–95, 116, 130
South of England (New) Music Hall 179, 192
South Shields 99, 164, 187, 194, 196, 199, 201
Southall 114
Southampton 31, 46, 69–70, 84, 96, 106–108, 117, 144–145, 187, 194, 201
Southampton (ship) 150
Southsea Beach 31
Southwell 67, 186
Southwold 74, 126
Soyer's Symposium 89
Spain 3, 149, 160, 169, 203
Spanish Bullfight 26
The Spanish Dancers; or, Two Lovers Too Many 140
Sparkbrook 207–208
Sparkhill 206, 210–211
Sparrow, Bill 94–95
Speaight, George 34
Spicer, Mary Ann 38
The Spirit of the Air 15–16
Sprake, Jacob 22
Sprake, Mary Ann Frances 22
Sprake, Oceana 168
Sprake, Susannah 22
Spring, Tom 43
The Springer of Rialto 85
Springfield, Ind. 148
Springthorpe's Waxworks and Promenade Concerts 184
The Sprite of the Morning Star 18–19
Stafford 100, 114
Stafford, George 209
Staffordshire 77–78
Stamford 77, 83, 100, 113
The Standard (London newspaper) 30, 64, 159, 167–168, 183, 189, 199
Standard Theatre (Shoreditch) 84
Stane Street 72
Stanley 82
Stanley, Mr. (theatre manager) 16
Star Hotel (Oxford) 30, 106

Index

Steeple Chase! or, England's Harvest Home 62–63
Stephens, J. and Mrs. 53
Stepney 14
Stevens, B. 146
Stevens, Jemmy 178
Stevens, Mrs. 86
Stevens, Peter 207
Stevens' Circus 178, 180
Stevens the barrel equilibrist 86
Stevenson, Robert Lewis Balfour 171
Stewarton 82
Steyning 108
Stickney, Sally 131
The Stiltonian Gymnast 190
Stirling 82, 99, 164
Stirling, Edward 140
Stockport 27, 42, 207
Stock's Croft, Bristol 104–105
Stockton-on-Tees 20, 31, 81, 99, 164
Stocqueler, J.H. 139
Stoke 114
Stokes (performer) 130
Stokes, Spencer 131
Stokesley 99
Stone, Den 142–143
Stone, Eaton 3, 116–117, 119, 121–129, 131–134, 135–138, 142
Stonehaven 99
Stonette, Charles (or Carl) 52–53, 87, 181, 193
Stourbridge 88, 100, 153, 163
Stourport 19, 153, 163
Stout, Bill 24
Stout, W.H. 146
Stow 101
Stowmarket 21, 110
Stradbroke 111
Stradsett 112
The Strand Ballet Company 140
The Strand Theatre (London) 140
Strang, King 146
Strange, Mr. 196
Strange & Pulleyn's Circus 196, 198–199
Strangers' Friend Society 64
Stranraer 99
Stratford, Essex 47, 71, 209
Stratford Road, Bordesley 208
Stratford Street, Sparkbrook 208
Stratford-upon-Avon 68–69, 162, 207–208
Strathaven 82
Strathspey Players, Past and Present 12

Stratton 94
Strichen 98
Stroud 163, 181
Strutt, Edward 36
Stuart, Lord James 44
Sudbury 52, 76, 109
Sudlow, Edward 31
Suffolk 16, 74, 110
Sun Tavern (Knightsbridge) 176
Sunderland 35, 76, 81, 85, 99–100, 102, 108, 164, 184, 187, 204
Surrey Gardens 183
Surrey Music Hall (Sheffield) 181, 188
The Sussex Chronicle 30
Sutcliffe the bandleader 119
Sutton Coldfield 100
Swaffham 76, 112, 186
Swallow, Mr. 180
Swan Inn Bowling Green, Derby 32, 66–67
Swann, Tom 19, 33, 58, 135–137, 150, 159, 176–178, 191
Swansea 89, 158, 162–163, 183, 186, 201
Swansea Fair 89
Sweden 3, 138, 179
Swindon 96, 163, 181
Swinson, F. 210
The Swiss Acrobats 7, 9
The Swiss Entree 79
The Swiss Milk Maid and Her Lover 16
Switzerland 206
Sycorrae 165
Sydney 159
The Sylph of the Circle 16
Sylvester the equestrian 38–39
The Syrian Acrobatiques 121

Tadcaster 65
Tain 98
Talliott Brothers 170
Tamborino Voy 86
Tamworth 77, 100
Tanner, William 176
The Tar of All Weathers 16
Tarporley 100
Tarratt, Sgt. 55
Tasmania 94
Taunton 38, 44, 83, 95, 110, 116, 130
Tavistock 46, 92, 116
Taylor, Job 45
Taylor, Mr. 190
Taylor, Robert 47
Taylor the vaulter 14
Tecumseh, Mich. 144
Teignmouth 44, 91, 116

Tempest, Colonel 59
Tempest, Sir Charles Robert 65
Templeton, R. 181
Tenbury 163
Tenby 89
Tenterden 71, 108
Teresita, Signora 202
Terre Haute, Ind. 148
Terry, Joseph and Emily 207
Tewkesbury 89, 101, 116, 162
Thame 30
Thames 29, 175
Thanet 71
Thaxted 52, 76
Thayer, Stuart 143
Theatre Royal (Bury St Edmunds) 54
Theatre Royal (Drury Lane) 44, 121, 131, 133, 140, 191
Theatre Royal (Dundee) 191
Theatre Royal (Edinburgh) 52, 202
Theatre Royal (Greenock) 166
Theatre Royal (Jersey) 20
Theatre Royal (Liverpool) 119, 154
Theatre Royal (Manchester) 86, 122, 136–137
Theatre Royal (Nottingham) 27
Theatre Royal (Plymouth) 134
Theatre Royal (Sheffield) 137
The Theatrical Examiner 129
Thetford 76, 110–111
3rd Dragoons 57, 58
Thirsk 82, 100, 164
13th Light Dragoons 170
Thompson, George 61, 138
Thorne 82
Thorne, James 140, 186–187, 192, 197, 199, 201–203
Thorner 82
Thornhill 82
Thrapston 100
Thumb, Tom 25–26, 112, 153–154, 163
Thurland Street, Nottingham 55, 56
Tichborne Street, Haymarket 175
Tickhill 100, 186
Tiffin, Oh. 144
Tike (horse) 186
Tillicoultry 82
The Times 129, 142, 201
Timour the Tartar 24–25, 35–36, 57, 137
Tinkham, Mr. 144
Tinsley Brothers (publisher) 50
Tipton, Ia. 147

236　Index

Tiverton 38, 97
Tivoli (Margate) 74
Tivoli, Copenhagen 160
Tivoli Gardens (Copenhagen) 138
Todmorden 31
Todmorden Road, Burnley 45
Toledo, Oh. 144
Tollhouse Hill, Nottingham 128
Tom of Coventry 98, 165
Tom Thumb 25–26, 112, 153–154, 163
Tomkinson the clown 31, 60, 87
Tomkinson the vaulter 24
Tony (horse) 207
Tooting 210
Torquay 44, 91, 105, 116, 134
Torrington 116
Totnes 46, 91, 116
Tottenham 186
Tourniaire, Francois 24, 42–43, 45, 60
Tourniaire, Louis 194
Towcester 100
Town Hall (Torquay) 134
Town Hall Assembly Rooms (Cardiff) 153
Town Malling 109
Town Meadows, Rochdale 19
Toxteth Park 80
The Toy Symphony 190
Trafford, Sir Humphrey de 195–196
"La Tranca" 172
La Tranca Hispaniola 24, 26, 172
The Transformation Dancer 190
Travis Brothers 181
Tredegar 89, 163, 186
Trelawny, Charles 102, 134
Tremadoc 100
Tremayne, Maj. 170
Tremont Circus 10
Trent Bridge Cricket Ground (Nottingham) 153
The Trewman's Exeter Flying Post see Flying Post
Trowbridge 96, 116, 163, 187
Truro 20, 46, 84, 92–94, 108
Tunbridge Wells 21, 109
Turf Moor, Burnley 45
Turner, John 31
Turnham, John 188, 190
Turnham's Grand Concert Hall 188–191
Turpin's Great Ride 58
Turpin's Ride to York 63, 80
12th Regiment 167
Twigg, James 195

Twist, Harry 168
Tyrian Lodge of Freemasons 36

Uncle Tom's Cabin 123
Uncle Tom's New Music Hall, Bradford 175
Union Docks, Plymouth 134
Union Poor House, Derby 32
Union Road, Plymouth 97
Union Street, Plymouth 92, 134
United States 3–4, 7–9, 27–28, 41, 46–47, 51, 61, 111, 138, 142, 145, 169, 177, 181, 208, 210
Unsworth, Mr. 189–190
Upper Banchory 99
Uppingham 77, 100
Upton-on-Severn 153
Usher, Dickie 29
Utley the mason 65
Uttoxeter 83
Uxbridge 178

Valentina, Seline & Augusta 197
Valparaiso 9
Valparaiso, Ind. 146
Van Amburgh, Isaac A. 13–14, 19–22, 27, 52, 142–143, 203
Van Amburgh's Circus 13, 19, 142–145, 148
Varney, Richard 34
Vauxhall 60, 124
Vauxhall Gardens 47, 87, 116
The Venetian Clown 85
Vernon, Webster 205
Verry, John 31
Vesta (pony) 103
Vickers (publisher) 41
Victoria (horse) 166
Victoria, Queen 13, 20, 36, 44, 54, 132, 163
Victoria Gardens, Norwich 52
Victoria Pavilion (Copenhagen) 139
Victoria Railway station (Sheffield) 187
Victoria Road, Sheffield 187
Victoria Rotundo, Copenhagen 138
Victoria Street, Belfast 200
The Victorian Arena 31
Vienna 165, 192
Vigro, Captain 60
The Village Lovers; or, The Old Ones Outwitted 80
Virginia 10
The Virginian Brothers 19
Virginie, Mademoiselle 161
Vivian, Mrs. 84

Volkerson, Mr. 160
Vollaire, Mr. 140
Vor Frue Kirke, Copenhagen 51

Wabash River 148
Wadebridge 46, 84, 94
Wakefield 42, 50, 65–66, 125, 132, 163
Wales 83, 89, 153, 199
Walker, Harry 15–16, 19–20, 41, 44, 49, 56, 62–63, 86, 88, 136, 159
Walker, Mary Ann 27
Wallace (dog) 118
Wallace (horse) 186
Wallack, H.J. 137
Wallett, Mrs. 50, 57, 59
Wallett, William F. 3, 15, 20, 27, 32, 34–35, 37, 42–44, 46–50, 54–62, 116, 132–134, 146, 150–151, 153, 156, 162–163, 166, 173, 177–178, 180–181, 183, 191, 194, 199, 201, 203, 210
Wallett's Circus 54–56, 58–59, 162–163
Wallingford 100, 106, 133
Walpole 111
Walsall 78, 100, 114, 187
Walters, Charles 145–146
Walton Close, Oxford 30
A Wander Through the Ocean 63
Wandsworth 109
Wantage 101
Wardlow, Captain 64
Warkworth 99
Warminster 20, 44
Warren Co., Ill. 147
Warwick 68, 162
Warwickshire 77, 210
Water Lane, Stratford, Essex 209
Watertown, Wisc. 147
Watford 114
Wath 100
Watlington 19
Watson, Charles 167, 177
Watson, Lizzie 189
Watton 76
Watts, Sarah 94
Waukegan, Ill. 146
Waupun, Wisc. 147
Webb, George 192
Wednesbury 100
Weeks, Chauncey R. 142, 148
Welby, Harry 197, 200
Welch, Hernandez & Co 109, 116–118
Welch, Rufus 111, 116
Welch & Lent's Circus 148

Index

Welch's Circus 111
Welch's Park Circus 10
Wellclose Square, Whitechapel 182
Wellesley, Arthur 5
Wellington 38, 44, 88, 97, 100, 116, 153
Wellington, the Duke of 5, 35, 70
Wellington Street, Hull 40
Wellington Street, Leicester 36
Wellington Street Station, Leeds 63
Wellington, Salop 206
Wells 44, 116
Wells, Emily Jane 166, 172
Wells, Infant 161
Wells, John 209
Wells, Miss 56, 59
Wells, Mr. 50, 56
Wells family 180
Wells-next-the-Sea 75
Wells's Circus 19
Welsh, Jemmy 186
Welsh Harp Hotel (Hendon) 186
Welshay 88
Wencart the clown 197
Wensum, River 75
West, Mr. 190
West Bromwich 83, 100, 187, 210
West Derby 165
West Derby Road, Liverpool 185
West Ham 47
West Woodlands 94
Westbar, Sheffield 181
Westbury 95
Westermann, H.J. 51
Westminster Bridge 4
Westminster Bridge Road 11
Westminster Hospital 27
Westminster Road, London 18
Weston, Edward 36
Weston, Elizabeth 37
Weston, Pitney 158
Weston's Music Hall 175
Weston-super-Mare 83, 90, 110, 116
Wetherby 20, 65, 186
Weymouth 90, 112, 116, 178, 183
Wharfe, River 65
What Acrobats Can Do 11
Whenca, or Hard Heart 104
Where's Your Ticket? 200
Whitby 81
Whitchurch 96
White & Sons 195
The White Gipsy 202

White Hart Inn, Chipping Norton 28
White Lion (public house) 188
White the lion tamer 30
Whitechapel 175, 182
Whitehaven 82, 99
White's Circus 43
Whithorn 99
Whittlesey 77
Whitton the acrobat 7
Widdicomb, Mr. 140
Wigan 42–43, 60, 116
Wight, Isle of 108
Wighton 82, 99
Wigton 99
Wild, Jim 35, 206
Wild, Mr. 130, 165
Wild, Samuel 35, 41
Wild, Sarah Ann 34–35
Wild, Selina 34–35
The Wild Horseman 173
The Wild Indian 33, 126
The Wild Indian of the Prairie 103
Wild's Circus 159–160
Wilkinson, W.B. 6–7
Williams, Edwin 176
Williams, Herbert 195
Williams, Jane 5
Williams, Mary 207
Williams the clown 6
Williams the equestrian 38, 41, 44–45, 86
Williamson, Hannahbella 15
Willio, Herr 201
Williton 95
Wilmington, Ill. 146
Wilmot, Sir Henry S. 35
Wilson, James 171, 180, 211
Wilson, Mr. (singer) 36
Wilson, Sarah 33
Wilton, John and Ellen 182
Wilton's Music Hall 175, 182
Wiltshire 96
Wimborne 96
Wincanton 95
Winchester 69–70, 84, 106, 187
Winchester, Ill. 148
Winder, E. 175
Windsor 20, 86
Winterbottom, Mrs. (singer) 63
Wirksworth 32, 68, 114, 126
Wisbech 54, 112
Wisconsin 146–147
Wishaw 201
The Witches' Glen and Waterfall 179
Witham 72, 109
Witney 105, 130
Wivelisscombe 95
Wolcott, N.Y. 173

The Wolf 178
Wolverhampton 83, 100, 109, 133, 139, 156, 162–163
Wombwell, Mr. 25
Wombwell's Menagerie 20, 25, 66, 118
Wood, Charles 39
Wood Street, Wakefield 42
Woodbridge 46, 74, 158
Woodbridge Road, Ipswich 73, 127
Woodford 71–72, 109
Woodhouse Lane, Leeds 59
Woodhouse Lane Cemetery, Leeds 50
Woodhouse Moor, Leeds 39
Woodman, Charles 176
Woods, Edward 26–27
Woodstock 69, 100
Wooler 99
Woolford, George 37
Woolford, Mrs. G. 62, 79–80
Woolford, Rebecca 37–38, 62, 67, 80, 88, 102
Woollidge, Mrs. 140
Woolmer the magistrate 92
Woolwich 15–19, 109, 117, 183
Woonsocket 144
Wootton Bassett 96
Wootton-under-Edge 20, 90, 116, 181
Worcester 19, 42, 88–89, 114, 116, 127, 133, 139, 153, 162, 172, 187, 211
Worcester College, Oxford 105
Worcestershire 153
Workington 82, 99
Worksop 32, 68, 114, 132
Worlds Fair 90
Worrell, Irene 142, 145–146
Worrell, Jennie 142, 145–146
Worrell, Sophia 142, 145–146
Worrell, William 142, 145–146
Worthing 70–71, 108
Wotton, James 142
Wratislaw, the Countess 20
Wrexham 83, 152–154, 158, 163
The Wrexham and Denbigh Weekly Advertiser 152–154
Wrigley, Joe 204
Wymondham 111
Wyoming 207

Yankee (horse) 186
Yankee Doodle on His Little Pony 63
Yarde-Buller, Baronet 134
Yardley 35, 207, 209
Yarm 99
Yarmouth 28–29, 54, 75, 102, 111

Yates, Police Sergeant 79
Yealm, River 91
Yealmpton 91
Yeo, River 91
Yeomanry Cavalry 35, 119
Yeovil 90, 130
York 20, 41, 82, 124–125, 159, 163, 186–187, 202
The York Herald 12, 31–32, 41–42
York Road, Finsbury 9
Yorkshire 45, 162
Young Felix 158

Young Godolphin 85, 88
Young Hernandez *see* Hernandez
Young Leon *see* Leon, Master
Young Meltonian 37
Young the equestrian 117, 121
Ypsilanti, Mich. 144

Zamezou, Fred 122–124, 42, 145–146
Zamezou, Jim 122–124
Zamezou, Josephine 103, 105, 122–124, 132, 142, 145–146

Zamezou, Madame 124, 142, 145–146
Zamezou, Signor (Tom Jameson) 42, 64, 83, 104–105, 110, 116, 122–124, 138, 142, 145–146, 173, 202, 209
Zanesville, Oh. 143–144
The Zanesville Aurora 143–144
Zorilda, Princess 35
Zoyara, Ella *see* Ella
Zweiker, Anna 168

www.ingramcontent.com/pod-product-compliance
Ingram Content Group UK Ltd.
Pitfield, Milton Keynes, MK11 3LW, UK
UKHW041941140426
5217IPUK00014B/597